Through Britain on Country Roads

Peter Brereton

Have fun with this one Joe
Love Stan & June + x
XMAS 1983.

M
MACMILLAN LONDON

Peter Brereton was educated at Wellington College and served in the Far East during the India and Burma campaign of 1941-45. After the war he took a regular commission, serving in Germany, Cyprus and Suez. In 1959 he retired with the rank of major, and after a spell with a finance company he entered community and social work, which took him first to Manchester and then to London. Now he spends most of his time travelling and writing, and his first book, *Through France on Minor Roads,* is in its third edition.

First published 1982 by Arthur Barker Limited

First published in paperback 1983 by
PAPERMAC
a division of Macmillan Publishers Limited
4 Little Essex Street London WC2R 3LF
and Basingstoke

Associated companies in Auckland, Dallas, Delhi, Dublin, Hong Kong, Johannesburg, Lagos, Manzini, Melbourne, Nairobi, New York, Singapore, Tokyo, Washington and Zaria

ISBN 0 333 35441 9

Printed in Hong Kong

Preface

What is this life, if full of care
We have no time to stand and stare.
No time to stand beneath the boughs
And stare as long as sheep or cows.
No time to see, when woods we pass
Where squirrels hide their nuts in grass.
No time to see, in broad daylight
Streams full of stars like skies at night.
A poor life this if full of care
We have no time to stand and stare.

(W. H. Davies)

In common with many European countries, the motorways and main roads of Britain are becoming increasingly overburdened with traffic. It must also be said that the best of the beautiful and varied scenery we possess is rarely enountered by travelling along the major roads. But Britain is fortunate in that it is endowed with a profusion of well maintained minor roads which are relatively traffic-free. The object of this guide is to assist the traveller, whether motorist, cyclist, or rambler, to explore these roads and get off the 'beaten track'.

Through Britain on Country Roads describes eighteen routes through England, Scotland and Wales as shown on the Contents page. Each of these routes covers a distance of around two to three hundred miles, as far as possible along roads with either a B classification or along unclassified roads. All the chosen routes are on properly surfaced roads, but many of them, owing to their width, are unsuitable for very large vehicles.

These minor roads meander past quiet villages, many consisting of little more than a church and pub, through scenery encountered by chroniclers such as Pepys, Johnson, Cobbett, Borrow and Stevenson who travelled the same paths centuries ago. By the wayside ancient forts and castles as well as medieval towns and villages bring history to life. Delightful inns tempt the traveller to pause and emulate the example of the essayist William Hazlitt who, on 10 April 1798, recorded that he 'sat down to a volume of the new Heloise, at the Inn at Llangollen, over a bottle of sherry and a cold chicken'.

This guide has not, therefore, been compiled for those in a hurry. It will, I hope, appeal to those who, at leisure, wish to visit some of the remoter parts of Britain – ready, as the spirit takes them, to dwell a while and find the time to simply 'stand and stare'.

Price Grading of Hotel Accommodation

The letters A, B, C or D which follow the listed hotels or guest houses refer to the lowest charge for bed and breakfast in a double room, including VAT and service charge where applicable, in 1982. However this grading system should only be treated as a guide and it is advisable to check with the hotel before making a firm booking.

A £20 and above B £15–£20 C £10–£15 D Below £10

Author's Note

Few books are without errors, and no guidebook can ever be completely up to date, for road numbers and road signs change, and hotels come under new management, which can affect standards. The author will be glad to receive, care of the publishers, any corrections and suggestions for improvements, which can be incorporated in the next edition.

Acknowledgements

The photographs in this book are reproduced by kind permission of:

British Museum: 316. *CHM Dobell:* 46(r), 222(al), 228(a), 234, 282. *SJ Dobell:* 222(bl), 228(b), 230(b), 232. *AF Kersting:* 62, 78–9, 88, 146, 226, 236, 276–7, 280, 284. *National Trust:* 104, 300. *Cressida Pemberton-Pigott:* 42–3, 46(l), 48, 50(l). *Charlie Waite:* 12–13, 20, 24, 32, 50–1, 92, 93, 96(r), 112, 134, 136, 138–9, 154, 162–3, 164, 166, 170–1, 172, 174–5, 178, 188–9, 222(r), 230(a), 230–1, 242–3, 254–5, 286, 312. *Weidenfeld & Nicolson:* 170, 176, 216, 218(l), 288.

All the remaining photographs were supplied by the *British Tourist Authority*.

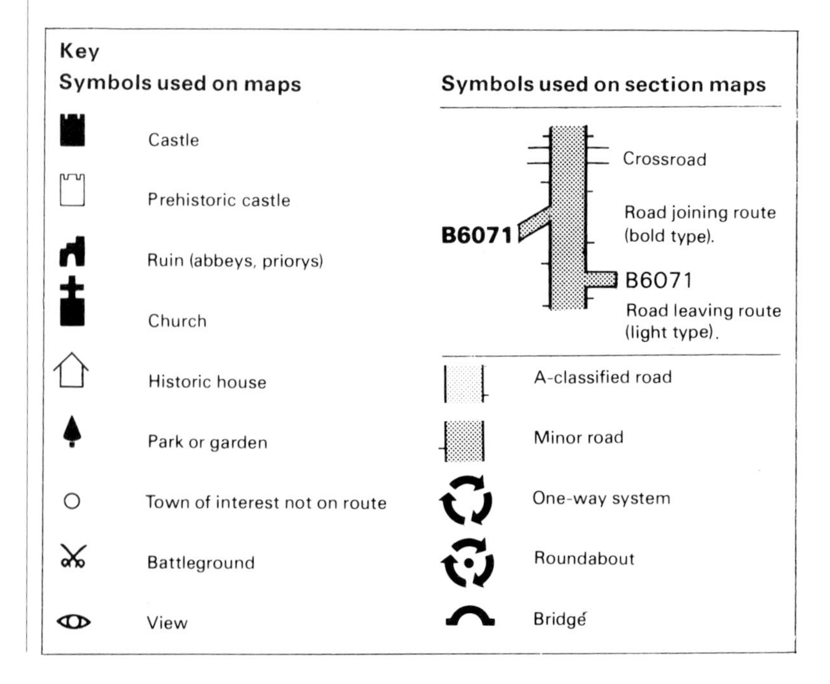

Contents

Preface 3

Key to Symbols, Acknowledgements 4

Introduction 6

The Routes

1 North Wales 10

2 Yorkshire: the Dales 26

3 Cumbria (the Lake District) 40

4 East Anglia (South): Cambridgeshire, Suffolk, Essex 56

5 Heart of England (East) 74

6 Devon, Cornwall, West Somerset 90

7 Wiltshire, Somerset, Dorset 110

8 Scotland 128

9 Yorkshire: the Wolds, the Coast, the Moors 156

10 The North-East: Durham, Northumberland 172

11 West Surrey, West Sussex, Hampshire (New Forest) 192

12 East Anglia (North): Norfolk 206

13 Oxfordshire, Berkshire, Gloucestershire, Buckinghamshire 220

14 South Wales 240

15 Heart of England (West) 262

16 East Surrey, Sussex, Kent 274

17 Cheshire, North Shropshire 292

18 Staffordshire, Derbyshire 304

Index 318

Introduction

The book describes eighteen routes throughout the length and breadth of Britain. These are shown in diagrammatic form in the outline map facing this page. Each of these routes starts and ends at a town of reasonable size and particular interest, where a variety of accommodation from hotels to guest houses is available. Each route is divided into sections of thirty-five miles (fifty-six kilometres), and all distances are shown. Each section occupies a pair of facing pages. Right-hand pages give a visual presentation of the route in the form of a straight-line 'route diagram', complemented by verbal instructions for finding the way. Left-hand pages give information about places of interest, accommodation and the general nature of the countryside.

Road numbers in Britain are preceded by the letters M (motorways), A (major roads), or B (secondary roads). The greater part of this country's road network, however, consists of unclassified minor roads. The chosen routes are confined as far as possible to the B or unclassified roads, although in the vicinity of towns or in the interest of continuity the occasional use of A roads proved necessary.

Right Hand Pages

The route is the thick vertical line which, it is emphasized, does not necessarily run from north to south. Towns and villages of any significance on the route have been inserted in their appropriate position. NB The figures to the left of the vertical line show miles (to the nearest mile); the figures to the right show kilometres (to the

---

As the map on the facing page shows, there is often a particular point on a route which lies close to one or two other routes. It is hoped that the brief route instructions below will assist those who wish to connect one route with another.

a. From Route 6 to Route 7. From *Exeter* take A30 and A35 to *Charmouth* – or alternatively take A3052 through Lyme Regis to *Charmouth.*
b. From Route 7 to Route 11. From *Sandleheath* take B3078 to *Fordingbridge.*
c. From Route 7 to Route 13. From *Wootton Bassett* take B4041 and A419 to *Cirencester.*
d. Note Routes 11 and 16 both start at *Guildford.*
e. From Route 13 to Route 5. From *Deddington* take A423 to *Banbury.*
f. From Route 5 to Route 4. From *Huntingdon* take A604 to *Cambridge.*
g. From Route 4 to Route 12. From *Eye* take B1077, A140, and A143 to *Harleston.*
h. From Route 14 to Route 1. From *Mallwyd* take A470 to *Dolgellau.*
i. Note Routes 1 and 17 both start at *Chester.*
j. From Route 17 to Route 15. from *Much Wenlock* take A458 to *Bridgnorth.*
k. From Route 17 to Route 18. From *Knutsford* take A537, A5002, and A6 to *Chapel-en-le-Frith.*
l. Note Routes 2 and 9 both start at *York.*
m. From Route 2 to Route 10. From *Leyburn* take A6108 to *Richmond.*
n. From Route 2 to Route 3. From *Hawes* take A684 to *Kendal.*

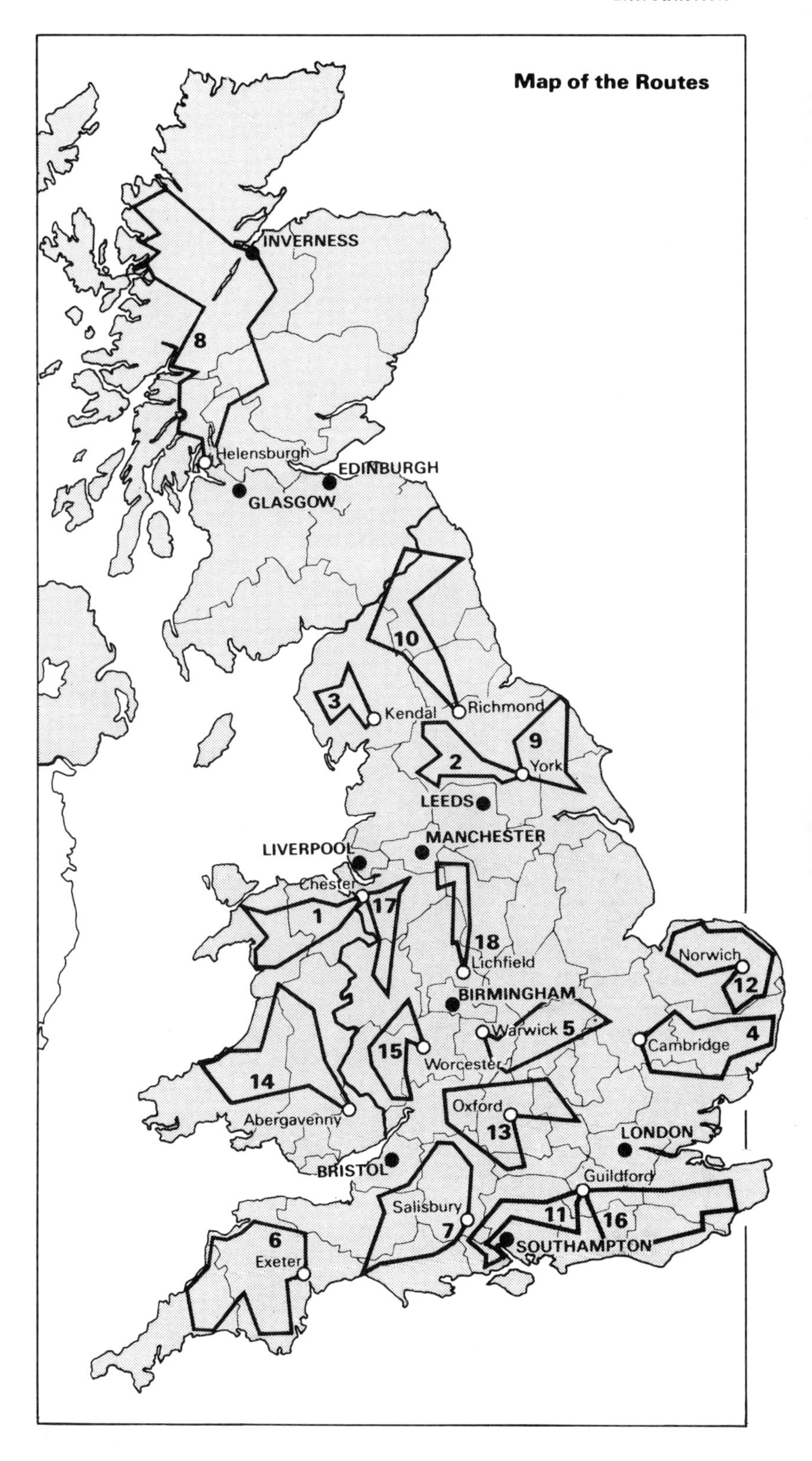
Map of the Routes
INVERNESS
8
Helensburgh
EDINBURGH
GLASGOW
10
3
Kendal
Richmond
9
2
York
LEEDS
MANCHESTER
LIVERPOOL
Chester
17
1
18
Lichfield
Norwich
12
BIRMINGHAM
Warwick
5
Cambridge
4
15
Worcester
14
Abergavenny
Oxford
13
LONDON
BRISTOL
Guildford
Salisbury
11
16
7
SOUTHAMPTON
6
Exeter

nearest two kilometres). Occasionally, in order to conserve space on uncomplicated sections of the route, the vertical line is broken to indicate that a short stretch has been omitted. Classified road numbers are shown alongside the vertical line, the darker shading indicating that this stretch of road is either a B road or unclassified. Whenever space permits signs at road junctions have been illustrated diagrammatically pointing straight, left, or right of the vertical line (always remembering that the map needs to be read from *top* to *bottom*). These diagrammatic signs have normally been inserted at points where classified road numbers change or where the route moves from one category of road to another. For example, on page 94 at EXETER the A377 is taken (light shading). After 2.6 m (see verbal instruction) STOCKLEIGH is signed to the RIGHT and a minor unclassified road is now taken (dark shading). Just past Stockleigh Pomeroy, TIVERTON is signed to the RIGHT and the A3072 (light shading) is now taken.

Beside each route diagram are verbal route instructions, partly to amplify tricky points which cannot be shown in detail on the diagrams, and partly for the benefit of those who prefer verbal to visual presentation. These instructions indicate the distance in miles from one point of change to another as well as at least one of the names of the towns or villages shown on the signpost. At road junctions where no signpost exists or, as is sometimes the case on minor roads, the sign has been damaged or is indecipherable, this has been indicated with the words 'no sign'. Along these routes there were a number of occasions where signposts had been damaged or repositioned incorrectly. It is impossible, therefore, to assure the reader that the named signs given in the guide are completely accurate – but it is hoped that their inclusion proves useful to compliment the route instructions which have been detailed in distance to one tenth of a mile. For those who wish also to use a map, the relevant RAC (Royal Automobile Club) navigator maps (scale 3 miles to 1 inch) are indicated for each route.

Finally it needs to be emphasized that roadworks or temporary diversions may entail the motorist diverting from the detailed route. But it is hoped that sufficient information has been given in order for the route to be rejoined without undue difficulty.

Left Hand Pages

Towns and villages on the route diagrams are mentioned on the left-hand pages when there are points of special interest or hotel or restaurant facilities where it is suggested that a comfortable night could be spent or a meal taken at reasonable cost. However, since this is not a comprehensive hotel guide, the reader may on occasions find an hotel of his choice that is not mentioned here. The purpose of listing hotels is only to reassure the traveller that although he may be far removed from a major town, he is always in a position to anticipate a halt within a reasonable space of time along the route. Addresses and telephone numbers of tourist offices (T.O.) passed along the route are shown – and at these offices there will be comprehensive details of hotels in the areas as well as facilities for hotel reservations.

Hotel details include address (except in smaller places where this is not necessary), telephone number and number of rooms. In addition each hotel has been given a price category with regard to the cost of a room on a bed and breakfast basis. These room costs have been categorized by a capital A, B, C or D, and it is stressed that they refer to the cost of a double room. Naturally the cost of a single room will be relatively less expensive. The key to this grading system will be found on page 4. Costs in Britain as elsewhere may rise from year to year, but relative costs are unlikely to vary greatly, and for this reason it should be possible with this grading system to select hotels from the guide with approximate prices in mind. In addition to hotels the addresses and phone numbers of youth hostels have been given.

Brief details of places of interest to be found along the route are given. However it would be misleading to include opening times of properties, gardens, etc., for as the National Trust point out these vary from one property to another and at times they are closed for repairs or other reasons. The National Trust publish annually a booklet entitled *Properties Open*, obtainable from 42 Queen Anne's Gate, London SW1H 9AS.

Index

The index lists all towns and villages encountered along the route or referred to in the text. It also includes the names of people mentioned in the text – and these names, placed alphabetically within the list, are distinguished from the names of towns and villages by their insertion in a lighter type.

The Pronunciation of Welsh Names

For those unfamiliar with Welsh, here is a guide to the pronunciation of some of the more difficult names encountered in Routes 1 and 14. Stressed syllables are printed in bold type.

Abbeycwmhir *Abbey-koom-***heer**
Beddgelert **Beth**-*gelert*
Betwys-y-Coed *Betoos-u-***Koyd**
Caernarvon *Car-***nār**-*von*
Capel Curig *Kappel* **Kir***rig*
Capel-y-Ffynn *Kappel-u-***Fin**
Cemaes **Kem**-*ice*
Clwyd *Kloo-id*
Coed-y-Brenin *Koyd-u-***Bren***in*
Cwellyn **Kwe**-*hlin*
Dolgellau *Dol-ge-hlay*
Dyfed **Duv***ed*
Glascwm *Glass-***coom**
Glyn Ceiriog *Glin* **Kay**-*ryog*
Gwaunceste *Gwine-***Kest**-*e*
Gwbert *Goobert*
Gwynedd *Gwin-eth*
Gwytherin *Gwith-***er***in*
Honddu *Hon-***thee**
Llanbedr *Hlan-***bedd***er*
Llanddwyn *Hlan-***thoo**-*in*
Llanidloes *Hlan-***id**-*loys*
Llanuwchllyn *Hlan-***uke**-*hlin*
Llwynmawr **Hloo***in-ma-oor*
Llyn Clywedog *Hlin-Klu-wedog*
Machynlleth *Mack-***un**-*hleth*
Mallwyd *Ma-hloo-id*
Mawddwy **Mow**-*thooy*
Moel Siabod *Moyl* **Sha***bod*
Mynach **Mun**-*ack*
Nant-y-Moch *Nant-u-***Mauk**
Penforddlas *Pen-***forth**-*las*
Penrhyndendraeth *Pen-rhin-***dye**-*dryth*
Pen-y-fan *Pen-u-***van**
Pen-y-Gwryd *Pen-u-***Goo**-*rid*
Pistyll Rhaeadr **Pis**-*tihl* **Rye**-*adder*
Pontrhydfendigaid *Pont-reed-ven-***dee**-*guide*
Pwllheli *Poohl-***hel***ly*
Rhos-y-Gwalian **Rhose**-*u*-**Gwali**-*ay*
Rhyd-ddu *Rheed-thee*
Tal-y-Llyn *Tal-u-***hlin**
Teifi **Tie**-*vee*
Tywy *Tu-wee*
Vyrnwy **Vur**-*noo-y*
Waenfawr *Wine-***vowr**

1 *North Wales*

A WIDE VARIETY of hotel accommodation is to be found in the beautiful city of Chester, making it an ideal starting-point for touring North Wales. One of the pleasures of travelling through Wales, whether in the north or the south, is that the perceptive visitor will readily learn about the history, mythology and folklore of this lovely country. Probably no other part of Britain is peopled with so many lovers of music and poetry – people who in the pubs, the shops and even the High Street delight in discussing not only the arts but wide varieties of topics such as politics, religion and local history. Thus, in the remotest of Welsh villages, it is always possible to learn of history and traditions that range over centuries – facts which are rarely found in the guidebooks.

North Wales is a land of mountains and valleys, lakes and forests. Along the coast there are stretches of fine sandy beach as well as historic castles like Harlech and Caernarvon, both of which are passed along this route. No route of 220 miles can possibly cover all that is beautiful in North Wales. The Lleyn Peninsula is not visited,

Park Street, Chester – a fine example of the town's timbered buildings.

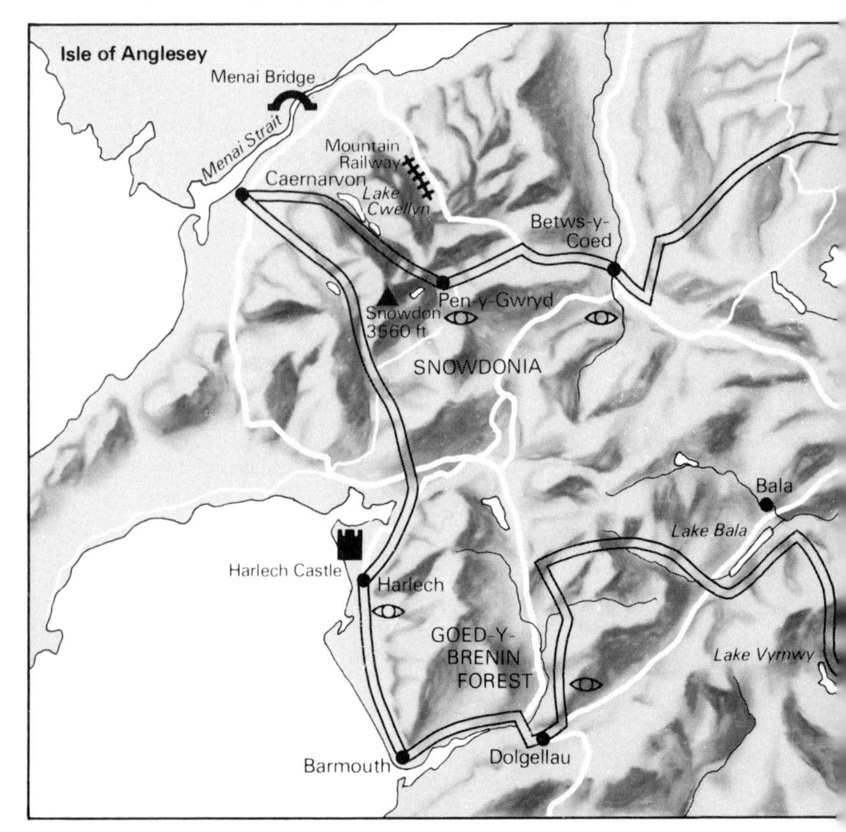

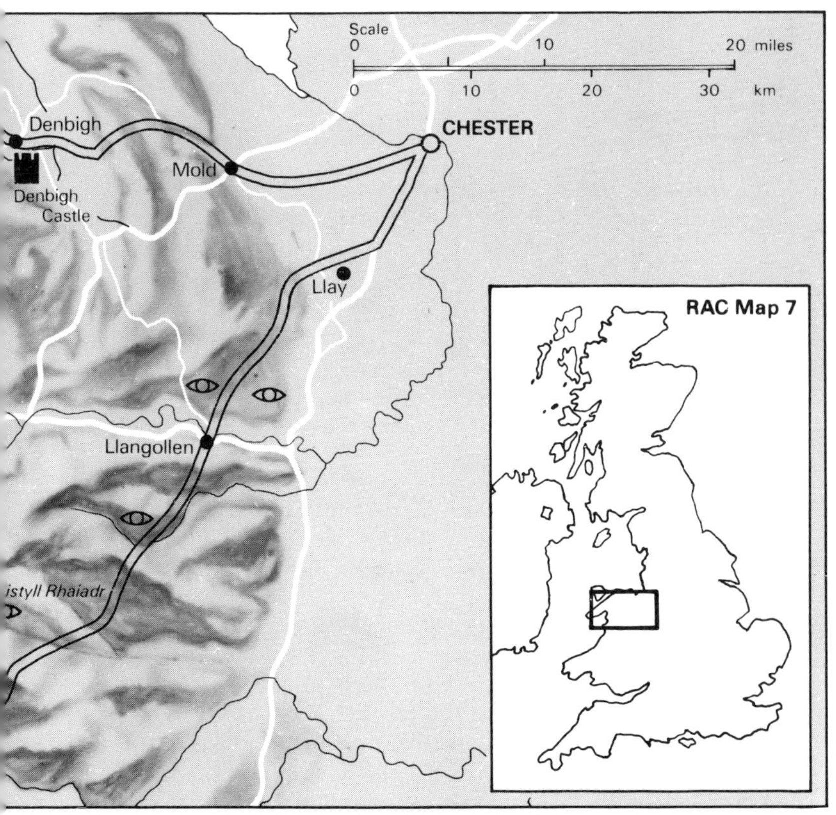
Scale
0
10
20 miles
0
10
20
30
km
Denbigh
CHESTER
Mold
Denbigh
Castle
Llay
RAC Map 7
Llangollen
istyll Rhaiadr

This delightful valley lies at the foot of Eglwyseg mountain, north of Llangollen.

and it has been suggested in the text that the best point of diversion for this area is at Penrhyndeudraeth. The isle of Anglesey, separated from the mainland by the Menai Straits, and where in particular the historic town of Beaumaris and Holy Island should be visited, can be reached across the Menai Bridge at Bangor after a nine-mile diversion from Caernarvon. The southernmost point of this route is Dolgellau – and those who decide to travel both the North Wales and the South Wales route should note that the northernmost point on the latter route, Mallwyd, lies only eleven miles from Dolgellau along the A470.

Those not conversant with the Welsh language may find that the names of towns, villages and features which appear on signposts and

maps tend to be complicated. In fact these names are usually descriptive, and for this reason it may be helpful to list the meanings of some place names encountered on the route:

Afon – river; Bach – little; Bedd – grave; Bont – bridge; Bwlch – pass; Capel – chapel; Coed – wood; Cwm – valley; Ddu – black; Fawr – great; Glyn – glen; Llan – enclosure (often a sacred enclosure or churchyard); Llech – flat stone; Llyn – lake; Moel – bare hill; Nant – black; Pen – head or top; Rhaiadr – water fall; Rhos – open moor; Rhyd – ford; Ty – house.

Numerous excellent hotels, guest houses and farm-houses that provide accommodation are to be found throughout North Wales. It is probably fair to say that prices in general tend to be lower than those charged in similar establishments in the south of England.

A street scene in Chester.

Chester (Cheshire)

Almost 2,000 years ago the Romans built a fortress here on the banks of the R. Dee. Much of the present city wall follows the line of the Roman defences, a circuit of two miles with a rampart walk from where there is a good view of both the city and the rugged hills of N. Wales through which the route runs. Interesting features of this rampart walk are the various gateways, towers and steps which form part of it. Among these are King Charles Tower, where King Charles I watched the defeat of his troops by the Parliamentarians in 1645, and which now contains a Civil War exhibition; the Water Tower, with an exhibition illustrating medieval Chester; the Goblin Tower, known also as Pemberton's Parlour after the rope-maker who worked there; and the Wishing Steps, where tradition has it that a wish is granted to those who can run up, down, and up again without drawing breath. East of the Newgate is the site of the Roman Amphitheatre. The walls also provide a good view of Chester racecourse, where meetings have been held since 1540.

A world-famous architectural feature of Chester is the design of the Rows – double tiers of shops allowing pedestrians to stroll along shop fronts and survey the passing traffic beneath. Among other places to see in the city are the Cathedral, the Castle, the Grosvenor Museum and the Zoo.

Plantation Hotel, Liverpool Rd, 64 rooms, T49221 (B)
Westminster Hotel, City Rd, 51 rooms, T25811 (B)
YHA, 40 Hough Green, T22231

Llangollen (Clwyd)

The town lies in a sheltered valley described by John Ruskin (1819–1900) as 'one of the most beautiful and delightful villages in Wales or anywhere else'. A house of particular interest is Plas Newydd (signed from centre of town), former home of two eccentric members of the Irish aristocracy known as the 'Ladies of Llangollen'. This whitewashed building, with elaborate wood carving in a delightful garden, is open to the public, and there is a display of gifts presented to the Ladies of Llangollen by many distinguished visitors. The international Eisteddfod takes place in the town annually each July, when thousands of visitors arrive from all over the world to join the Welsh choirs and make music.

Royal Hotel, Bridge St, 39 rooms, T860202 (B)
Chain Bridge Hotel, 35 rooms, T860215 (C)
YHA, Tyndwr Hall, Birch Hill, T860330
T.O. Town Hall, T860828

Glyn Ceiriog (Clwyd)

In the Institute is a memorial tablet to the third President of the USA, Thomas Jefferson (1743–1826), who was of Welsh descent. This much visited Institute is a memorial to local Welsh poets.

Golden Pheasant Hotel, Llwynmawr, 17 rooms, T281 (B)
Royal Oak Inn, 4 rooms, T243 (D)

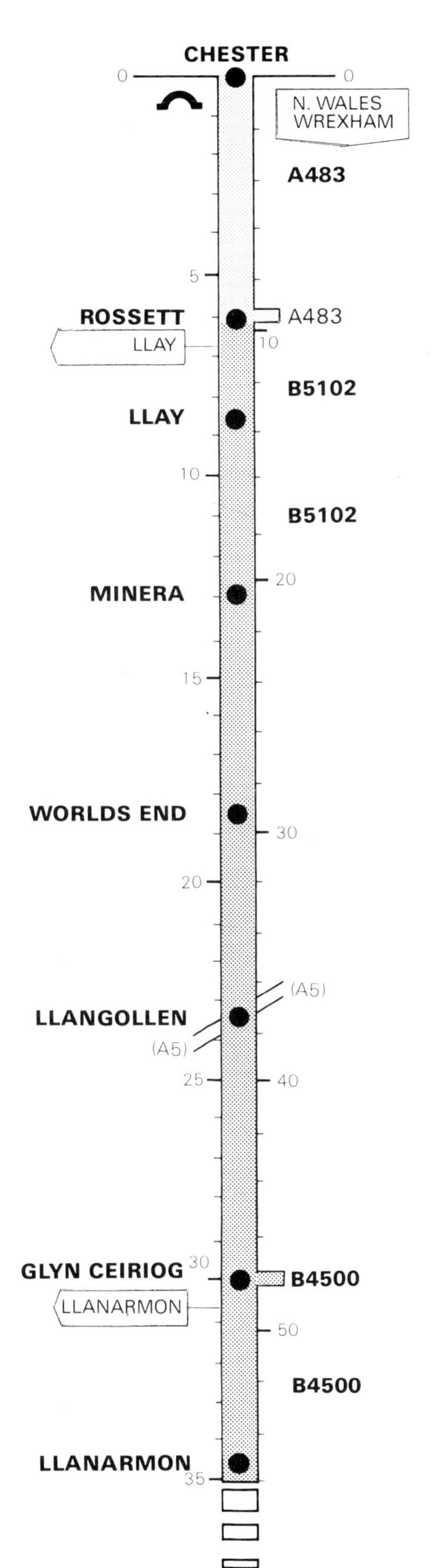

In Chester take A483 (signs N. Wales and Wrexham). Cross river and in 6.0 m bear right on to B5102 (sign Llay).

Continue straight on B5102 (signs Llay, later Wrexham) and in 2.5 m keep straight (sign Mold). In 1.1 m turn right and almost immediately left (sign Minera). In 1.2 m keep straight (no sign) and in further 1.0 m continue straight (sign Minera). In 1.1 m keep straight across A525 (no sign) and in 0.1 m at T junction turn right and immediately left (no sign). In 0.4 m keep straight and immediately right (sign Worlds End). In 0.6 m turn right (signs Worlds End and Llangollen).

Keep straight for 4.6 m into Worlds End valley. In 1.8 m bear left (sign Llangollen) and in 1.1 m bear right (sign Llangollen). In 0.8 m bear left (sign Llangollen) and continue straight for 1.2 m crossing river into Llangollen.

Keep straight through Llangollen and at traffic lights turn right (sign Betwys-y-Coed). In 1.0 m fork left (no sign). In 0.4 m bear left (no sign). In 0.8 m turn left (sign Ceiriog) and in 0.3 m turn right (sign Ceiriog). In 2.5 m turn left at T junction (sign Ceiriog via Church Hill) and in 0.1 m turn right (sign Ceiriog).

In 1.1 m at Glyn Ceiriog turn right on to B4500 (sign Llanarmon) and continue straight for 4.8 m through Pandy and Tregeiron to Llanarmon.

Llanrhaeadr-ym-Mochnant (Clwyd)

A diversion from the route can be made from this small village by turning right where Pistyll Rhaiadr Fall is signed. This waterfall caused the author of *Wild Wales*, George Borrow (1803–81) to write, 'I never saw water falling so gracefully, so much like beautiful threads as here.'

The dramatic Pistyll Rhaiadr Fall.

Llanwddyn (Powys)

Lies to the south-eastern edge of Lake Vyrnwy. The Vyrnwy Estate, an area that includes the man-made lake and surrounding moorlands and woodlands, covers almost 23,000 acres at the head of the R. Vyrnwy in the Berwyn mountains. The lake, five miles in length and about half a mile across, supplies Liverpool with water. The chosen route follows the eastern edge of the lake, while the alternative road which can be reached by crossing over the vast dam. Fishing rights are leased to the Lake Vyrnwy Hotel, who administer them from there.

Lake Vyrnwy Hotel, 30 rooms, T Llanwddyn 244 (C)

Rhos-y-Gwaliau (Gwynedd)

YHA, Plas Rhiwaedog, T Bala 215

Bala (Gwynedd)

The town with its broad tree-lined main street and prominent statue of Thomas Ellis (1859–99) who was Chief Liberal Whip at the end of the 19c, lies to the immediate north east of Lake Bala. The lake, 4½ miles long and 130 feet at its deepest point, is smaller than Lake Vyrnwy but is nevertheless the largest natural sheet of water in Wales. No less than 14 species of fish are stocked in it – among them trout, pike and a breed of salmon unique to this lake. Other popular sports on the lake include boating, swimming and skin diving. Train lovers will find the narrow gauge railway between Bala and Llanuwchllyn of interest – there are 13 locomotives, which include two steam engines, *Holy War* (1902) and *Maid Marian* (1903).

White Lion Hotel, 23 rooms, T314 (C)
Bala Lake Motel, 14 rooms, T344 (C)
Goat Hotel, 10 rooms, T432 (D)
YHA, see Rhos-y-Gwaliau
T.O. High St, T367

Llangower (Gwynedd)

Outside the church is a tiny yew tree, said to be the oldest in Wales. In the church can be seen one of only two horse-biers known to exist in Wales.

The Route

The descent to Glyn Ceiriog is very steep but quite safe if care is taken (the alternative route is signed via Nantyr and adds several miles).

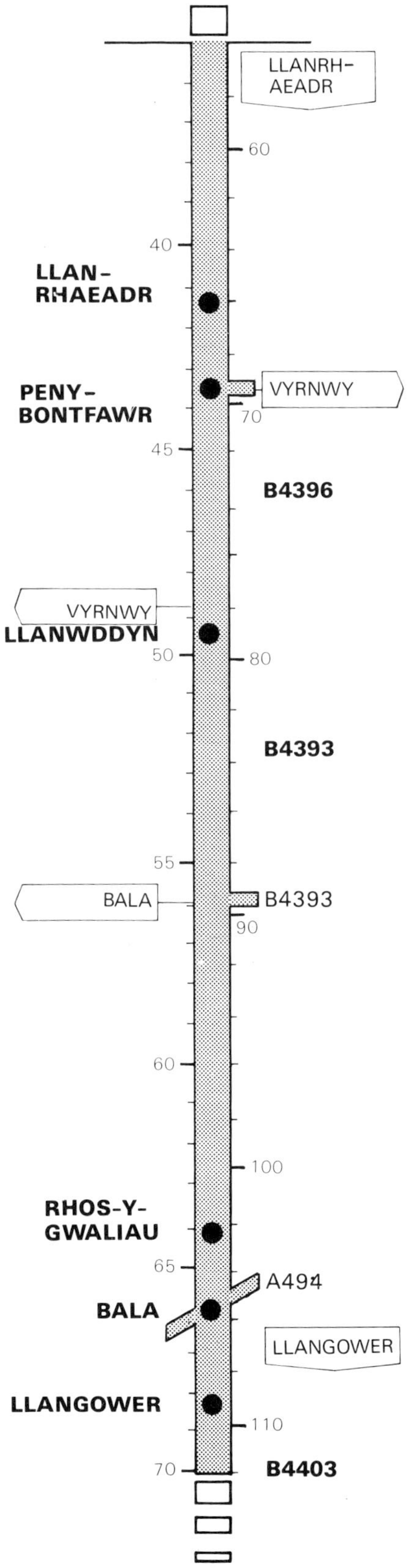

LLANRH-AEADR

60

40

LLAN-RHAEADR

At Llanarmon continue straight (sign Llanrhaeadr). In 1.7 m bear left (sign Llanrhaeadr) and keep straight for 4.5 m to Llanrhaeadr.

PENY-BONTFAWR

VYRNWY

70

45

B4396

Here keep straight (sign Llanginog) for 2.6 m to Penybontfawr, and here turn right and immediately left on to B4396 (sign Lake Vyrnwy). Keep straight for 5.9 m through Hirnant to Llanwyddyn.

VYRNWY

LLANWDDYN

50

80

B4393

On entering Llanwddyn bear right on to B4393 (sign Lake Vyrnwy). Continue straight and in 6.0 m bear right on to minor road (sign Bala). Keep straight (signs Bala) for 10.0 m for Bala town centre.

55

BALA

B4393

90

60

100

RHOS-Y-GWALIAU

65

A494

BALA

LLANGOWER

LLANGOWER

110

70

B4403

From here return to southern edge of lake Bala and take B4403 (sign Llangower) for 2.4 m to Llangower.

The Route

After leaving Llanuwchllyn, if time permits, it is worth taking the mountain road which circles indirectly towards Dolgellau in preference to the more direct but busy A494. Initially the road climbs high, with a huge waterfall to the left and the peaks of Arennig Fawr (2,800 ft) and Moel Llynfnant (2,460 ft) to the right. The early part of this road is gated (5 gates) but thereafter, fortunately, only cattle grids are encountered. There is ample compensation for the somewhat bleak mountain road as it descends southward through the lovely forest of Coed-y-Brenin.

Llanuwchllyn (Gwynedd)

At the far end of the village a fine monument has been erected depicting the figures of Sir Owen Edwards, prominent educationalist and man of letters, and his son Sir Ifan ab Owen Edwards. Both father and son are buried in the old cemetery of the village. There is a pleasant old inn, the Eagle (non-residential).

Dolgellau (Gwynedd)

Grey stone houses cluster round a variety of small squares connected by narrow streets in the town described by H. V. Morton, author of *In Search of Wales*, as being 'the most foreign corner in Wales'. Dolgellau is tucked neatly in a valley beneath the slopes of Cader Idris (2,927 ft) which towers above it to the south. It is an ideal base for climbers and ramblers, for apart from the challenge of the five peaks of Cader Idris there are numerous well-signed walks to the north of the town – among them the 'Precipice Walk' and the 'Torrent Walk'. The ruins of Cymer Abbey lie just outside the town.

Golden Lion Hotel, 29 rooms, T422579 (B)
Royal Ship Hotel, 23 rooms, T422209 (B)
T.O. The Bridge, T422888

Barmouth (Gwynedd)

This seaside resort lies beneath the Llawr Llech range of hills on the northern side of the Mawddach estuary, across which there is a rail- and footbridge, half a mile in length with a good overall view of the town. The promenade extends along a fine sandy beach to Llanaber. High up in the hills is a footpath, appropriately named 'Panorama Walk', with views of the estuary and the hills beyond.

Marine Mansion Hotel, 38 rooms, T280459 (C)
T.O. The Promenade, T280787

Llanbedr (Gwynedd)

The Maes Artro Craft Village is signed out of Llanbedr to the left. Apart from a variety of craft workshops there is also a miniature model village and a sea life aquarium. Two miles away is the peninsula of Mochras, known as Shell Island because it becomes an island at high tide and many rare shells are found there.

Victoria Hotel, 8 rooms, T213 (D)
Cae Nest Hall, 10 rooms, T349 (C)

Harlech (Gwynedd)

The town with its historic 13c castle stands on a hill overlooking Cardigan Bay. There is a panoramic view of the bay and the Snowdonia mountain range from the castle, scene of the surrender by the Welsh to the English in 1647 after a gallant defence which inspired the ballad 'March of the Men of Harlech'. Beneath the town is one of the finest sandy beaches in Wales and an excellent golf course.

St David's Hotel, 73 rooms, T366 (B)
T.O. High St, T658

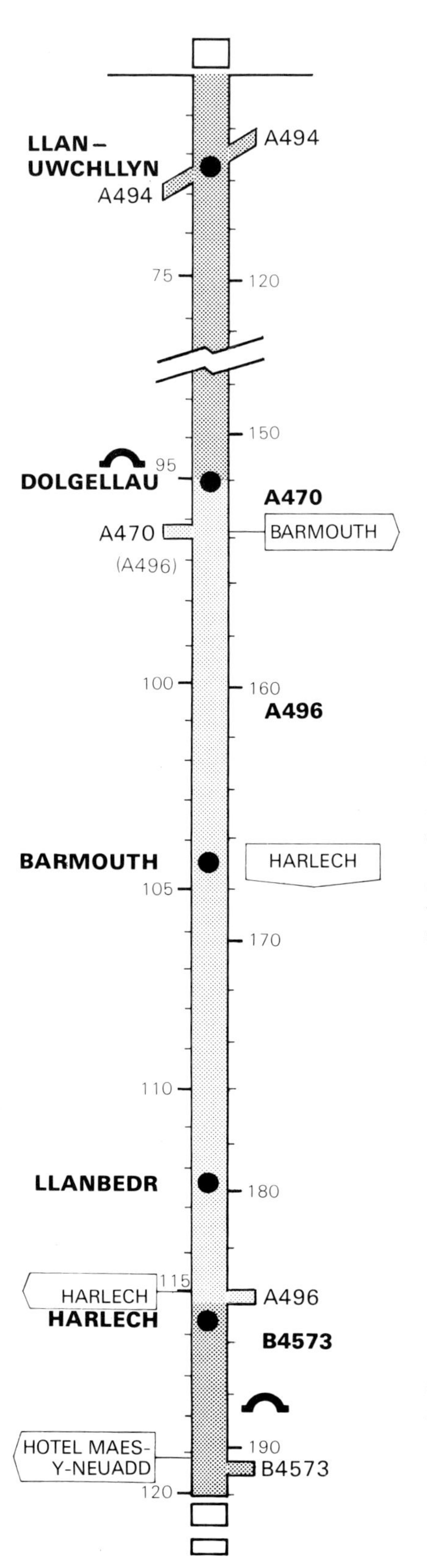

From Llangower continue straight for 3.0 m and at extremity of Llanuwchllyn turn right on to A494 (sign Bala) and in 0.1 m before crossing river turn left on to minor road (no sign). In 1.3 m turn right (no sign) and almost immediately left (local sign Trawsfynydd).

In 7.8 m bear left (no sign) and in 1.3 m turn left (sign Dolgellau). In 0.7 m fork right (sign Dolgellau). In 2.9 m keep straight (sign Dolgellau). In 2.4 m bear left (sign Dolgellau).

In 2.2 m keep straight (sign Dolgellau) and in 0.3 m bear right (sign Dolgellau). In 0.9 m turn right (sign Dolgellau) for 2.5 m and cross river into Dolgellau town centre.

In Dolgellau re-cross river and turn left on to A470 (sign Barmouth). In 1.5 m turn left on to A496 (sign Barmouth) and keep straight for 8.0 m to Barmouth town centre. Here keep straight through town on A496 (signs Harlech) and continue for 7.7 m to Llanbedr. Keep straight and in 2.6 m fork right on to B4573 (sign Harlech) for 0.5 m into Harlech town centre.

Here continue straight on B4573 (no sign) and in 3.7 m on crossing small bridge turn right on to minor road (sign Hotel Maes-y-Neuadd). In 0.4 m turn left (sign Llandecwyn).

Beddgelert (Gwynedd)

A picturesque village set in the midst of rocky heights, woodlands and mountain streams. The village name comes from the Bedd(grave) of Gelert, the legendary hound of Prince Llewelyn. Gelert's grave is signed out of the village to the right, lying in a meadow some 400 yards away. The story goes that Llewelyn went on a hunting expedition, leaving his infant son in the charge of Gelert. When the prince returned he found that the child was missing, and seeing blood on the hound's mouth suspected Gelert had killed him. In a rage Llewelyn slew Gelert, only to find later that his child was safely asleep near the body of a wolf – killed by his faithful hound.

Royal Goat Hotel, 29 rooms, T224 (C)
Saracens Head Hotel, 24 rooms, T223 (C)

Rhyd-Ddu (Gwynedd)

Snowdon, the highest mountain in England and Wales, is made up of five peaks – the loftiest being Wyddfor (3,560 ft) which lies some 3½ miles to the east of Rhyd-Ddu. One of several recommended signed walks to the summit of Snowdon starts here (3-hour walk). Another of these walks starts a mile or so further along the road from the youth hostel at Lake Cwellyn (2 hours).

YHA, Snowdon Ranger, Lake Cwellyn, T Waenfawr 391

Caernarvon (Gwynedd)

This ancient town and port at the end of the Menai Straits boasts one of Britain's most historic castles. Built in 1283 as one of King Edward I's fortresses, its massive walls enclose an area of about three acres. The remains include the entry gate, Kings Tower; the imposing Eagle Tower with three turrets, where it was once thought that Edward II was

Cottages at Beddgelert.

born; the Queen's Tower, housing the regimental museum of the Royal Welsh Fusiliers; and the North-East Tower, with an Investiture exhibition.

Muriau Park Hotel, Pwllheli Rd, 14 rooms, T4647 (D). This hotel has the advantage of a pleasant position about a mile from the town. A quite excellent menu is served at modest prices.
T.O. Slate Quay, T2232

Llanberis (Gwynedd)

The main part of the village lies off the road to the right on the slope of the hill. To the left of the road the lakes Padarn and Perris can be seen. The easiest ascent of Snowdon starts from here (3-hour walk), and the Snowdon Mountain railway station is at the southern end of the village.

Gallt-y-Glyn Hotel, 10 rooms, T370 (C)
YHA, Llwyn Celyn, T280

The Route

After a pleasant drive from Dolgellau to Barmouth, the coastal road to Harlech is somewhat spoilt by caravan sites. After Harlech the beautiful hillside minor road drops to cross the toll bridge (10p) into Penrhyndeudraeth. From here the road runs northward through the heart of Snowdonia.

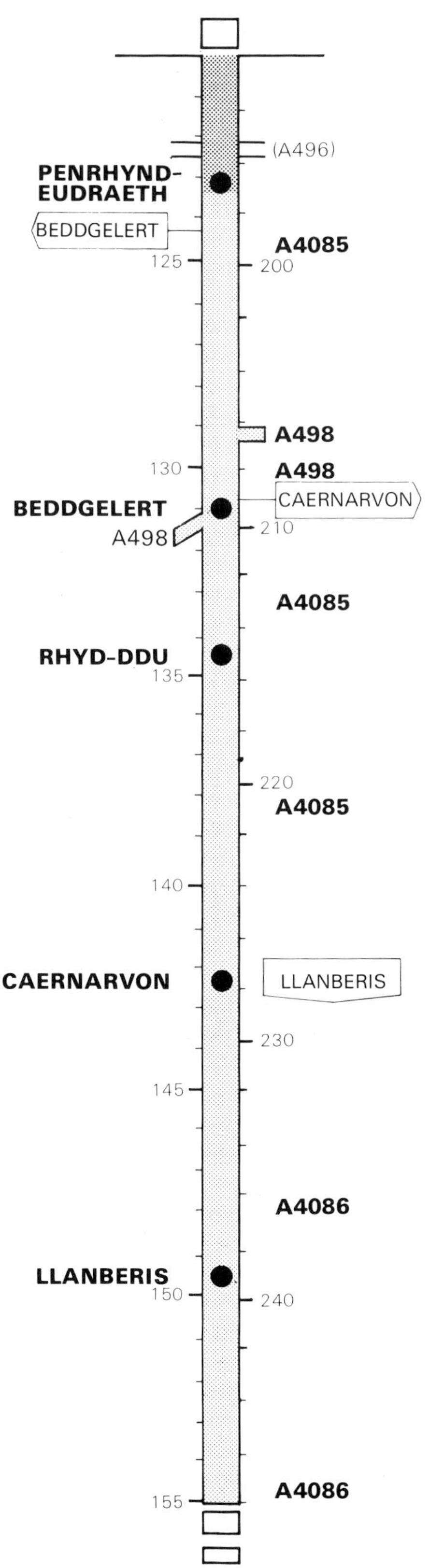

In 1.0 m keep straight (no sign) and in 0.7 m continue straight (no sign). In 0.2 m bear left (no sign) and in 0.7 m keep straight (sign Penrhyndeudraeth). In 1.1 m turn right on to A4085 (sign Beddgelert) and in 0.1 m continue straight (sign Beddgelert).

In 6.1 m turn right on to A498 (sign Beddgelert) for 1.5 m into Beddgelert. Here turn left on to A4085 (sign Caernarvon) for 3.6 m to Rhyd-Ddu.

Continue straight for 7.4 m and at roundabout keep straight for further 1.0 m into Caernarvon. In Caernarvon take A4086 (sign Llanberis) and in 6.8 m continue straight (sign Capel Curig).

The Route

Fine mountain and lake scenery most of the way from Caernarvon to Betws-y-Coed. Thereafter the minor roads are narrow but well surfaced, allowing traffic-free motoring through peaceful green pasture land – a contrast to the severity of the earlier mountain scenery.

Pen-y-Gwryd Hotel
(Gwynedd)

Whether deciding to stay here or not, it is certainly worth stopping off to visit this hotel with its historic associations in the fields of both mountaineering and literature. The successful 1953 Everest expedition team stayed here during their preparation. The signatures of the mountaineers are to be found on the ceiling of the Everest room, and there are numerous interesting relics connected with climbing. A well-known ascent of Snowdon starts opposite the hotel by a track named after it – the PYG track.

Pen-y-Gwryd Hotel, 21 rooms, T Llanberis 211 (D)

Capel Curig (Gwynedd)

A number of hotels are strung along the main Bangor/Shrewsbury road in this pretty village which is a popular headquarters for climbing, fishing and boating. In addition to Snowdon, other well-known peaks to climb include the Glyders to the west (3,279 ft) and Moel Siabod to the south (2,860 ft).

Cobdens Snowdonia Hotel, 17 rooms, T243 (C)
Bryn Tyrch Hotel, 14 rooms, T223 (C)
YHA, Plas Curig, T225

Betws-y-Coed (Gwynedd)

As the name implies, the village is entirely surrounded by wooded hills. It is one of the most popular spots in Wales for naturalists, artists, ramblers, anglers – all those in fact who want to pursue their particular activity in idyllic surroundings. Space only permits reference to a few of the local attractions. Among several waterfalls the most impressive are the Swallow Falls, which were signed to the left before entering the village. Still nearer to the village is the Miners Bridge, a solid wooden structure originally built by miners who used it as a short cut across a narrow part of the stream to the mines on the other side.

Royal Oak Hotel, Holyhead Rd, 38 rooms, T219 (B)
Park Hill Hotel, Llanrwst Rd, 10 rooms, T540 (C)
T.O. T426

Capel Garmon (Gwynedd)

Just past this small hillside village is a sign to the right directing to bronze-age burial chambers. These are of the long barrow type, about forty feet in length, and are to be found in a field not far from the road.

Gwytherin (Clwyd)

This remote village possesses a small inn, the Lion, which offers bed and breakfast accommodation.

Denbigh (Clwyd)

The prominent feature of this market town is the 13c castle, best approached on foot by a lane which leads off from the back of the Bull Hotel, a pleasant old coaching inn. A short climb towards the castle passes the wall of Leicester's church, a building begun in 1579 by the Earl of Leicester and intended as a cathedral, though never completed. The ruins of the castle lie among well-tended lawns at the

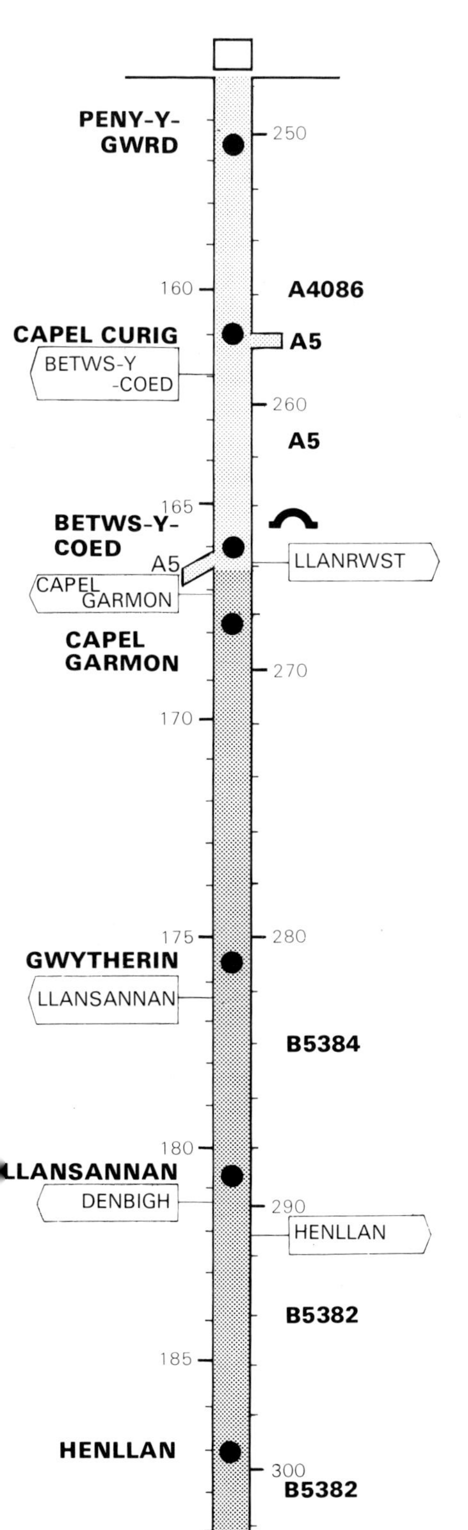

In 7.0 m at Pen-y-Gwryd Hotel turn left (sign Capel Curig) for 4.3 m to Capel Curig.

Here turn right on to A5 (sign Betws-y-Coed) and in 4.9 m cross Waterloo bridge and immediately turn left on to A470 (sign Llanrwst). In 0.3 m turn right on to minor road (sign Capel Garmon) and in 1.2 m at T junction turn right (no sign). In 0.2 m at Capel Garmon continue straight and in 1.0 m turn left (no sign). In 1.0 m bear left (sign Llanrwst) and in 0.1 m bear right (no sign). In 0.5 m keep straight and then immediately turn left (sign Llangernyw).

In 0.5 m bear right (no sign) and in 0.8 m keep straight (no sign). In 0.2 m bear right (sign Gwythern) and in 3.0 m bear left (sign Gwythern). In 0.5 m at Gwythern turn right on to B5384 (sign Llansannan). In 1.4 m bear left (sign Llansannan). Keep straight for 2.6 m and turn right (sign Llansannan).

In 0.8 m on entering Llansannan turn right (sign Denbigh) and in 0.6 m turn left on to B5382 (sign Henllan). In 0.2 m bear left (signs Denbigh and Henllan). In 1.5 m bear right (sign Denbigh). Keep straight for 4.5 m to Henllan and here bear right (sign Denbigh). Continue straight for 2.5 m into Denbigh town centre.

The Clwyddian Hills.

crown of the hill, presenting views over a great distance. The castle was begun by the Earl of Lincoln after Edward I had granted the town of Denbigh to him. Over the centuries it was held by a variety of people and causes, featuring as an object of siege in both the Wars of the Roses and the Civil War before being abandoned and left to decay in the 17c. The best preserved part of the castle is the gatehouse, from where a steep path leads back to the High Street, passing under the 13c Burgess Gate, entrance to the outer ward of the castle.

Bull Hotel, 14 rooms, T2582 (C)

Mold (Clwyd)

A busy little town with a wide tree-shaded High Street. Near the council offices is a statue of Daniel Owen, a native of the town who wrote many novels set in this part of Wales.

Denbigh's 13c castle.

The Route

The minor roads out of Denbigh are narrow but traffic-free. The road then rises sharply to cross the Clwyddian hills before descending to meet the A541 into Mold. The final stretch back to Chester has inevitably to follow the main road and is less interesting.

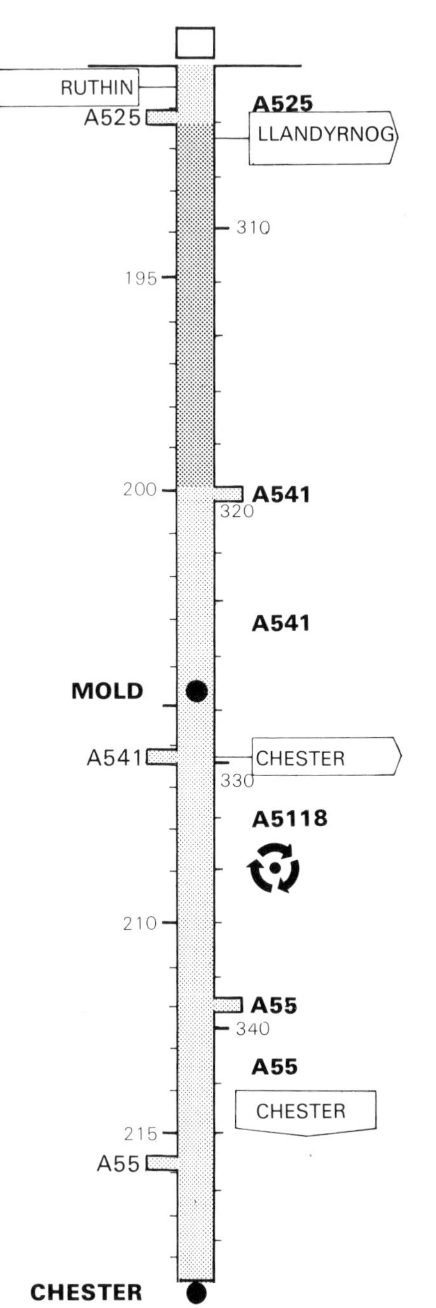

In Denbigh town centre follow signs for Ruthin and at traffic lights at end of town bear right on A525 (sign Ruthin). In 0.6 m at roundabout bear left on to minor road (sign Llandyrnog). In 2.6 m at roundabout continue straight (sign Llangwyfan hospital). In 0.4 m keep straight (no sign) and in 1.6 m at Swan Inn T junction turn left (sign Llangwyfan hospital).

In 1.0 m turn right (sign Star Crossing) and in 3.7 m turn right on to A541 (no sign). Continue straight for 5.0 m and bear right into Mold town centre. Here turn left on to A541 (sign Chester) and in 1.5 m bear left on to A5118 (sign Chester).

In 3.2 m at roundabout keep straight (sign Chester) and in 2.6 m turn right on to A55 (sign Chester). In 3.0 m bear left (sign Chester) for 3.0 m into Chester town centre.

2 *Yorkshire: the Dales*

FROM YORK the chosen route runs westward in the general direction of the Dales. The road to Wetherby crosses a plain, a little to the north of which is Marston Moor, scene of the defeat of Prince Rupert and the Royalists in 1644 by the Parliamentarians led by Lord Fairfax. Equipment from this famous battle can be seen at the Castle museum in Knaresborough, from where the route runs through Pateley Bridge and ascends to Greenhow, Yorkshire's highest village, before descending to Grassington.

The road has now entered the Yorkshire Dales National Park, one of the two National Parks in the county – the other being the North Yorkshire Moors National Park (Route 9). The Dales consist of a series of valleys carved into the Pennine hills, taking their names from the rivers which flow through them, except in the case of Wensleydale – named after the village of Wensley. It would be impossible within the scope of one progressive tour to see more than a limited number of the Yorkshire Dales – areas of unspoilt grandeur which compare with any others in the whole of England. This particular route runs through large sections of Wharfedale and Swaledale, crossing Wensleydale at Hawes and at Leyburn, while Nidderdale can be explored by diverting northward from Pateley Bridge.

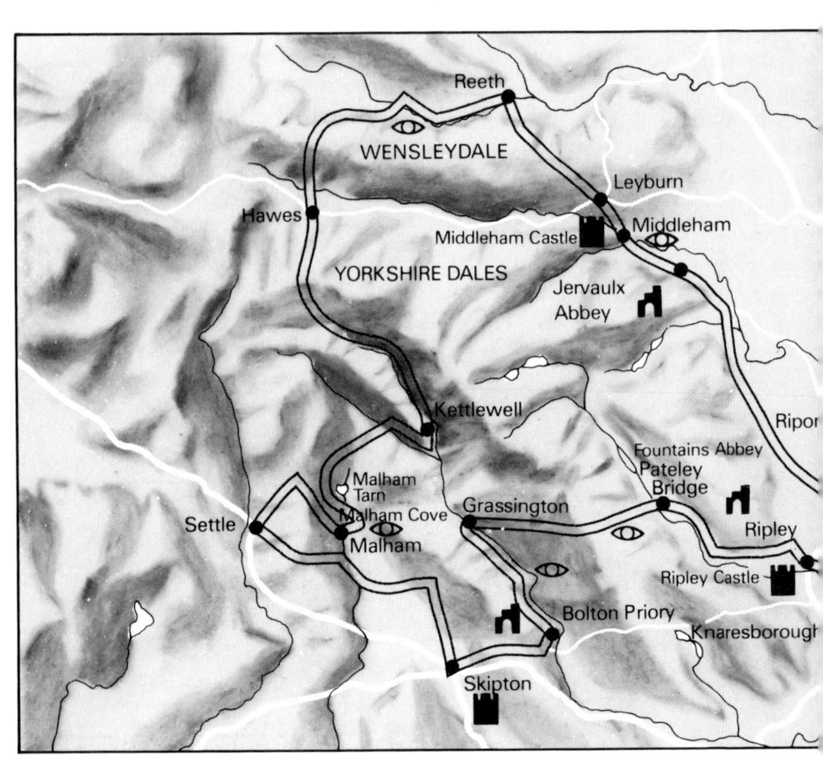

From Grassington the road passes by way of the beautiful village of Burnsall; Bolton Abbey; Skipton and its well-preserved castle; Malham with the nearby tarn and gorge; and then runs northwards through what is perhaps the finest section of Wharfedale around Kettlewell. After the beauty of this lush valley scenery the road climbs high over Buttertubs Pass before reaching Swaledale, one of the wildest of the Yorkshire Dales and hemmed in by wooded hills on both sides. On leaving Swaledale at Grinton the road crosses the moors once more to Leyburn and then proceeds by way of Middleham, passing the ruined Jervaulx Abbey before arriving at the attractive little town of Masham and the quiet remote villages of Grewelthorpe and Kirkby Malzeard to the south of it. The huge Fountains Abbey, adjoining the Studley Royal Park, occupies a peaceful setting in the lovely Skell valley, and is the last place of real interest along the route which from here returns to York. Those wishing to linger here should bear in mind that Ripon lies only three miles to the north. This is a cathedral town of great traditions where the night watchman, or Wakeman as he is called, sounds his horn in the market square – an event which has taken place nightly for a thousand years.

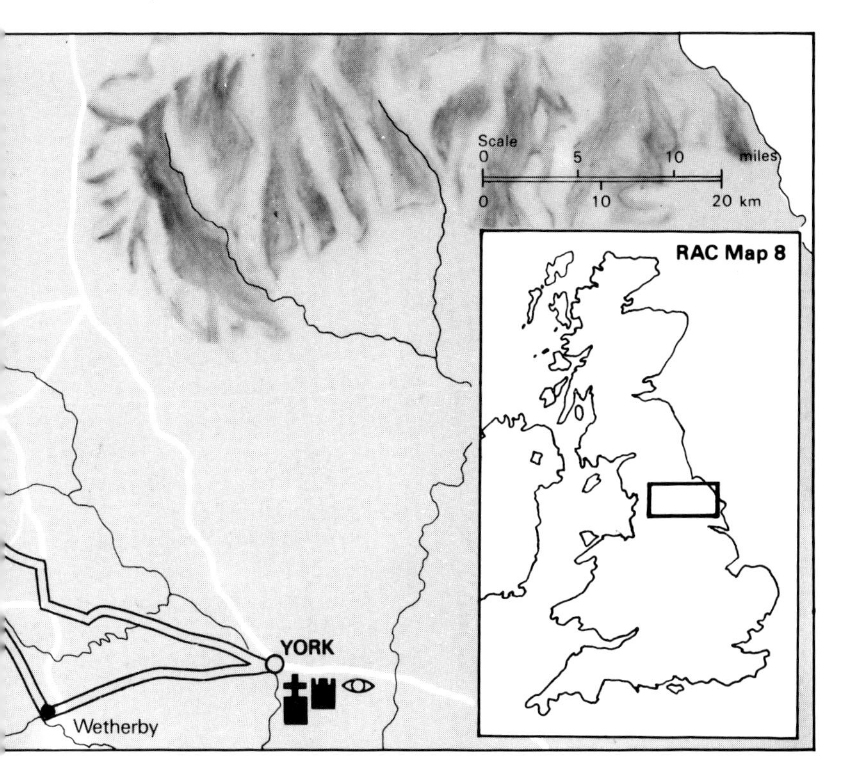

York (N. Yorks)

See Route 9, page 158.

Wetherby (W. Yorks)

A market town entered by a picturesque bridge across the R. Wharfe where boating is popular. The race course can be seen on the left of the road before entering the town.

Wetherby Turnpike Hotel, Leeds Rd, 70 rooms, T63881 (A)
T.O. Council Houses, 24 Westgate, T62706

Knaresborough (N. Yorks)

The town commands a fine position above the R. Nidd with a market square (to left of route), surrounded by old houses and shops. Only a minute's walk away are the castle ruins, set amidst pleasant gardens and standing magnificently above the river. From the ramparts there is a glorious view of the huge viaduct and the houses built in tiers along the hillside. Many prisoners languished in Knaresborough Castle, among them King Richard II on his way to a mysterious death at Pontefract. The castle keep is occupied by a museum that includes armour worn at Marston Moor. Boats can be hired on the river, where other attractions include Conyngham Hall, in the grounds of which is a zoo; Mother Shipton's Cave, dwelling of a 15c prophetess who foretold the coming of the car and the aeroplane; and the Dropping Well, a petrifying spring.

Dower House, Bond End, 20 rooms, T Harrogate 863302 (B)
T.O. Market Place, T Harrogate 866886

Ripley (N. Yorks)

Ripley Castle and All Saints Church face each other across the cobbled tree-shaded square of this tiny village. The castle, home of the Ingilbys, has entertained both James I and Oliver Cromwell, the latter watched over throughout the night he spent there by Lady Ingilby armed with a pistol. The castle lies in landscaped gardens and is open to the public on specified occasions. Among interesting features of the church are the tombs of Sir Thomas and Sir William Ingilby.

The stocks at Ripley.

In the churchyard is one of the few remaining 'weeping' crosses, a pedestal with a hole in the top for the reception of a larger cross and surrounded by recesses where penitents could kneel – the narrowness of the recesses ensuring that they did so in pain.

Pateley Bridge (N. Yorks)

The main street drops sharply to the R. Nidd. From this small town it is possible to divert northwards and explore Upper Nidderdale by way of such pretty villages as Warth and Ramsgill, between which lies the Garthwaite reservoir and bird sanctuary. This road is a cul de sac, but worth taking, and there is a YHA at Ramsgill (below).

YHA, Longside House, T Harrogate 75207.

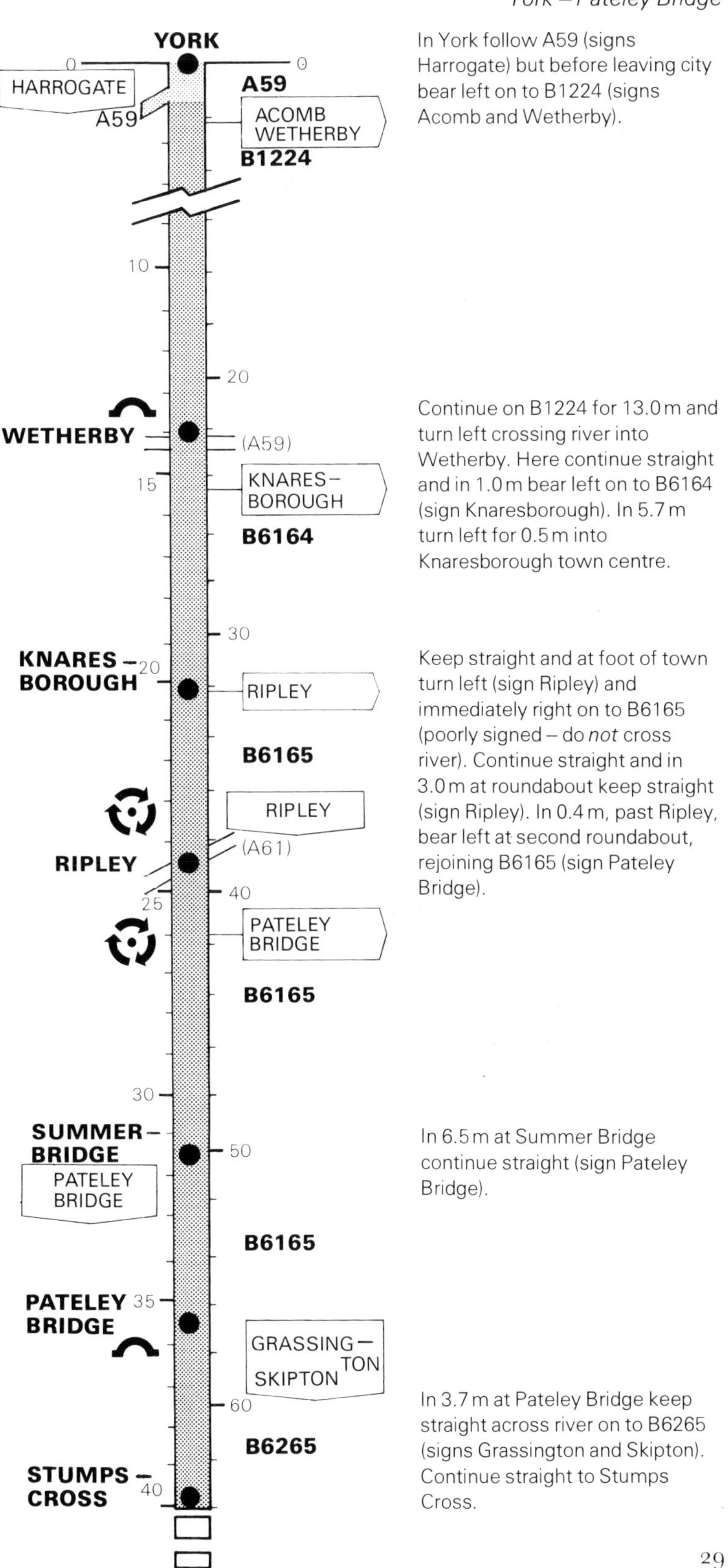

In York follow A59 (signs Harrogate) but before leaving city bear left on to B1224 (signs Acomb and Wetherby).

Continue on B1224 for 13.0 m and turn left crossing river into Wetherby. Here continue straight and in 1.0 m bear left on to B6164 (sign Knaresborough). In 5.7 m turn left for 0.5 m into Knaresborough town centre.

Keep straight and at foot of town turn left (sign Ripley) and immediately right on to B6165 (poorly signed – do *not* cross river). Continue straight and in 3.0 m at roundabout keep straight (sign Ripley). In 0.4 m, past Ripley, bear left at second roundabout, rejoining B6165 (sign Pateley Bridge).

In 6.5 m at Summer Bridge continue straight (sign Pateley Bridge).

In 3.7 m at Pateley Bridge keep straight across river on to B6265 (signs Grassington and Skipton). Continue straight to Stumps Cross.

Stump Cross Cavern
(N. Yorks)

These caves, to the left of the road, were discovered by miners in 1860, and there are now a number of illuminated caverns through which there are guided tours, taking about 20 minutes. These show caverns have been given descriptive names such as the Butcher's Shop, the Twins, the Jewel Box, and the Chamber of Pillars.

Grassington (N. Yorks)

This small hill town above the R. Wharf is a popular centre for touring the Dales, and in high season does appear to be rather overcrowded. Numerous hotels and guest houses surround a tiny square where access and parking are difficult. Among many old houses is a 16c barn where John Wesley (1703–91) once preached.

Devonshire Hotel, The Square, 11 rooms, T752525 (C)
Black Horse Hotel, The Square, 12 rooms, T752770 (D)

Bolton Abbey (N. Yorks)

The Priory, the bulk of which is in ruins, occupies an enchanting position above the river, where a bridge – and fifty-seven stepping-stones – connect with the wooded hills beyond. Fine examples of Norman and Early English architecture can be seen – but for its setting alone the Priory is well worth visiting.

Skipton (N. Yorks)

This large market town was once called 'Sceptone' (sheep town), and now, owing to its position, it is known as the 'Gateway to the Dales'. At the top of the High Street is one of England's most imposing and well-preserved castles. Skipton Castle, now privately owned and open to the public on occasions, was formerly the home of the Cliffords. An 18c room lined with shells and the castle dungeon are among those parts of the castle which can be viewed.

The ruins of Bolton Abbey.

Snaygill House Hotel, Keighley Rd, 18 rooms T2970 (C)
T.O. High St Car Park, T2809

Rylstone (N. Yorks)

The church is tucked away in the trees, and apart from a manor house, a few farm-houses, and a duck-pond there is little to see in this romantic village, the scene of Wordsworth's 'White Doe of Rylstone'.

Airton (N. Yorks)

On the hillside just before reaching this pretty village is a solid grey house with a superlative view – Calton Hall. This was the birthplace of the Parliamentarian general, John Lambert (1619–84).

The Route

The road strikes westward from York and until it reaches Wetherby is somewhat featureless. From here, however, beautiful scenery is encountered as the road undulates toward the Dales. From Pateley Bridge there is a steep ascent to Greenhow Hill, from where there are magnificent views.

Stump Cross Cavern – Airton

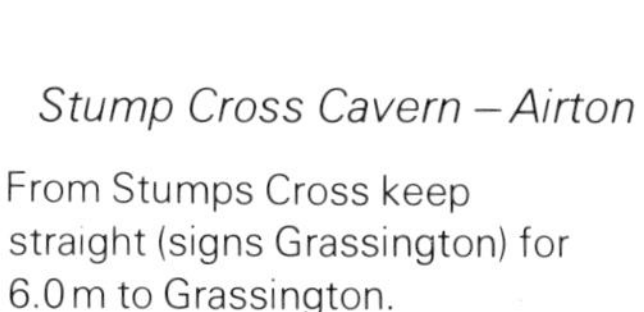

From Stumps Cross keep straight (signs Grassington) for 6.0 m to Grassington.

Here continue straight across river and immediately turn left on to minor road (sign Burnsall). In 0.6 m turn left on to B6160 (sign Burnsall) for 2.6 m to Burnsall. Here continue straight for further 6.0 m to Bolton Abbey.

In village turn right on to minor road (sign Embsay) and continue on minor road (signs Skipton) through Embsay for 5.8 m to Skipton.

Here at first roundabout turn right on to B6265 (sign Grassington). In 4.7 m at Rylstone turn left on to minor road (sign Hetton). In 0.5 m at T junction turn left (sign Gargrave) and in 0.3 m at Hetton bear right (sign Malham). In 1.8 m keep straight (sign Airton) and almost immediately turn right over bridge (sign Airton). In 1.9 m turn left (sign Malham) and in 0.4 m at Airton turn right (sign Malham). In 0.2 m turn left (sign Settle) and continue straight for Settle.

The Route

Initially runs southward through Wharfedale to Bolton Abbey. The road from Rylstone to Settle is narrow but there are plenty of passing places. There is a sharp descent to Settle, from where the road rises once more with fine views as it drops down to Arncliffe. There are numerous cattle grids and one gated road (two gates only) between Malham and Arncliffe.

Settle (N. Yorks)

The small town, immediately overlooked by a massive cliff, has some quaint arcaded shops over which are living quarters. Victoria Cave, to the east of the town, was discovered in 1838 and many ancient relics from there are to be seen in the museum. The well-known school, Giggleswick, lies a mile away.

Falcon Manor Hotel, Skipton Rd, 12 rooms, T2357 (A)

The precipice of Malham Cove.

Malham (N. Yorks)

From the little village can be explored both Malham Cove, a limestone cliff almost 300 feet in height – the tallest inland precipice in England – and Malham Tarn, a 150-acre lake owned by the National Trust which is a bird sanctuary and where there is a field centre open to the public. Another attraction is Gordale Scar.

Buck Inn, 10 rooms, T Airton 317 (C)
Beck Hall Guest House, 10 rooms, T Airton 332 (D)
Sparth House, 10 rooms, T Airton 315 (C)
YHA, John Dower Memorial Hostel, T Airton 321

Arncliffe (N. Yorks)

There is a magnificent view of the village as the road descends to it. Most of the houses overlook the rough village green, and although the road continues without passing the church it is well worth parking here and strolling to the R. Skirfare (left). St Oswald's Church has a superb position on the banks of the river – on a site which has been occupied by a variety of churches since Saxon times.

Kettlewell (N. Yorks)

The two recommended hotels face each other in this charming village on the R. Wharfe.

Racehorses Hotel, 16 rooms, T233 (B)
Bluebell Hotel, 6 rooms, T230 (C)
YHA, Whernside House, T232

Hubberholme (N. Yorks)

In this tiny village there is an inn on the left and a church beyond the bridge on the right. In common with the church at Arncliffe the little church here occupies an idyllic position on the river in the heart of Wharfedale. Inside the church is a proud but possibly justified boast:

*Hubberholme Church in beautiful
Wharfedale,
Wharfedale so sweet and fair
Nothing in England can with
Thee compare.*

As the river flows placidly past the little church, once a simple forest chapel, one is tempted to agree.

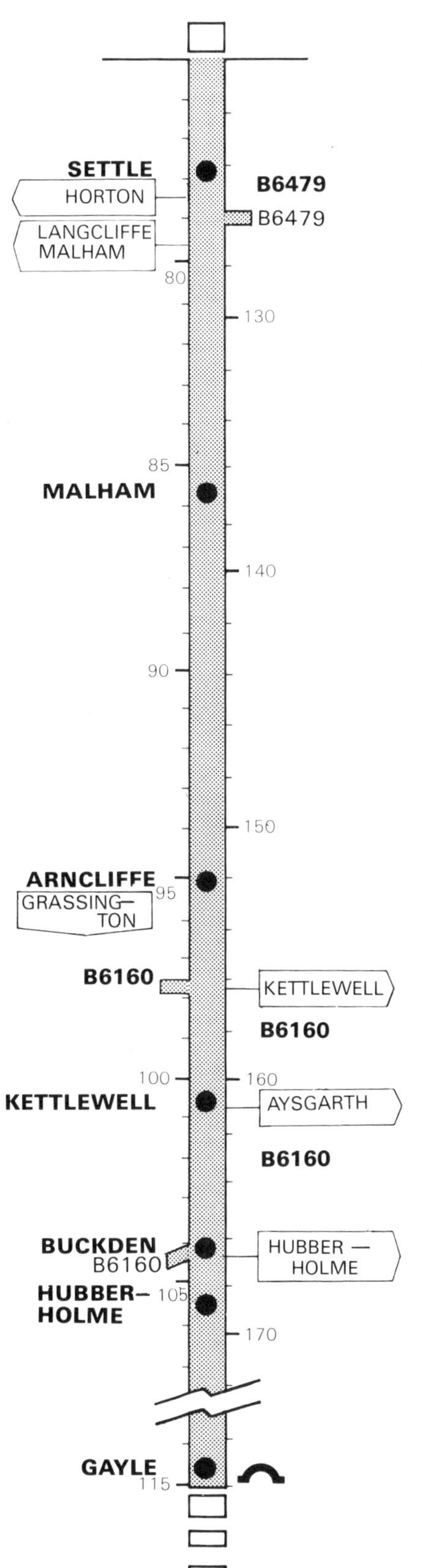

In Settle, entering town centre at T junction turn right (no sign). In 0.4 m turn right on to B6479 (sign Horton) and in 0.6 m turn right on to minor road (sign Langcliffe and Malham). In 2.8 m bear right (sign Malham) and in 1.1 m bear right (sign Arncliffe). In 0.5 m turn right (sign Malham) and continue straight for 2.7 m to Malham.

At Malham turn left (sign Gordale and Malham Tarn) and in 0.2 m turn left (sign Malham Tarn). In 2.0 m bear left (sign Settle) and in 1.6 m turn right (sign Arncliffe). Keep straight for 5.8 m to Arncliffe.

In Arncliffe continue straight (sign Grassington) and in 3.1 m turn left on to B6160 (sign Kettlewell). In 2.3 m at Kettlewell bear left on B6160 (sign Aysgarth). In 3.5 m at Buckden turn left on to minor road (sign Hubberholme) and in 1.2 m at Hubberholme keep straight.

In 10.2 m at Gayle bear right through village and immediately turn left over bridge (sign Hawes) for 0.5 m into Hawes.

Hawes (N. Yorks)

The little grey market town lies at the head of Wensleydale – the famous cheese being made at factories here. At the Ropemaker near the station it is possible to watch ropes made in the traditional fashion. To the north of the town at the village of Hardrow (half a mile off the route) is one of England's most impressive waterfalls. Hardrow Force, as the falls are known, is approached through the grounds of the Green Dragon Inn.

Fountain Hotel, Market Place,
12 rooms, T206 (A)
YHA, Lancaster Terrace, T368 (A)

Muker (N. Yorks)

The first of a number of villages passed as the road turns eastward through Swaledale. Houses perched on the hillside overlooking the valley are linked by narrow alleys and steps. At one time the only consecrated ground in the valley lay far away at Grinton and this meant that bodies for burial from Muker and other Swaledale villages had to be transported manually to the Grinton churchyard – giving that road the macabre title of the 'Corpse Way'.

The Route

From Kettlewell the road runs northwards through Wharfedale, crossing Wensleydale at Hawes. Beyond Hawes the road crosses Buttertubs Pass – so called because of geological features; some of them 50 feet deep and shaped like buttertubs.

NB The high moorland road between Grinton and Leyburn runs through a practice range which is very occasionally closed when in use. It would then be necessary to take the longer signed route to Leyburn by the major road.

An attractive scene near Muker.

Feetham/Low Row (N. Yorks)

There are a number of hotels and inns along the valley. Among the most pleasant and one which commands a fine view is the Punch Bowl.

Punch Bowl Hotel, 17 rooms, T Gunnerside 233 (C)

Reeth (N. Yorks)

There is a spacious green around which a number of hotels stand. Reeth is a larger village than those passed earlier in Swaledale, and boasts an Art Gallery and Folk Museum. The museum is well organized, and among points of interest are a genealogical tree of a Swaledale family and an account of the life of the local doctor which illustrates the dedication needed by a GP working and travelling through these remote parts.

Kings Arms Hotel, The Green, 5 rooms, T259 (C)
Arkleside Hotel, 8 rooms, T200 (C)

Leyburn (N. Yorks)

The hill town stands round a huge market square. Behind the Bolton Hotel a sign directs to the 'Shawl', a mile-long terrace overlooked by oaks and sycamores from where there is a fine view of Wensleydale. Mary Queen of Scots was reputed to have been captured on the 'Shawl' after her escape from Bolton Castle.

Golden Lion Hotel, Market Place, 5 rooms, T22161 (D)

Middleham (N. Yorks)

Centuries ago horses were bred here by monks from Jervaulx Abbey, and today racehorses are trained in an establishment older than Newmarket. Middleham Moor, where the training gallops take place, has a remote spot known as 'Courting Wall Corner', where it is said that a jealous lover murdered and buried his girlfriend.

Jervaulx Abbey.

The town boasts two small market squares. One of these has a market cross; the other contains a strange monument comprising two stone blocks and over them a carving which despite its age has some resemblance to a boar – perhaps a representation of the boar of Richard III. Although the castle was largely dismantled in the 17c, the immense 12c keep remains almost in its entirety. This was the castle where Richard's son was born and died.

Miller's House, Market Place, 7 rooms, T Wensleydale 22630 (C)

Jervaulx Abbey (N. Yorks)

The car park is on the right of the road, and the ruins of the Cistercian Abbey are to be found opposite after a walk of a few hundred yards. These remains occupy a charming site amidst shrubs and trees, and from the stonework it is possible to detect the overall layout of the monastery where, although little of the church exists, it is easy to make out the well-defined area that was once the monks' quarters. The monastery was founded in 1156 and destroyed in the 16c, after the Abbot had been hanged for complicity in the Pilgrimage of Grace.

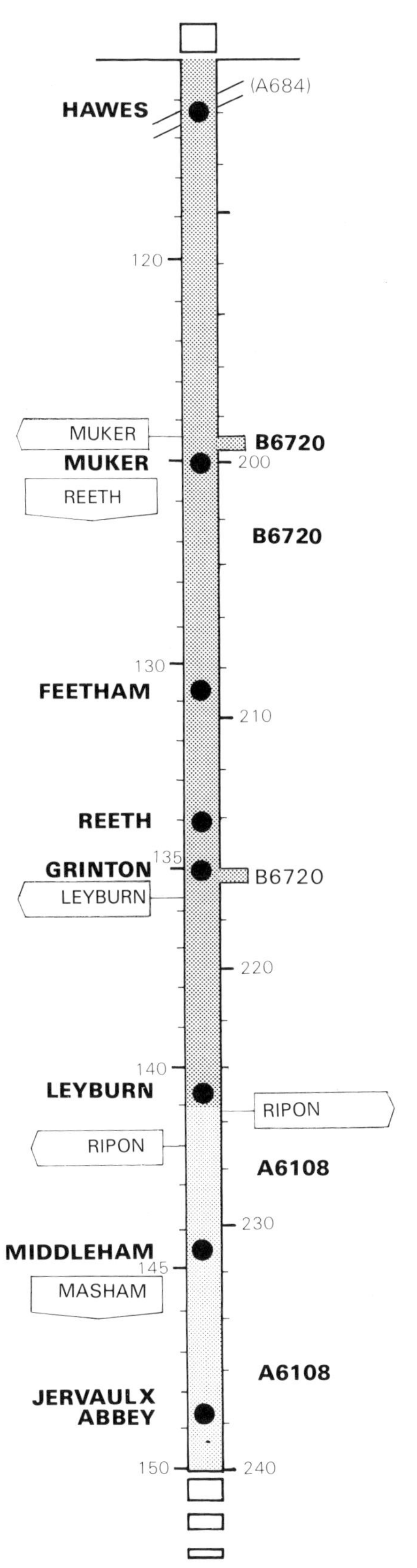

In Hawes turn right (sign Aylsgarth), following one-way circuit, and in 0.3 m turn left on to minor road (sign Hardrow). In 0.8 m bear left (sign Hardrow) and almost immediately right (sign Muker).

In 5.6 m turn right on to B6270 (sign Muker). In 1.2 m at Muker continue straight (sign Reeth). Keep straight on B6270 (signs Reeth) for 5.9 m to Feetham and here continue straight for 3.5 m to Reeth.

Continue straight (sign Leyburn) and in 0.9 m at Grinton bear right on to minor road (sign Leyburn).

In 5.2 m keep straight (sign Leyburn) for 1.8 m into Leyburn. Here turn right and immediately left (sign Ripon). In 0.3 m turn right on to A6108 (sign Ripon) for 1.8 m to Middleham. In Middleham take A6108 (sign Masham) for 3.7 m to Jervaulx Abbey car park.

The extensive remains of Fountains Abbey stand in a magnificent setting.

Masham (N. Yorks)

Solid Georgian houses surround the spacious square of this small town, a quiet and placid place due to the fact that no main road passes through it. St Mary's Church in the square retains in the churchyard part of an Anglo-Saxon cross (9c).

Kings Head Hotel, Market Place, 13 rooms, T295 (C)

Grewelthorpe (N. Yorks)

The village is the home of the Grewelthorpe Weavers, and in their craft shop can be seen fine examples of hand-loom weaving.

Kirkby Malzeard (N. Yorks)

Here lived for a great part of his life one Henry Jenkins. He was buried at Bolton on Swale, where records show him to have been born in 1500 and to have died in 1669!

Fountains Abbey (N. Yorks)

This famous Cistercian Abbey, founded in 1132, stands in the lovely valley of the R. Skell, and so much of it remains that at least half a day needs to be spent here to appreciate not only the Abbey but the adjoining Studley Royal Park. The church, 370 feet in length and with a 168-foot tower, lies by the extraordinary cellarium undercroft with its twenty-two bays. Other surviving features of interest include the Chapel of Nine Altars, Chapter House, Refectory, Warming House, and a wishing-well.

The Route

The minor roads from Masham run south-eastward in a complicated pattern but the verbal route instructions should be sufficient to guide the traveller through this unspoilt country.

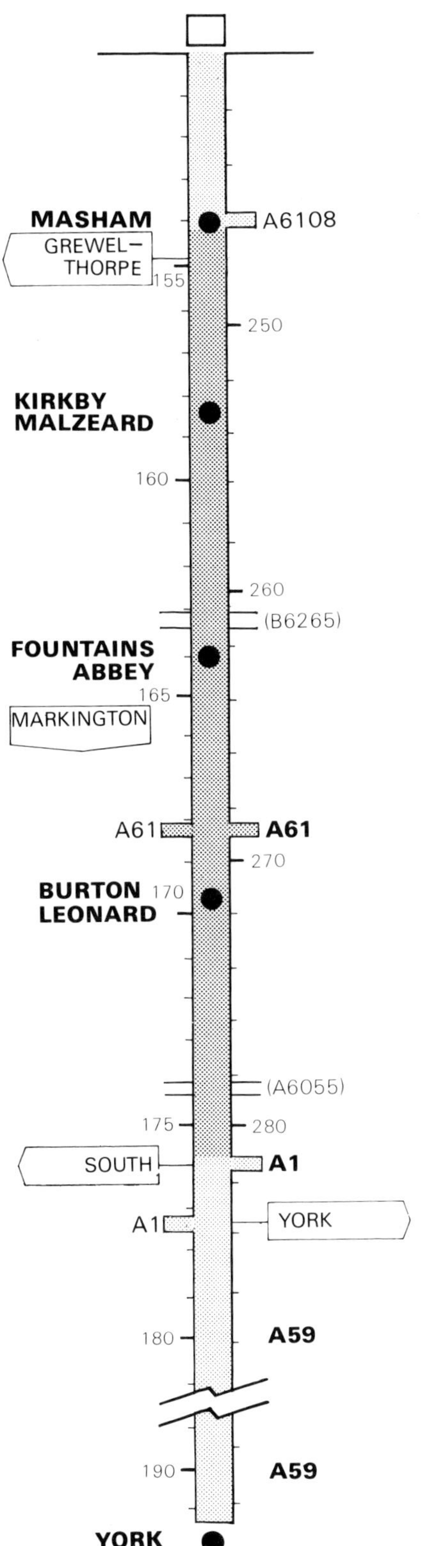

From Jervaulx Abbey keep straight and in 5.2 m turn right (sign Masham) into Masham. Here bear right on to minor road (sign Grewelthorpe) for 3.3 m and on entering Grewelthorpe bear left (sign Kirkby Malzeard). At centre of Grewelthorpe turn right (sign Kirkby Malzeard). In 0.9 m bear left and in 0.3 m at Kirkby Malzeard keep straight (signs Grantley).

In 1.3 m bear right (sign Grantley) and immediately bear left (sign Winksley). Keep straight for 1.2 m to Winksley and here continue straight, in 0.7 m bear right and in 0.5 m bear left (signs Aldfield). In 0.3 m turn left and immediately right (sign Aldfield). In 0.7 m at T junction turn right (sign Fountains Abbey) for 1.0 m to abbey car park.

Here continue straight, and in 1.5 m turn left (signs Markington). In 1.0 m at Markington turn left (sign Wormald Green) and in 0.3 m bear right (sign Wormald Green). In 0.9 m turn left on to A61 (sign Ripon) and in 0.2 m turn right on to minor road (sign Burton Leonard). There, in 1.5 m turn right (sign Copgrove).

In 1.3 m at Copgrove keep straight, and in 1.0 m turn left (signs Staveley). In 0.5 m at Staveley bear right, and in 1.1 m keep straight (signs Arkendale). In 0.8 m at Arkendale turn left (sign Marton). In 0.2 m turn right (sign Allerton). In 1.1 m turn left and immediately right on to A1 (sign South) and in 1.7 m turn left on to A59 (sign York) for 14.0 m into York.

3 *Cumbria (the Lake District)*

THE BEAUTY of this National Park of lakes, mountains and valleys is best appreciated on foot. This guide, of course, has been compiled primarily for the motorist or cyclist who probably wishes to see as much as possible of the area within a limited time. However, this tour of less than two hundred miles may encourage the traveller to return to an area of his choice for a more detailed exploration.

Planning a route by minor roads through this area of mountains and valleys is no easy task, as inevitably the roads tend to become channelled, sometimes confining the tourist to a single road with no alternative choice. So far as possible, however, minor roads have been taken to link, progressively, a great variety of lakes and lakeland scenery. As a result thirteen of the fifteen largest lakes are passed directly along the route – the exceptions being Bassenthwaite and Thirlmere. Bassenthwaite, the most northerly of the lakes, can be seen at a distance from the road between Keswick and Caldbeck. Thirlmere, which like Hawes Water is now a reservoir, lies along the A591 south-east of Keswick. Among those lakes that are passed the largest are Windermere and Ullswater; the broadest is Derwentwater; the most remote are Ennerdale and Hawes Water; the most beautiful, perhaps, is Crummock Water.

No introduction to the Lake District would be complete without reference to the poets of the romantic school who lived here and, in particular to William Wordsworth, who was born at Cockermouth, just to the north of the route, educated at Hawkshead, and spent the greatest part of his adult life at Grasmere and later Rydal, where he died in 1850. In addition to his poetry he produced, in 1810, his *Guide to the Lakes*, in relation to which hangs an amusing tale. Wordsworth visited a lakeland clergyman who congratulated him on the excellence of his *Guide* and who asked the world-famous poet, in all innocence, 'Have you, Sir, written anything else?' Wordsworth and John Ruskin, the artist and critic, were among the foremost of the 19th-century conservationists who did much to protect Lakeland from spreading industrialization. Although the area was not defined as a National Park until 1915, it is worth remembering that as early as 1846 Wordsworth was bombarding the national Press with protest in both verse and prose, asking, 'Is there no nook of England ground secure from rash assault?' His aspirations for his native land were expressed in the wish that he should 'be joined by persons of pure taste throughout the whole island who, by their visits (often repeated) to the Lakes of the North of England, testify that they deem the district a sort of national property, in which every man has a right and interest who has an eye to perceive and a heart to enjoy'. Sixty years after Wordsworth's death, Lakeland became national property and the poet's dream had become a reality.

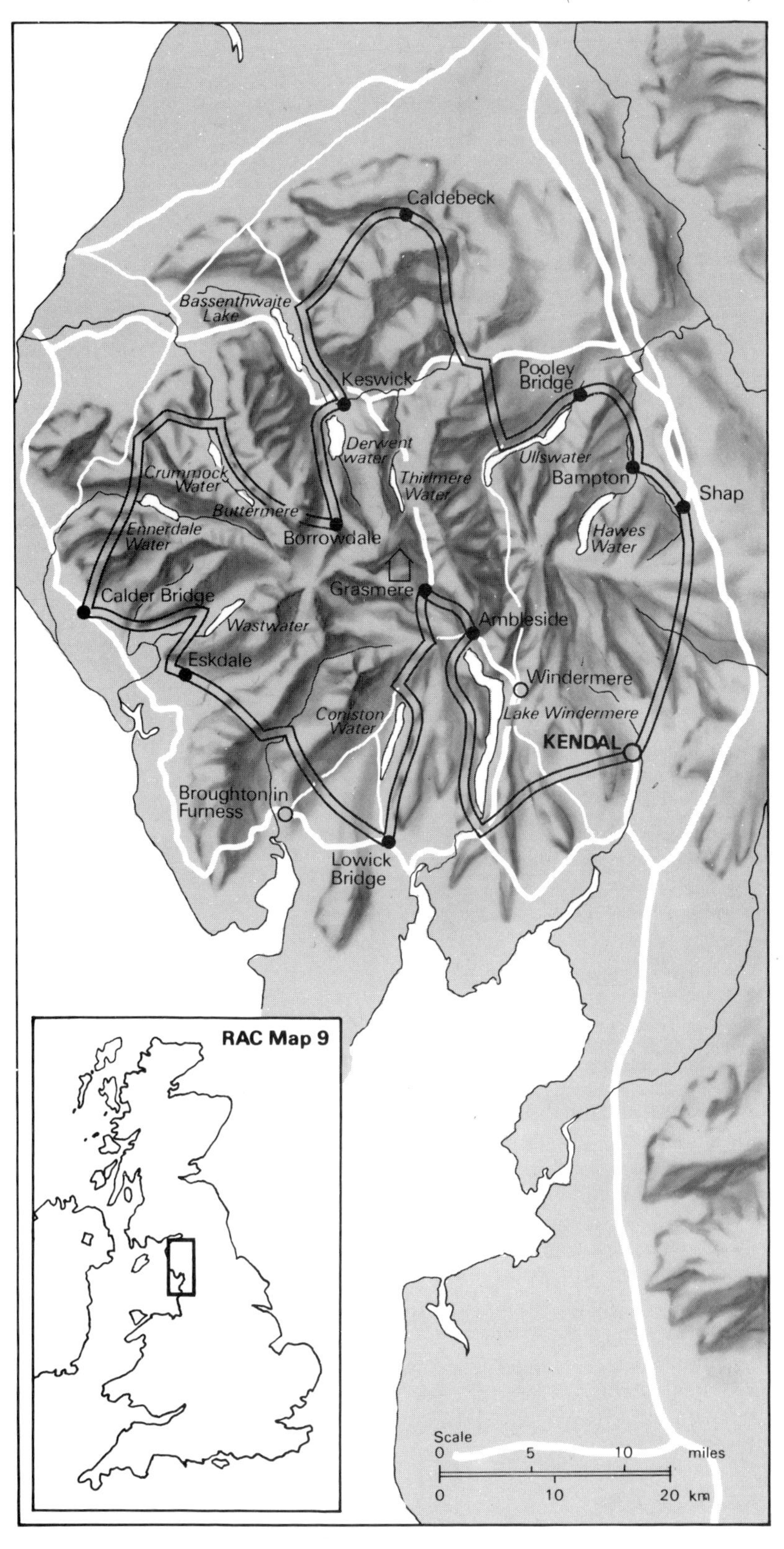
Caldebeck
Bassenthwaite Lake
Keswick
Pooley Bridge
Derwent water
Thirlmere Water
Ullswater
Bampton
Shap
Crummock Water
Buttermere
Ennerdale Water
Borrowdale
Hawes Water
Grasmere
Calder Bridge
Wastwater
Ambleside
Eskdale
Windermere
Coniston Water
Lake Windermere
KENDAL
Broughton in Furness
Lowick Bridge
RAC Map 9
Scale
0 5 10 miles
0 10 20 km

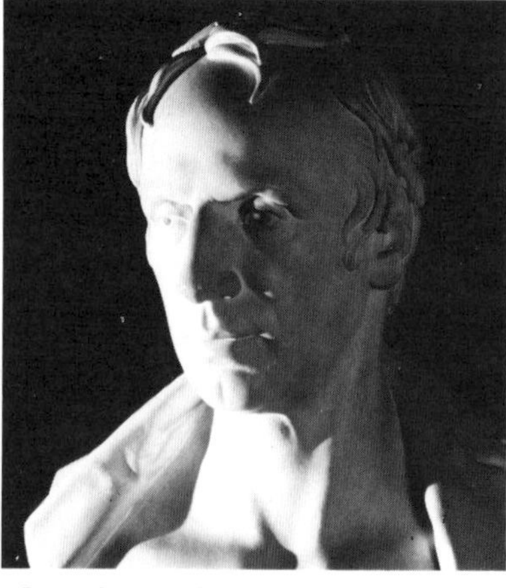

Dove Cottage (top) *contains a bust of William Wordsworth* (below).
Right: *Borrowdale.*

Kendal (Cumbria)

The R. Kent meanders past grey stone buildings, centuries old, which earned Kendal the nickname of the 'Auld Grey Town'. Dominating the town to the east of the river is the ruined castle, birthplace of Katherine Parr (1512–48), whose prayer book can be seen at the Town Hall. Lying to the east of Lakeland, Kendal makes an ideal starting-point for touring the area.

There are numerous hotels and guest houses as well as many buildings of historic interest. Among these are the house where Prince Charlie, the Young Pretender, stayed in 1745 when pursued by the Duke of Cumberland (the 'Butcher'), who occupied the Prince's bed two days after he had fled; Romney House, now a guest house, named after the celebrated portrait painter George Romney (1734–1802), who spent his last years here; and the Castle Dairy in Wildman St, another old building with rich oak beam carvings. Among the products of the town is the famous Kendal mint cake – rarely absent from the haversacks of mountaineers the world over.

Woolpack Hotel, Stricklandgate, 67 rooms, T23852 (B)
Headlands Private Hotel, 53 Milnthorpe Rd, 7 rooms, T20424 (D)
YHA, 107 Milnthorpe Rd, T24066
T.O. Town Hall, T25758

Bowland Bridge (Cumbria)

Hare and Hounds Inn, 12 rooms, T Crosthwaite 333 (D)

Lake Side (Cumbria)

Windermere is England's largest lake, stretching for 10½ miles from north to south. The shores of the lake are dense in woodland, so that views of it are restricted. This village, however, lies right on the banks of the extreme southern edge of Windermere.

Lake Side Hotel, Newby Bridge, 96 rooms, T Newby Bridge 207 (B)
Knoll Guest House, Lakeside, 10 rooms, T Newby Bridge 347 (D)

Hawkshead (Cumbria)

One of Lakeland's most enchanting villages, where old cottages surround courtyards linked by narrow passages. William Wordsworth (1770–1850) attended the grammar school here over a period of 9 years, and carved his name on a desk which can stll be seen in the school which now acts as a museum and library.

Tarn Hows Hotel, 30 rooms, T330 (A)
Red Lion Hotel. 10 rooms, T213 (D)
YHA, Esthwaite Lodge, T293
T.O. Main Car Park, T525

Ambleside (Cumbria)

Occupies a central position on the Lake District and has therefore become a leading tourist centre with a great variety of hotels, guest houses, and gift shops.

Salutation Hotel, Lake Rd, 29 rooms, T2244 (C)
Copper Coins Hotel and Restaurant, Compston Rd, 15 rooms, T2210 (C)
YHA, Waterhead, T2486
T.O. Old Court House, Church St, T3084

Grasmere (Cumbria)

William Wordsworth moved here with his sister, Dorothy, when he was 29 years of age. Much of his best work originated during his nine-year stay at Dove Cottage, which has been preserved much as it was when the poet lived there, although it later became the home of another poet, de Quincey (1785–1859). After moving from Dove Cottage Wordsworth occupied two further houses in Grasmere before finally moving to Rydal where he spent the last 37 years of his life. He lies buried in the parish church of St Oswalds.

Swan Hotel, 31 rooms, T551 (A)
Beck Steps Guest House, 9 rooms, T348 (D)
YHA, Butharlyp, T316
T.O. Broadgate Newsagency, T245

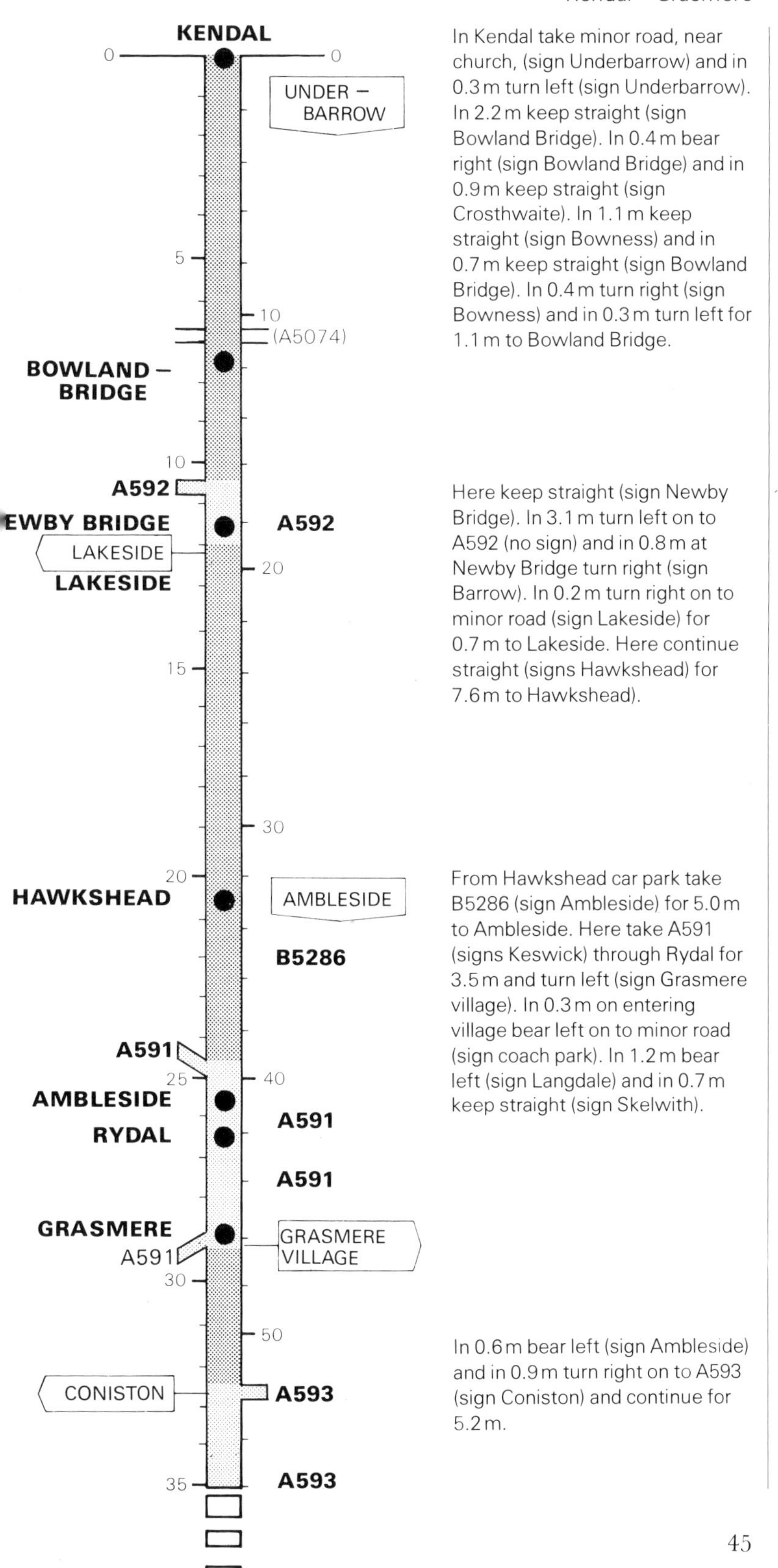

In Kendal take minor road, near church, (sign Underbarrow) and in 0.3 m turn left (sign Underbarrow). In 2.2 m keep straight (sign Bowland Bridge). In 0.4 m bear right (sign Bowland Bridge) and in 0.9 m keep straight (sign Crosthwaite). In 1.1 m keep straight (sign Bowness) and in 0.7 m keep straight (sign Bowland Bridge). In 0.4 m turn right (sign Bowness) and in 0.3 m turn left for 1.1 m to Bowland Bridge.

Here keep straight (sign Newby Bridge). In 3.1 m turn left on to A592 (no sign) and in 0.8 m at Newby Bridge turn right (sign Barrow). In 0.2 m turn right on to minor road (sign Lakeside) for 0.7 m to Lakeside. Here continue straight (signs Hawkshead) for 7.6 m to Hawkshead).

From Hawkshead car park take B5286 (sign Ambleside) for 5.0 m to Ambleside. Here take A591 (signs Keswick) through Rydal for 3.5 m and turn left (sign Grasmere village). In 0.3 m on entering village bear left on to minor road (sign coach park). In 1.2 m bear left (sign Langdale) and in 0.7 m keep straight (sign Skelwith).

In 0.6 m bear left (sign Ambleside) and in 0.9 m turn right on to A593 (sign Coniston) and continue for 5.2 m.

Coniston's superbly restored steam gondola. Lakeland is ideal for family holidays.

Coniston (Cumbria)

Some good views of Coniston Water are obtained from the road which runs above the east bank, and there are plenty of parking areas in the woods. The lake is $5\frac{1}{2}$ miles long, and it was here in 1967 that Donald Campbell was killed in an attempt to break the water speed record. High above the lake stands Brantwood House, where John Ruskin (1819–1900) spent the last years of his life and which is now a museum.

Sun Hotel, 9 rooms, T248 (C)
YHA, Holly How, T323
T.O. Main Car Park, T533

Lowick Bridge (Cumbria)

Consists of only a few houses where the chosen route crosses the B5084. The road from here to Eskdale is an isolated one – climbing high across fells where sheep graze, with occasional descents into valleys. Although some small wayside inns can be seen, there does not appear to be anywhere to stay between here and Eskdale. For this reason a pleasant guest house has been shown which lies just off the route on the A595 – at Duddon Bridge, the other side of Broughton in Furness. The guest house lies high up, in a tranquil position affording glorious views, and is highly recommended to those who wish to halt a while and explore the beautiful Duddon Valley.

High Duddon Guest House, Duddon Bridge, T Broughton in Furness 279 (C)

Eskdale Green (Cumbria)

Lies in a valley between the rivers Esk and Mite. Because of its proximity to the Cumbrian mountains it provides an excellent base for the Outward Bound Mountain School – an organization which gives young people, particularly those from urban areas, opportunities to partake in a variety of outdoor pursuits.

Bower House Inn, Holmrook, T244 (B)
Woolpack Inn, Boot, 7 rooms, T230 (C)
YHA, Boot, Homerook, T219

The Route

Main roads are avoided apart from a four-mile stretch on the A591 between Ambleside and Grasmere, which does tend to get crowded. Most of the route runs through wooded, hilly countryside, and the roads are narrow in places. Along this stretch there are views of five of the lakes – Windermere, Esthwaite Water, Rydal Water, Grasmere and Coniston Water.

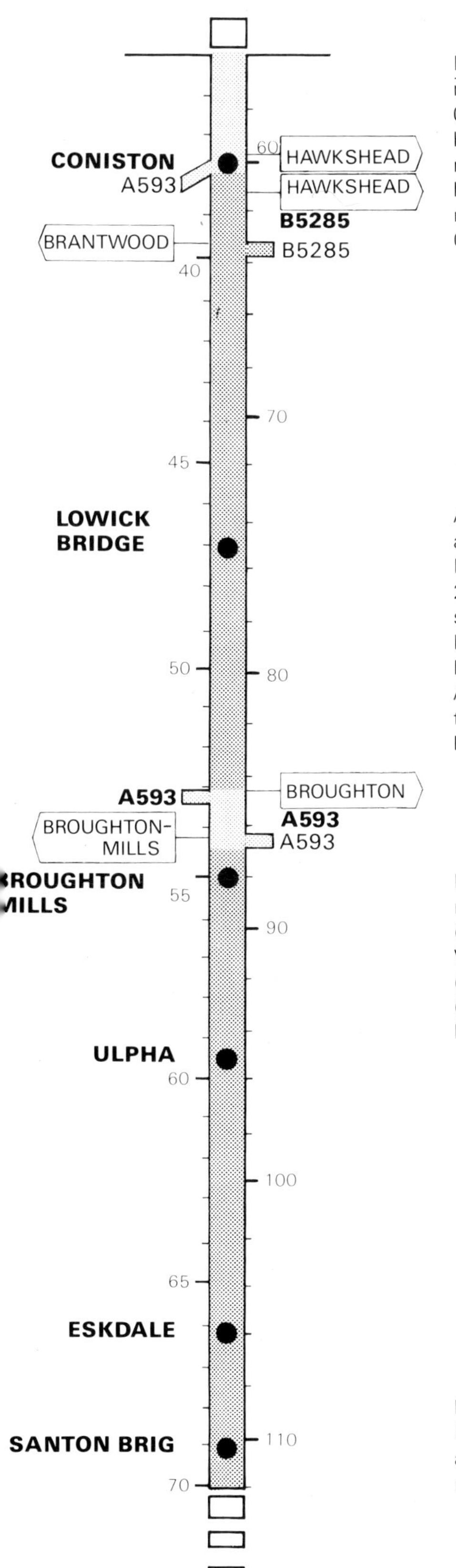

Entering Coniston turn left on to minor road (sign Hawkshead). In 0.2 m turn left on to B5285 (sign Hawkshead) and in 0.7 m turn right on to minor road (sign east of lake and Brantwood). In 7.9 m turn right (sign Newby Bridge) for 0.1 m to Lowick Bridge.

At Lowick Bridge keep straight across A5084 (sign Gawthwaite). In 0.7m turn right (no sign). In 2.3 m at T junction turn right (no sign). In 1.3 m turn right (sign Broughton). In 0.8 m turn left (sign Broughton). In 1.1 m turn left on to A593 (sign Broughton). In 0.8 m turn right on to minor road (sign Broughton Mills).

In 1.0 m at Broughton Mills turn right (sign Ulpha). In 3.3 m turn left (sign Broughton via Duddon Valley). In 1.5 m at Ulpha turn right (sign Eskdale). Keep straight (signs Eskdale) for 6.2 m and turn left (sign Holmrock).

In 1.3 m bear right (sign Gosforth). In 1.7 m bear right (sign Gosforth) and in 0.1 m at Santon Brig turn right (sign Wasdale).

The Route

The narrowness of the minor roads on this section present few problems as the roads are relatively free of traffic. The road between Lowick Bridge and Broughton Mills is gated (three gates) and there are numerous cattle grids. After leaving Broughton Mills there is a particularly fine view of the Duddon valley.

Wastwater

Although one of the smaller lakes, three miles in length and half a mile across, it is the deepest in England, reaching depths, in parts, of 260 feet. The road runs for about a third of the length of the lake, close to the west bank, before turning off to the left. It is possible, however, to continue along the full length of the lake as far as Wasdale Head – a popular headquarters for climbers as it lies immediately beneath Scafell Pike (at 3,210 feet being the highest mountain in England), Sca Fell (3,162 ft) and Great Gable (2,949 ft). Sheer, almost vertical, cliff lines the south-east bank of Wastwater for almost its entire length.

Wasdale Head Inn, 10 rooms, T229 (B)
YHA, Wasdale Hall, Wasdale, Seascale, T222

Calder Bridge (Cumbria)

The ruins of Calder Abbey, founded AD1135, occupy a beautiful position to the east of the village on the R. Calder. The site is open to the public and the remains include the nave and the church aisles.

Stanley Arms Hotel, 9 rooms, T Beckermet 235 (C)

Ennerdale Bridge (Cumbria)

Ennerdale Water can be reached in the car via a rough track that leads

A wintry scene at Wastwater.

off to the right between the village and Lamplugh. The lake, 2½ miles long and quite broad at the western end, is one of Cumbria's least visited lakes – perhaps owing to its inaccessibility and the fact that it is the most westerly of all the lakes.

Shepherds Arms Hotel, 5 rooms, T249 (D)
YHA, Cat Crag, T Lamplugh 237

Loweswater (Cumbria)

A few scattered hotels and houses lie above the small lake, about a mile in length. A footpath runs along the south-west side of Loweswater through Holme Wood, both lake and wood being the property of the National Trust.

Scale Hill Hotel, 13 rooms, T Lorton 232 (C)
Kirkstile Inn, 10 rooms, T Lorton 219 (B)

Crummock Water (Cumbria)

Rounding a bend in the hills the lake suddenly comes into view far beneath, presenting a spectacular view. Crummock Water, 2½ miles in length, was once joined to Buttermere, and this lake, and the impressive peaks above it, are a favourite subject for artists.

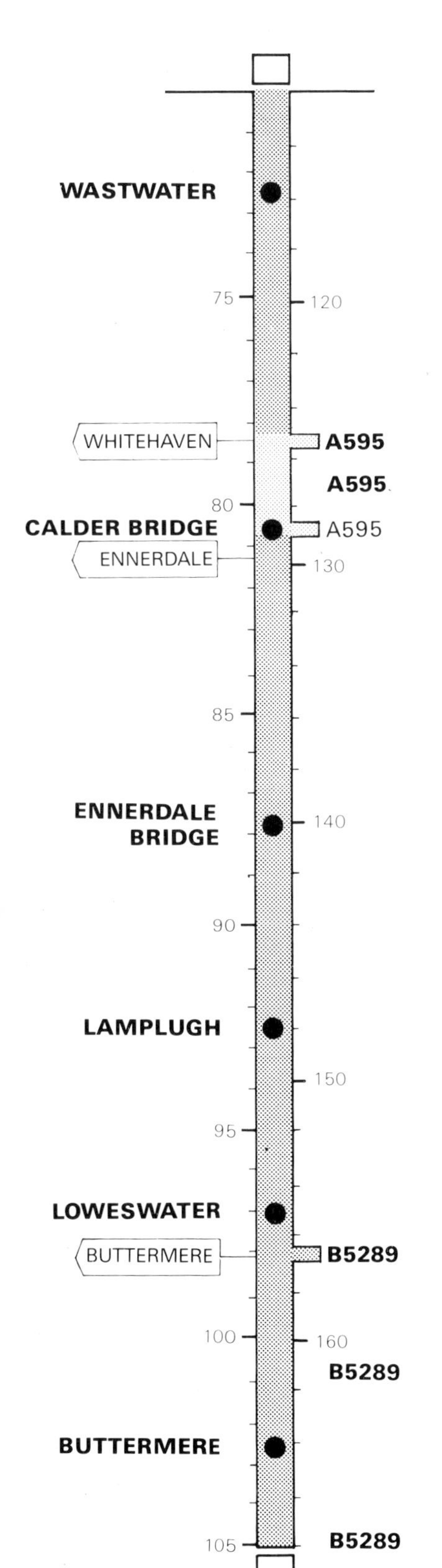

In 1.8 m turn right (sign Wasdale) and in 0.1 m turn right (sign The Lake). In 1.8 m turn left (sign Gosforth).

In 2.7 m keep straight (sign Gosforth). In 3.0 m entering Gosforth bear right (sign Whitehaven). In 0.2 m bear right (sign Whitehaven) and in further 0.2 m turn right on to A595 (sign Whitehaven). In 2.1 m at Calder Bridge turn right (sign Ennerdale). In 0.6 m turn left and immediately right (sign Ennerdale).

Keep straight for 6.4 m and turn right (sign Ennerdale Bridge). In 0.4 m bear right (sign Ennerdale Water). In 1.0 m keep straight (sign Lamplugh) and in further 1.0 m turn left (sign Lamplugh). In 2.4 m turn right (sign Loweswater) and in further 0.4 m turn right (sign Loweswater). In 1.6 m bear right (sign Loweswater) for 3.0 m to Loweswater.

From Loweswater continue straight (sign Buttermere) and in 1.0 m turn right on to B5289 (sign Buttermere). Keep straight for 4.2 m past Crummock Water to Buttermere.

In 0.1 m continue straight on B5289 (sign Keswick via Honiston Pass).

Top: *Wastwater.*
Above: *Hunting at Mungrisdale.*
Right: *Buttermere.*

Buttermere (Cumbria)

The village lies between Crummock Water and the smaller lake of Buttermere. The area is much favoured by climbers, as there are a multitude of mountain paths to explore which vary in severity but from which there are magnificent views of both lakes.

Bridge Hotel, 24 rooms, T252 (C)
Fish Hotel, 11 rooms, T253 (C)
YHA, King George VI Memorial Hostel, T254
YHA, Honister House, Honister Pass, T267

Borrowdale (Cumbria)

Lies in what is perhaps Lakeland's most beautiful valley – the only drawback being the fact that this area has the highest annual rainfall in England. The village was reached by way of Honister Pass, where there are one in four gradients on both the ascent and descent. At the top of the pass is the highest YHA in the Lake District, from where there are marvellous views (see Buttermere).

Borrowdale Hotel, 38 rooms, T224 (B)

Rosthwaite (Cumbria)

Just past the village, on the right of the road, the famous Bowder Stone is signed. This 30-foot-high rock is believed to weigh around 2,000 tons, and can be climbed by ladder. It is owned by the National Trust.

Derwentwater (Cumbria)

The minor road to the west of the lake was chosen because of the marvellous views of the lake from high above it. The lake is oval in shape, 1½ miles wide at one point, making it the broadest of all the lakes. From the road above the lake there is a good view of the islands, which include St Herbert's Island and Lord's Island, once the home of the Earls of Derwentwater.

Keswick (Cumbria)

The beautiful town contains many attractive grey stone buildings. Keswick was much favoured by the poets. Coleridge and Southey both lived at Greta Hall, and Shelley rented a house on Chestnut Hill with his sixteen-year-old runaway bride, Harriet Westbrook. The town is overshadowed by Skiddaw to the north, which at 3,053 feet is England's third highest mountain. The numerous narrow streets mean that it is best to park the car and appreciate on foot a town which John Ruskin described as 'almost too beautiful to live in'.

Keswick Hotel, Station Rd, 76 rooms, T64200 (A)
Chaucer House Hotel, Ambleside Rd, 36 rooms, T72318 (C)
YHA, Station Rd, T24066

Caldbeck (Cumbria)

In the churchyard is the tomb-stone of John Peel, decorated with a hunting horn. The song which made Peel famous was composed by his friend John Graves. He lived at Caldbeck and hunted his own pack in his 'coat so gray' through the moorlands which surround the village.

Mungrisdale (Cumbria)

The tiny village is situated on the banks of the R. Glendermackin at the foot of the Skiddaw range of fells. Those seeking solitude in these remote surroundings might be advised to spend a night or two in the 16c Mill Inn, where John Peel is reputed to have stayed and hunted.

Mill Inn, 9 rooms, T Threlkeld 659 (D)

The Route

Before reaching Keswick there are good views of Crummock Water, Buttermere and Derwentwater. The steep climb and descent of Honister Pass is not too difficult as the road is reasonably broad. After leaving Keswick the road runs through rugged fell country. Bassenthwaite lake can be seen at a distance to the left of the road a few miles out of Keswick, and a little further along the route, also on the left, is a small and little-known lake called Overwater.

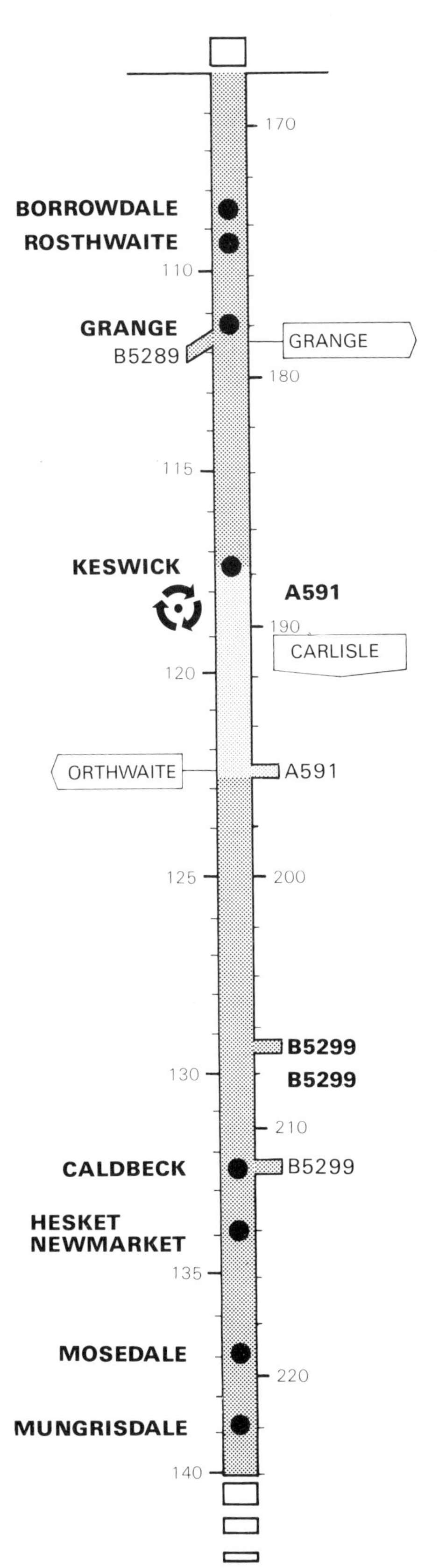

In 5.9 m at foot of pass bear left (sign Keswick) and in 0.9 m keep straight (sign Keswick) for 0.4 m to Rosthwaite.

In 1.8 m turn left on to minor road (sign Grange). In 2.7 m turn right (sign Keswick) and in 0.5 m bear right (sign Keswick). In 1.7 m turn right (sign Keswick) and in further 0.2 m turn right for 0.8 m to Keswick town centre.

In Keswick town centre take A66 (sign Cockermouth) and in 0.6 m bear right (sign Carlisle). In 0.4 m at roundabout keep straight on A591 (sign Carlisle). In 4.8 m bear right on to minor road (sign Orthwaite). In 0.9 m keep straight (sign Uldale). In 1.2 m keep straight (sign Uldale). In 1.5 m keep straight (sign Caldbeck).

In 2.0 m turn right (sign Caldbeck) and in 0.8 m keep straight on B5299 (sign Caldbeck). In 1.5 m bear left (sign Caldbeck) and keep straight for 1.6 m to Caldbeck. Here continue straight (sign Hesket Newmarket) and in 1.8 m at Hesket Newmarket bear right (sign Mungrisdale).

In 0.9 m turn left (sign Mungrisdale) and in 1.5 m bear right (sign Mungrisdale). Continue straight for 3.6 m past Mosedale to Mungrisdale. Here continue straight (sign Keswick).

Troutbeck (Cumbria)

Not to be confused with the well-known beauty spot near Ambleside. In fact Troutbeck station is merely a point on the A6 which the route crosses. The recommended hotel does, however, occupy quite a pleasant position off the main road.

Troutbeck Hotel, 5 rooms, T Greystoke 243 (D)

Ullswater (Cumbria)

Wordsworth described Ullswater as being 'perhaps, upon the whole, the happiest combination of beauty and grandeur, which any of the lakes affords'. The lake, seven miles in length, is second only in size to Windermere. The road follows the west bank, passing Gowbarrow Park, where Wordsworth was inspired to write his poem 'Daffodils'. In a preface to his famous poem Wordsworth wrote, 'The Daffodils grew and still grow on the margin of Ullswater, and probably may be seen to this day as beautiful in the month of March, nodding their heads beside the dancing and foaming waves.'

Leeming on Ullswater Country Hotel, Watermillock, 17 rooms, T Pooley Bridge 444 (A)
Knotts Mill Guest House, Watermillock, 5 rooms, T Pooley Bridge 328 (D)

Pooley Bridge (Cumbria)

Lies beside the R. Eamont to the extreme north-eastern point of Ullswater, where there are good views of the lake and from where boat trips are arranged.

Askham (Cumbria)

Queens Head Inn, 8 rooms, T Hackthorpe 225 (D)

Bampton Grange (Cumbria)

The small villages of Bampton and Bampton Grange lie half a mile apart, divided by the R. Lowther. The hotel at Bampton Grange stands opposite the church in this quiet village. Hawes Water can be reached by taking a diversion of about two miles from Bampton. It is clearly signed. This long stretch of water is now a reservoir, supplying Manchester, and can only be seen from the car by driving along the eastern bank. The hotel lies above the lake, half-way along it, and where the road finishes at the extreme southern end of the lake there is also a car park. From this point there is a footpath which runs along the west bank to Bampton – while more adventurous paths are signed through the hills to Kentmore and Llongledale. On the slopes of High Street, a mountain range to the west of Hawes Water, is a tarn known as Blea Water. Some 200 feet deep, it is the deepest tarn in Lakeland.

Crown and Mitre Hotel, Bampton Grange, 6 rooms, T225 (D)
Haweswater Hotel, Haweswater, 16 rooms, T Bampton 235 (C)

Shap (Cumbria)

A long straggling village at the highest point of the A6. Some two miles before reaching Shap, the Abbey ruins, mainly 13c, are worth diverting half a mile to see, for they occupy a beautiful position amidst farm lands on the banks of the R. Lowther.

The Route

Follows minor roads whenever possible. Ullswater, however, can only be seen from the A592; and owing to the Shap range of mountains the return route must inevitably follow the A6 for the final sixteen miles back to Kendal.

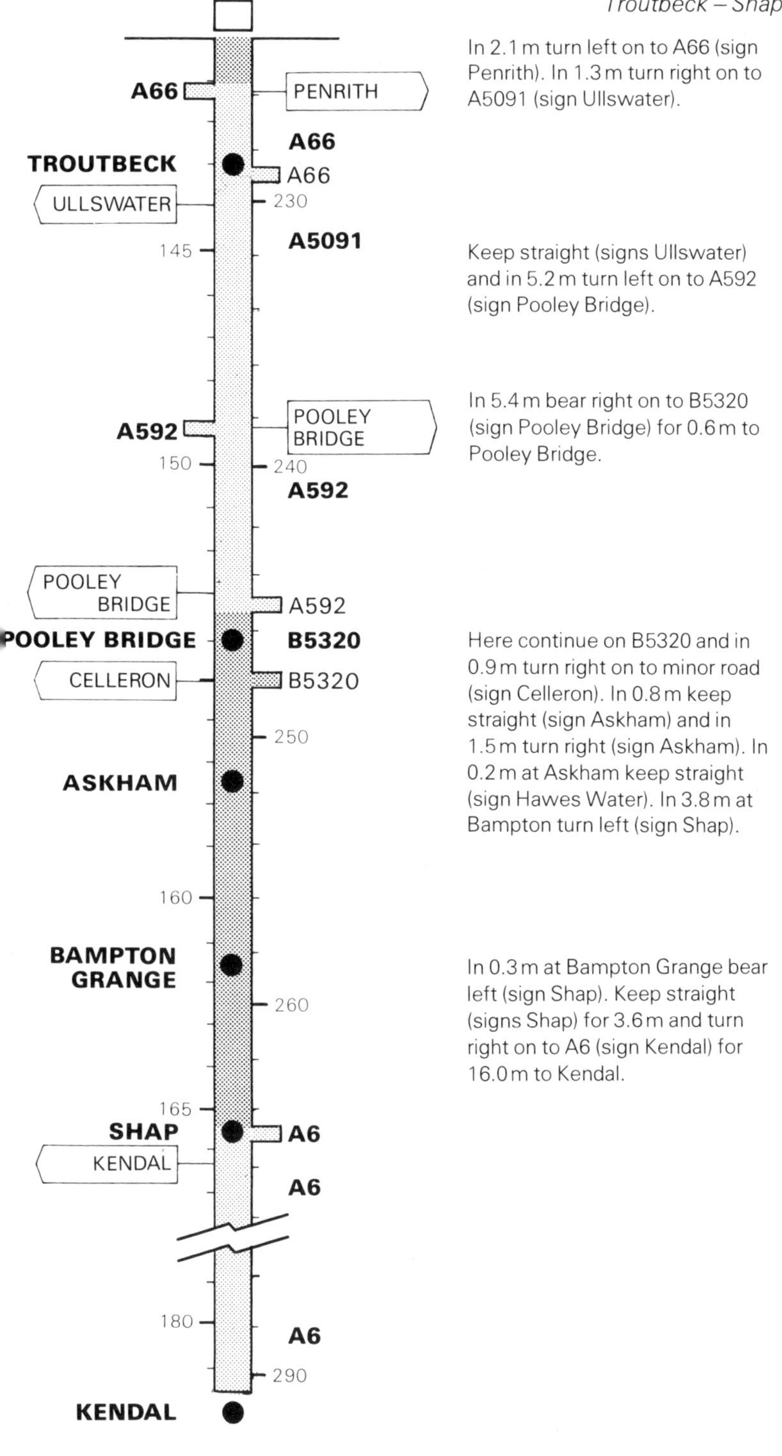

In 2.1 m turn left on to A66 (sign Penrith). In 1.3 m turn right on to A5091 (sign Ullswater).

Keep straight (signs Ullswater) and in 5.2 m turn left on to A592 (sign Pooley Bridge).

In 5.4 m bear right on to B5320 (sign Pooley Bridge) for 0.6 m to Pooley Bridge.

Here continue on B5320 and in 0.9 m turn right on to minor road (sign Celleron). In 0.8 m keep straight (sign Askham) and in 1.5 m turn right (sign Askham). In 0.2 m at Askham keep straight (sign Hawes Water). In 3.8 m at Bampton turn left (sign Shap).

In 0.3 m at Bampton Grange bear left (sign Shap). Keep straight (signs Shap) for 3.6 m and turn right on to A6 (sign Kendal) for 16.0 m to Kendal.

4 *East Anglia (South): Cambridgeshire, Suffolk, Essex*

HISTORICALLY, EAST ANGLIA is taken to mean an area roughly corresponding to Norfolk and Suffolk. It was in these parts that the Saxons and Angles settled after their invasion from Schleswig-Holstein – eventually establishing themselves among the North Folk and South Folk of Norfolk and Suffolk respectively. Nowadays, however, although the total area of East Anglia is not precisely defined, it is generally assumed to embrace four counties: Cambridgeshire, Essex, Norfolk and Suffolk.

East Anglia is among the less populated and less well-known areas of Britain. Its sparse population stems from the fact that this is primarily a rural as opposed to an industrial locality; it is not well

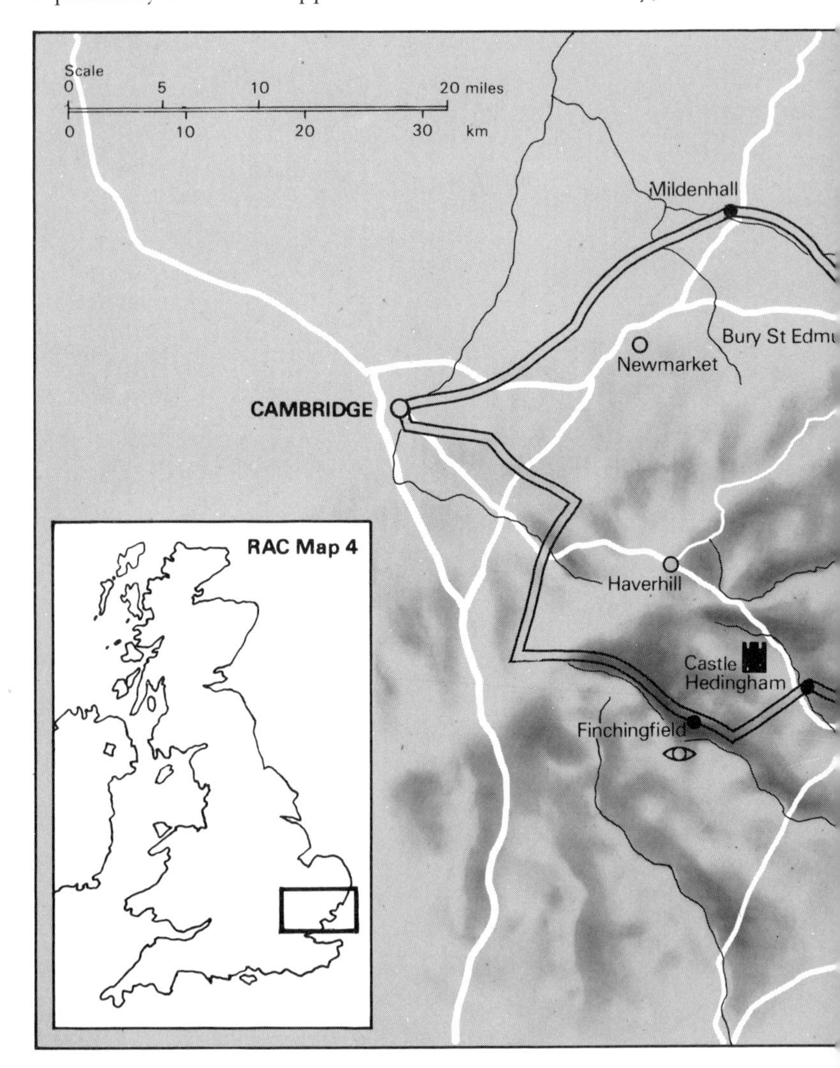

known because it is not on the way to anywhere and consequently receives no casual visitors. It is sometimes depicted as a flat and treeless area. This chosen route through Cambridgeshire, Suffolk and Essex (Norfolk forms Route 12) runs through some 230 miles of remote countryside by way of streams and small valleys, and shows that these parts are by no means totally flat and far from treeless.

After leaving the beautiful university town of Cambridge the route runs eastward towards the coast, avoiding the big A45 road and therefore missing Newmarket, headquarters of British horse racing. Those wishing to call in at Newmarket should note that Burwell, on the route, lies only two miles to the north of it. The road from Bury St Edmunds to the coast at Southwold runs almost due east, between two major roads, A143 and A1120, and roughly parallel to them. From Southwold to Aldeburgh, via Walberswick and Dunwich, there are glimpses of some of the best of the Suffolk coastline. On leaving the coast the route returns by way of the Constable country in the extreme south of Suffolk and later through some pretty villages in the north of

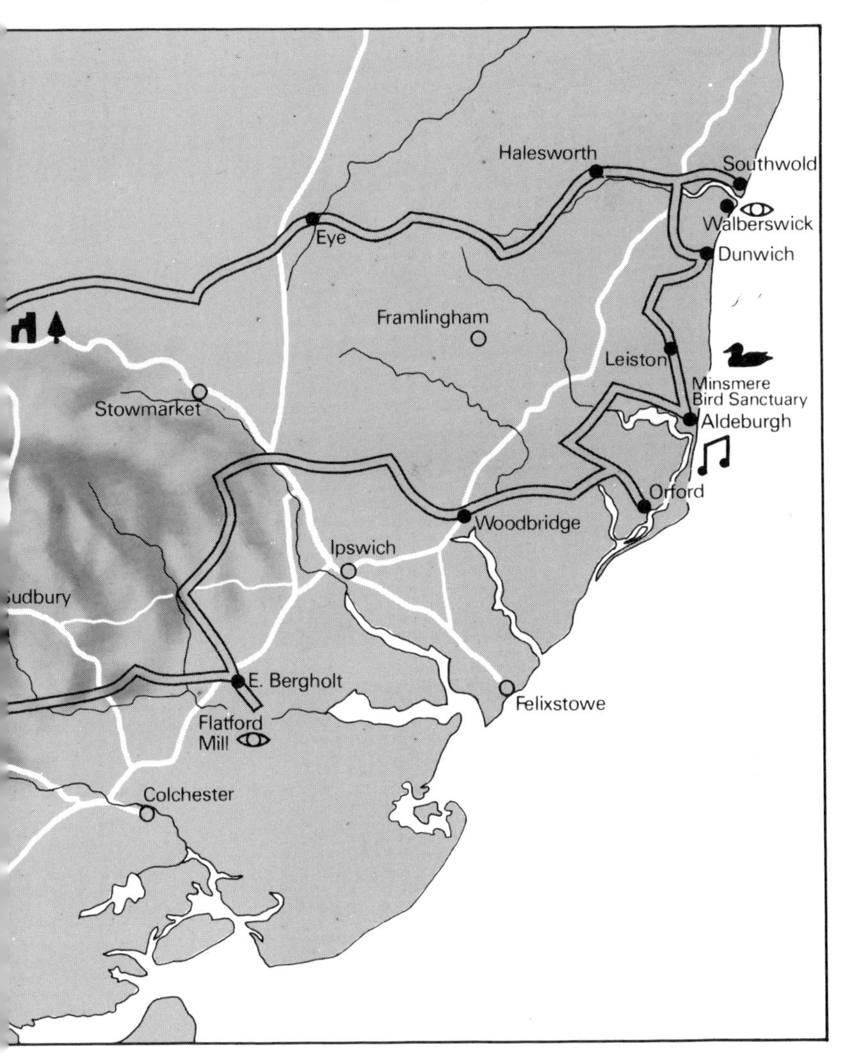

The famous Flatford Mill, immortalized by Constable.

Essex before returning to Cambridgeshire. Planning the final leg of this route presented difficulties, as to visit such places as Finchingfield and Saffron Walden meant omitting other beautiful villages like Lavenham. This can, however, be easily reached from Hadleigh.

Final impression of this part of East Anglia is the extreme cleanliness of the towns and villages. Vandals, all too prevalent in more

built-up areas, have not reached here yet. Thus the only reference to vandalism appears at Stradbroke (page 62) where it is noted that one George Dowsing did havoc here and in many neighbouring churches. Fortunately, Dowsing, a Puritan who was affectionately nicknamed 'Smasher', died more than 300 years ago.

Cambridge (Cambridgeshire)

Cars are prohibited from entering the centre of this university town which, in any case, is best seen on foot or by hiring a boat. For those with only a limited time in Cambridge, here is a suggested itinerary. Starting at King's College, with its famous chapel, it is but a short walk by way of Caius College to the university's largest college, Trinity, where after passing through the Great Court the river is reached. From this point, at King's Bridge, there is a good view of the Bridge of Sighs that connects the buildings of St John's College. Many foot bridges lead from the well-kept college lawns to the meadows on the other side of the Cam – an area appropriately named the 'Backs'. Close to St John's College is the Church of the Holy Sepulchre (The Round Church) and Magdalene College, where in the Pepysian library are books and manuscripts left by the diarist Samuel Pepys (1633–1703).

University Arms Hotel, Regent St, 120 rooms, T51241 (B)
Royal Cambridge Hotel, Trumpington St, 85 rooms, T51631 (C)
All Seasons Guest House, 219 Chesterton Rd, 10 rooms, T53386 (D)
YHA, 97 Tenison Rd, T56401
T.O. Wheeler St, T58977

Lode (Cambridgeshire)

Little remains of the original 12c Augustinian priory known as Anglesey Abbey other than the chapter-house and vaulted Canon's Parlour. These relics form part of what is now a country house with landscaped garden, in the care of the National Trust and open to the public on specified occasions. Within the house is a wide variety of furniture that includes Sir Robert Walpole's writing desk and paintings by Claude, Cuyp, Gainsborough and Constable. Anglesey Abbey lies to the left of the road before entering the village.

Swaffham Bulbeck (Cambridgeshire)

The Black Horse Inn (good bar snacks) overlooks the large green.

Freckenham (Suffolk)

To the right of the road lies the church, where an interesting feature is the carved figure of the village blacksmith who, according to legend, is St Eloy, patron saint of blacksmiths.

Mildenhall (Suffolk)

The village occupies a pleasant position on the R. Lark. It sprang to fame in 1946 with the discovery of the Mildenhall Treasure – more than 30 pieces of silver tableware, now displayed in the British Museum.

Bell Hotel, High St, 19 rooms, T712134 (C)

Bury St Edmunds (Suffolk)

The outskirts of the town, burial place of St Edmund, King of E. Anglia, have been taken over by industry, but the centre remains unmolested. Little remains of the Benedictine abbey, but it is worth strolling through Abbey Gate for a glimpse of the fine gardens. The tiny Nutshell Inn is claimed to be England's smallest inn.

Angel Hotel, Angel Hill, 46 rooms, T3926 (A)
Everards Hotel, 2 Cornhill, II rooms, T5384 (C)

The Route

By way of traffic-free roads and numerous unspoilt villages with old, well preserved thatched cottages.

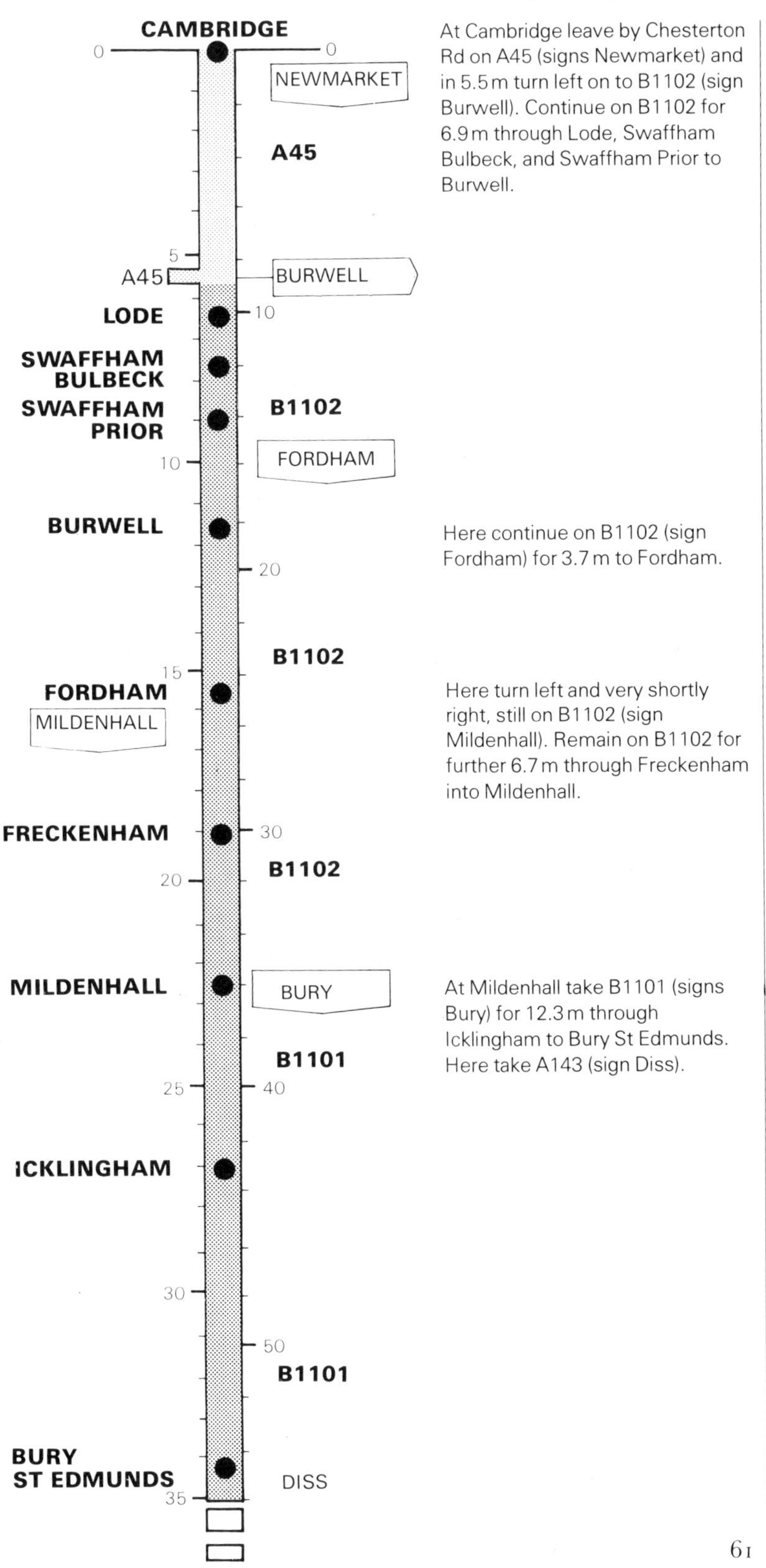

At Cambridge leave by Chesterton Rd on A45 (signs Newmarket) and in 5.5 m turn left on to B1102 (sign Burwell). Continue on B1102 for 6.9 m through Lode, Swaffham Bulbeck, and Swaffham Prior to Burwell.

Here continue on B1102 (sign Fordham) for 3.7 m to Fordham.

Here turn left and very shortly right, still on B1102 (sign Mildenhall). Remain on B1102 for further 6.7 m through Freckenham into Mildenhall.

At Mildenhall take B1101 (signs Bury) for 12.3 m through Icklingham to Bury St Edmunds. Here take A143 (sign Diss).

Finningham (Suffolk)

Just another small village among many in this beautiful but remote part of Suffolk. Nowhere to stay here, but the White Horse Inn serves good bar snacks.

Wickham (Suffolk)

Although the route does not pass through the centre of this village, it is worth a diversion to the right for a glimpse of the village green and the willow-clad duck-pond near to attractive cottages. Down a country lane the small church with 14c tower lies in the midst of meadows. A mile further along the road, back on the route, is a pleasant thatched inn, the Four Horseshoes, serving good food.

Eye (Suffolk)

After many miles of small villages the route at last enters a town of reasonable size – and an attractive one at that. The 16c White Lion Inn, typical of the coaching inns of that period, was selected for the filming, in 1980, of 'An Innkeeper's Diary', in which the actor Robert Hardy appeared. New proprietors are attempting to bring the White Horse up to former standards – and the pleasant dining-room provides French cuisine about which local people enthuse. The 100-foot church tower has been described as one of the 'wonders of Suffolk' and next to the church is a handsome, beam-fronted Tudor house. The ruins of the old Norman castle are perched forlornly on the hill above the town.

White Lion Inn, 9 rooms, T264 (C)

Cottages at Eye.

Stradbroke (Suffolk)

The history in the 14c church reminds us that vandalism is not just a modern disease, for as long ago as 1650 a local Puritan named Dowsing took pleasure in recording, '8 angels off the Roof and Cherubins in wood to be taken down; and 4 crosses on the Steeple; and 17 pictures in the upper window; and organs which I break'. Dowsing was responsible for creating havoc in many nearby churches as well as this one – but the church history hastens to point out that he did not hail from Stradbroke but from Laxfield.

Laxfield (Suffolk)

A charming, compact village, its focal points are the church and adjacent inn, opposite to which is the small timbered guildhall. The Royal Oak Inn (T Ubbeston 446) does not provide accommodation but contains a comfortable, spacious bar where a huge log fire burns and good food is provided.

The Route

Quiet country roads almost all the way from Finningham to Halesworth. Nearing the coast the green landscape gives way to the yellow and brown tints of heather and gorse that encompass the road. Approaching Dunwich the road runs through Forestry Commission land, where there are good picnic sites.

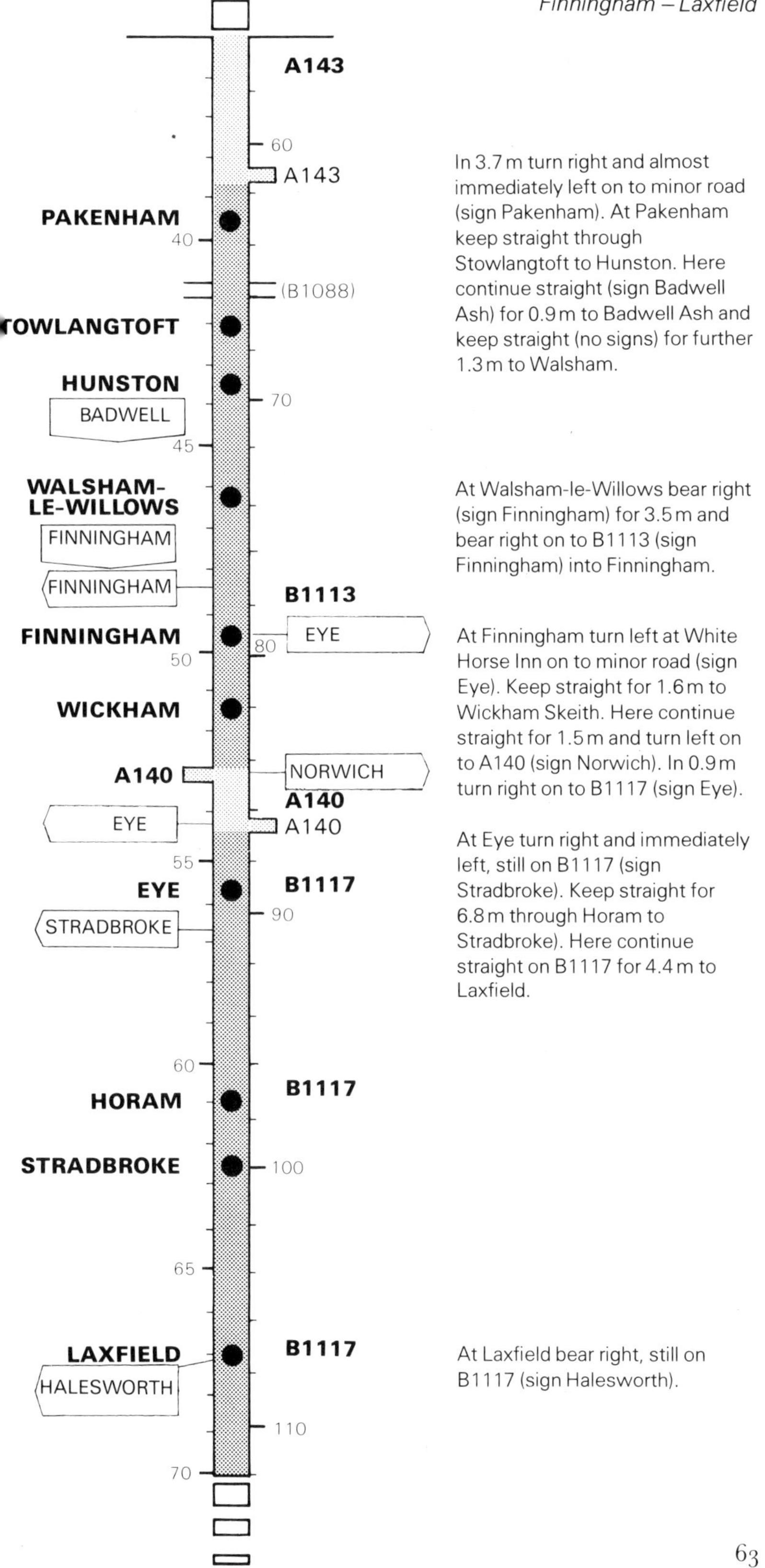

In 3.7 m turn right and almost immediately left on to minor road (sign Pakenham). At Pakenham keep straight through Stowlangtoft to Hunston. Here continue straight (sign Badwell Ash) for 0.9 m to Badwell Ash and keep straight (no signs) for further 1.3 m to Walsham.

At Walsham-le-Willows bear right (sign Finningham) for 3.5 m and bear right on to B1113 (sign Finningham) into Finningham.

At Finningham turn left at White Horse Inn on to minor road (sign Eye). Keep straight for 1.6 m to Wickham Skeith. Here continue straight for 1.5 m and turn left on to A140 (sign Norwich). In 0.9 m turn right on to B1117 (sign Eye).

At Eye turn right and immediately left, still on B1117 (sign Stradbroke). Keep straight for 6.8 m through Horam to Stradbroke). Here continue straight on B1117 for 4.4 m to Laxfield.

At Laxfield bear right, still on B1117 (sign Halesworth).

The Swan Hotel at Southwold.

Walberswick, artists' paradise.

Halesworth (Suffolk)

Fenway Guest House, School Lane, 3 rooms, T3574 (D)

Southwold (Suffolk)

A seaside resort with long sandy beach, several good hotels and a small harbour on the mouth of the R. Blyth. There is no car ferry across to Walberswick.

Swan Hotel, Market Place, 52 rooms, T722186 (B)

St Edmunds Private Hotel, Marlborough Rd, 7 rooms, T723222 (D)

Walberswick (Suffolk)

Small, picturesque seaside village where attractive greens are surrounded by pretty cottages – favourite subjects for the many artists who have come to the area.

Anchor Hotel, 16 rooms, T Southwold 722112 (C)

Dunwich (Suffolk)

Once a thriving town with nine churches, all that remains of Dunwich today is a handful of cottages, an inn, a modern church, a fisherman's hut on the beach, and the ruins of the old priory on the cliff above the village. Everything else has been washed away by the sea over the centuries, making it fascinating to gaze seaward and reflect upon what must be buried beneath.

Westleton (Suffolk)

Across from the inn is a village green with a large duck-pond.

Crown Inn, 8 rooms, T273 (C). Recommended for comfort, good food, and friendly service

Theberton (Suffolk)

A German zeppelin crashed in this small village in 1917 – a fragment of the plane is preserved in the porch of the church.

The Route

Pleasant traffic-free roads for most of the way. The famous Minsmere bird sanctuary lies on the left between Dunwich and Westleton.

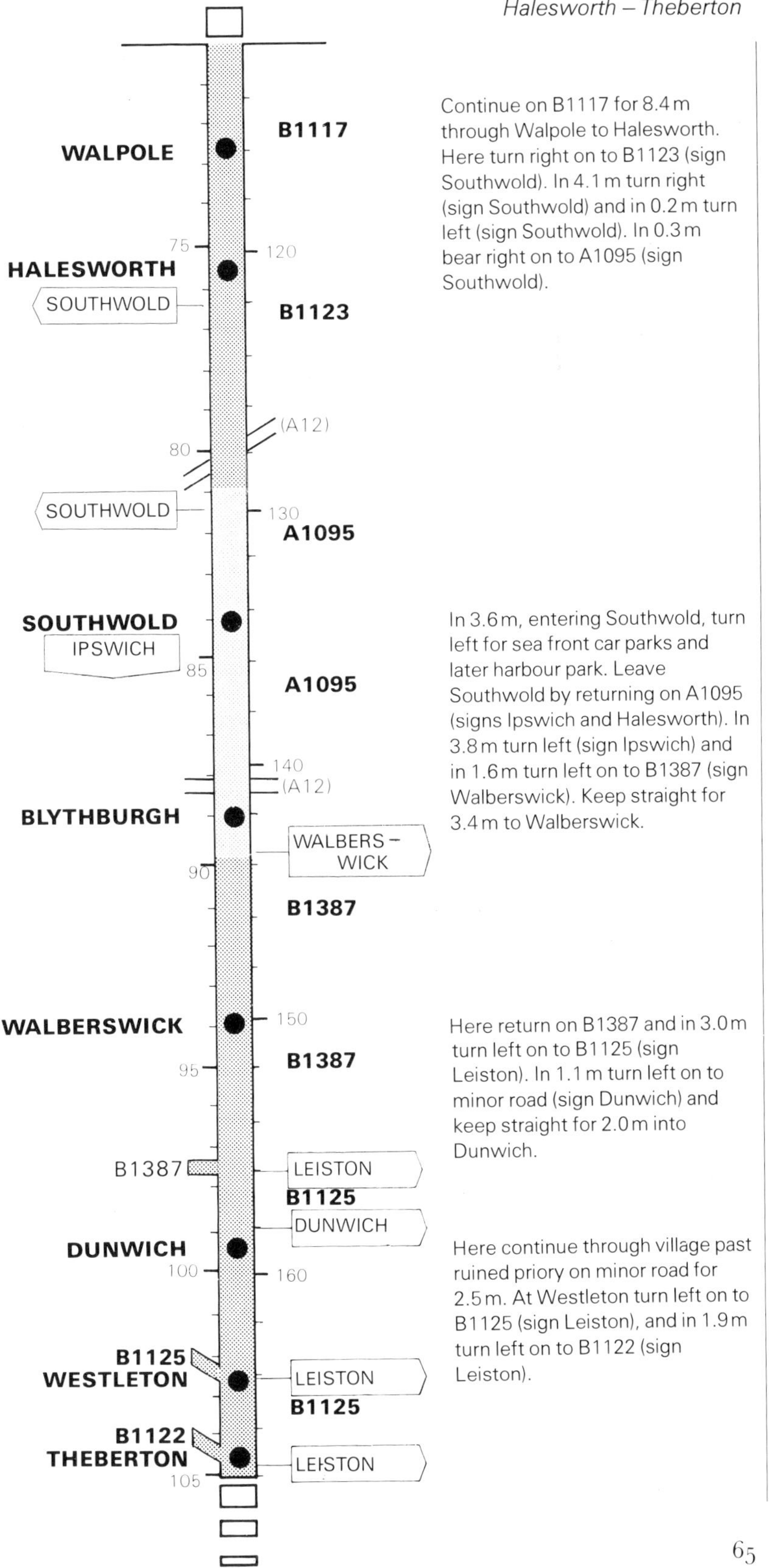

Continue on B1117 for 8.4 m through Walpole to Halesworth. Here turn right on to B1123 (sign Southwold). In 4.1 m turn right (sign Southwold) and in 0.2 m turn left (sign Southwold). In 0.3 m bear right on to A1095 (sign Southwold).

In 3.6 m, entering Southwold, turn left for sea front car parks and later harbour park. Leave Southwold by returning on A1095 (signs Ipswich and Halesworth). In 3.8 m turn left (sign Ipswich) and in 1.6 m turn left on to B1387 (sign Walberswick). Keep straight for 3.4 m to Walberswick.

Here return on B1387 and in 3.0 m turn left on to B1125 (sign Leiston). In 1.1 m turn left on to minor road (sign Dunwich) and keep straight for 2.0 m into Dunwich.

Here continue through village past ruined priory on minor road for 2.5 m. At Westleton turn left on to B1125 (sign Leiston), and in 1.9 m turn left on to B1122 (sign Leiston).

Aldeburgh, seaside resort and cultural centre.

Leiston (Suffolk)

The route does not run through the main part of the town. Signed to the right of the road are the well-preserved ruins of Leiston Abbey (14c).

Aldeburgh (Suffolk)

Attractive seaside resort and venue for the music festival started in 1948 by the world famous composer, Benjamin Britten (1913–76). The Aldeburgh Music Festival takes place annually in June. Much of the old part of the town has been washed away by the sea but the Moot Hall, a small 16c timbered building, stands defiantly on the sea front opposite another old building, the Mill Inn. The sea-front road, Crabbe Rd, is named after the poet, George Crabbe (1754–1832), who was born here and who wrote: 'The ocean roar, whose greedy waves devour the lessening shore.'

Brudenell Hotel, The Parade, 45 rooms, T2071 (A)
Uplands Hotel, Victoria Rd, 19 rooms, T2420 (C)

Orford (Suffolk)

Attractive old houses surround the square above the quay. At the end of the square, towering above it, is a Norman keep which can be climbed for magnificent views across both land and water. It is worth visiting the Jolly Sailor Inn by the quay for a good welcome and talk of the smugglers who used to use the inn as a retreat.

Kings Head Inn, Front St, 4 rooms, T271 (C)
Crown and Castle Hotel, 20 rooms, T205 (A)

Woodbridge (Suffolk)

After visiting many quiet towns and villages, there seems to be a great deal of bustle along the crowded, narrow streets of this very old town. There is a complicated one-way traffic system and it is essential to park in a recognized car park and explore the town on foot.

Bull Hotel, Market Hill, II rooms, T2089 (B)

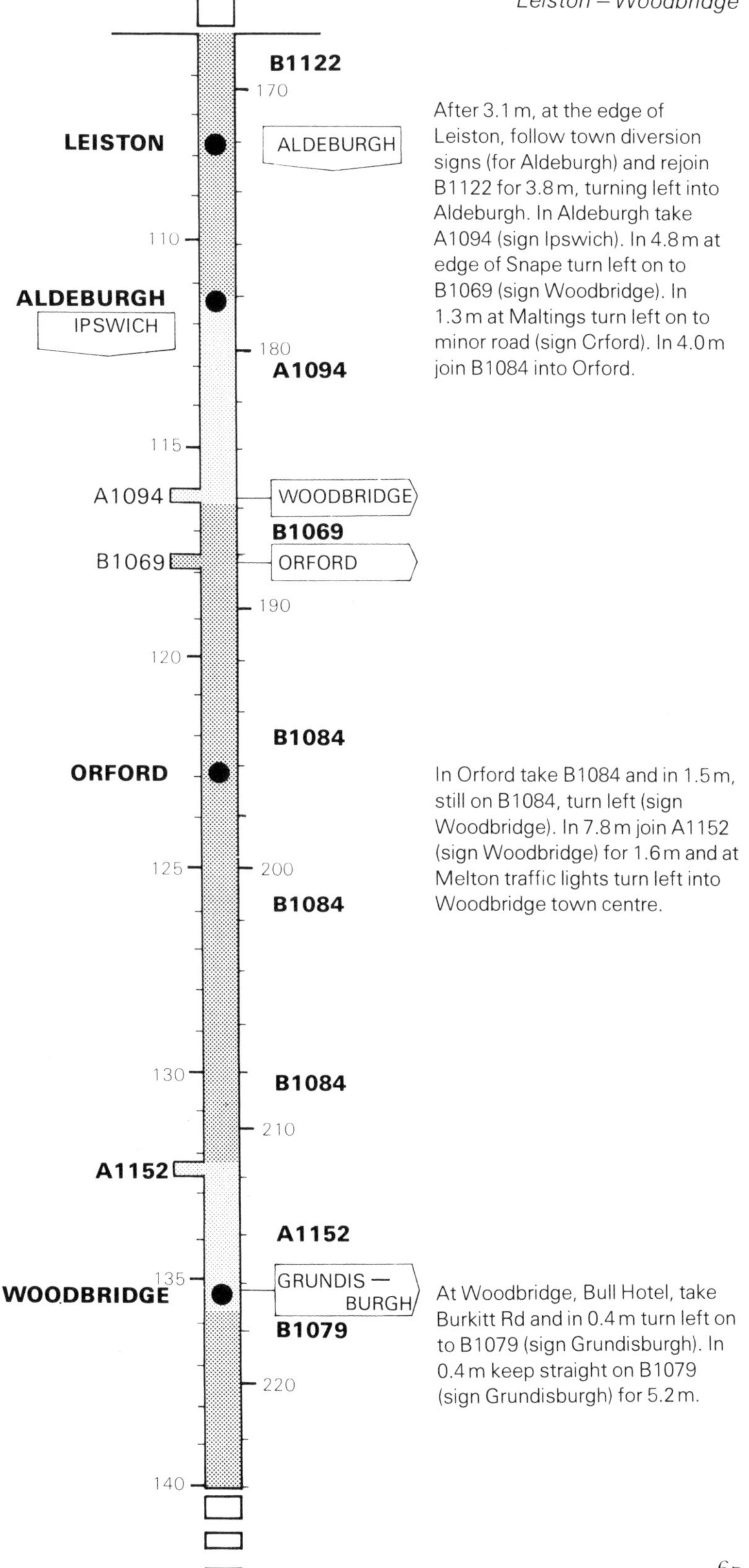

After 3.1 m, at the edge of Leiston, follow town diversion signs (for Aldeburgh) and rejoin B1122 for 3.8 m, turning left into Aldeburgh. In Aldeburgh take A1094 (sign Ipswich). In 4.8 m at edge of Snape turn left on to B1069 (sign Woodbridge). In 1.3 m at Maltings turn left on to minor road (sign Orford). In 4.0 m join B1084 into Orford.

In Orford take B1084 and in 1.5 m, still on B1084, turn left (sign Woodbridge). In 7.8 m join A1152 (sign Woodbridge) for 1.6 m and at Melton traffic lights turn left into Woodbridge town centre.

At Woodbridge, Bull Hotel, take Burkitt Rd and in 0.4 m turn left on to B1079 (sign Grundisburgh). In 0.4 m keep straight on B1079 (sign Grundisburgh) for 5.2 m.

Coddenham (Suffolk)

A small, picturesque village on the slope of a hill. The attractive houses are mainly washed in pink, green and white. There used to be several inns here, but now only the Dukes Head remains, with a public bar which displays what must surely be the oldest wooden darts scoreboard in the land.

Needham Market (Suffolk)

The name is misleading for there is no longer a market here, though there used to be one when this was a wool town. Along the long, narrow High Street the few shops appear to straggle rather untidily.

Aldham (Suffolk)

The church is signed to the left before reaching the village. It is worth a visit and has a marvellous situation on a rise amidst farmhouses and barns, overlooking a huge expanse of countryside.

Hadleigh (Suffolk)

This was once a noted wool town and it lies on the R. Brett, a tributary of the R. Stour. Fine medieval buildings cluster around the church of the Blessed Virgin Mary where, in the South Chapel, there is an interesting bench carving illustrating the legend of St Edmund – the saint's head in the jaws of a wolf. A stained glass window of the south wall commemorates Rowland Taylor, the martyr who was burned at the stake on Aldham common in 1555, where there is a plaque marking the scene of his death. A huge beer jug (once known as a 'gotch') is preserved in a glass case and is a reminder that the 18c bell-ringers must have had a healthy thirst, for the jug is engraved: If ye love me due not lend me, Use me often keep me clenly, Fill me full or not at all, And that with Strong and not with small.'

Edgehill Hotel, 2 High St, 6 rooms, T2458 (C)

East Bergholt (Suffolk)

John Constable (1776–1837), son of a miller, was born here and many of his finest paintings, including that of nearby Flatford Mill, were composed in the area. The pretty Essex village of Dedham, where Constable was educated, can only be reached by car after returning to the main road – although there are boats for hire at Flatford for those who wish to row there. Flatford Mill is approached by way of a narrow one-way system, and probably the area is best avoided in mid-summer on account of the crowds.

Higham (Suffolk)

The village is made up of handsome old houses and lies where the Stour joins the Brett.

The Old Vicarage, 5 rooms, T248 (D)

Stoke by Nayland (Suffolk)

The tower of the church here forms a background to many of Constable's landscape paintings. There is a pleasant, spacious old inn, The Crown, with a reputation for good food.

Thorington Hall, 3 rooms, T Higham 329 (D)

Nayland (Suffolk)

Another old cloth town on the R. Stour with many of the original weavers' houses and cottages.

White Hart Hotel, 5 rooms, T262382 (D)

The Route

Much of the route undulates past trees and meadows near to the R. Stour and its tributaries, passing numerous picturesque villages.

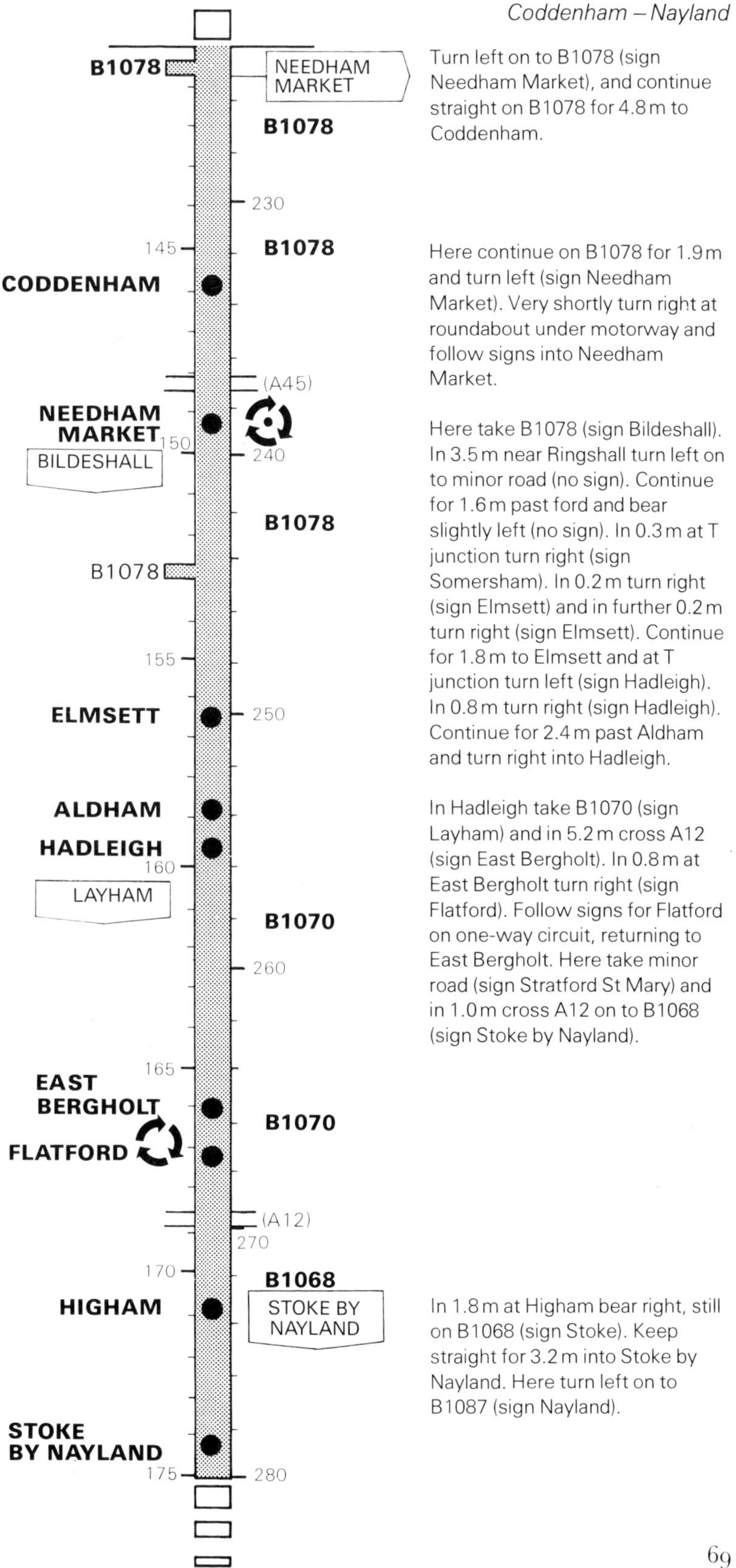

Turn left on to B1078 (sign Needham Market), and continue straight on B1078 for 4.8 m to Coddenham.

Here continue on B1078 for 1.9 m and turn left (sign Needham Market). Very shortly turn right at roundabout under motorway and follow signs into Needham Market.

Here take B1078 (sign Bildeshall). In 3.5 m near Ringshall turn left on to minor road (no sign). Continue for 1.6 m past ford and bear slightly left (no sign). In 0.3 m at T junction turn right (sign Somersham). In 0.2 m turn right (sign Elmsett) and in further 0.2 m turn right (sign Elmsett). Continue for 1.8 m to Elmsett and at T junction turn left (sign Hadleigh). In 0.8 m turn right (sign Hadleigh). Continue for 2.4 m past Aldham and turn right into Hadleigh.

In Hadleigh take B1070 (sign Layham) and in 5.2 m cross A12 (sign East Bergholt). In 0.8 m at East Bergholt turn right (sign Flatford). Follow signs for Flatford on one-way circuit, returning to East Bergholt. Here take minor road (sign Stratford St Mary) and in 1.0 m cross A12 on to B1068 (sign Stoke by Nayland).

In 1.8 m at Higham bear right, still on B1068 (sign Stoke). Keep straight for 3.2 m into Stoke by Nayland. Here turn left on to B1087 (sign Nayland).

This row is typical of Saffron Walden's attractive old houses.

Pebmarsh (Essex)

The road skirts the edge of Bures before approaching this tiny village through remote countryside. Thus Pebmarsh is something of an oasis, and it is a pleasure to come across an attractive old inn, the King's Head, which offers a warm welcome and bar snacks.

Castle Hedingham (Essex)

This is the smaller and more attractive of the two Hedinghams – the route only skirting Sible Hedingham, a mile away. The village is named after the 12c castle on the hill above it, where the 100-foot tower can be visited on specific occasions. Among many old buildings is a 15c pink-washed restaurant, Old Moat House (T60342), which provides a good menu.

Finchingfield (Essex)

Wethersfield, through which the road ran, is quite an attractive village but certainly not in the same class as Finchingfield where the village green and pond, together with the windmill and a variety of buildings of historic interest, make it one of the county's best-loved villages. On the east wall of the church of St John's is an inscription which refers to the strange story of William Kemp, one-time owner of Spains Hall, a manor house to the west of the village. After unjustly accusing his wife of adultery, Kemp was struck with remorse and paid penance by keeping a seven-year silence and digging ponds in the grounds of the mansion – one for each year of penance. Later, in 1760, Spains Hall became the home of the Ruggles-Brise family, and a plaque in the church to Sir Evelyn Ruggles-Brise is inscribed: 'We shall remember him as one who had faith in his fellow men' – a reminder that Sir Evelyn was the prison reformer who devised the system for Borstal training.

Saffron Walden (Essex)

Saffron was once grown here for use in dyes and medicine – hence the name of this old town, where a maze of narrow streets and passages lead from the market-place. Among the many old houses is the beam-fronted Cross Keys Inn.

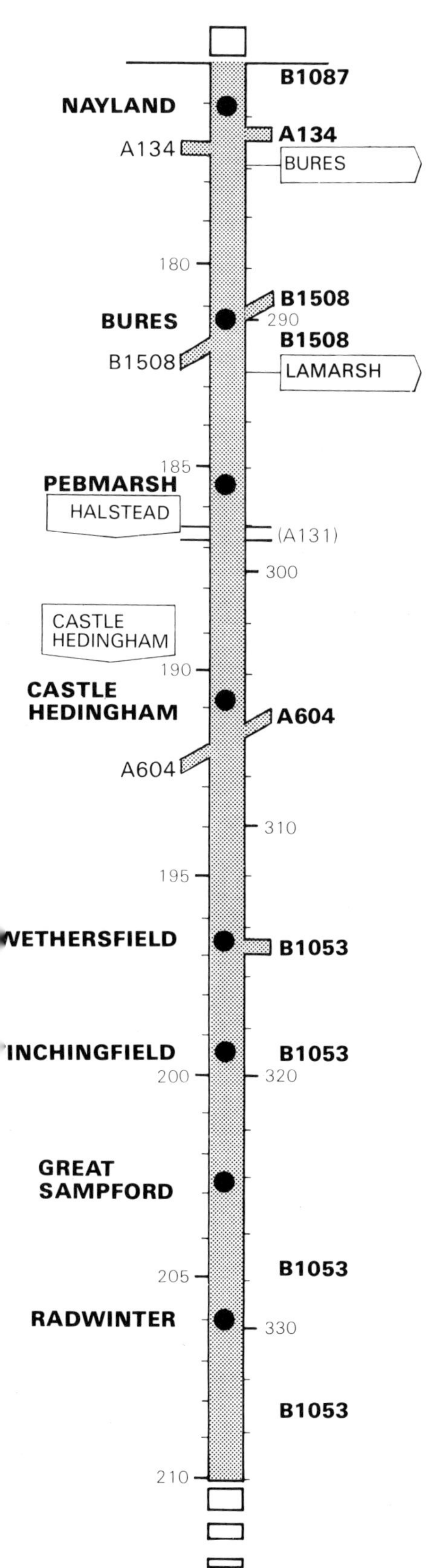

At Nayland keep left through village and in 0.7 m turn right and almost immediately left across A134 on to minor road (sign Bures).

In 4.8 m at Bures turn left and almost immediately bear right (sign Lamarsh). In 0.1 m turn left (sign Pebmarsh). In 1.2 m turn right (sign Pebmarsh). In 0.5 m at Hornes Green bear left (no sign). In 0.7 m bear right (no sign). In 0.5 m at T junction turn left (sign Pebmarsh) and continue for 1.0 m to Pebmarsh.

Here keep straight (sign Halstead) and in 1.6 m keep straight across A131 (sign The Hedinghams). In 0.3 m turn right and immediately left (sign Maplestead). In 0.8 m turn right (sign Castle Hedingham). Follow signs for Castle Hedingham for 2.5 m into Castle Hedingham.

Here keep straight (sign Sible Hedingham) and in 0.7 m turn left and immediately right (sign Wethersfield). In 0.3 m turn right (sign Wethersfield). In 0.1 m turn left (sign Wethersfield). Keep straight for 4.7 m to Wethersfield.

Here take B1053 (sign Finchingfield) for 2.3 m to Finchingfield and here continue on B1053 (sign Saffron Walden) for 3.5 m to Great Sampford.

Here turn right, still on B1053, and continue for 2.5 m. Turn left (sign Saffron Walden) and in 0.4 m at Radwinter keep straight (sign Saffron Walden) for 5.1 m into Saffron Walden.

Punting along the 'Backs' at Cambridge, with the Bridge of Sighs on the right.

Hadstock (Essex)

The last village before leaving Essex – but certainly not the least, for it is a beautiful one that nestles in the hollow after crossing the plain from Saffron Walden. The church on the hill approaching the village has a Saxon door considered to be the oldest church door in England.

Linton (Cambridgeshire)

There is a small zoo on the left of the road before it crosses the main road into the village itself. The steep village High Street is flanked by many old houses and inns.

Fulbourn (Cambridgeshire)

Quite a large village where the houses are spread along a number of tree-lined lanes.

The Route

As far as Saffron Walden the roads continue to undulate and twist past woods, meadows and streams. Thereafter the road climbs and runs straight across a bare plain which is, nevertheless, interspersed with several attractive villages.

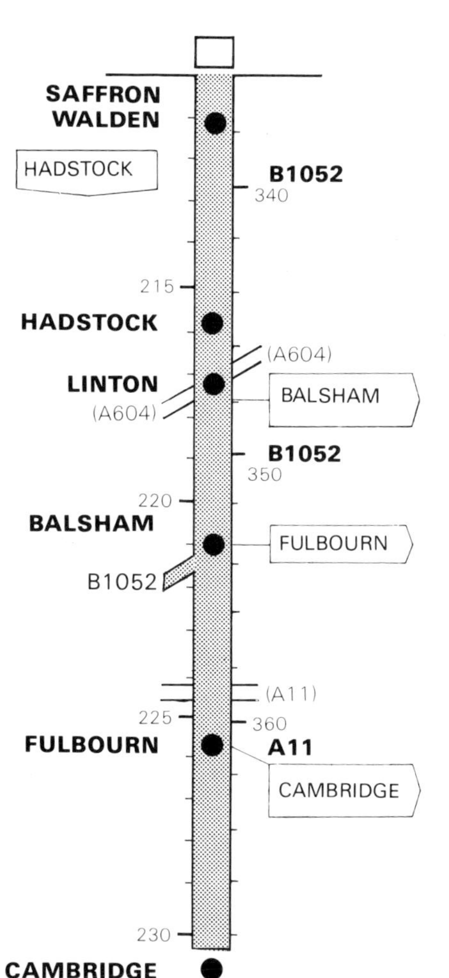

In Saffron Walden take B1052 (sign Hadstock) and continue straight for 4.7 m to Hadstock.

Here keep straight on B1052 (sign Linton) for 1.0 m and cross A604 into Linton. Here, at foot of hill, turn left (signs Balsham and Newmarket). Keep straight for 2.9 m to Balsham.

At Balsham turn left on to minor road (sign Fulbourn). In 2.9 m keep straight across A11 (sign Fulbourn) for 1.8 m into Fulbourn.

Here bear left (sign Cambridge) and continue to follow signs for Cambridge for further 5.0 m into Cambridge.

5 *Heart of England (East)*

THE TITLE FOR THIS ROUTE is somewhat arbitrary, for although the route begins at Warwick, a town that can certainly be said to lie in the heart of England, it stretches as far east as Huntingdon, passing through or at least touching no less than seven counties, namely Warwickshire, Oxfordshire, Northamptonshire, Buckinghamshire, Bedfordshire, Cambridgeshire, and Leicestershire.

Warwick makes a good starting-point. The town lies only a few miles to the north of Stratford-on-Avon, birthplace of William Shakespeare (1564–1616) and, apart from London, England's principal tourist centre. About the same distance to the north of Warwick is Kenilworth with its famous 14th century castle, subject of Sir Walter Scott's novel. A little to the east is the pleasant spa town of Leamington. All these places are worth visiting if time permits before departing on the mapped route.

The route sets off in the rough direction of Banbury through some fine Warwickshire countryside, nearing the scene of the first battle of the Civil War. In fact throughout the route there are associations with

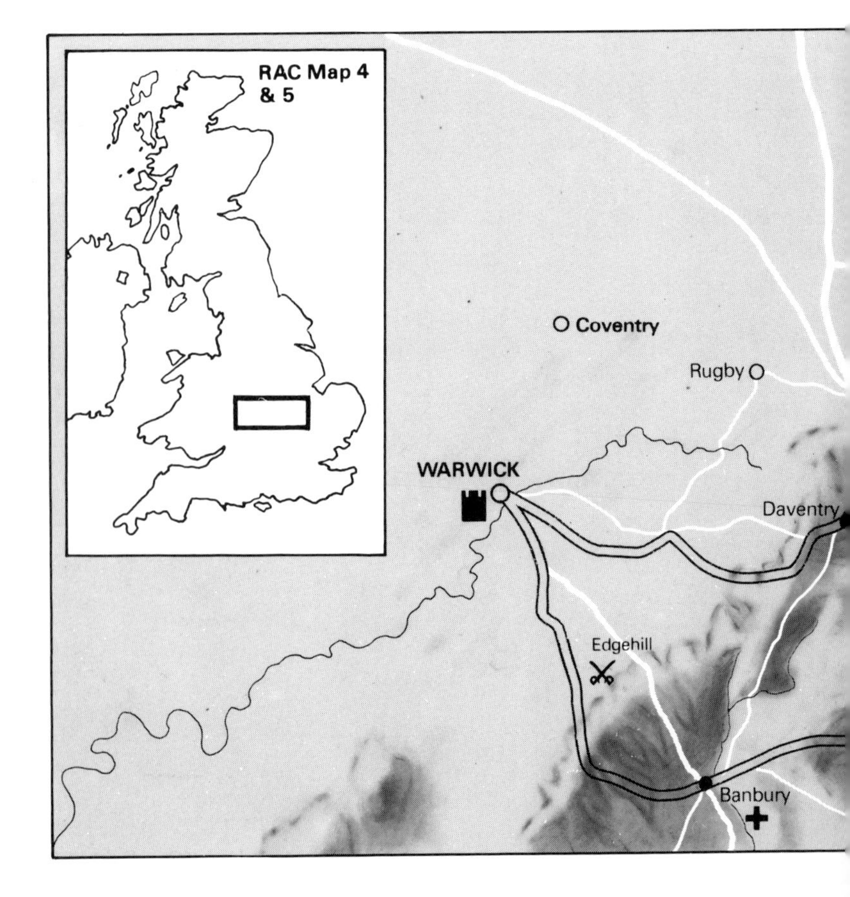

the Civil War, for not only does it pass near the battlefields of Edgehill and Naseby but it also visits the birthplace of Oliver Cromwell at Huntingdon and the town where King Charles I spent his last nights before the Battle of Naseby at Daventry.

Much of the country which William Cowper (1731–1800) loved and wrote about lies along the route, as well as his last two homes.

The old Roman road known as Watling Street is touched at Towcester. This road was a 'happy hunting-ground' for Dick Turpin and other notorious highwaymen, who hid in the nearby villages.

Almost the whole of this route runs through agricultural country, where there is little industry apart from that found in the immediate vicinity of Huntingdon, Daventry and Market Harborough. Farm mechanization has led to the depopulation of many small rural villages, resulting in the closure of churches, schools, and inns. But although these remote villages are quieter places than in former times, it is evident that the remaining inhabitants are doing their best to preserve their heritage and traditional way of life.

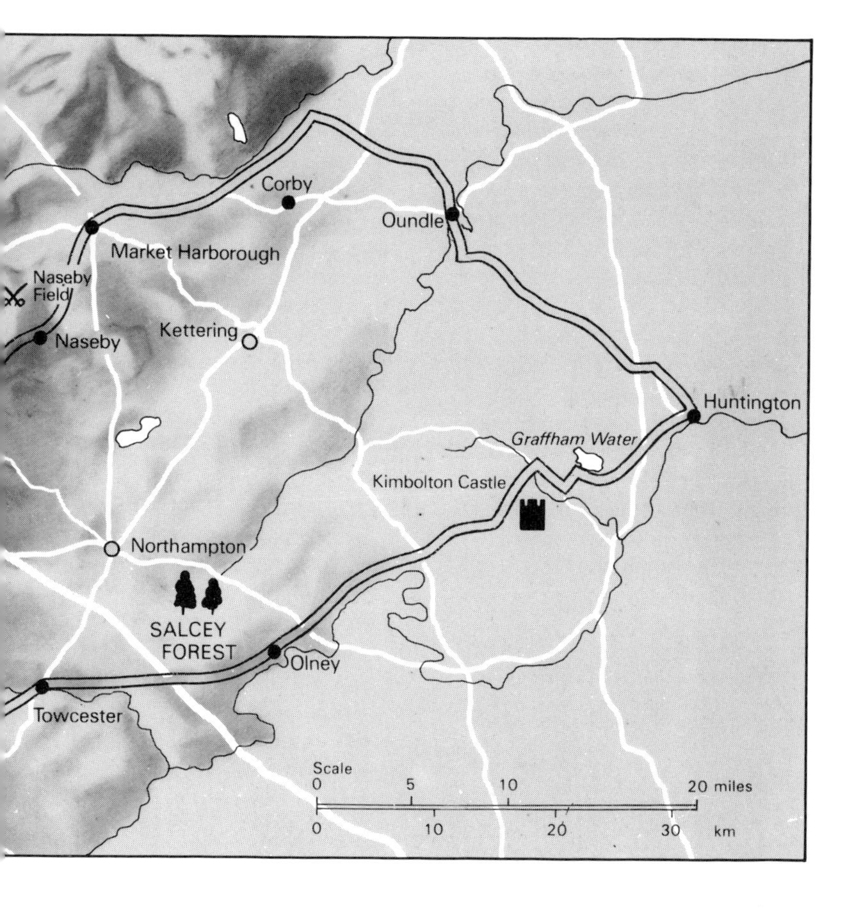

Warwick

There can be few towns in the whole of England where such a multitude of historic buildings lie in so compact a space. This, coupled with the fact that Stratford-upon-Avon, Kenilworth and Leamington Spa lie close at hand, makes Warwick an ideal centre for the start of this tour.

There is a good overall view of Warwick Castle from the river bridge, and from here it is worth strolling past the beautiful Tudor houses in Mill street for a close-up view of the Castle from beneath. From this point the three huge towers (Caesar's Tower, Guy's Tower and the Clock Tower) soar upwards, and the sheer solidity of this immense fortress castle is apparent. The Castle is open to the public daily and here can be seen many fine furnished rooms and classical paintings – as well as the torture chamber and dungeons, with the terrifying pit down which prisoners were thrown and forgotten – the 'oubliette'.

Among other buildings of interest are St Mary's Church with its world-famous Beauchamp Chapel, and the Leycester Hospital, which since 1571 has been a home for retired soldiers and where a visit is best concluded by taking the excellent cream tea served in the ancient Bretherens' Kitchen. An old timbered house in Castle Street now serves as a museum for dolls in period dress, and nearby is Landor House, birthplace of the poet W. S. Landor.

Lord Leycester Hotel, Jury St, 43 rooms, T23241 (B)
Avon Guest House, 7 Emscote Rd, 7 rooms, T41367 (D)
T.O. Court House, Jury St, T42212

Kineton (Warwickshire)

A spacious old town of broad streets, near to the ridge known as Edgehill which can be seen on the left of the road between here and Tysoe. It was at Edgehill that the first battle of Civil War took place.

The Manor House Hotel, 4 rooms, T Warwick 640113 (D)

Tysoe (Warwickshire)

This is in fact made up of three villages – the road running from Lower Tysoe through Middle Tysoe, where there is a splendid 11c church, to Upper Tysoe.

Compton Wynyates (Warwickshire)

Home of the Marquis of Northampton. The immense house, begun in 1480, is beautifully situated in a fold in the Warwickshire hills. The grounds and parts of the house are open to the public on specific occasions.

Shutford (Oxfordshire)

It is quite usual in English villages for church and inn to lie close together, but the proximity of these buildings in this attractive, remote little village must be almost a record. The George and Dragon Inn backs on to the church – less than three yards separating the inn from the church tower.

Banbury (Oxfordshire)

The 'Fine lady upon the White Horse' who according to the nursery rhyme came to Banbury Cross may have hailed from nearby Broughton Castle. The original Banbury Cross was destroyed by the Puritans in 1602, and the existing one was erected near to where the original was supposed to have stood.

Whateley Hall Hotel, Horsefair, 78 rooms, T3451 (A)
Lismore Private Hotel, 61 Oxford Dr, 12 rooms, T 2105 (C)

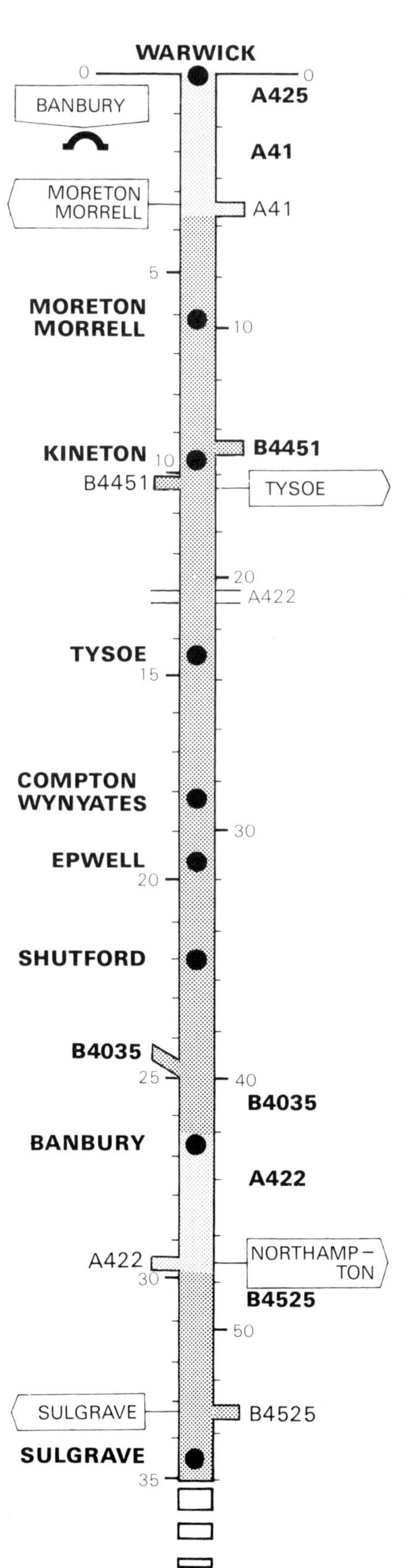

At Warwick follow signs Banbury and cross river. Keep straight on A425, later A41, and in 3.5 m turn right on to minor road (sign Moreton Morrell). Keep straight and in 1.9 m turn left (sign Moreton Morrell) for 0.5 m to Moreton Morrell. Here keep straight for 0.7 m and at T junction turn left (sign Lightorne). In 0.4 m keep straight (sign Lightorne) but immediately after cross-roads bear right (no sign). Keep straight for 2.6 m and turn right into Kineton.

In Kineton take B4451 (sign Halford) and in 0.4 m turn left on to minor road (sign Tysoe). Keep straight for 3.7 m and bear right (sign Compton Wynyates). Continue to follow signs Compton Wynyates for further 3.4 m to entry of Compton Wynyates. Here keep straight (sign Epwell) and in 1.0 m turn right (sign Epwell) for 0.5 m to Epwell.

Here bear right (sign Banbury) and in 0.1 m turn left (sign Banbury). In 0.7 m turn right (sign Banbury). In 1.4 m at Shutford bear left (sign Banbury). Keep straight (signs Banbury) for 2.9 m and turn left on to B4035 into Banbury.

Keep straight at Banbury Cross (signs Daventry and Brackley) and in 1.0 m continue straight (sign Brackley). In 1.5 m bear left on to B4525 (sign Northampton). In 4.3 m bear right on to minor road (sign Sulgrave) for 0.6 m to Sulgrave. Here bear right (sign Helmdon).

Above: *The Grand Union Canal at Stoke Bruerne.*
Right: *Warwick Castle.*

Wappenham (Northants)

This little village with church but no pub remains as peaceful as it must have been in the 15c, when an anonymous poet described his visit to the valley in which the village lies as follows:

And so down to the valley – I didn't stop again,
But such a noise of nestlings nor such sweet birdsong
I haven't heard this half year, nor such heavenly sounds,
As I did in that valley among the hedges.

Abthorpe (Northants)

The church, inn and village green lie just off to the left of the road, and are worth visiting, as is the old stone school building (1642), now used as a village hall.

The Route

Very quiet, traffic-free roads through numerous peaceful villages. The road is particularly narrow as it approaches Epwell.

Towcester (Northants)

This very old town lies along the A5, a Roman road known as Watling Street. The nearby M1, takes most of the northbound traffic which used to pass through Towcester – making the town a quieter and more peaceful place. The Saracen's Head Hotel has an attractive bar where much local history is displayed on the walls.

Saracen's Head Hotel, 12 rooms, T50414 (C)

Stoke Bruerne (Northants)

Just before reaching the village, signed to the right, are Stoke Pavilions. The two pavilions which originally flanked a great Inigo Jones house, burned to the ground a hundred years ago, still stand in magnificent countryside and the grounds and parts of the buildings are open to the public, normally at weekends. The village is a delightful place. The road descends past thatched houses until reaching the bridge over the Grand Union Canal. Here, constructed from a number of old terraced cottages, is the Boat Inn (T Towcester 31760). On the opposite bank is the British Waterways Museum.

Hartwell (Northants)

It is hard to believe that this little village lies so close to the M1 motorway, which in fact now separates it from the Salcey Forest. A number of very old oak trees can be found at the extremity of the village, including the Grafton Oak under which the Duke of Grafton was reputed to have rested on his way to church. Beyond the motorway the road runs through the heart of the Salcey Forest. The village boasts a pleasant old inn, the Rose and Crown.

Ravenstone (Bucks)

The church can be found on the left and can be approached by a rose-bordered path which runs under an enormous chestnut tree. The Finch chapel in the church is named after the Lord Chancellor of that name who founded the almshouses which lie nearby.

Weston Underwood (Bucks)

This beautiful village has much to connect it with the poet William Cowper (1731–1800), for he spent the last years of his life here after moving from nearby Olney. His stone house with seven first-floor front windows stands on the left of the road just before reaching the inn, the Cowper Oak. Shortly after the inn there is a path to the left which leads for half a mile to Cowper's Alcove, in which he wrote some of his later poetry, and from where there is a fine view.

Olney (Bucks)

A pleasant market town on the Great Ouse. By the market square is the house where Cowper lived before retiring to Weston Underwood. The house is now known as the Cowper Newton museum, for it was here that Cowper collaborated with his friend John Newton to write a number of well-known hymns. There is a good restaurant here – the Four Pillars, T Bedford 711563.

Harrold (Beds)

There is a small village green surrounded by pretty thatched cottages on which lies the old market house and a tiny hive-shaped gaol-house, used in the old days for locking up 'drunks' overnight. There are three inns in this lengthy village, among them Oakley Arms (T Bedford 720478) which serves excellent meals.

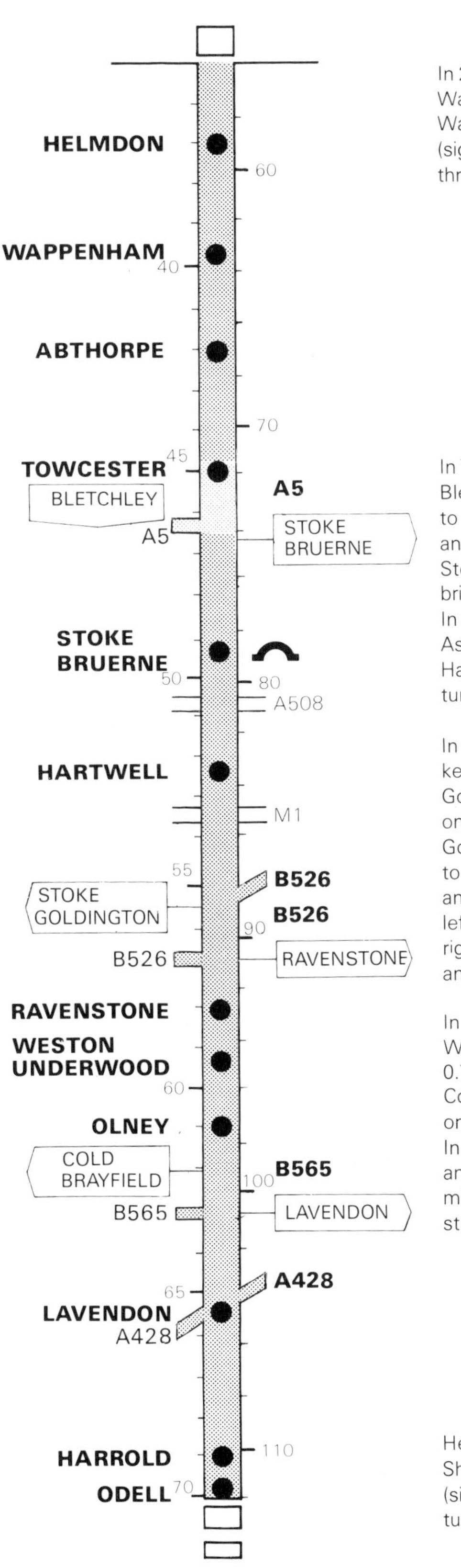

In 2.4 m bear left (sign Wappenham) for 2.8 m to Wappenham. Here bear right (signs Towcester) for 5.0 m through Abthorpe to Towcester.

In Towcester take A5 (sign Bletchley) and in 1.3 m turn left on to minor road (sign Stoke Bruerne) and keep straight for 3.2 m to Stoke Bruerne. Here cross canal bridge and bear left (sign Ashton). In 0.5 m keep straight (sign Ashton). In 0.9 m turn right (sign Hartwell) and in 0.4 m at Hartwell turn left (sign Stoke Goldington).

In 0.8 m, after crossing motorway, keep straight (sign Stoke Goldington) and in 1.5 m turn right on to B526 (sign Stoke Goldington). In 1.8 m turn left on to minor road (sign Ravenstone) and in 1.3 m at Ravenstone turn left (sign Olney). In 0.3 m bear right (sign Weston Underwood) and in 1.0 m turn left (sign Olney).

In 1.5 m at Olney turn left (sign Wellingborough) and in further 0.7 m turn right on to B565 (sign Cold Brayfield). In 1.4 m turn left on to minor road (sign Lavendon). In 0.6 m at Lavendon turn right and almost immediately left on to minor road (sign Harrold). Keep straight for 3.0 m to Harrold.

Here keep straight (sign Sharnbrook). In 0.5 m turn left (sign Sharnbrook) and in 0.3 m turn right (sign Sharnbrook).

The Route

Quiet minor roads all the way except for the last few miles into Huntingdon.

Kimbolton (Cambridgeshire)

The route runs half a mile from the town in the direction of Graffham Water. Those wishing to divert will find Kimbolton is a pleasant little town with many old houses along the main street and in narrow lanes near the church. Kimbolton Castle is now a school, but can be visited on occasions. It was here that Catherine of Aragon (1485–1536), Henry VIII's first queen, died when virtually a prisoner.

Graffham Water (Cambridgeshire)

Sailing takes place on this huge stretch of water (1,570 acres), which is the largest man-made reservoir in England.

Huntingdon (Cambridgeshire)

Though once a county town, Huntingdon has now been absorbed into Cambridgeshire. Although industry has sprung up around the town the central part is of interest. Huntingdon was the birthplace of Oliver Cromwell (1599–1658) and the Cromwell museum is located in an old church near to the town's spacious car park. Cromwell was educated at the grammar school here, a school later attended by the diarist Samuel Pepys (1633–1703). All Saints Church, 15c, stands near the museum and a footpath through the churchyard leads to George Street and an old coaching inn, the George, near to which another old inn, the Falcon, is reputed to have been Cromwell's headquarters during the Civil War.

Old Bridge Hotel, High St, 25 rooms, T52681 (B)
YHA, Houghton Mill, Mill St, Houghton, T62336 (3 miles out of town)

Great Stukeley (Cambridgeshire)

The first three or four miles out of Huntingdon are rather featureless. However, the guest house (below) deserves mention, for the rooms are better appointed than in many hotels and there is an excellent restaurant.

Stukeleys Guest House, 6 rooms, T Huntingdon 56927 (C)

Kimbolton Castle.

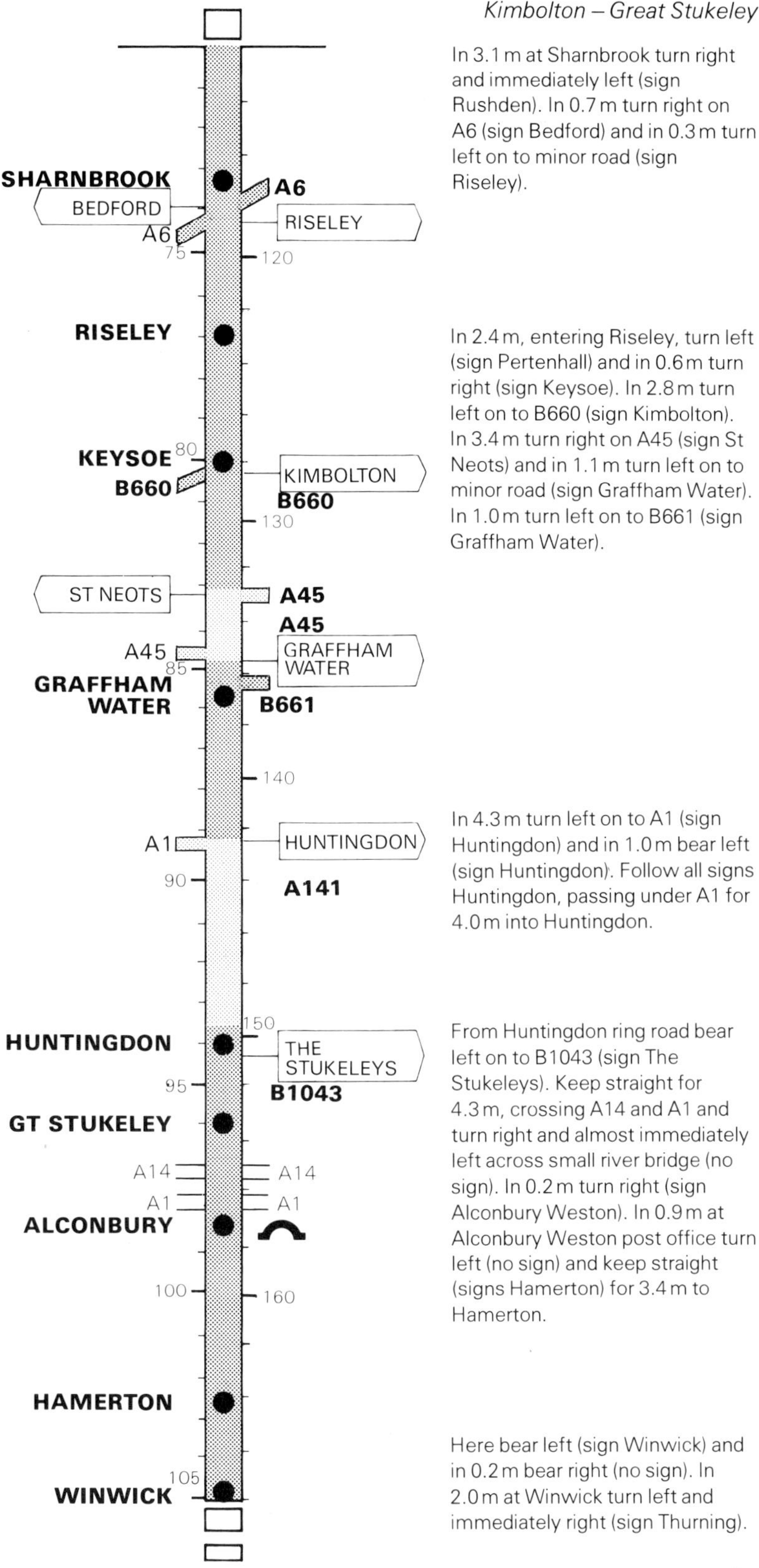

In 3.1 m at Sharnbrook turn right and immediately left (sign Rushden). In 0.7 m turn right on A6 (sign Bedford) and in 0.3 m turn left on to minor road (sign Riseley).

In 2.4 m, entering Riseley, turn left (sign Pertenhall) and in 0.6 m turn right (sign Keysoe). In 2.8 m turn left on to B660 (sign Kimbolton). In 3.4 m turn right on A45 (sign St Neots) and in 1.1 m turn left on to minor road (sign Graffham Water). In 1.0 m turn left on to B661 (sign Graffham Water).

In 4.3 m turn left on to A1 (sign Huntingdon) and in 1.0 m bear left (sign Huntingdon). Follow all signs Huntingdon, passing under A1 for 4.0 m into Huntingdon.

From Huntingdon ring road bear left on to B1043 (sign The Stukeleys). Keep straight for 4.3 m, crossing A14 and A1 and turn right and almost immediately left across small river bridge (no sign). In 0.2 m turn right (sign Alconbury Weston). In 0.9 m at Alconbury Weston post office turn left (no sign) and keep straight (signs Hamerton) for 3.4 m to Hamerton.

Here bear left (sign Winwick) and in 0.2 m bear right (no sign). In 2.0 m at Winwick turn left and immediately right (sign Thurning).

Thurning (Northants)

This little village, just across the border from Cambridgeshire, has seen greater days and in this respect has much in common with the two villages just passed – Hamerton and Winwick. There is a declining population in these areas, demonstrated at Thurning by the old inn sign outside a building no longer in use as an inn, which stands next to another vacant building – once the village school. At the back of the old Wheatsheaf Inn is a spinney where a great manor house once stood. The innkeeper still lives in the village and can recall the days when he did a thriving trade in this quiet remote place.

Barnwell (Northants)

This delightful village seems busy indeed compared with Thurning, boasting an inn as well as a shop. There is a pleasant walk past the churchyard down to the willow-lined brook which runs beneath Barnwell Castle. From here the towers of the 13c castle can be seen in the grounds of the Elizabethan manor house which is the home of the Duke of Gloucester. Further along the brook, in the village, is an attractive inn, the Montagu Arms, and in the church there are many memorials to the Montagu family who originally owned the manor.

Oundle (Northants)

A busy market town which is made up of many old houses, including the 17c Talbot hotel near the market square. The well-known public school here was founded by William Laxton, a native of the town and one-time Lord Mayor of London.

Talbot Hotel, New St, 23 rooms, T3621 (B)

Bulwick (Northants)

An ancient inn, the Queen's Head, stands opposite the church in an attractive village, marred only by the busy A43 which runs through the centre of it.

Harringworth (Northants)

Descending to the village there is a good view of the huge railway viaduct which lies beyond it. In the centre of the village is yet another very old inn, the White Swan, behind which is a medieval cross mounted on stone steps.

Gretton (Northants)

The village green stands at the top of the High Street, which descends to the Welland valley. On the green, in addition to the war memorial, are the village stocks and whipping post.

Rockingham (Northants)

The village lies on the left of the route, the broad main street climbing up to Rockingham Castle, which is still owned by the family to whom it was presented by Henry VIII. Dickens once stayed as a guest at the castle, where he is reputed to have written much of *Bleak House*. Although there are relics of the Norman castle, the present building is Elizabethan and is open to the public on occasions. The village was once a central point of a huge hunting area, Rockingham Forest, which at one time stretched from Kettering to Stamford.

The Route

Apart from the first three or four miles out of Huntingdon, the route is composed of quiet winding roads in an area which is almost entirely agricultural.

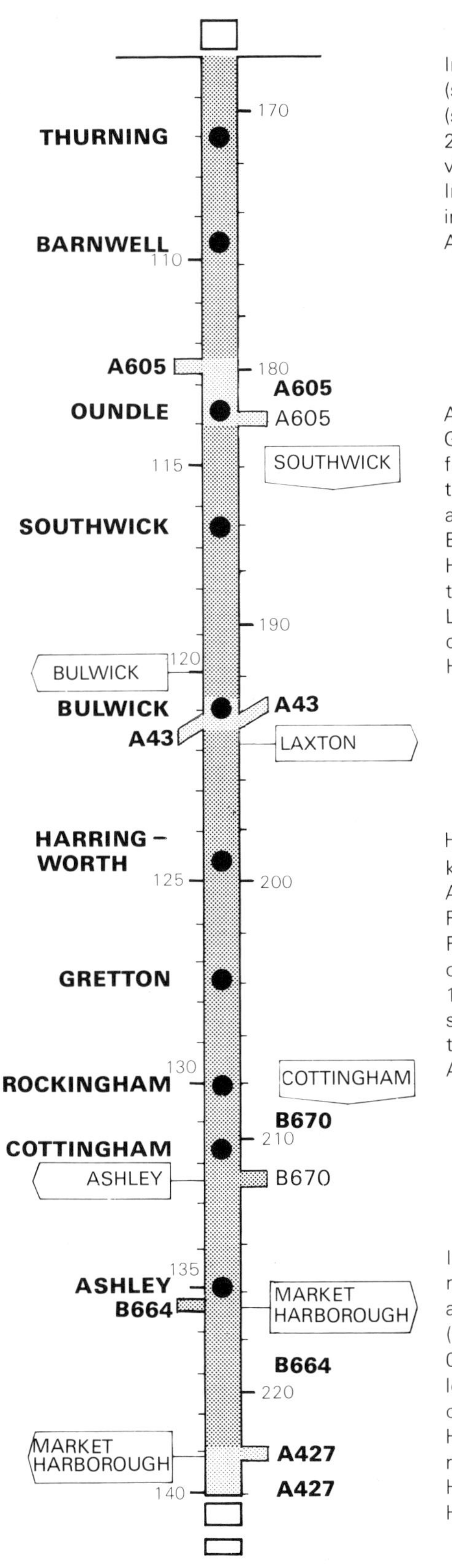

In 1.9 m at Thurning turn right (sign Oundle) and in 0.1 m turn left (sign Oundle). Keep straight for 2.7 m to Barnwell and at end of village turn right (sign Polebrook). In 2.0 m turn left (sign Oundle) and in further 1.2 m turn left on to A605 into Oundle.

At Oundle town centre take Glapthorne Rd (sign Southwick) for 2.9 m to Southwick and here turn left (sign Bulwick) for 4.0 m and turn right on A43 (sign Bulwick) for 0.3 m into Bulwick. Here keep straight for 0.4 m and turn left on to minor road (sign Laxton). In 1.0 m at Laxton continue straight for 2.2 m to Harringworth.

Here turn left (sign Gretton) and keep straight for 2.5 m to Gretton. At Gretton continue straight (sign Rockingham) for 2.6 m to edge of Rockingham. Here keep straight on B670 (sign Cottingham) and in 1.8 m at Cottingham continue straight for 0.3m to Middleton and turn right on to minor road (sign Ashley).

In 3.5 m at end of Ashley bear right (sign Market Harborough) and in 0.2 m turn left on to B664 (sign Market Harborough). In 0.8 m at Weston by Welland bear left (sign Market Harborough) and continue on B664 (signs Market Harborough) for 2.5 m. Here bear right on A427 (sign Market Harborough) for 2.0 m into Market Harborough.

Market Harborough (Leicestershire)

The town lies in the midst of fox-hunting country which contains such famous hunts as the Fernie, the Quorn and the Pytchley. In the market square, close to the 14c church with its beautiful spire, is the quaint old timbered grammar school (1613), on pillars, beneath which there was once a butter market.

Three Swans Hotel, 21 High St, 14 rooms T66644 (B)
Angel Hotel, 37 High St, 21 rooms, T3123 (B)
T.O. Public Library, 53 The Square, T62469

Cold Ashby (Northants)

This small village (pop. 200) is the highest in the county and from Honey Hill, on the Stanford road, it is possible to see seven counties. The church stands off to the left of the road, and the churchyard, beautifully maintained, has recently won awards for being the best kept in the area. The tiny church is well worth a visit – an interesting feature being the verse inscribed near a north window by a former rector.

Clipston (Northants)

The greater part of this beautiful village lies off to the left of the road behind the green. There is a fine building in brown stone, on the front of which is a reminder that 'This free grammar school and hospital was built and endowed by Sir George Buswell.'

Naseby (Northants)

In the fields near the village the final and decisive battle of the Civil War took place. Before arriving in the village, on the left of the road, is a tall monument commemorating the Battle of Naseby. The authors of the inscription on the monument appear to be warning both sides: '. . . leaving a useful lesson to British kings never to exceed the bounds of their just prerogative and to British subjects never to swerve from the allegiance due to their legitimate monarch.' The monument does not, however, lie on the battlefield which in fact is to be found 1½ miles on the other side of the village on the road to Sibbertoft. In the village there is a pleasant inn, the Fitzgerald Arms, with an invitation to wine and dine at the King Charles I Hostelry.

Daventry (Northants)

The old part of the town stands on a hill. Here is a huge dilapidated building, the Wheatsheaf Hotel, where Charles I spent five nights before the battle of Naseby. Legend has it that in this place Charles encountered the ghost of Lord Strafford, executed by his order, who warned him not to engage the Roundheads at Naseby.

Abercorn Hotel, 97 Warwick St, 32 rooms, T3741 (C)

Staverton (Northants)

The highwayman, Dick Turpin (1706–39), once used a local barn as a hideaway after his hold-ups along Watling Street. There is a nice little inn, the Countryman, where meals are served.

Hellidon (Northants)

The bulk of this picturesque village lies off the route to the right, behind the Red Lion Inn. In 1980 an excellent *à la carte* restaurant was established as an annexe to the inn – something of a 'find' in this out of the way place (T Byfield 60469).

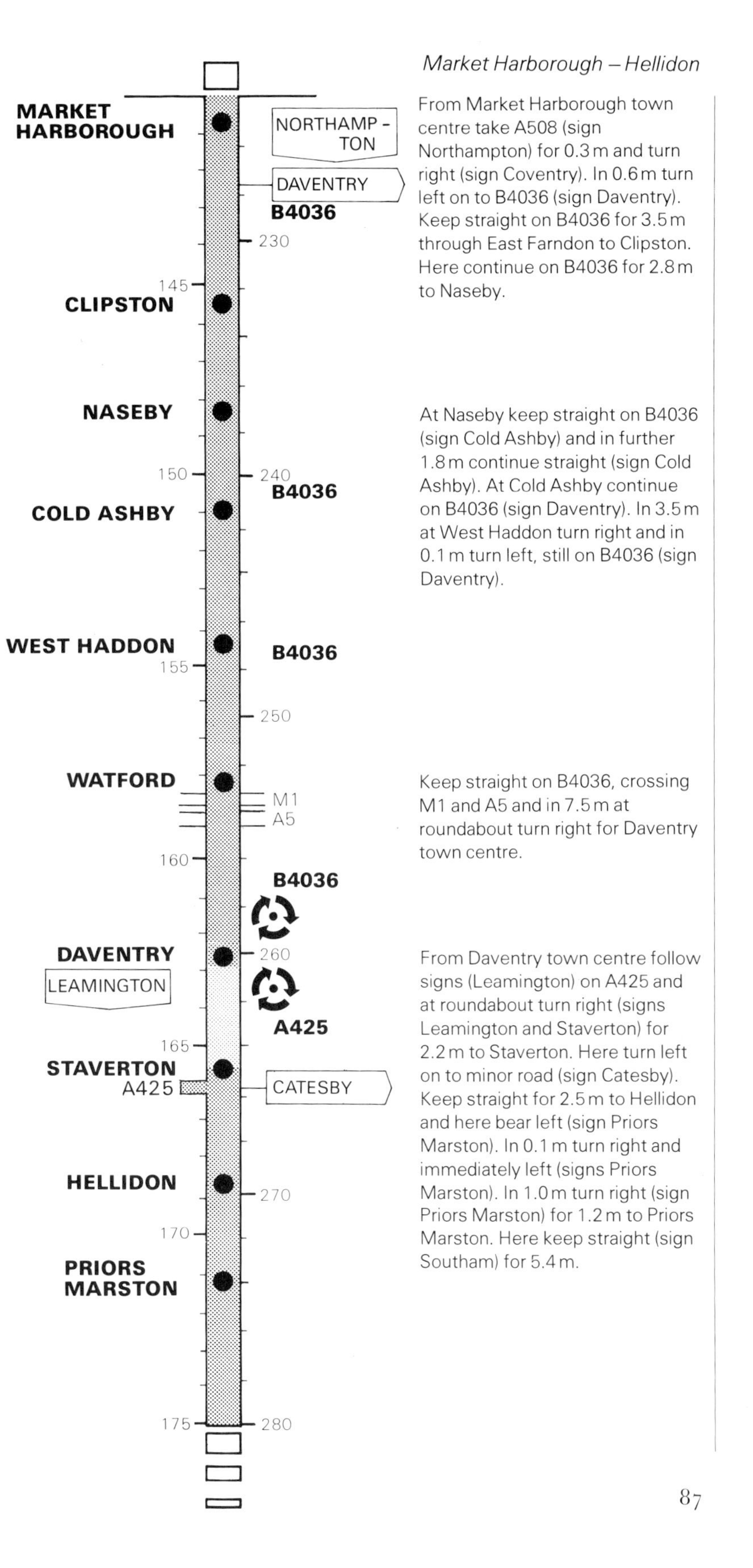

From Market Harborough town centre take A508 (sign Northampton) for 0.3 m and turn right (sign Coventry). In 0.6 m turn left on to B4036 (sign Daventry). Keep straight on B4036 for 3.5 m through East Farndon to Clipston. Here continue on B4036 for 2.8 m to Naseby.

At Naseby keep straight on B4036 (sign Cold Ashby) and in further 1.8 m continue straight (sign Cold Ashby). At Cold Ashby continue on B4036 (sign Daventry). In 3.5 m at West Haddon turn right and in 0.1 m turn left, still on B4036 (sign Daventry).

Keep straight on B4036, crossing M1 and A5 and in 7.5 m at roundabout turn right for Daventry town centre.

From Daventry town centre follow signs (Leamington) on A425 and at roundabout turn right (signs Leamington and Staverton) for 2.2 m to Staverton. Here turn left on to minor road (sign Catesby). Keep straight for 2.5 m to Hellidon and here bear left (sign Priors Marston). In 0.1 m turn right and immediately left (signs Priors Marston). In 1.0 m turn right (sign Priors Marston) for 1.2 m to Priors Marston. Here keep straight (sign Southam) for 5.4 m.

Back at Warwick, the courtyard of Lord Leycester Hospital (above), *and Eastgate* (below).

Southam (Warwickshire)

A busy town with pleasant High Street and several inns, among them the Old Mint Inn where, as the name implies, coins of the realm used to be minted.

Harbury (Warwickshire)

The Chesterton Mill, seen to the left of the road after leaving the village, was designed by Inigo Jones (1573–1652). It is supported by six arches and has a revolving dome roof which acts as an observatory.

The Route

Remote and traffic-free roads with some fine views between Staverton and Warwick.

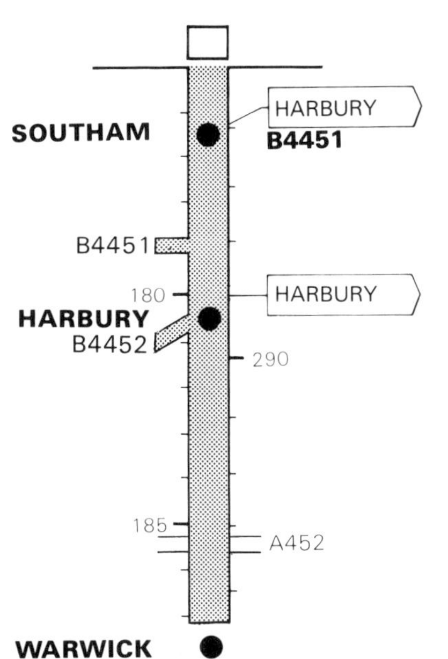

Entering Southam turn left (sign Leamington). In 0.4 m turn right (sign Leamington) and in further 0.2 m turn left on B4451, later B4452, for 3.0 m (signs Harbury). Turn left on to minor road (sign Harbury) and entering Harbury keep straight, shortly turning right (sign Warwick).

Keep straight on minor road (all signs Warwick) for 7.0 m to Warwick.

6 *Devon, Cornwall, West Somerset*

THOUGHTS OF DEVON AND CORNWALL range across a wide canvas. The county of Devon has a coastline that is wild and rocky to both north and south, broken up, nevertheless, with creeks, estuaries, and enchanting bays of golden sands. To the north-east of the county is romantic Exmoor, the 'Lorna Doone country' and the home of red deer and a native breed of pony; and to the south is the lofty expanse of Dartmoor, noted for its wild aspect and crowned by blocks of granite known as tors. Contrasting with these rugged coastal and upland areas, the sheltered parts of the county give way to pastureland and expanses of rich red soil interwoven with a vast complex pattern of winding high banked country lanes. Among the principle industries of

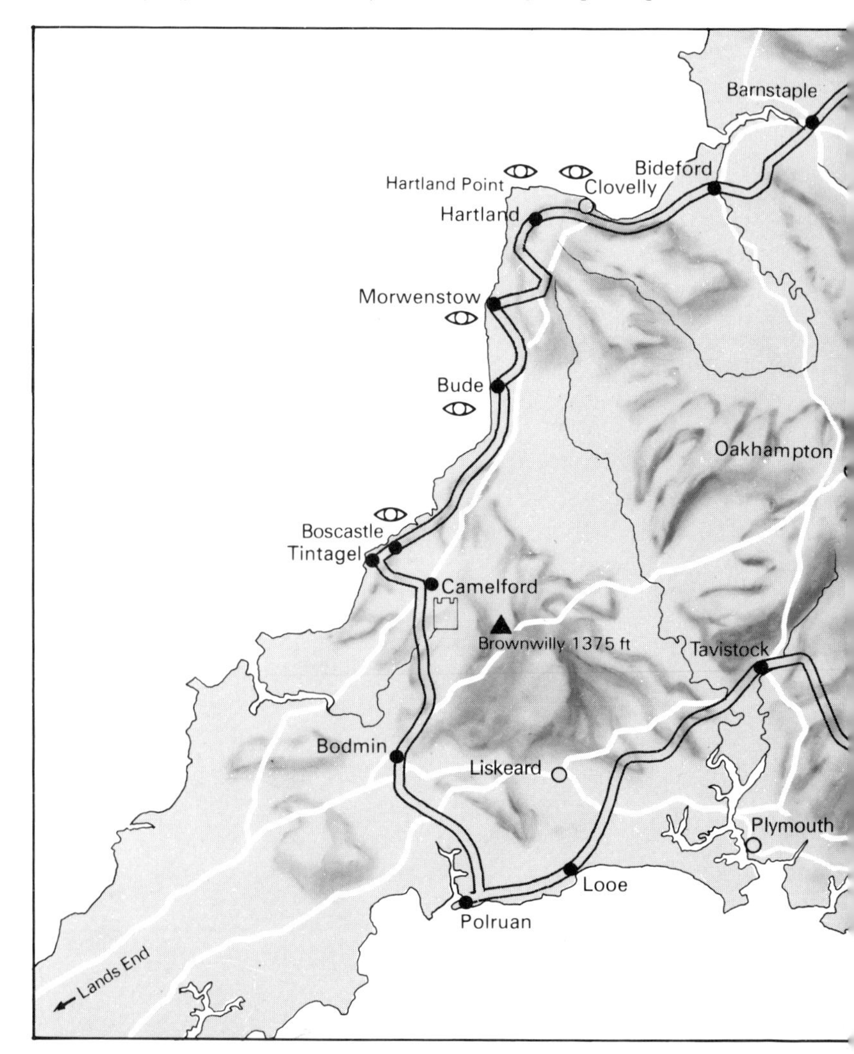

Devon are ship building and lace making, while of course the county is renowned for its cream and cider.

Cornwall occupies the extreme south-west corner of England and like Devon is rich in fine coastal scenery – with the high Atlantic cliffs to the north and a less rigorous coastline to the south. Cornwall is a place of legend, a place that abounds with ancient crosses and holy wells, the scene of King Arthur's birth as well as his death at Camelford (believed by many to be Camelot). Inland Cornwall includes Bodmin Moor, a peaty upland where from Brown Willy (1,375 ft), the highest hill in the county, there are spectacular views across both Devon and Cornwall. Sections of rich agricultural land specialize in early vegetables. Minerals such as tin, copper and lead are mined, and china clay for pottery is a considerable source of income. This route of less than three hundred miles cannot possibly cover more than a small sample of West Country landscape. Initially the road runs northward from Exeter by way of typical Devonshire lanes towards the National Park of Exmoor, the eastern part of which lies in

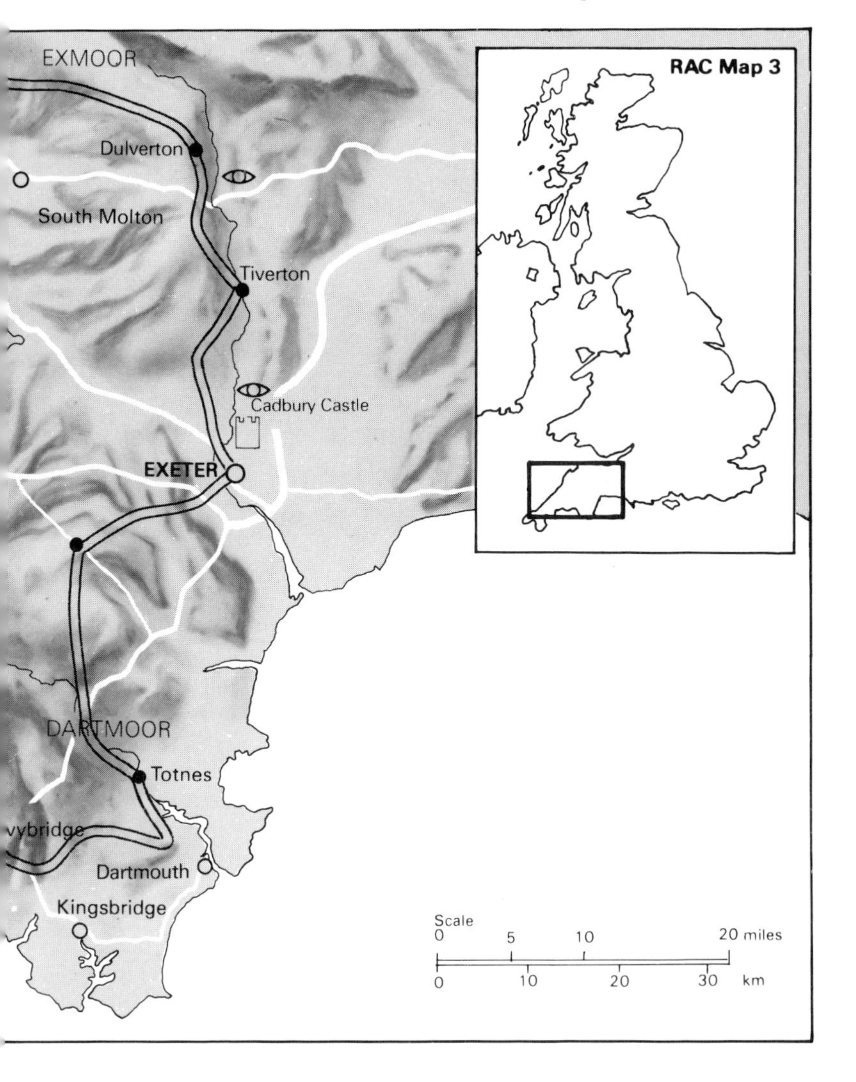

Two faces of Devon: Hartland Point (left) *and Clovelly* (right).

Somerset. From Dulverton the route runs westward through the moors to Barnstaple, ignoring the North Devon coast which is perhaps best approached by diverting to Simonsbath (signed to the right at various points) and from there taking the B3223 for some seven miles to Lynmouth.

After a variety of views of the Devon/Cornwall coast between Hartland and Tintagel the route turns inland to Bodmin and Lostwithiel before returning to the coast at Polruan. It would of course be impossible to explore the narrow 'toe' of Cornwall by minor roads, but those wishing to visit the extreme south-western part of the county might be advised to divert from the route at Bodmin, taking the main road to Land's End. Places of interest along both the north and south coasts between Bodmin and Land's End are too numerous to list in detail but include St Ives, in the north, and Porthcurno, Mousehole, Penzance, and the Lizard peninsula in the south.

After leaving the seaside resort of Looe on the south Cornish coast the route veers inland in the general direction of the River Tamar, which divides Cornwall from Devon before crossing the south-west fringe of Dartmoor. From Modbury the road runs eastward and those with time to spare may wish to divert by way of the B3196 to Kingsbridge (signed right) or consider visiting Dartmouth, a fascinating port which is almost reached at the point where the minor road leaves the B3207 for Dittisham. After following the River Dart to Totnes, the road runs northward through the Dartmoor National Park to Moretonhampstead before returning to Exeter on the relatively traffic-free B3212.

As elsewhere in the guide, price graded hotels and youth hostels have been indicated. But it is worth remembering that both Devon and Cornwall pride themselves on the excellence of their farmhouse accommodation, often much less expensive than that encountered even in the more modest hotels.

Exeter (Devonshire)

In May 1942 bombs flattened much of the centre of this ancient city which, today, is very much a blend of the old and new. Sections of the Roman wall, built around AD 200, intermingle with well laid out modern streets that are bordered by flowers and shrubs. Among many historic buildings to be seen in Exeter are the Cathedral, founded in 1050 but rebuilt in the 13/14c; the Guildhall, 14c and possibly the oldest municipal building in England; and St Nicholas Priory, a monastic guest house with a display of 16 and 17c furniture. Mol's Coffee House, now an art gallery near the Cathedral, was once a meeting-place for Drake, Hawkins and other seafaring men. Interesting old inns include the White Hart, Turk's Head and the Ship – also frequented by Sir Francis Drake (1546–96), who said of it: 'Next to mine own shippe I do most love that old Shippe in Exon, a tavern in St Martins Lane.'

Royal Clarence Hotel, Cathedral Yard, 65 rooms, T58464 (A)
Bystock Hotel, Bystock Terrace, 25 rooms, T72709 (C)
YHA, 47 Countess Weare Rd, T Topsham 3329
T.O. Civic Centre, Dix's Field, T77888

Stockleigh Pomeroy (Devonshire)

The Norman church and a few thatched cottages nestle beneath wooded hills down the lane to the left of the route. Origin of the name Stockleigh is 'the farm in the clearing'.

Cadbury (Devonshire)

The village lies to the right of the route. A sign indicates the footpath to Cadbury Castle, the Iron Age earthworks on the hilltop, from where there are fine views.

Bickleigh (Devonshire)

Bickleigh Castle is signed to the right before the edge of the village is reached. The restored castle, once a fortified manor house, stands on the bank of the R. Exe amidst picturesque gardens that are open to the public on occasions in the summer. The hotel, below, also occupies a fine position on the river.

Fisherman's Cot, 8 rooms, T237 (D)

Tiverton (Devonshire)

The route bypasses the centre of this textile producing town by way of some rather ugly suburbs. The Norman church, partly rebuilt in the last century, and the Greenway Almshouses, 16c, are worth visiting. Among the pupils of Blundells School was R. D. Blackmore (1825–1900), author of the novel *Lorna Doone*, a romance of Exmoor in the 17c.

Boars Head Hotel, Bampton St, 10 rooms, T2313 (C)
T.O. Tiverton Museum, St Andrews St, T56295

Dulverton (Somerset)

Beautifully situated in a valley of wooded hills to the extreme south of the Exmoor National Park at a point near the junction of the rivers Exe and Barle. The R. Barle, flanked by tall trees, can be seen to advantage by the roadside to the north of Dulverton before the road ascends sharply to cross the moors. An old packhorse bridge across the Barle, the Tarr Steps, is preserved by the National Trust and worth visiting but unfortunately the ford here is not always motorable – the reason that the alternative route south of Hawkridge has been indicated.

Lamb Hotel, 26 rooms, T23369 (C)

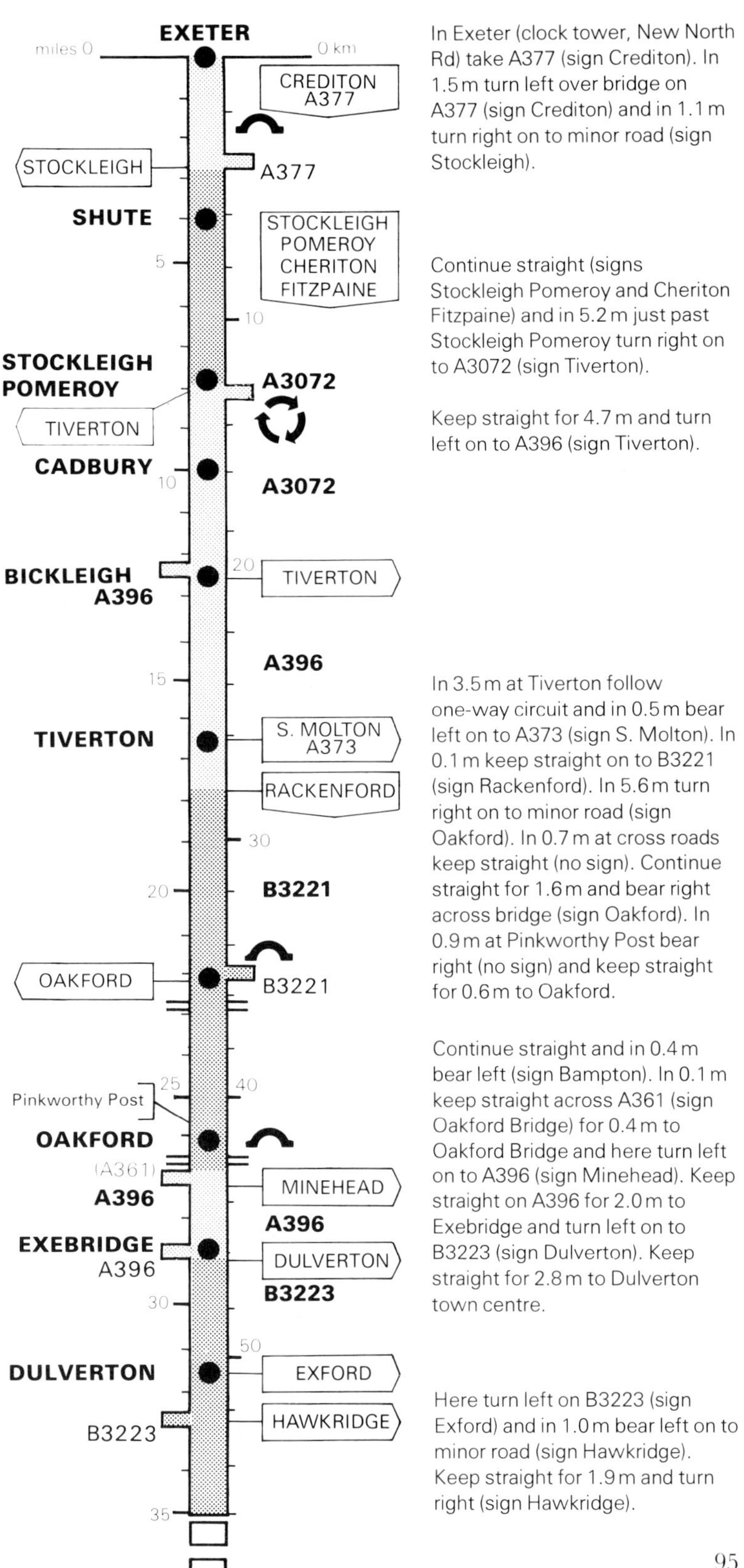

In Exeter (clock tower, New North Rd) take A377 (sign Crediton). In 1.5 m turn left over bridge on A377 (sign Crediton) and in 1.1 m turn right on to minor road (sign Stockleigh).

Continue straight (signs Stockleigh Pomeroy and Cheriton Fitzpaine) and in 5.2 m just past Stockleigh Pomeroy turn right on to A3072 (sign Tiverton).

Keep straight for 4.7 m and turn left on to A396 (sign Tiverton).

In 3.5 m at Tiverton follow one-way circuit and in 0.5 m bear left on to A373 (sign S. Molton). In 0.1 m keep straight on to B3221 (sign Rackenford). In 5.6 m turn right on to minor road (sign Oakford). In 0.7 m at cross roads keep straight (no sign). Continue straight for 1.6 m and bear right across bridge (sign Oakford). In 0.9 m at Pinkworthy Post bear right (no sign) and keep straight for 0.6 m to Oakford.

Continue straight and in 0.4 m bear left (sign Bampton). In 0.1 m keep straight across A361 (sign Oakford Bridge) for 0.4 m to Oakford Bridge and here turn left on to A396 (sign Minehead). Keep straight on A396 for 2.0 m to Exebridge and turn left on to B3223 (sign Dulverton). Keep straight for 2.8 m to Dulverton town centre.

Here turn left on B3223 (sign Exford) and in 1.0 m bear left on to minor road (sign Hawkridge). Keep straight for 1.9 m and turn right (sign Hawkridge).

Poltimore Arms (Devonshire)

This inn (below) is among the very few buildings encountered on Exmoor. It is under new ownership and bed and breakfast is available to those who are prepared to shrug aside the legend that the ghost of Charles II haunts this ancient hostelry. In any case it is worth pausing at the Poltimore Arms, frequent meeting place of the Devon and Somerset Staghounds and the Exmoor Foxhounds, for the view at the rear of the inn, where on fine days distant Hartland Point can be seen.

Poltimore Arms, 2 rooms, T Brayford 381 (D)

Barnstaple (Devonshire)

One of the oldest boroughs in Britain where many of the buildings lie close to the R. Taw, among them the John Gay theatre which acts as a reminder that the dramatist John Gay (1685–1732), author of *The Beggar's Opera*, was born here. The town is noted for Queen Anne's Walk, a small arcade with statue of Queen Anne, and the huge covered Pannier Market.

Royal and Fortescue Hotel, Boutport St, 63 rooms, T2289 (C)

Queen Anne's Walk, Barnstaple.

Alverdiscott (Devonshire)

The name means 'Alfred's outlying farm' and indeed the village comprises little more than a farm and a church with a good view of the countryside beneath.

Statue of Charles Kingsley.

Bideford (Devonshire)

Occupies a lovely position on the R. Torridge, spanned by a bridge more than 200 yards in length with 24 arches of differing widths. Charles Kingsley (1819–75), the author, wrote part ofhis *Westward Ho* in the Kingsley suite of the hotel (below) and there is a statue of him by the river. Another interesting feature of the hotel are the former prison cells.

Royal Hotel, Barnstaple St, 33 rooms, T2005 (C)
T.O. The Quay, T77676

The Route

Initially by way of narrow hedged lanes of the kind that abound in Devon. Similar lanes are encountered between Tiverton and Oakford Bridge before the route runs momentarily into Somerset, crossing Exmoor from east to west and re-entering Devonshire.

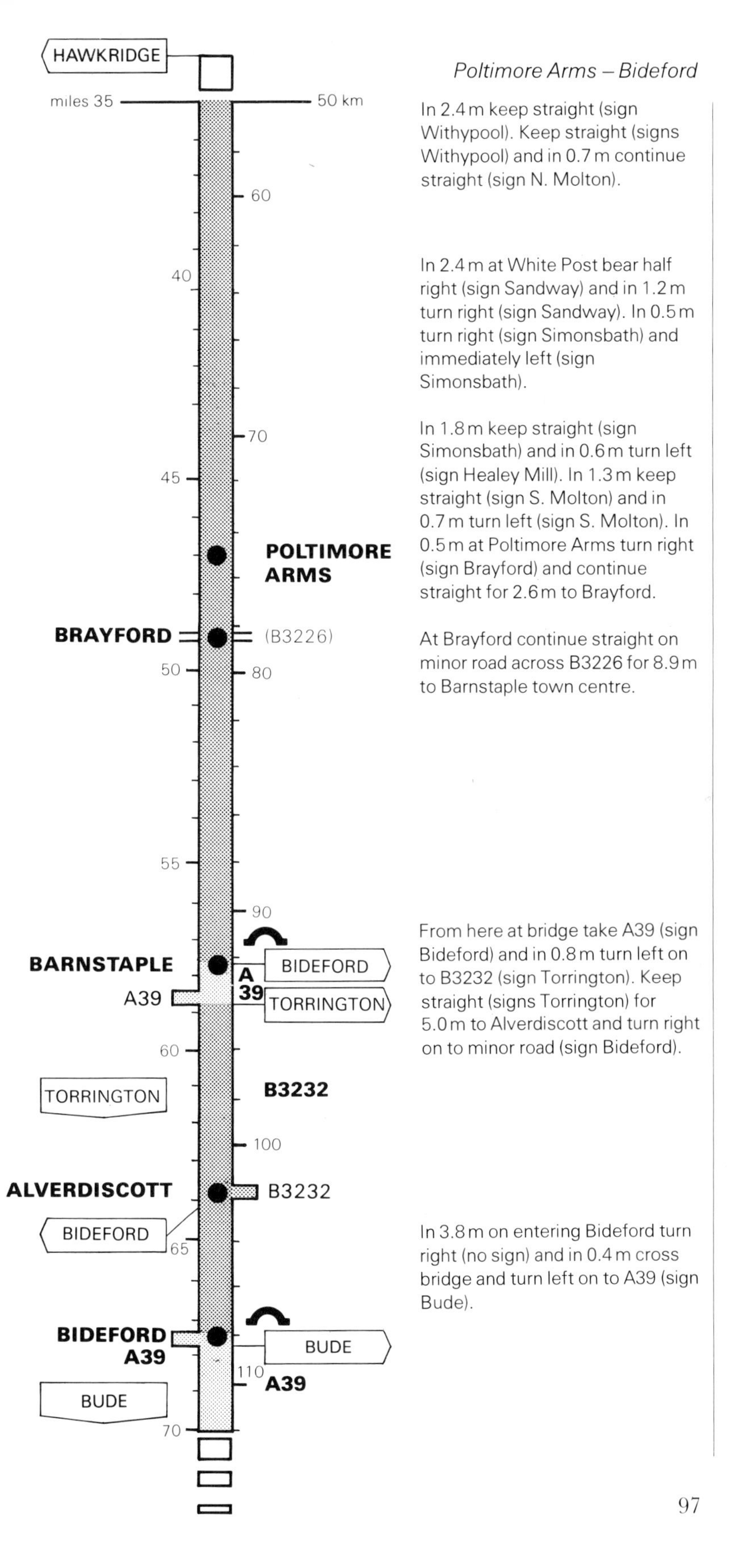

Poltimore Arms – Bideford

In 2.4 m keep straight (sign Withypool). Keep straight (signs Withypool) and in 0.7 m continue straight (sign N. Molton).

In 2.4 m at White Post bear half right (sign Sandway) and in 1.2 m turn right (sign Sandway). In 0.5 m turn right (sign Simonsbath) and immediately left (sign Simonsbath).

In 1.8 m keep straight (sign Simonsbath) and in 0.6 m turn left (sign Healey Mill). In 1.3 m keep straight (sign S. Molton) and in 0.7 m turn left (sign S. Molton). In 0.5 m at Poltimore Arms turn right (sign Brayford) and continue straight for 2.6 m to Brayford.

At Brayford continue straight on minor road across B3226 for 8.9 m to Barnstaple town centre.

From here at bridge take A39 (sign Bideford) and in 0.8 m turn left on to B3232 (sign Torrington). Keep straight (signs Torrington) for 5.0 m to Alverdiscott and turn right on to minor road (sign Bideford).

In 3.8 m on entering Bideford turn right (no sign) and in 0.4 m cross bridge and turn left on to A39 (sign Bude).

Hartland (Devonshire)

Before leaving the main road to approach this village a diversion of 1½ miles could be made to visit famous Clovelly, a 'picture postcard' village and cove which unhappily can get overrun with tourists in the high season. Hartland is a delightful inland village in a remote area of Devonshire where, round the square, are two inns, the Kings Arms and the Hart, that offer bed and breakfast. Near to Hartland at Stoke is the parish church with a 128-foot pinnacled tower offering a magnificent view. From Stoke the route proceeds southwards along the coast; but it is worth diverting by the toll road for a mile to Hartland Quay where there is an hotel (below) with a pleasant bar, the Green Ranger, which supplies draft cider from a local farm. From Hartland Quay footpaths lead across the cliffs through some of England's most exciting coastal scenery to both Hartland Point in the north and to Bude in the south. Although Bude only lies 12 miles away as the crow flies, one must remember that the Cornwall coastal path to it is much longer.

Hartland Quay Hotel, 17 rooms, T371 (D)

Elmscott (Devonshire)

YHA, T Hartland 367

Welcombe Mouth (Devonshire)

Set amidst attractive scenery there is a small beach backed by a handful of farmhouses. The guest house (below) is run by a family who recently took over the delightfully situated old hermitage and modernized it. The comfortable rooms and excellent food are highly recommended.

The Hermitage, Welcombe Mouth, 9 rooms, T Morwenstow 258 (D)

Morwenstow (Cornwall)

A footpath leads beyond the church to the cliffside hut where the eccentric cleric and poet R. S. Hawker (1803–75), famed in particular for his poem 'And shall Trelawney die', wrote much of his poetry. Hawker, vicar here for 41 years, was responsible for building the vicarage near the church. Hawker's financial generosity was matched by his concern for seamen in an area of many shipwrecks – he would preach in his oilskins in order to be among the first of the rescue teams.

Bude (Cornwall)

A seaside resort where the town stands well back from the sea with a good golf course but some rather higgledy-piggledy building. Good surf bathing takes place along this part of the coast.

Grenville Hotel, Belle Vue, 73 rooms, T2121 (D)
Burn Court Hotel, Burn Court, 35 rooms, T2872 (C)
T.O. Caravan, The Castle, T4240

Widemouth (Cornwall)

Little here other than a broad beach and one or two hotels – the hotel (below) being near the beach.

Trelawney Hotel, Marine Drive, 10 rooms, T328 (C)

The Route

It was found necessary to use a short stretch of the main A39 after Bideford. The lanes from Stoke southward are very narrow in places and unfortunately the minor road from Welcombe to Morwenstow is not normally motorable – adding several miles to the journey.

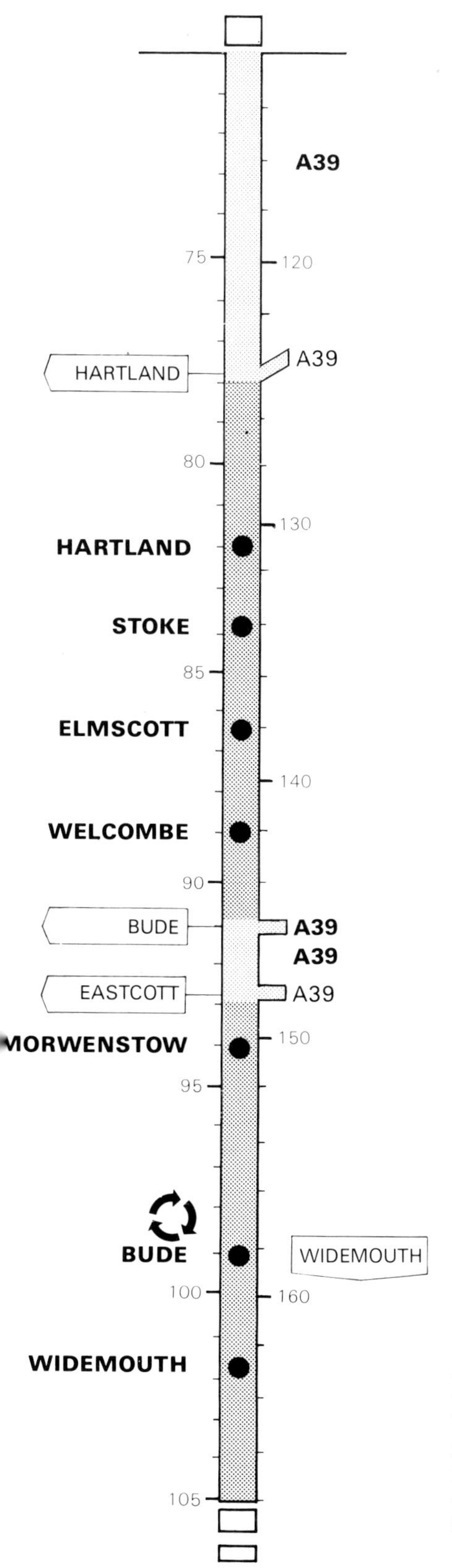

Remain on A39 (signs Bude) and in 10.6 m turn right (sign Hartland). Keep straight (signs Hartland and Stoke) for 3.6 m to Hartland village centre and continue straight (signs Stoke and Hartland Quay).

In 1.5 m at Stoke turn left (sign Elmscott) and in 0.9 m turn right (sign Elmscott). In 0.3 m turn right (sign Elmscott) and in further 0.3 m turn left (sign Elmscott).

In 0.4 m keep straight (sign Elmscott). In 0.5 m keep straight (sign Welcombe Mouth) and in 0.3 m turn right (sign Welcombe Mouth). In 0.6 m bear right (sign Welcombe Mouth) and continue straight for 1.6 m. Here keep straight (sign Welcombe Mouth) and in 0.6 m at Welcombe bear left (sign Bude).

In 0.6 m turn left (sign Bude) and in 1.5 m keep straight (sign Bude). In 1.3 m turn right on to A39 (sign Bude) and in 1.4 m turn right on to minor road (sign Eastcott). Continue straight (signs Morwenstow) for 3.1 m and turn left (sign Coombe Valley). In 3.7 m turn left (sign Kilkhampton) and in 0.4 m turn right (sign Bude). In 1.9 m turn right (sign Bude) and keep straight, following one-way circuit for 1.5 m to town centre.

In Bude bear left on A39 and very shortly (past Strand Hotel) turn right on to minor road (sign Widemouth). Keep straight for 2.7 m to Widemouth Bay. In 0.8 m keep straight (sign Millook) and in 4.0 m turn right (sign Crackington Haven).

Crackington Haven (Cornwall)

After leaving Bude and Widemouth the coast becomes more interesting and from here onwards there are exciting cliff walks along footpaths that have been well signed and preserved by the National Trust. The minor road that ascends from Crackington Haven is gated and runs near Cornwall's highest cliff (731 feet).

Coombe Barton Hotel, 11 rooms, T St Gennys 345 (D)

Boscastle (Cornwall)

Fishermen still put out from the strong-walled harbour of this classic beauty spot. The Palace Stables (National Trust) at the head of the harbour once housed cart-horses that worked the capstans in busier times. Nearby is a Museum of Witchcraft. The main part of the village lies in the wooded hills some way back from the harbour.

Valency House Hotel, 7 rooms, T288 (C)
YHA, Palace Stables, T287

The spectacular ruins of Tintagel Castle.

Tintagel (Cornwall)

According to legend the infant King Arthur was thrown by the waves on to the beach by Merlin's cave beneath Tintagel Castle. Within the village itself is the National Trust preserved Old Post Office, a small 14c manor house used as a post office in Victorian times; and King Arthur's Hall, where the legend of King Arthur and the Knights of the Round Table is illustrated.

Bossiney House Hotel, 20 rooms, T240 (D)
YHA, Dunderhole Point, T334

Camelford (Cornwall)

A mile to the north of the town, though not along the precise route, is Slaughter Bridge, said to be the scene of the famous battle where Arthur slew Mordred.

Lanteglos Farmhouse Hotel, 20 rooms, T3551 (C)
Higherhead Hotel, College Rd, 10 rooms, T3325 (D)

Blisland (Cornwall)

Village greens are a rarity in Cornwall, but here church, inn and sturdy stone cottages surround a spacious green graced by ash and sycamore trees. The church, partially Norman, has a painted rood screen with intricate carving that formed part of the restoration in the late 19c.

Bodmin (Cornwall)

This would be a suitable point to divert from the route to reach Land's End by the main road (see Introduction). The town possesses a fine indoor swimming pool and in the former barracks of the Duke of Cornwall's Light Infantry is a museum of that regiment's history. St Petroc's Church, the largest in the county, was built in the 15c.

The Route

The coast road is particularly narrow and gated past Crackington Haven and the road narrows again between Camelford and Blisland.

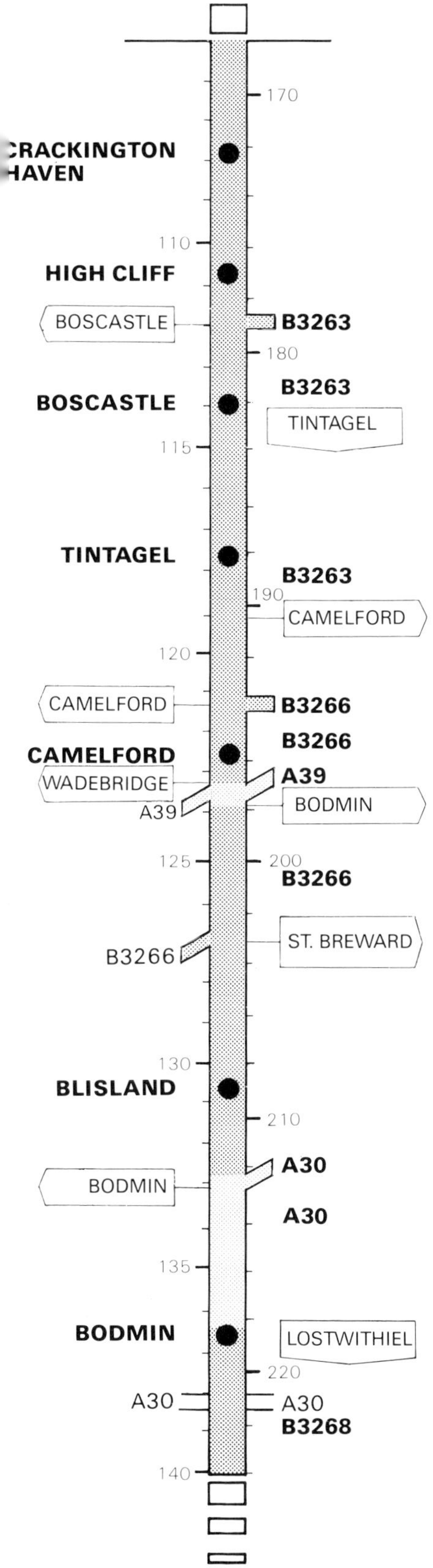

170
CRACKINGTON HAVEN
110
HIGH CLIFF
BOSCASTLE
B3263
180
B3263
BOSCASTLE
TINTAGEL
115
TINTAGEL
B3263
190
CAMELFORD
120
CAMELFORD
B3266
B3266
CAMELFORD
WADEBRIDGE
A39
A39
BODMIN
125
200
B3266
B3266
ST. BREWARD
130
BLISLAND
210
A30
BODMIN
A30
135
BODMIN
LOSTWITHIEL
220
A30
A30
B3268
140

In 0.5 m turn right (sign Crackington Haven) and keep straight for 1.1 m to Crackington Haven. Here bear right (sign High Cliff). Keep straight for 2.4 m to High Cliff car park and in further 0.7 m turn right on to B3263 (sign Boscastle). Continue straight on B3263 (signs Boscastle) for 2.8 m to Boscastle car park and from here continue on B3263 (signs Tintagel) for 3.8 m to Tintagel car park.

Continue for 0.1 m and turn left on B3263 (sign Camelford). In 4.0 m turn left and shortly right on to B3266 (sign Camelford).

In 1.3 m at entry to Camelford turn left (sign Camelford) and in 0.3 m turn right on to A39 (sign Wadebridge). In 0.7 m turn left on to B3266 (sign Bodmin). In 3.4 m turn left on to minor road (signs St Breward and Wenfordbridge). In 0.9 m keep straight (no sign) and in 0.7 m at T junction turn left and cross river (no sign). Immediately turn right (sign Blisland).

In 0.5 m keep straight (sign Blisland) and in 0.3 m turn left (sign Blisland). In 0.2 m turn sharp left (sign Blisland) and keep straight for 0.8 m to Blisland. Here continue straight (sign Bodmin) and in 1.1 m turn left (sign Bodmin). In 0.8 m turn right on to A30 (sign Bodmin).

In 2.3 m turn left (sign Bodmin) and in 1.4 m turn right (sign Bodmin) for 0.4 m to Bodmin town centre. Here take B3268 (sign Lostwithiel) for 5.5 m to Lostwithiel.

Lostwithiel (Cornwall)

Three miles before reaching Lostwithiel, signed to left, is Llanhydrock House (National Trust), approached by an avenue of beeches and sycamores with a picturesque two-storey gatehouse. This 17c granite manor house, rebuilt after a fire in 1881, contains period furniture as well as family portraits that include works by Kneller and Romney. Lostwithiel lies astride a busy main road, but a pleasant part of this small town is to be found near the R. Fowey, and a mile to the north is Restormel Castle, dating from the 11c and considered to be the best preserved castle of that period in the county.

Royal Talbot Hotel, 9 rooms, T872498 (D)

Polruan (Cornwall)

The car park lies at the top of the steep narrow main street at the foot of which, on the quay, is the pleasant small guest house (below) and the Lugger Inn where Cornish folk singers entertain. From the quay the foot passenger ferry connects with Fowey, a town with a maze of crooked cobbled streets described by the sea rat in Kenneth Grahame's *Wind in the Willows* as 'the little grey sea town that clings along one side of the harbour'. Those wishing to take their cars to Fowey should note that there is a car ferry at Bodinnick (signed before reaching Polruan).

Quayside Guest House, 6 rooms, T377 (D)

Polperro (Cornwall)

This delightful village, once a smuggler's paradise, has become something of a haven for tourists but, fortunately, cars have to be parked at the head of the village, so wandering around the quaint narrow streets that lead to the

The harbour, Polperro.

harbour is still a pleasure. An Elizabethan house, once the home of the village doctor, contains an interesting smugglers' museum, and near the quay is a house studded with a variety of shells collected by a local fisherman.

Claremont Hotel, 11 rooms, T241 (D)

Looe (Cornwall)

East and West Looe, separated by the river, make up what is both an important fishing port and a seaside resort. East Looe is the home of a fine Cornish museum.

Hannafore Point Hotel, Marine Drive, 40 rooms, T3273 (B)
Portbyhan Hotel, The Quay, 44 rooms, T2071 (D)
T.O. Guildhall, Fore St, E. Looe, T2672

Menheniot (Cornwall)

This remote village has grown recently and has an attractive inn, the White Hart, where a limited amount of accommodation is available. Many of the Cornish Trelawney family are buried in the church.

Pillaton (Cornwall)

This isolated village is approached after crossing the clapper bridge across a beautiful stretch of the R. Lynher.

Weary Friar Hotel, 13 rooms, T St Dominick 238 (B)

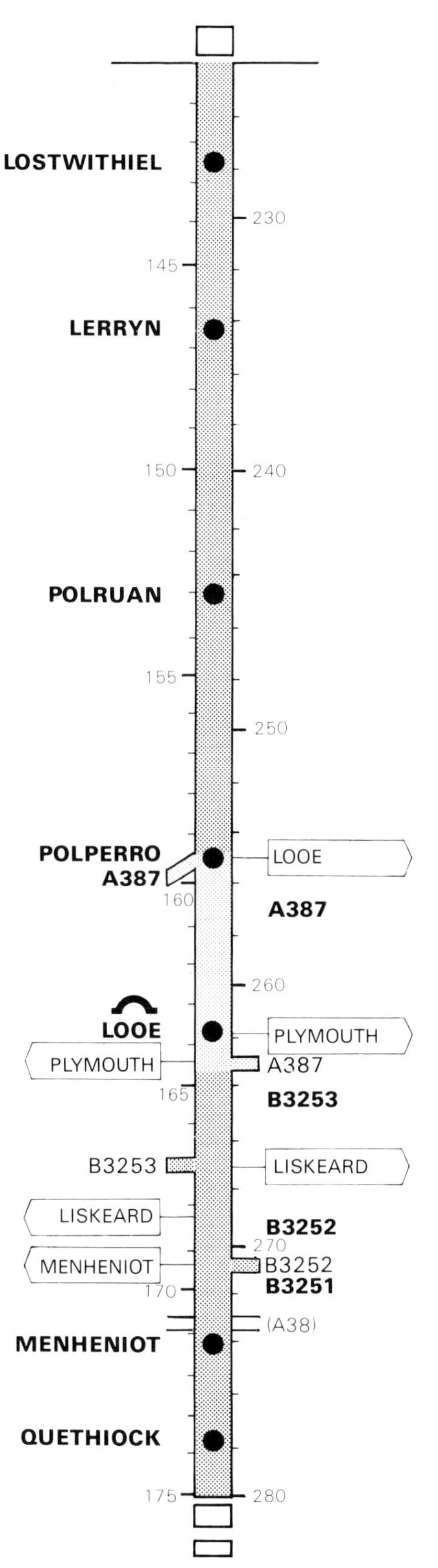

On entering Lostwithiel turn left on to A390 (sign Liskeard) and in 0.5 m turn right on to minor road (sign Lerryn). In 0.1 m continue straight (sign Lerryn) for 2.9 m to Lerryn. Here cross river and shortly keep straight (sign Boddinick). In 0.6 m bear left (sign Boddinick) and in 0.2 m keep straight (sign Polruan). In 0.6 m keep straight (one way road) and in 0.4 m at T junction turn right (sign Polruan).

In 0.5 m turn right (sign Polruan) and in 0.8 m turn left (sign Polruan). In 0.4 m turn left (sign Polruan) and in 0.9 m turn right (sign Polruan) for 2.2 m to Polruan car park. From here return by entry road for 0.5 m and keep straight (sign Polperro). Continue straight (signs Polperro and Looe) and in 3.6 m turn right (sign Polperro). In 0.1 m turn left (sign Polperro) and in further 0.8 m turn left (sign Polperro) for 1.2 m to Polperro car park.

Here turn left on to A387 (sign Looe) for 4.2 m to Looe. Cross river at Looe and turn left on A387 (sign Plymouth). In 0.4 m bear right on to B3253 (sign Plymouth). Continue on B3253 (sign Plymouth) for 2.2 m and turn left on to minor road (sign Liskeard). In 1.0 m keep straight (sign Liskeard) and in 0.2 m bear right on to B3252 (sign Liskeard). In 0.8 m turn right on to B3251 (sign Menheniot) and in 1.1 m keep straight across A38 on to minor road (sign Menheniot for 1.4 m to Menheniot.

Here at Inn turn immediately right (no sign). In 0.4 m bear left (no sign) and in 0.3 m turn right (no sign). In 0.1 m bear left (sign Quethiock) and in 1.3 m turn right (sign Quethiock) for 0.4 m to Quethiock. Here continue straight and in 0.3 m keep straight (sign Blunts). In 0.9 m turn right (sign Saltash) and in 0.8 m turn left (sign Callington).

The 17c tower of Cotehele House.

Cotehele House (Cornwall)

In a wooded setting above the steep banked R. Tamar stands this magnificent early Tudor manor house which from 1353 until its transference to the National Trust in 1944 was the home of a famous Cornish family, the Edgecumbes. The house has one of the most impressive Great Halls to be found in the country, as well as many tapestry-lined rooms with a rich collection of Jacobean and Stuart furniture. The chapel in the garden was built by Richard Edgecumbe to mark the spot where he hid from the soldiers of Richard III before defeating them for Henry VII at Bosworth Field.

Tavistock (Devonshire)

A market town on the R. Tavy that grew, originally, around a 10c Benedictine Abbey of which only a few fragments are now visible. The town is the scene of a famous county event, the Goose Fair, that takes place annually in the second week of October.

Bedford Hotel, Plymouth Rd, 35 rooms, T 3221 (B)
YHA, Abbotsfield Hall, T2529

Sampford Spiney (Devonshire)

Here, on the fringe of the Dartmoor National Park, the little 13c church lies in splendid isolation amongst scattered farmhouses where sheep and Dartmoor ponies wander freely.

Meavy (Devonshire)

At the gates of St Peter's Church is propped an ancient oak tree, believed to date from the 12c and possibly a 'Gospel Oak' planted when the church was built. There is an interesting epitaph on a grave in the churchyard to the memory of the village blacksmith who died in 1826, aged 80:

My sledge and hammer both declined
My bellows too have lost their wind
My fire's extinct, my forge decayed
And in the dust my vice is laid.
My coal is spent, my iron's gone,
My nails are drove – my work is done.

The Route

The minor roads in this part of Cornwall are particularly narrow, and this applies throughout a large part of this section of the route.

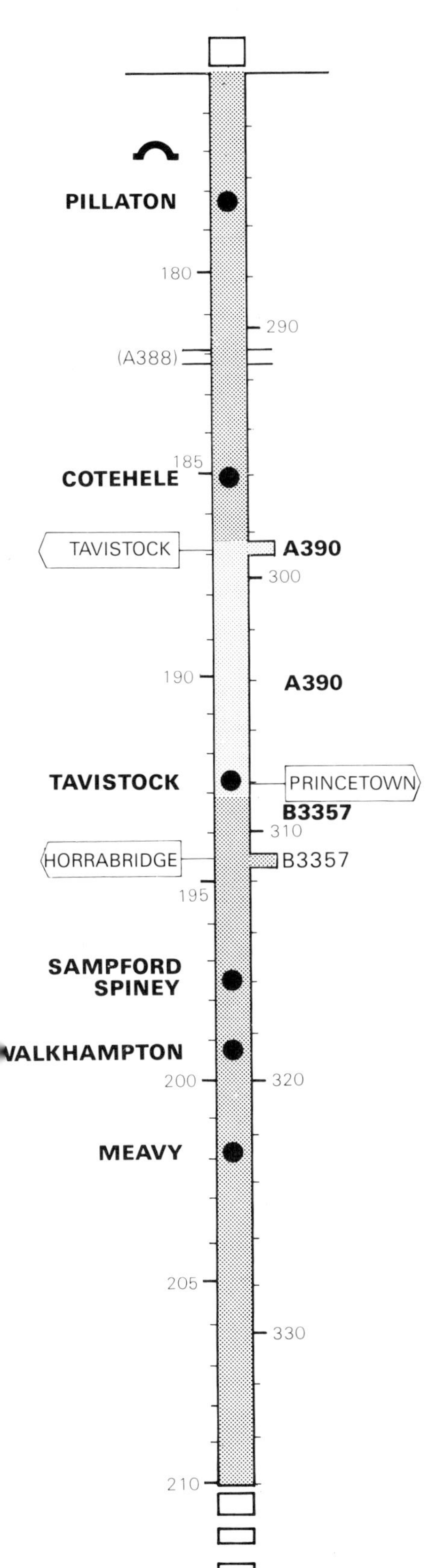

In 1.6 m after crossing bridge turn right (sign Pillaton) for 1.2 m to Pillaton.

Here at Inn turn left (sign Callington). In 0.5 m turn left (no sign) and in 1.3 m at multi junction turn right (sign St Dominick). In 0.8 m bear slightly (not fully) left at multi junction (no sign). In 0.5 m keep straight across A388 (signs St Dominick and Cotehele) and in 1.3 m at St Dominick turn right (sign Cotehele). In 0.2 m bear left (sign Cotehele) and in 0.3 m bear right (no sign). In 0.1 m turn left (sign Cotehele) and in 0.4 m turn left and immediately right (sign Cotehele).

In 0.3 m turn right (sign Cotehele) and keep straight for 0.7 m to Cotehele car park. Here return by entry route and in 0.7 m turn right (sign Gunnislake). Keep straight (signs Gunnislake) and in1.0 m turn right (sign Gunnislake). In 0.6 m turn right on to A390 (sign Tavistock) for 5.8 m to Tavistock town centre.

In Tavistock town centre continue straight and shortly turn right and immediately left on to B3357 (sign Princetown). In 1.9 m turn right on to minor road (sign Horrabridge). Keep straight for 0.8 m to T junction and turn left (sign Sampford Spiney). Keep straight (signs Sampford Spiney) for 1.7 m to Sampford Spiney church and from here continue straight. In 0.6 m bear right (sign Horrabridge) and in further 0.6 m turn left (sign Walkhampton). Keep straight for 0.9 m to Walkhampton.

Here bear left (sign Dousland) and in 0.5 m keep straight across B3212 (sign Burrator). Keep straight for 1.2 m and bear right (sign Yelverton) for 0.2 m to Meavy. In 0.1 m past Meavy post office turn left (no sign) and in 0.5 m turn left (sign Cornwood). Keep straight (signs Cornwood and Wotter) and in 3.8 m turn left (sign Cornwood) for 4.3 m to Cornwood.

Ivybridge (Devonshire)

A dormitory town for Plymouth, pleasantly situated on the R. Erme.

Ermington (Devonshire)

The church is famous for its crooked spire, and the nearby inn of this delightful village, appropriately named the Crooked Spire Inn, is a pleasant place with good bar snacks that include grills and omelettes. The hotel lies on the route beyond the village.

Ermewood House Hotel, 12 rooms, T Modbury 321 (C)

Modbury (Devonshire)

Once an important wool centre, this is now mainly a residential town with a good shopping area of 18c houses and a 15c church.

Modbury Inn, Brownston St, 8 rooms, T275 (D)

Dittisham (Devonshire)

A pretty village of thatched cottages surrounded by plum orchards and standing above a wide section of the R. Dart where, on a rock known as Anchor Rock, it is said that Sir Walter Raleigh (1552–1618) used to sit and ponder while smoking tobacco. The little slate church has a fine red sandstone font.

Tuckenhay (Devonshire)

The Maltsters Arms has a small cider factory beneath it and overlooks a broad and placid section of Bow creek off the R. Dart. A little further on is another nice inn, the Waterman's Arms.

Totnes (Devonshire)

The historian William Camden (1551–1623) described this Anglo-Saxon town as 'hanging from east to west on the side of a hill' – and indeed the main street is a steep one as it climbs past timbered shops through a clock-mounted gateway. Above the town are the well preserved ruins of Totnes Castle with extensive views and other features of Totnes include the 15c red sandstone church with a magnificent stone rood-screen and the 16c Guildhall.

The clock and gateway in Totnes.

Royal Seven Stars Hotel, 18 rooms, T862125 (B)
Seymour Hotel, 30 rooms, T864686 (B)
T.O. The Plains, T863168

Dartington (Devonshire)

Dartington Hall, a 14c manor house built by John Holland, half brother of Richard II, was acquired by the American philanthropists Dr and Mrs Elmshirst, who set up a Trust in 1925 to provide adult and youth education as well as experimental business and agricultural activity in surrounding farms and forests. In the terraced gardens of the Hall is an open-air theatre.

The Route

At first through the western edge of the Dartmoor National Park, only marred by mine works around Cornwood. From Ivybridge the route veers eastward before following the course of the R. Dart by a very narrow road into Totnes.

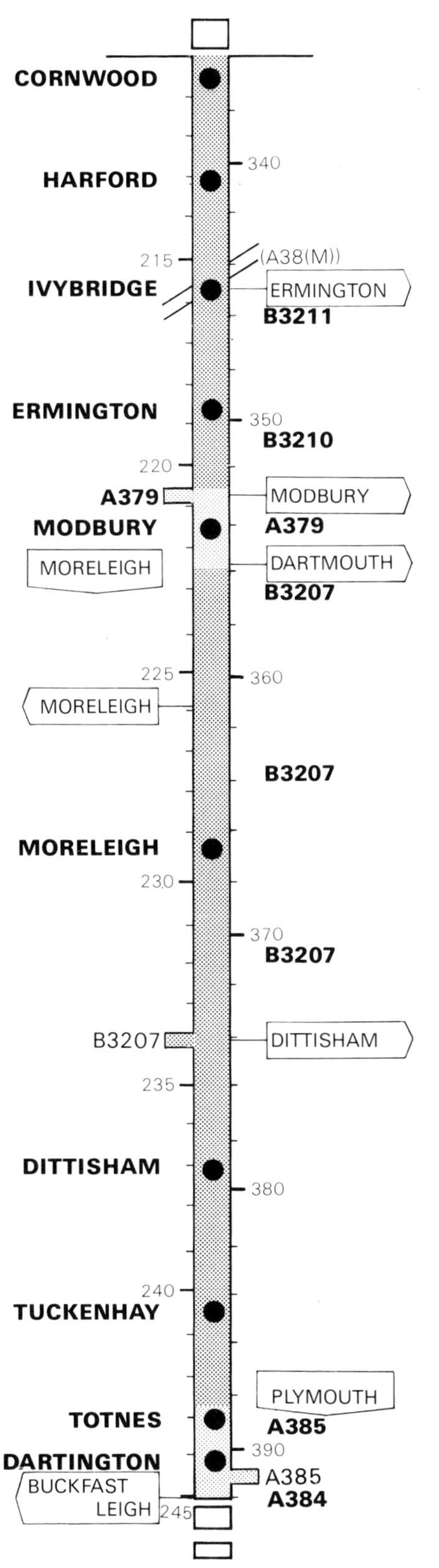

At Cornwood turn left (sign Torr) and in 0.3 m keep right (no sign). In 0.4 m continue straight (sign Torr) and in 0.2 m keep straight (sign Harford) for 1.7 m to Harford. Here turn right (sign Ivybridge) for 2.4 m to Ivybridge. At Ivybridge turn right (sign Plympton) and in 0.6 m cross motorway and turn left on to B3211 (sign Ermington). Keep straight for 2.4 m to Ermington village square and here continue straight. In 0.1 m turn right (sign Modbury) and in 0.6 m turn left (sign Modbury). In 0.1 m turn left on to A379 (sign Modbury) for 1.8 m to Modbury.

Here turn left on to B3207 (sign Dartmouth). Keep straight (signs Moreleigh) and in 3.6 m turn right on B3207 (sign Moreleigh). Keep straight (signs Moreleigh and Totnes) for 4.4 m to Moreleigh. Here continue straight (sign Kingsbridge) and in 0.5 m turn left and almost immediately left again (signs Dartmouth). In 0.5 m bear right (sign Dartmouth) and in 3.8 m bear left on to minor road (sign Dittisham). In 2.7 m at Dittisham keep straight (sign Cornworthy).

In 2.1 m continue straight (sign Totnes). In further 0.3 m keep straight (sign Totnes). In 0.3 m bear left (sign Totnes) and in 0.5 m bear right (sign Totnes). In 0.8 m at Tuckenhay keep straight for 0.4 m and here continue straight (sign Totnes). In 0.6 m keep straight (sign Totnes light traffic) and keep straight down hill into Totnes town centre.

In Totnes do not cross river but at Royal Seven Stars hotel take A385 (sign Plymouth). In 1.5 m at Dartington bear right on to A384 (sign Buckfastleigh).

Buckfast Abbey (Devonshire)

The site of what was once a Saxon Abbey was bought by French monks of the Benedictine order who set to work to build the existing Abbey church in 1906 and completed it in 1938. In 1960 Buckfast Abbey became affiliated to the English Benedictine Congregation. The Abbey occupies a superb position on the banks of the R. Dart where there is a preparatory school staffed by the monks, a nearby co-operative woollen mill, and a museum of shells. A mile or so further along the route, set in the midst of National Trust woodland and signed to the right, is Hembury Castle, an iron-age hill fort.

Buckland in the Moor
(Devonshire)

The route does not run directly through this pretty village of thatched cottages – but it does pass the church, from where there are extensive views across the moors. The church clock is of particular originality as the hours on the face are not depicted numerically but instead show twelve letters, MY DEAR MOTHER, a memorial presented by a Buckland family.

Widecombe in the Moor
(Devonshire)

Famed for the September fair and the ballad which describes the attendance of 'Uncle Tom Cobbleigh and All'. A statue on the green by the church is engraved with the figures of Uncle Tom and his friends being led in on their mare and above the entrance to the Old Inn, opposite the church, is a painted sign of the party in a more bibulous mood. The church has a prominent 120-foot pinnacled tower and the 15c

Widecombe in the Moor.

granite Church House, used as a village hall, is preserved by the National Trust.

Moretonhampstead
(Devonshire)

Has a 15c granite church and a row of almshouses that date from 1637. The Manor House Hotel (below) is passed before the town and has its own golf course.

Manor House Hotel, 68 rooms, T355 (A)
White House Inn, 9 rooms, T242 (C)

Exeter Cathedral.

The Route

Most of this section passes through the Dartmoor National Park, and contains a stretch of particular beauty between Buckfast Abbey and Buckland.

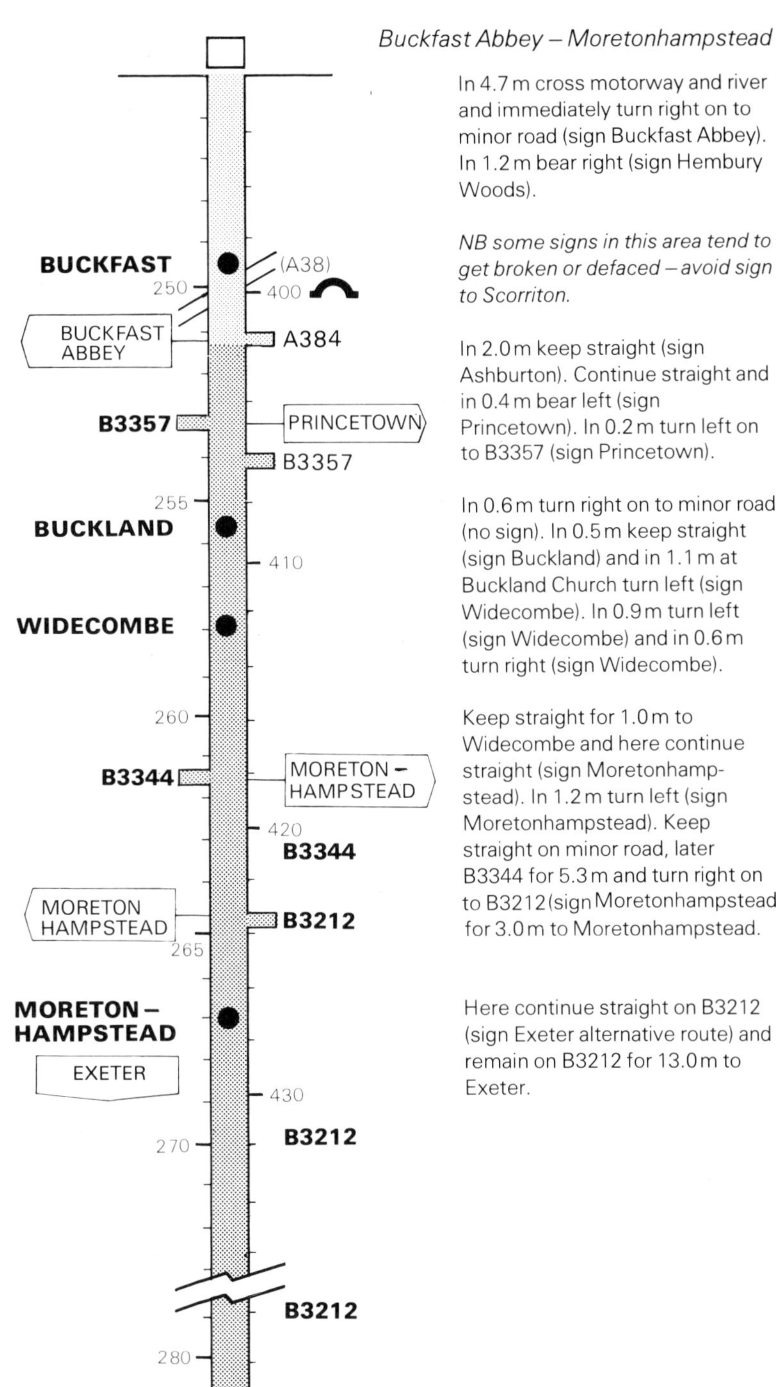

In 4.7 m cross motorway and river and immediately turn right on to minor road (sign Buckfast Abbey). In 1.2 m bear right (sign Hembury Woods).

NB some signs in this area tend to get broken or defaced – avoid sign to Scorriton.

In 2.0 m keep straight (sign Ashburton). Continue straight and in 0.4 m bear left (sign Princetown). In 0.2 m turn left on to B3357 (sign Princetown).

In 0.6 m turn right on to minor road (no sign). In 0.5 m keep straight (sign Buckland) and in 1.1 m at Buckland Church turn left (sign Widecombe). In 0.9 m turn left (sign Widecombe) and in 0.6 m turn right (sign Widecombe).

Keep straight for 1.0 m to Widecombe and here continue straight (sign Moretonhampstead). In 1.2 m turn left (sign Moretonhampstead). Keep straight on minor road, later B3344 for 5.3 m and turn right on to B3212 (sign Moretonhampstead) for 3.0 m to Moretonhampstead.

Here continue straight on B3212 (sign Exeter alternative route) and remain on B3212 for 13.0 m to Exeter.

7 *Wiltshire, Somerset, Dorset*

ALTHOUGH THE ROUTE is confined almost entirely to the counties of Wiltshire, Somerset and Dorset, it is necessary to remember that Bath, originally part of Somerset, now lies in the county of Avon. And for a few miles between Cranborne and Salisbury the road touches the fringe of Hampshire.

After leaving Salisbury, where the lofty spire rising from the Cathedral in the water meadows is a memorable sight, the road runs northward by way of the Avon valley past Old Sarum, location of the original Norman cathedral and castle, in the direction of Stonehenge and Salisbury Plain. Much of Salisbury Plain, regrettably, is used for

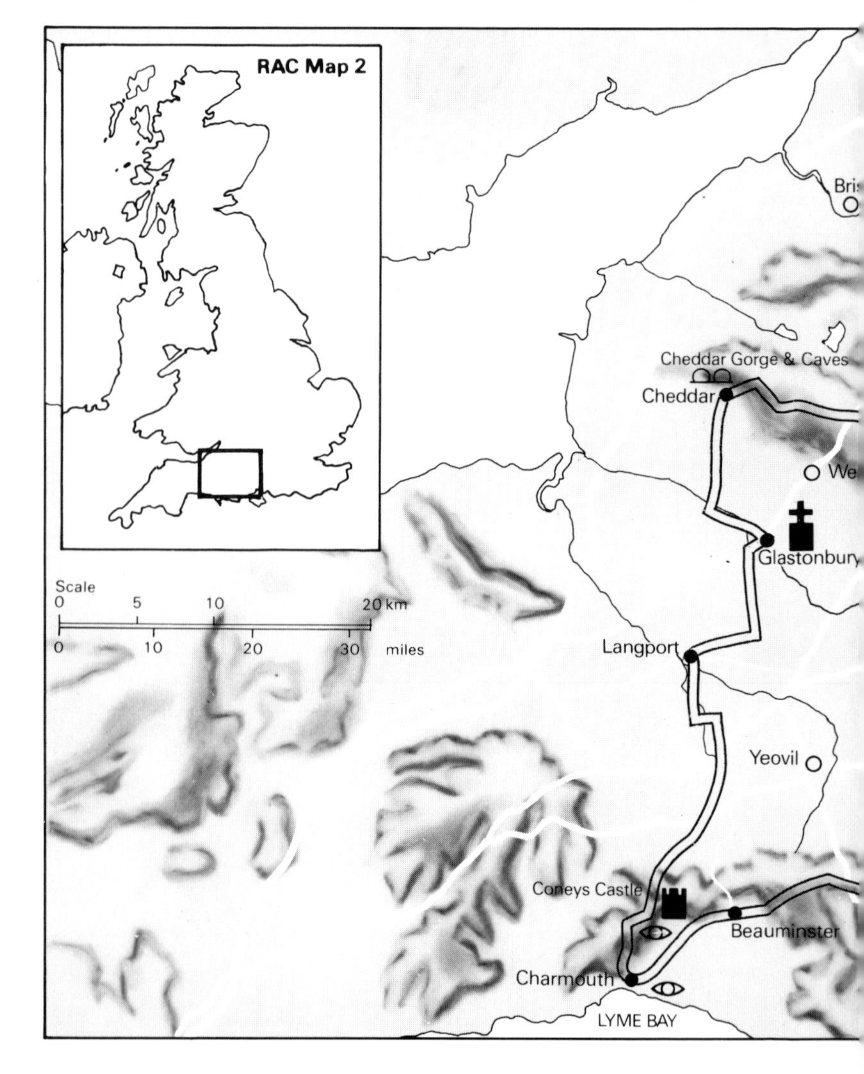

military purposes; yet villages like Shrewton, Tilshead and Lavington remain peaceful and unspoilt.

The road now runs through the heart of the North Wessex Downs and the Marlborough Downs, passing along the way two of Wiltshire's celebrated White Horses cut out of the turf near Alton Barnes and Broad Hinton. The Alton Barnes horse is the larger and more easily visible of the two horses which were both designed in the last century – much younger creations than the Cerne Giant, passed later on the route, which dates from Roman times. After passing through historic Malmesbury the road reaches the spa town of Bath, from here veering southward through England's miniature Grand Canyon to Cheddar in Somerset. The southward route from Cheddar must inevitably cross somewhat flat, marshy, featureless land close to an area known as King's Sedge Moor, where the Monmouth rebellion was crushed at the end of the 17th century. The traveller with time to spare might do well to divert from this route at Wedmore to visit the beautiful city of Wells, rejoining the route at Glastonbury.

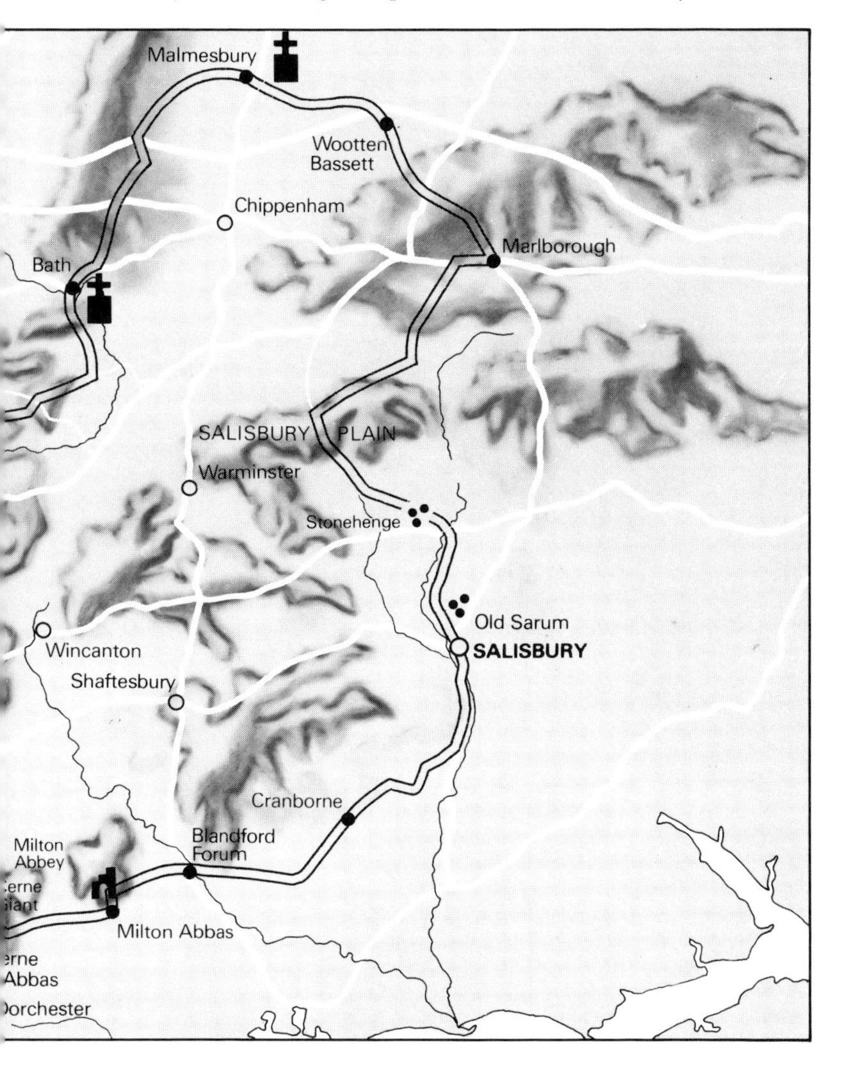

Above: *Pulteney Bridge, Bath.*
Right: *Marlborough's Tudor bookshop.*

From Glastonbury the route runs southward until it reaches the coast at Charmouth (near to other pleasant seaside resorts such as Bridport, Lyme Regis and Sidmouth) before turning north-eastward through the unspoilt Dorsetshire countryside. The fact that Dorset remains a quiet and little visited county is probably due to the completion of the motorway – creating a tendency on the part of the tourist to speed in the direction of Devon and Cornwall and allowing Dorset to remain, much as it was in the days of its native novelist Thomas Hardy (1840–1928), 'far from the madding crowd'. The route crosses Dorset almost in its entirety from Charmouth in the west to Cranborne in the east, passing many enchanting villages in an area where traffic of any significance is only likely to be encountered at Blandford Forum. After leaving Cranborne the route shortly passes through the edge of Hampshire before returning to Salisbury.

In common with Devon and Cornwall the counties passed on this route are well served with a variety of bed and breakfast accommodation in farmhouses and inns that are likely to be less expensive than the hotels recommended in the guide.

Although the minor roads along this route are not, in most cases, as narrow as the typical Devonshire or Cornish lane, there are sections which would certainly *not* prove suitable for very wide vehicles.

THE WHITE HORSE BOOKSHOP
136

A peaceful scene at Salisbury.

Salisbury (Wiltshire)

The Cathedral, surmounted by its 404-foot tower, occupies a Close considered to be among the most beautiful in England. Apart from the magnificence of the Cathedral there is much to see in this city, where medieval bridges span the river and the streets are flanked by gabled houses and inns of all periods. Mompesson House (National Trust) in the Cathedral Close has a finely carved staircase that dates from around 1700.

Red Lion Hotel, Milford St, 60 rooms, T22788 (B)
County Hotel, Bridge St, 36 rooms, T20229 (B)
YHA, Milford Hill, T27572
T.O. Fisherton St, City Hall, T27676

Old Sarum (Wiltshire)

Remnants of the foundations of the old castle and cathedral can be seen on the lonely hilltop here – signed to the right at a point where the route crosses the river.

The Woodfords (Wiltshire)

Lower, Middle and Upper Woodford are attractive small villages that lie along the R. Avon. Heale House, signed between Middle and Upper Woodford, has pleasant gardens which are occasionally open to the public.

Stonehenge (Wiltshire)

The road passes directly by this world-famous monument where circles of massive upright stones were probably erected as early as 2000BC.

Shrewton (Wiltshire)

The village nestles on the R. Till in the heart of Salisbury Plain, with a sinister little beehive-shaped building, 300 years old, known as the Blind House. It was used to confine those awaiting execution at the nearby gibbet.

Catherine Wheel Inn, High St, 4 rooms, T229 (D)

Market Lavington (Wiltshire)

A quiet and not unattractive old town where a variety of inns offer bed and breakfast. The recommended hotel (below) is a large 18c house that occupies beautiful grounds on the right of the road before it reaches Market Lavington.

Clyffe Hall Hotel, 10 rooms, T3310 (C)

Urchfont (Wiltshire)

The best part of the village can be seen by turning off the route to the left, where there is a pretty duck-pond and attractive thatched and Georgian houses. Pitt the Elder (1708–78) once lived at the manor house here.

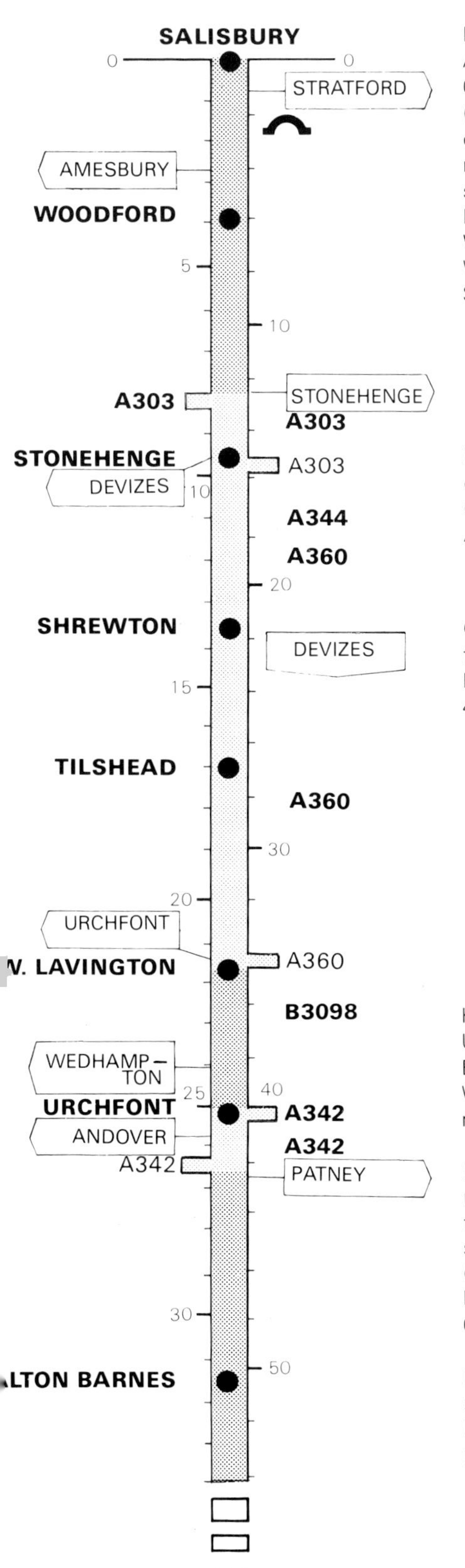

From Salisbury ring road take A345 (sign Amesbury) and in 0.1 m bear left on to minor road (sign Stratford). In 1.5 m bear left over river (no sign). In 0.9 m bear right (sign Amesbury). Keep straight (signs Amesbury) through Lower, Middle and Upper Woodford and in 6.0 m at W. Amesbury turn left (sign Stonehenge).

In 1.0 m at Stonehenge bear right on to A344 (sign Devizes). Continue straight on A344, later A360, for 4.0 m to Shrewton.

Continue on A360 (sign Devizes) for 3.5 m to Tilshead and from here remain on A360 for further 4.6 m to W. Lavington.

Here turn right on to B3098 (sign Urchfont) for 3.5 m to Urchfont. Bear right on B3098 (sign Wedhampton) and in 1.2 m turn right on to A342 (sign Andover).

In 1.0 m at Chirton turn left on to minor road (sign Patney). In 0.1 m turn right (sign Marden). Keep straight for 2.1 m and turn right (sign Woodborough). In 0.5 m turn left (sign Woodborough) and in 0.3 m keep straight (sign Alton).

In 1.6 m at Alton Barnes keep straight (sign Lockeridge and Marlborough) for 4.6 m to Lockeridge.

Marlborough (Wiltshire)

Marlborough College, the famous public school founded in 1843, was built on the site of the old castle where, according to legend, Merlin is buried. The town has a fine broad main street which allows central parking.

Ailesbury Arms Hotel, High St, 33 rooms, T53451 (A)
Castle and Ball Hotel, High St, 30 rooms, T52002 (A)
T.O. St Peter's Church, High St, T53989

Broad Hinton (Wiltshire)

Before reaching the village another of Wiltshire's white horses is carved near the ridgeway path that runs across Marlborough Downs. The hotel (below) is under new ownership and gets a particular recommendation for friendly service, comfort and good food at reasonable prices.

Crown Inn, 8 rooms, T302 (C)

Wootton Bassett (Wiltshire)

A rather busy small town consisting, in the main, of one long street where beneath the half-timbered town hall, originally built in 1700, there are relics on display such as the old stocks and ducking stool.

Malmesbury (Wiltshire)

This historic hillside town with its famous Abbey has a number of old inns, among them the Bell, with a 13c window and believed to have once formed part of the old castle, and the White Lion, originally part of the Abbey buildings. The Norman Abbey dominates the town and here is the tomb of King Athelstan, grandson of Alfred the Great, who was crowned king in 925. Volumes of the Bible written by monks in the 15c are stored in the Abbey and can be seen on request. The nearby market cross was erected to 'allow poore folkes to stande dry when rayne cummeth'.

Carvings of the Apostles in the porch of Malmesbury Abbey.

Old Bell Hotel, Abbey Row, 19 rooms, T2344 (B)
Kings Arms, 29 High St, 6 rooms, T3383 (D)

Sherston (Wiltshire)

A large village with a pleasant broad High Street where parking is easy as there seems to be very little activity in this 'sleepy' place. A legendary hero, John Rattlebone, fought a battle here under Edmund Ironside against the Danes, and the Rattlebone chest in the church once contained his armour. There is a Rattlebone Inn near the church, and the attractive old inn, the Angel, serves bar snacks.

The Route

The road runs peacefully along the banks of the R. Avon, later crossing Salisbury Plain and dropping into the villages of Shrewton and Tilshead. The white horse on the hillside near Alton Barnes can be seen for many miles. It was carved on the instruction of a local farmer three years before the battle of Waterloo.

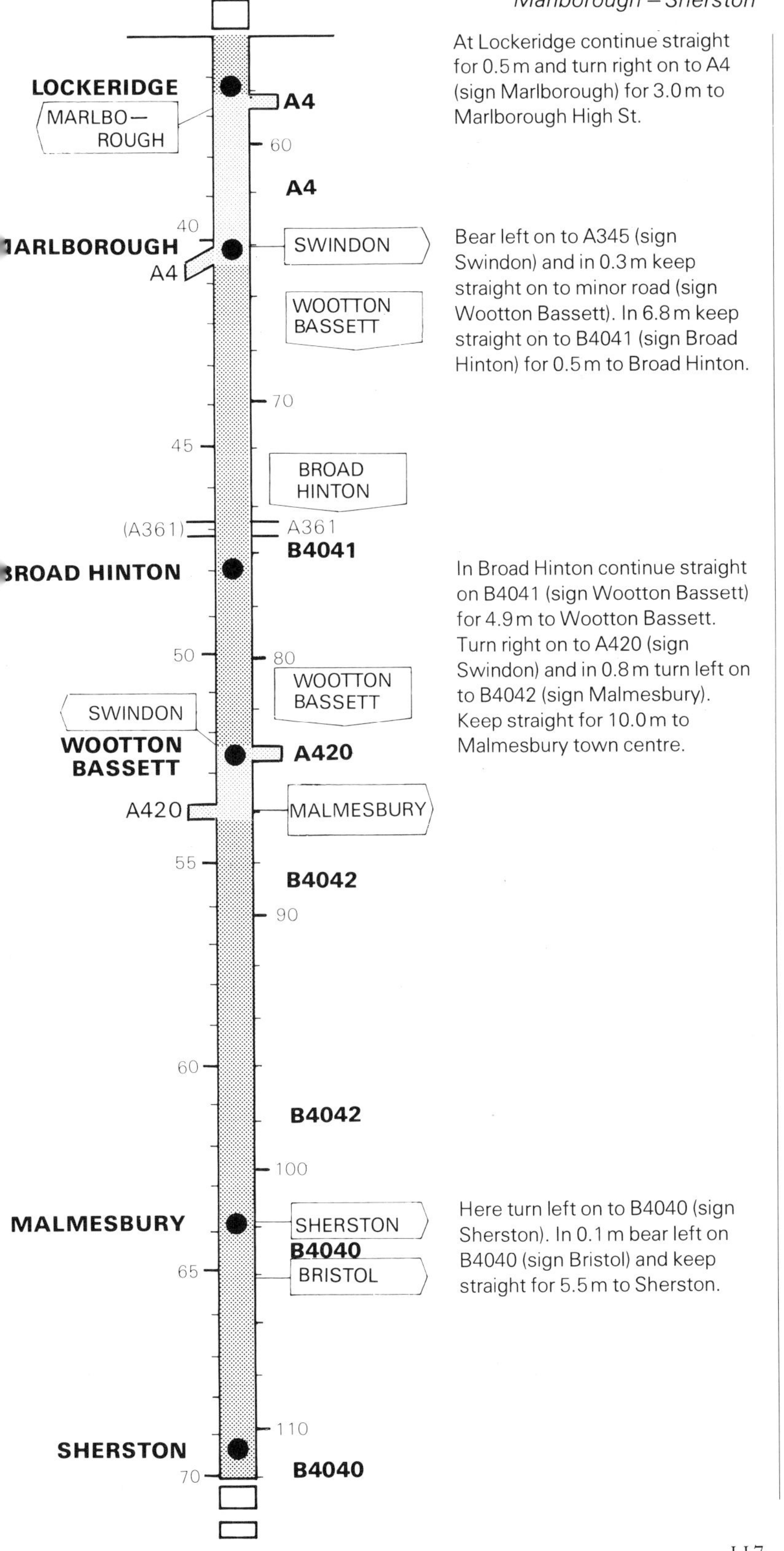

At Lockeridge continue straight for 0.5 m and turn right on to A4 (sign Marlborough) for 3.0 m to Marlborough High St.

Bear left on to A345 (sign Swindon) and in 0.3 m keep straight on to minor road (sign Wootton Bassett). In 6.8 m keep straight on to B4041 (sign Broad Hinton) for 0.5 m to Broad Hinton.

In Broad Hinton continue straight on B4041 (sign Wootton Bassett) for 4.9 m to Wootton Bassett. Turn right on to A420 (sign Swindon) and in 0.8 m turn left on to B4042 (sign Malmesbury). Keep straight for 10.0 m to Malmesbury town centre.

Here turn left on to B4040 (sign Sherston). In 0.1 m bear left on B4040 (sign Bristol) and keep straight for 5.5 m to Sherston.

The Abbey, Bath.

One of Bath's fine Georgian streets.

Luckington (Wiltshire)

Luckington Court, a Queen Anne house, is occasionally open to the public.

Bath (Avon)

The mineral waters of this celebrated spa town are still used in the treatment of rheumatic disease. The many places of interest include the Roman Baths (1st c. AD), where hot springs rise at a temperature of 51 °C and yield a daily flow of half a million gallons of mineral water; the Pump Room, famous 18c assembly room; the Museum of Costume, established in the Assembly Rooms in 1963 with an internationally famous collection that includes shirts and doublets worn when Shakespeare was alive; Royal Crescent and Lansdown Crescent with fine Georgian houses; and Pulteney Bridge, designed by Robert Adam in 1771 as a carriageway over the Avon, with shops on either side.

Fernley Hotel, North Parade, 46 rooms, T61603 (B)
Redcar Hotel, Henrietta St, 35 rooms, T65432 (A)
YHA, Bathwick Hall, T65674
T.O. Abbey Churchyard, T62831

Norton St Philip (Somerset)

Has a famous medieval inn, the George, half timbered with oriels and bay windows, where the diarist Samuel Pepys (1633–1703) and his wife dined in 1688 for a cost of ten shillings and where the Duke of Monmouth stayed twenty years later. Across the fields from the inn is the 15c church, built at the same time as the inn and also visited by Pepys, for there is a plaque here to 'twin ladies' on which the diarist reported, strangely, that they had 'only one stomach between them'.

Kilmersdon (Somerset)

A village of sturdy stone buildings that lies beneath wooded hills where the church is graced by a 100-foot tower with quaint gargoyles and where, near to the school, the old 'lock-up' has been retained.

The Route

Relatively traffic-free roads except in the immediate vicinity of Bath.

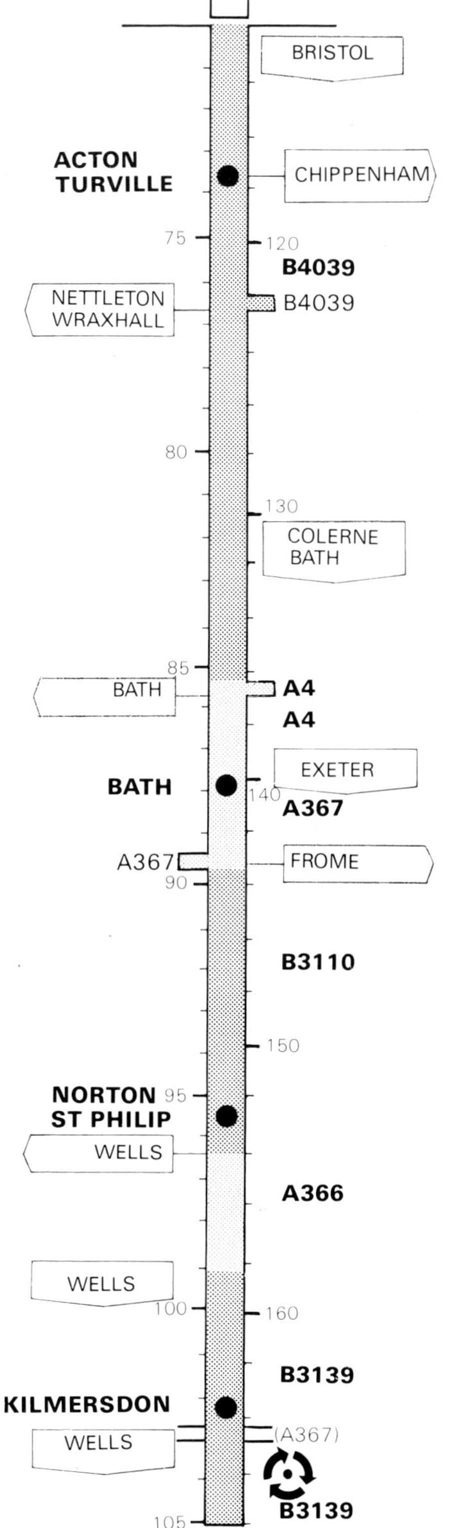

In 1.7 m at Luckington continue straight on B4040 (sign Bristol) and in 2.6 m at Acton Turville turn left on to B4039 (sign Chippenham). In 0.1 m turn left on B4039 (sign Chippenham). In 2.4 m turn right on to minor road (signs Nettleton and Wraxhall) and keep straight for 3.8 m to junction with A420 at the Shoe. Here keep straight on minor road (sign Colerne).

In 2.4 m keep straight (sign Bath) and in 2.5 m turn right on to A4 (sign Bath) for 3.0 m to Bath city centre. Here take A367 (sign Exeter) and in 1.7 m turn left on to B3110 (sign Frome). Keep straight on B3110 for 5.4 m to Norton St Phillip.

Here turn right on to A366 (sign Wells) and in 4.4 m keep straight on to B3139 (sign Wells) for 1.9 m to Kilmersdon.

Here continue straight on B3139 (sign Wells) and in 2.0 m at roundabout keep straight on B3139 (sign Wells).

Emborough (Somerset)

The hotel (below) lies along the route outside the village.

Court Hotel, 9 rooms,
T Stratton-on-the-Fosse 232237 (C)

Chewton Mendip (Somerset)

The route only skirts the village, dominated by the 126-foot church tower that was built by Carthusian monks and is considered one of the finest in the county. Within the church is a stone seat where criminals 'on the run' sought sanctuary.

Cheddar (Somerset)

The road runs through the mile-long Cheddar Gorge where vertical limestone cliffs rise on either side to a height of 450 feet.

Cheddar Gorge.

Bones of prehistoric man as well as Roman coins have been discovered in the famous Cheddar caves, and the well-known cheese is still made in local farmhouses.

Gordons Hotel, Cliff St, 14 rooms,
T742497 (D)
Market Cross Hotel, 6 rooms,
T74264 (D)
YHA, Hillfield, T742294
T.O. The Library, Union St, T742769

Meare (Somerset)

The village straggles through flat marshy country. The Abbots' Fish House (signed to the left in farm land where the key to view is obtainable from the farm) is a preserved 14c building where fishermen stored and salted fish for the supply of the monks of Glastonbury.

Glastonbury (Somerset)

'Arimathean Joseph, journeying brought to Glastonbury, where the winter thorn blossoms at Christmas, mindful of Our Lord.' With these words Tennyson recalled the legend that it was here that Joseph of Arimathea thrust his staff into the ground where it blossomed to produce the winter flowering tree known as the Glastonbury Thorn. It was here, also, that Joseph built the chapel which was later to be the site of the famous Abbey where it is said that the bones of King Arthur were reburied. The surrounds of the town are industrialized and there is a certain amount of ugly building.

George and Pilgrims Hotel, 1 High St,
15 rooms, T31146 (B)
Hawthorn House Hotel, 8 Northload St,
12 rooms, T31255 (D)
T.O. 7 Northload St, T32954

Street (Somerset)

There is a shoe museum here, for the town became a centre for shoe-making more than a century ago. South of the town, along the route, is Ivythorne Hill (National Trust land) with fine views over Sedgemoor, and a tree known as Marshall's Elm where thirty of Monmouth's followers were hanged in 1685.

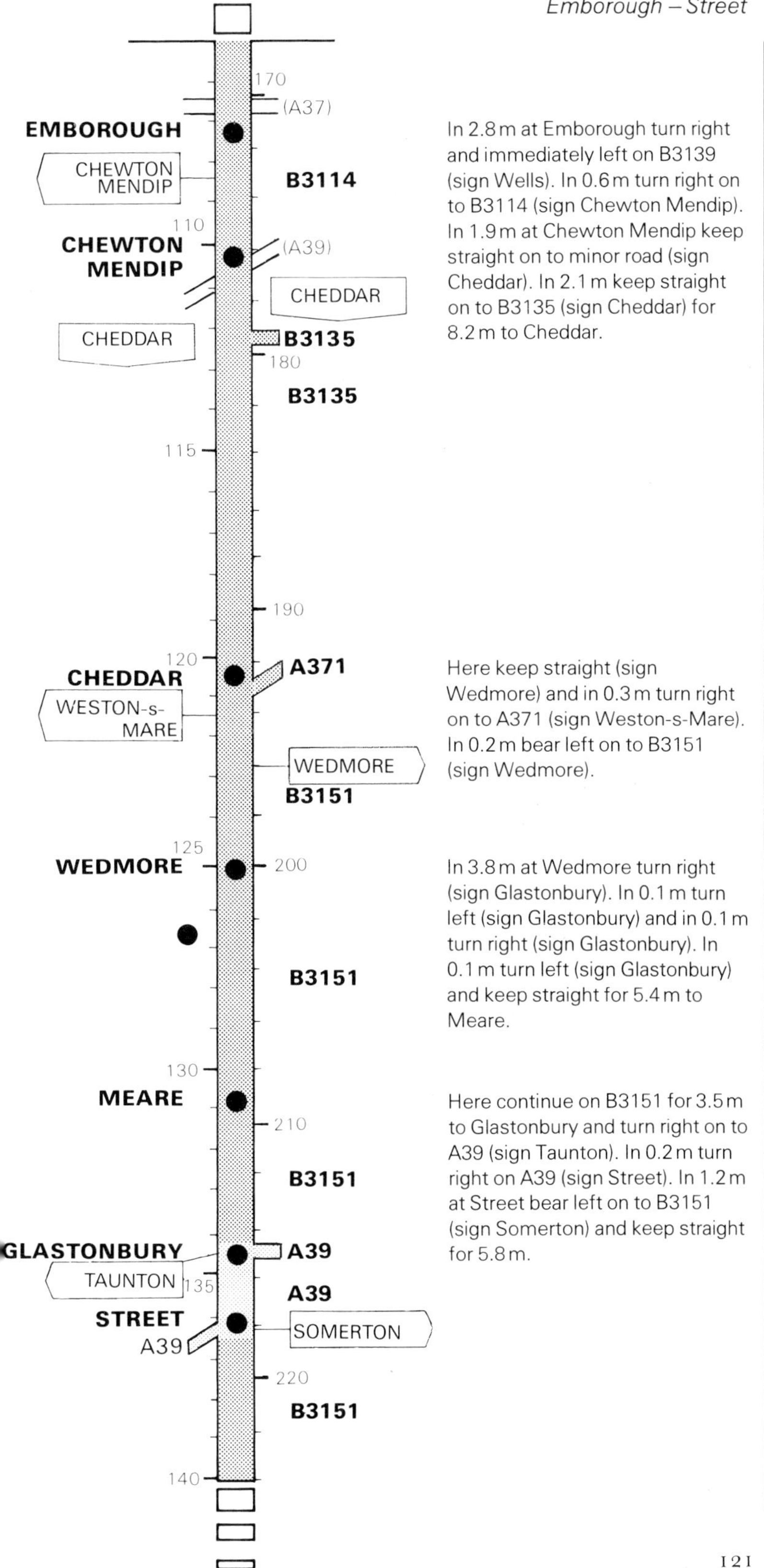

In 2.8 m at Emborough turn right and immediately left on B3139 (sign Wells). In 0.6 m turn right on to B3114 (sign Chewton Mendip). In 1.9 m at Chewton Mendip keep straight on to minor road (sign Cheddar). In 2.1 m keep straight on to B3135 (sign Cheddar) for 8.2 m to Cheddar.

Here keep straight (sign Wedmore) and in 0.3 m turn right on to A371 (sign Weston-s-Mare). In 0.2 m bear left on to B3151 (sign Wedmore).

In 3.8 m at Wedmore turn right (sign Glastonbury). In 0.1 m turn left (sign Glastonbury) and in 0.1 m turn right (sign Glastonbury). In 0.1 m turn left (sign Glastonbury) and keep straight for 5.4 m to Meare.

Here continue on B3151 for 3.5 m to Glastonbury and turn right on to A39 (sign Taunton). In 0.2 m turn right on A39 (sign Street). In 1.2 m at Street bear left on to B3151 (sign Somerton) and keep straight for 5.8 m.

The Route

Pleasant traffic-free roads, although the 11-mile stretch between Wedmore and Street runs through flat and somewhat featureless country.

Somerton (Somerset)

The pleasant compact town clusters round the square with a 17c Town Hall and market cross. There are some attractive old inns, almshouses built at the beginning of the 17c, and a church with a glorious 15c roof.

Red Lion Hotel, Broad St, 16 rooms, T46240 (B)

Langport (Somerset)

An old market town with narrow main street. The minor road ascends sharply from the town, passing the parish church and running beneath a 15c building known as the 'hanging chapel' which bridges the road.

Langport Arms, Cheapside, 9 rooms, T250530 (C)

Muchelney (Somerset)

Here lie the remains of a monastery almost as old as that founded at Glastonbury. The Abbot's House is among the surviving buildings and not far from the Abbey ruins is the Priest's House, a charming thatched 15c house, preserved by the National Trust but only to be visited by appointment.

Martock (Somerset)

Among the many old buildings of this beautiful town are the Treasurer's House, 13c and once the property of the Treasurer of Wells Cathedral; and the Church House, formerly the grammar school, with an inscription above the door that reads 'Martock neglect not thy opportunities'. An interesting feature of the 15c church is the Fives Place where a mutilated buttress near the north porch was used as a fives court. It appears that the fives players did much damage while retrieving balls from the roof and the game was abandoned in 1758, when an entry in the church warden's account ran 'For digging up ye Fives Place 3/6d.'

White Hart Hotel, Market Place, 9 rooms, T2825 (C)

Crewkerne (Somerset)

Best building in this old semi-industrialized town is the 15c church that lies tucked away in a remote corner. The Church Hall was formerly the grammar school where Captain Hardy (1769–1833), flag captain in the *Victory* who attended Nelson when he died, was educated.

George Hotel, Market St, 16 rooms, T73650 (D)

Coneys Castle (Dorset)

The remains of this iron-age fort on the top of a wooded hill are preserved by the National Trust. A car park is provided on the left of the road.

Charmouth (Dorset)

The town lies about half a mile from the pleasant sheltered sea front that looks south with a good easterly view of Golden Cap, so called because the hilltop is faced with a patch of yellow sandstone that glints vividly when the sun shines on it.

Queens Arms Hotel, The Street, 17 rooms, T60339 (C)

The Route

Sections of the route that are particularly narrow lie between Marshwood and Charmouth and

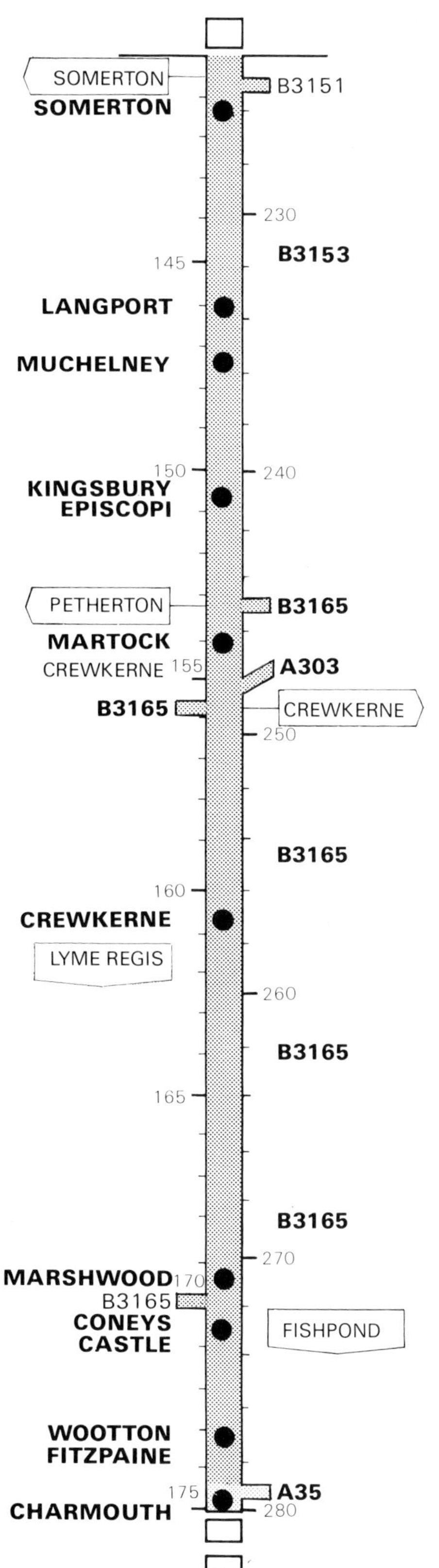

Turn right on to B3153 (signs Somerton and Langport) for 0.5 m to Somerton. Here keep straight on B3153 for 4.6 m to Langport.

In Langport turn left on to minor road by post office (no sign). In 0.4 m turn right (sign Mulcheney) for 1.0 m to Mulcheney. Keep straight (sign Petherton) and in 0.2 m bear right (sign Kingsbury) for 2.6 m to Kingsbury Episcopi. Here turn left (sign Martock). In 1.1 m turn left (sign Martock) and in 0.6 m turn right (sign Martock). In 0.6 m turn right on to B3165 (sign Petherton) for 0.8 m to Martock.

Here continue straight on B3165 (sign Crewkerne) and in 1.3 m turn right on to A303 (sign Honiton). In 0.3 m turn left on to B3165 (sign Crewkerne). In 0.1 m keep straight across A3088 (sign Crewkerne). Continue straight for 4.3 m and turn left on to A356 for 0.8 m to Crewkerne town centre. Here take B3165 (sign Lyme Regis).

Keep straight on B3165 (signs Lyme Regis) for 8.5 m when on leaving Marshwood turn left on to minor road (no sign, NB do *not* turn left on minor road that passes church but take the next minor road). In 0.2 m keep straight (sign Fishpond). In 0.7 m fork left (no sign) and immediately turn left (sign Wootton Fitzpaine). In 1.5 m turn right (sign Wootton Fitzpaine) and in 0.7 m turn left (sign Charmouth). In 0.1 m at Wootton Fitzpaine village hall bear left (sign Charmouth) and in 1.5 m turn right on A35 into Charmouth.

between Whitchurch Canonicorum and Stoke Abbot. It should be noted that the B3165 south of Martock crosses the A3088, at which point a two-mile diversion (left along the A3088) leads to Montacute House. This house, built in the late 16c and now in the care of the National Trust, is among the finest Elizabethan houses to be found in Britain.

Whitchurch Canonicorum (Dorset)

This remote village boasts the only parish church in England with a shrine agreed to contain the bones of its patron saint. These are the bones of St Wite, a lady said to have been murdered by the Danes when they landed at Charmouth.

But beauty vanishes; beauty passes;
However rare – rare it be;
And when I crumble, who will remember
This lady of the West Country?
(Walter de la Mare)

Shave Cross (Dorset)

The 14c Shave Cross Inn was once the resting place of travelling monks and pilgrims who were shaved here – hence the name of this delightful inn. Hot and cold snacks are served in the bar, which retains the original stone floor and inglenook fireplace (T Broadwindsor 358).

Stoke Abbot (Dorset)

Another charming village of picturesque houses, some of them 17c.

Beaminster (Dorset)

An ancient market town where several pleasant inns cluster round the square and market cross.

White Hart Hotel, 8 Hogshill St, 7 rooms, T862779 (D)

Evershot (Dorset)

The main street of this small village is lined with bow-windowed shops on raised pavements.

Cerne Abbas (Dorset)

Cut into the turf of a limestone hill to the left of the road before entering the village is the figure of a giant, 180 feet in length and brandishing a club. The Cerne Giant, believed to be some 1,700 years old and possibly a fertility figure associated with religious rites, is now in the care of the National Trust. Cerne Abbas is one of Dorset's most attractive villages, where a row of Tudor cottages stand near a fine Georgian house. Little remains of Cerne Abbey apart from the ornamental gateway beyond the privately owned Abbey House.

Piddletrenthide (Dorset)

The village straggles for almost two miles along the sheltered Piddle Valley, the 'Longpuddle' of Thomas Hardy's *Far from the Madding Crowd.* In fact the name of the village originates from the days of William the Conqueror, when a knight was leased thirty (trente) hides of land along the R. Piddle. The church lies to the north of the village, and its funds are assisted by an excellent cookery book, compiled by the villagers, entitled *The Piddle Valley Cook Book* (obtainable from the hotel or church). The hotel (below) does not lie directly on the route but can be found at the extreme southern end of the village. It has comfortable chalet rooms and a first-class restaurant.

Old Bakehouse Hotel, 7 rooms, T305 (B)

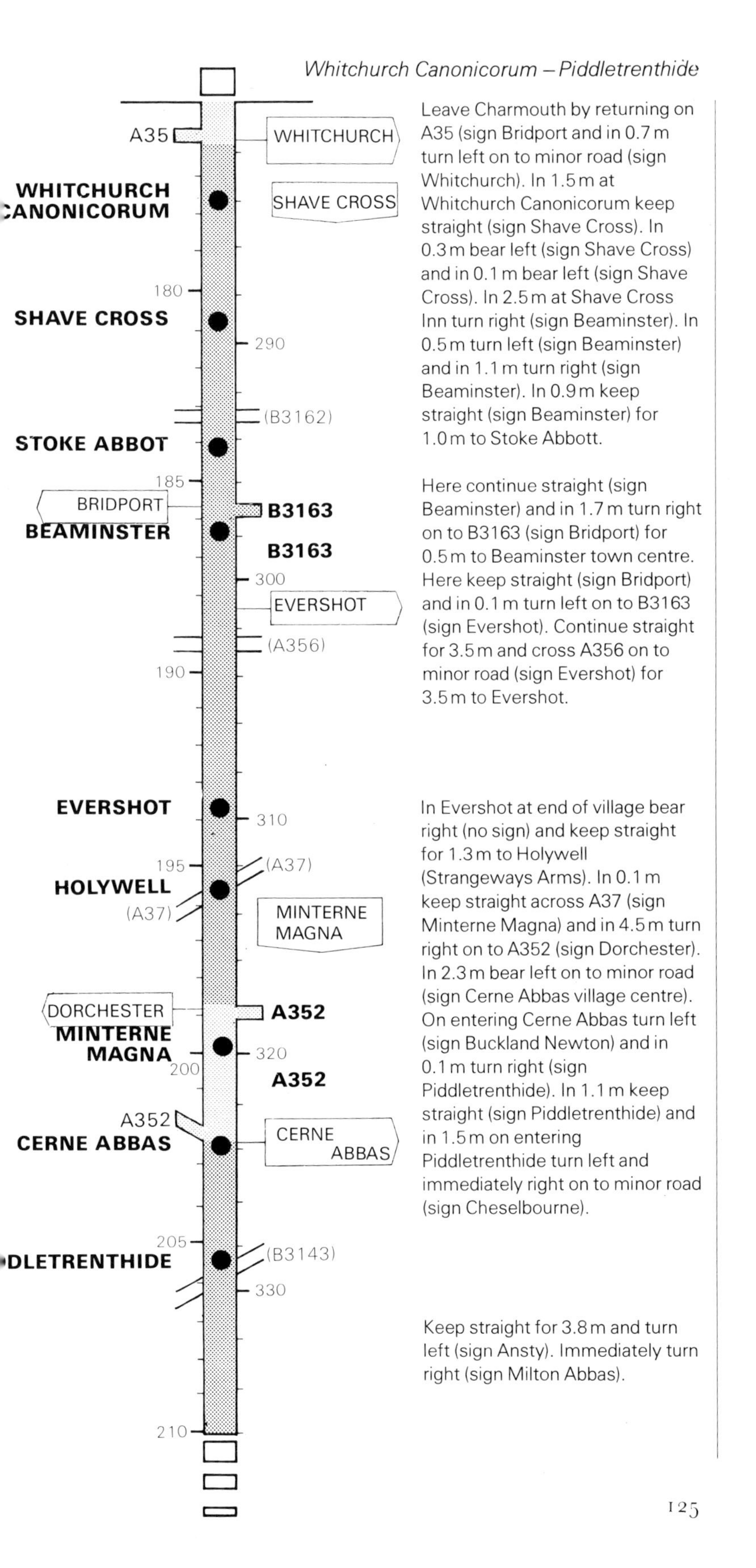

Leave Charmouth by returning on A35 (sign Bridport and in 0.7 m turn left on to minor road (sign Whitchurch). In 1.5 m at Whitchurch Canonicorum keep straight (sign Shave Cross). In 0.3 m bear left (sign Shave Cross) and in 0.1 m bear left (sign Shave Cross). In 2.5 m at Shave Cross Inn turn right (sign Beaminster). In 0.5 m turn left (sign Beaminster) and in 1.1 m turn right (sign Beaminster). In 0.9 m keep straight (sign Beaminster) for 1.0 m to Stoke Abbott.

Here continue straight (sign Beaminster) and in 1.7 m turn right on to B3163 (sign Bridport) for 0.5 m to Beaminster town centre. Here keep straight (sign Bridport) and in 0.1 m turn left on to B3163 (sign Evershot). Continue straight for 3.5 m and cross A356 on to minor road (sign Evershot) for 3.5 m to Evershot.

In Evershot at end of village bear right (no sign) and keep straight for 1.3 m to Holywell (Strangeways Arms). In 0.1 m keep straight across A37 (sign Minterne Magna) and in 4.5 m turn right on to A352 (sign Dorchester). In 2.3 m bear left on to minor road (sign Cerne Abbas village centre). On entering Cerne Abbas turn left (sign Buckland Newton) and in 0.1 m turn right (sign Piddletrenthide). In 1.1 m keep straight (sign Piddletrenthide) and in 1.5 m on entering Piddletrenthide turn left and immediately right on to minor road (sign Cheselbourne).

Keep straight for 3.8 m and turn left (sign Ansty). Immediately turn right (sign Milton Abbas).

Milton Abbas (Dorset)

A handsome and spacious village where symmetrical white thatched houses, lawn fronted, lie well apart along the broad main street with the church, museum, inn, and village shop. The Abbey Church and the Abbey House (now a school) are signed out of the village past the lake in a superb setting.

Thatched houses at Milton Abbas.

Blandford Forum (Dorset)

This busy market town in the midst of rich agricultural land was badly damaged by a great fire in 1731. Among the few surviving buildings are the Ryves Almshouses in Salisbury St. The town centre, however, contains many notable Georgian houses constructed after the fire.

Crown Hotel, 1 West St, 26 rooms, T2366 (B)

Witchampton (Dorset)

Among the many interesting features to be seen in the church (to the left of the route) are the Saxon chessmen, made of whalebone, displayed under glass.

Cranborne (Dorset)

The village was at one time a centre where huntsmen gathered in pursuit of fallow deer that roamed in Cranborne Chase, an area of a hundred square miles to the north-west that was heavily wooded and under royal patronage. The gardens of the Jacobean manor house run down to the river and are open to the public on occasional weekends throughout the summer. This quiet village has a pleasant old inn that provides bed and breakfast and good food in the Badger bar, where the visit of the poet, Rupert Brooke (1887–1915), is recorded:

Prince, it was dark to left and right,
Waits there an inn for you and me,
Fine hoppy ale and red fire light
These things are at the Fleur-de-Lys.

Roman Villa (Rockbourne, Hampshire)

The route runs to the south-east of Rockbourne, one of Hampshire's prettiest villages, past the remains of the Roman villa discovered in 1942. The villa consisted of some 46 rooms and yielded coins and a geometrical mosaic floor.

Breamore (Hampshire)

Outside the village, set in parkland near the Elizabethan manor house, is a Saxon church of outstanding beauty built around AD 980. Breamore House is open on occasions to the public, and has a splendid display of pictures, furniture and works of art as well as a carriage museum showing the development of agricultural machinery.

The Route

The road runs from west to east through the heart of Dorset's unspoilt countryside before reaching the fringe of Hampshire beyond Cranborne. After leaving Breamore House the minor road joins with the A338 for the final few miles back to Salisbury. Very little traffic encountered throughout.

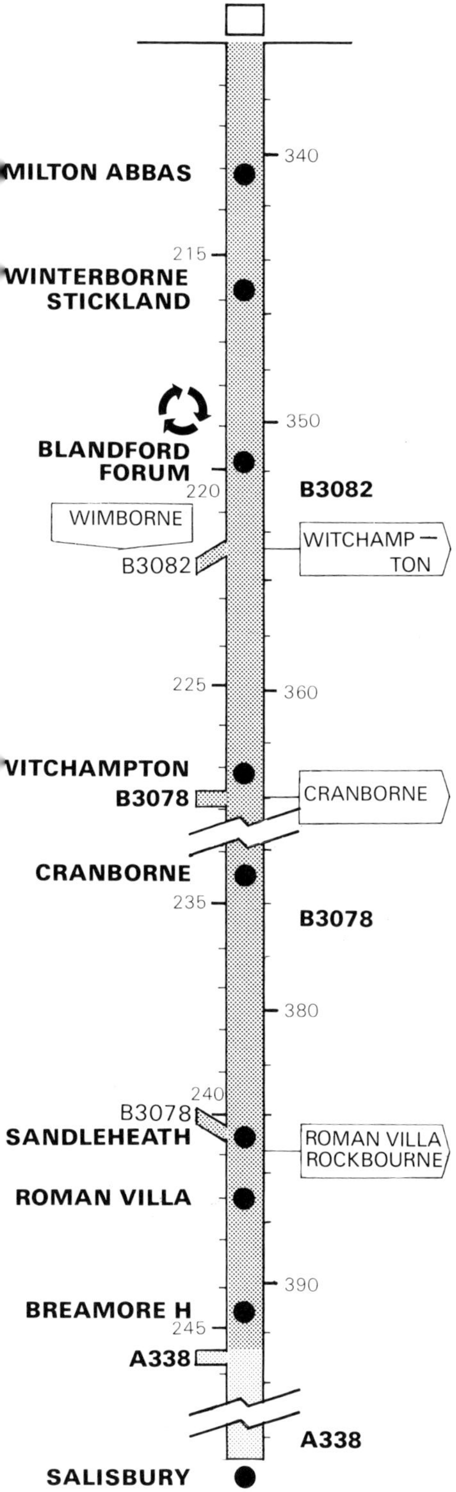

MILTON ABBAS
WINTERBORNE STICKLAND
BLANDFORD FORUM
WIMBORNE
B3082
WITCHAMPTON
B3078
CRANBORNE
B3078
SANDLEHEATH
ROMAN VILLA
BREAMORE H
A338
SALISBURY
B3082
WITCHAMP-TON
CRANBORNE
B3078
ROMAN VILLA ROCKBOURNE
A338
215 220 225 235 240 245
340 350 360 380 390

In 0.9 m turn right (sign Milton Abbas) and in 0.2 m turn left (sign Milton Abbas). In 1.0 m turn right (sign Milton Abbas) and in 0.3 m turn left (sign Milton Abbas). Keep straight (signs Milton Abbas) for 1.3 m to Milton Abbas and from here continue straight. In 0.3 m turn left (sign Stickland) and in 0.6 m bear right (sign Stickland).

In 1.9 m at Winterborne Stickland bear left (sign Blandford) and in 0.4 m turn right (sign Blandford). In 1.0 m bear right (sign Blandford) and in 2.8 m turn left into Blandford Forum. Here follow one-way circuit (signs Wimborne) and take B3082 (sign Wimborne). In 1.7 m bear left on to minor road (sign Witchampton). In 1.3 m turn left (sign Witchampton) and in 0.5 m bear right (sign Witchampton). Continue straight (signs Witchampton) and in 3.5 m at T junction turn right (sign Wimborne). In 1.0 m turn left on to B3078 (sign Cranborne) and keep straight (signs Cranborne) for 6.4 m to Cranborne.

Here turn right on to B3078 (signs Damerham and Fordingbridge). In 5.5 m at Sandleheath turn left on to minor road (signs Roman Villa and Rockbourne). In 1.4 m turn right (sign Breamore). In 0.8 m keep straight (sign Breamore) and in 1.2 m bear left (sign Breamore). Continue straight for 0.6 m and keep straight (sign North Street). In 0.7 m turn left on to A338 (no sign) for 8.0 m to Salisbury.

8 *Scotland*

'A SCOTCHMAN is one of the proudest things alive,' wrote the 18th century novelist Oliver Goldsmith, who in his twenties studied medicine at Edinburgh. Today Scotland is one of Europe's most popular tourist centres, and the tens of thousands who flock there annually from all over the world cannot fail to be struck both by the hospitality of the people of that country and their pride in the traditions and beauty of their native land.

This route of around five hundred miles cannot do more than allow a glimpse of Scotland, being confined to the western and central areas of the mainland. Almost eight hundred islands are scattered around the Scottish shores, among the largest of these being Arran, Bute, Islay, Jura, Mull, Skye and the Hebrides off the west coast and the Orkneys and Shetlands to the north. The reader with time to spare might well wish to divert from this route and take a ferry to one or more of these islands.

Dumfries and Galloway in the extreme south-west form an area which is relatively ignored by tourists and yet has much to offer – in particular the superb 200-square-mile Galloway Forest Park, which contains numerous mountain peaks that exceed two thousand feet in altitude. Those motoring from England can of course explore the area 'en route'.

The northernmost point of this particular route is Little Loch Broom, and the eastern extremity is reached around Carrbridge and Aviemore – approximate points where consideration might be given to extending the tour either northward or eastward. Faced with the fact that time and space only permitted a journey of five hundred miles, great difficulty was encountered in choosing the route, and the final decision was only made after consultation with numerous Scottish friends. I am grateful, in particular, to Dr R. S. Stevenson and the members of his Scottish Medical Golfing Association for their advice. After a lengthy meeting with Dr Stevenson and his colleagues, who all have a wide knowledge of the country, it became obvious that the Scotsman's pride in his country is as apparent today as when observed by Goldsmith – and it was only after much argument and confrontation that general agreement was reached as to the best possible route within the limitations. Some discussion took place as to whether the return route from Inverness should be by way of the Great Glen and Loch Ness or via the Spey valley. The former idea was discarded because it would have meant that after Fort Augustus some of the outward roads would need to be used again. Moreover there would have been no opportunity to divert to such areas as the Cairngorms and Loch Tummel.

It is necessary to emphasize that owing to the nature of the landscape the choice of roads used in Scotland is more limited than in England and Wales. But although much of this route is confined to A roads, it needs to be remembered that such roads in Scotland are often little more than single track roads with passing places.

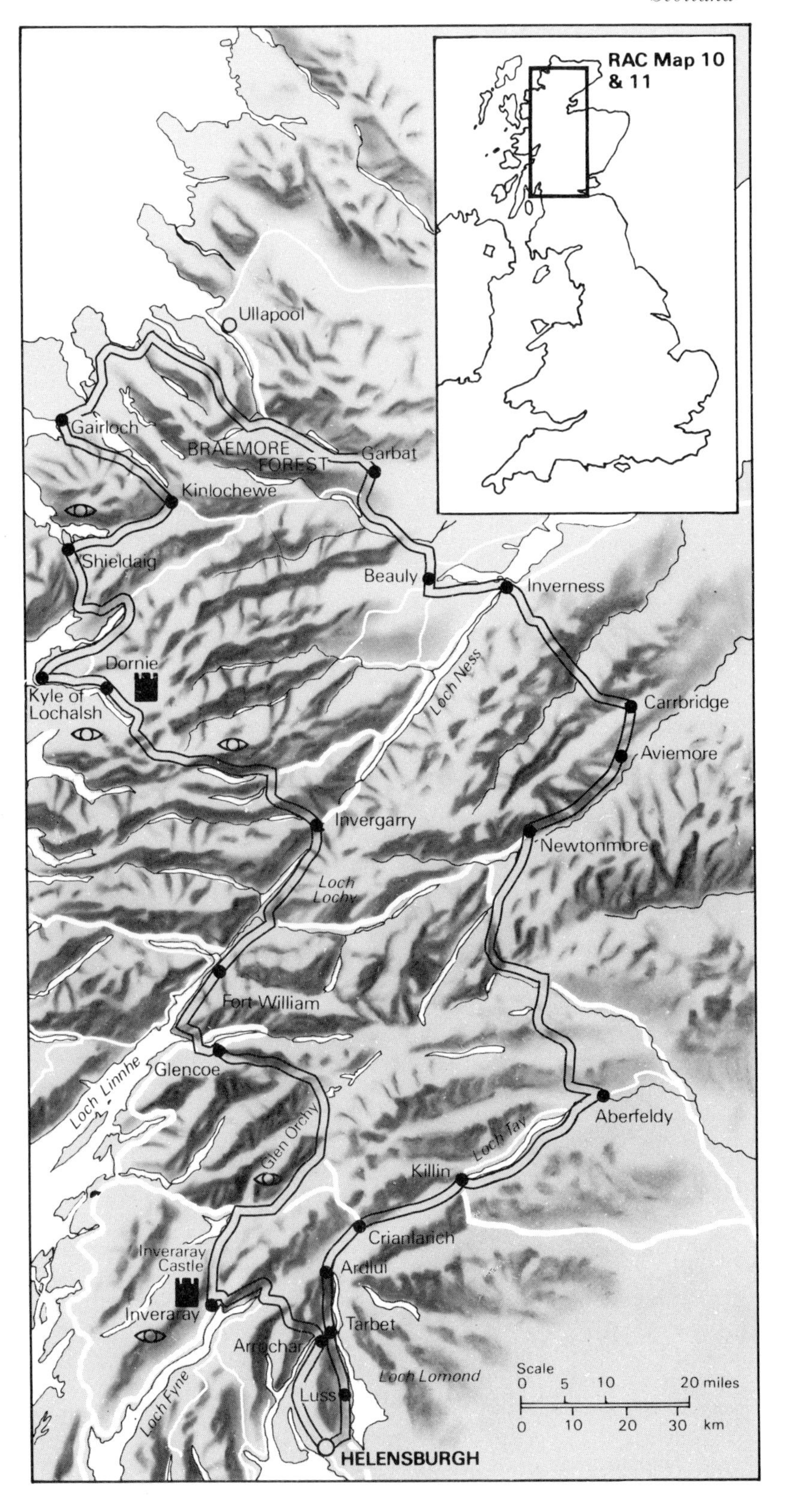
RAC Map 10
& 11
Ullapool
Gairloch
BRAEMORE
FOREST
Garbat
Kinlochewe
Shieldaig
Beauly
Inverness
Dornie
Kyle of
Lochalsh
Loch Ness
Carrbridge
Aviemore
Invergarry
Newtonmore
Loch
Lochy
Fort William
Glencoe
Loch Linnhe
Glen Orchy
Aberfeldy
Loch Tay
Killin
Crianlarich
Inveraray
Castle
Ardlui
Inveraray
Tarbet
Arrochar
Loch Lomond
Loch Fyne
Luss
HELENSBURGH
Scale
0 5 10 20 miles
0 10 20 30 km

Loch Tummel, Tayside.

The Scottish economy depends upon a wide field of activity ranging from stock raising, fishing and farming to mining, ship building, engineering and general industry. No reference to Scotland, however, would be complete without mention of the world-famous Scotch whisky, distilled from water peculiar to the country and with properties extolled by Scotland's most renowned poet, Robert Burns (1759–96): 'It gies us mair than either school or college; it kindles wit, it waukens lair [learning], it pangs [stuffs] us fu' o' knowlege.'

The poet Burns is only one of a number of Scottish men and women whose names spring to mind as one travels through their lovely country. In the literary field one thinks of Sir Walter Scott, R. L. S. Stevenson, James Barrie and John Buchan. Among scientists and engineers, Alexander Bell, inventor of the telephone; Alexander Fleming, who discovered penicillin; John McAdam, the road surveyor, and

John Logie Baird the television pioneer. Robert Adam, the architect, Sir Francis Chantry the sculptor, and David Livingstone the missionary and explorer were all Scotsmen born and bred. Sir Harry Lauder, son of a miner, and Jack Buchanan have enriched the stage, and among politicians both Ramsay Macdonald and Harold Macmillan served as prime ministers. Nor can one forget Flora Macdonald (1722–90), the Scottish heroine who rescued Prince Charles Edward after the Battle of Culloden, disguising him as her maid and escorting him from her home in the Hebrides to the mainland.

Perhaps, finally, it is worth recalling to mind that dour Scotsman James Boswell, for it was he, accompanied by the subject of his biography, Samuel Johnson, who travelled through western Scotland in 1733 and recorded the trip in his *Journal of the Tour to the Hebrides*. At this time Boswell was only thirty-three, but as one travels through the same rugged countryside it is impossible not to marvel at the stamina of Johnson, who made this arduous journey at the age of sixty-four.

Helensburgh (Dunbartonshire)

A holiday resort and centre for boat-building and yachting at the southern extremity of Gare Loch. Here and at neighbouring Rhu there are several well sited hotels, making the area a good starting-point for the journey north. The older part of the town was laid out in a draughtboard pattern at the end of the 18c by Sir James Colquhoun of Luss, who named it after his wife. There is an obelisk on the waterfront to Henry Bell (1767–1830), designer of Europe's first passenger steamer. The television pioneer, John Logie Baird (1888–1946), was born here – his birthplace honoured by a bust.

Queens Hotel, 114 East Clyde St, 24 rooms, T3404 (A)
Cairndhu Hotel, 14 rooms, T3388 (B)
T.O. Pier Head Car Park, T2642

Rhu (Dunbartonshire)

The village almost adjoins Helensburgh. The hotel shown below is under new management and has already built up an excellent reputation for good food.

Waters Edge Hotel, 8 rooms, T276 (B)

Garelochhead (Dunbartonshire)

Lies at the northern tip of Gare Loch. Just after leaving the town the road rises to a point where there is a pleasant picnic area on the right of the road.

Garelochhead Hotel, 6 rooms, T810263 (C)

Arrochar (Dunbartonshire)

The town is situated on Loch Long, with Loch Lomond less than two miles to the east. In 1263 King Haakon of Norway sailed his invading ships into Loch Long before transporting them across land to Loch Lomond.

Loch Long Hotel, 53 rooms, T434 (D)

Cairndow (Argyll)

The village stands on Loch Fyne and, as the map indicates, is bypassed by the main road. The short diversion is worth while, however, in order to see the 'pinetum' of Strone Gardens – and Scotland's tallest tree. The poet John Keats (1795–1821) breakfasted in the hotel here after bathing in the loch, recording his visit thus: 'We were up at four this morning and have walked fifteen miles through two tremendous glens, at the head of the first is a place called "Rest and be Thankful", which we took for an inn. It was nothing but a stone and we were cheated into doing five more miles for breakfast.'

Cairndow Inn, 9 rooms, T286 (D)

Inveraray (Argyll)

The white buildings of this enchanting town on Loch Fyne are fronted by a pleasant green and war memorial. Inverary Castle, seat of the Duke of Argyll, stands in wooded parkland on the right of the road before reaching the town. The castle was damaged by fire in 1975, but is once again open to the public on specified occasions. It contains magnificent paintings and a display of ancient Highland arms.

Argyll Arms Hotel, 30 rooms, T2466 (C)
Fern Point Hotel, 8 rooms, T2170 (C)
T.O. Town Hall, T2063

The Route

Initially good views of Gare Loch. After leaving Garelochhead there are even finer views of Loch Long and the wooded hills beyond. Past Arrochar the road runs through forest land, ascending the Rest and be Thankful pass before descending to Inverary and Loch Fyne.

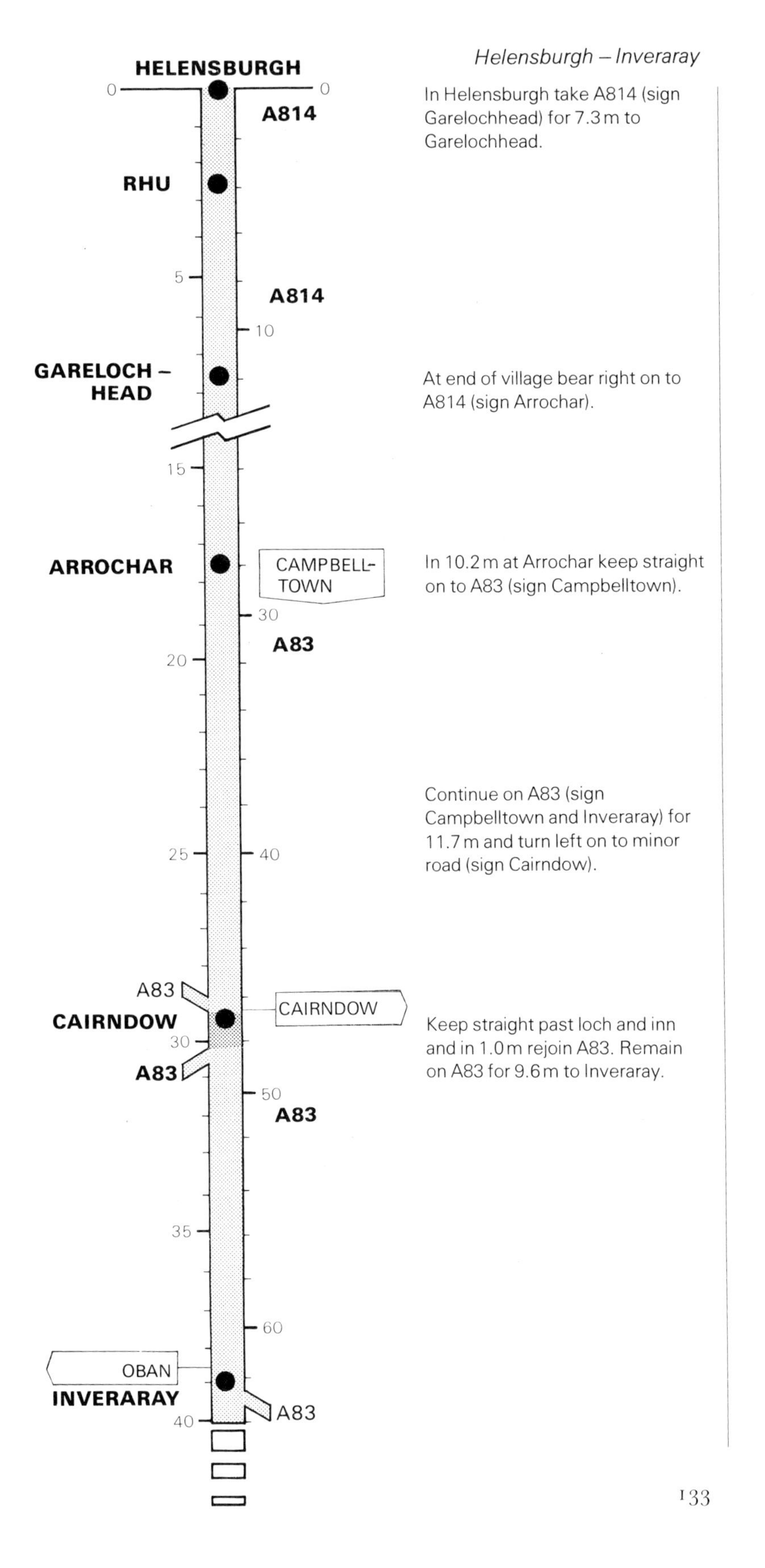

In Helensburgh take A814 (sign Garelochhead) for 7.3 m to Garelochhead.

At end of village bear right on to A814 (sign Arrochar).

In 10.2 m at Arrochar keep straight on to A83 (sign Campbelltown).

Continue on A83 (sign Campbelltown and Inveraray) for 11.7 m and turn left on to minor road (sign Cairndow).

Keep straight past loch and inn and in 1.0 m rejoin A83. Remain on A83 for 9.6 m to Inveraray.

Cladich (Argyll)

As the route instructions indicate, there is little point in diverting to this tiny place, once a weaving village, which is only mentioned as a point of reference. From the main road there are good views of Loch Awe and the little islands dotted around the northern part of the loch. Before reaching Dalmally road junction on a marshy site at the tip of the loch is Kilchurn Castle, once the home of the Campbells of Glenorchy and garrisoned by Hanoverian troops at the time of the Jacobite rebellion. The castle towers were damaged by the great gale of 1879 that destroyed the Tay Bridge.

Dalmally (Argyll)

The bulk of the village lies to the right of the road in the woods above the River Orchy – although the Dalmally Hotel stands outside the village on the main road. On Monument Hill, two miles to the south-west of the village, is the monument to Duncan Ban MacIntyre (1724–1812), known as the Robert Burns of the Highlands.

Dalmally Hotel, 56 rooms, T249 (D)

Bridge of Orchy (Argyll)

Before reaching the Bridge of Orchy Hotel the B road has followed the R. Orchy through beautiful Glen Orchy.

Bridge of Orchy Hotel,
T Tyndrum 208 (D)

Glencoe (Argyll).

Near to the Clachaig Inn which lies some two miles out of the village of Glencoe is Signal Rock, where on 13 February 1692 the Campbells received their orders for the massacre of the Macdonalds to commence. The massacre, instigated by King William III, resulted in the murder of some

Looking south from the Bridge of Orchy.

200 inhabitants of the Glen and the burning of their houses. Today, in the entry hall of the Clachaig Inn, is a prominent notice, 'No Hawkers and Campbells'. Quite apart from historical associations the Glen is a popular haunt of climbers, and lies amidst some of Scotland's finest mountain scenery. The area is noted for red deer, wild cat, and golden eagle.

Kings House Hotel, 22 rooms,
T Kingshouse 259 (C)
Clachaig Inn, 13 rooms, T Ballachulish 252 (D)

The Route

Particularly fine scenery through Glen Orchy, where the river cascades merrily past weird rock formations, the green of the trees and overhanging shrubs making a pleasant contrast with the rugged mountains that tower above the glen. After joining the main road at the Bridge of Orchy the road runs westward towards Glencoe, the entry to which is close to the Kings Head hotel (off the road to the right). Further along the glen a sign to the right indicates the minor road which leads to the Cladich Inn and Glencoe village. Both this road and that through Glen Orchy are single-track roads, but there are numerous well-marked passing-places.

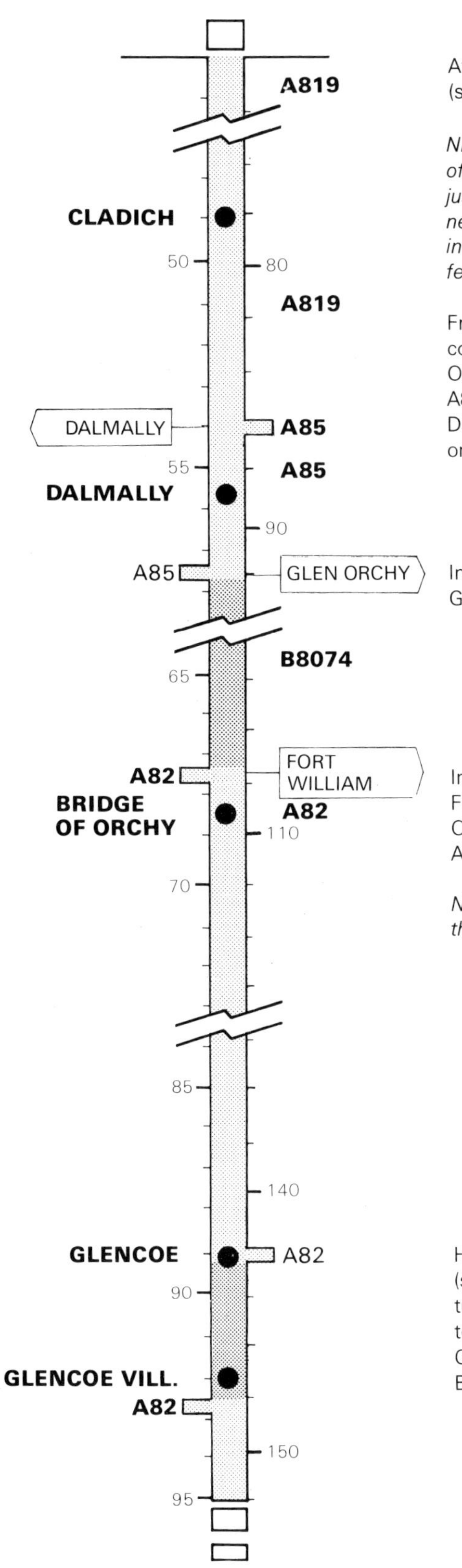

At Inveraray turn right on to A819 (sign Oban) for 9.2 m.

NB Cladich consists of only a post office and a few houses in a glen just off to the left of the road. No need to divert here unless interested in some particular feature mentioned.

From Cladich road junction continue straight on A819 (sign Oban) and in 5.1 m turn right on to A85 (sign Dalmally). In 1.7 m at Dalmally hotel continue straight on A85 (sign Crialarich).

In 1.8 m turn left on to B8074 (sign Glen Orchy).

In 10.2 m turn left on to A82 (sign Fort William) for 0.6 m to Bridge of Orchy. Here continue straight on A82.

NB Glencoe Village is signed off to the right in 20.7 m.

Here turn right on to minor road (sign Glencoe Village) and in 3.3 m turn left and immediately right on to A82 (sign Fort William). Continue straight for 3.6 m to Ballachulish bridge).

Ben Nevis from the west.

Ballachulish Bridge (Argyll)

The bridge across the mouth of Loch Leven was built in 1975, replacing the ferry service which used to ply between North and South Ballachulish. The chosen route makes direct for Fort William, but if time allows an addition of thirteen miles to the journey, it is worth noting that there is a road encircling Loch Leven by way of Kinlocheven – through spectacular scenery. Shortly after crossing Ballachulish bridge a ferry service (signed to the left) crosses Loch Linnhe for Coran and the Ardgour district, from where the islands of Mull and Iona can be reached by ferry.

Ballachulish Hotel, 35 rooms, T239 (B)

Fort William (Inverness-shire)

A number of roads converge on this tourist centre, which tends to get crowded in summer. The Fort, built by William III as a bastion against rebel Highlanders, was demolished in 1890 to give access to the railway. The West Highland Museum contains items of historic interest, among them a typical crofter's kitchen; a bed once used by the Young Pretender; and the helmet worn by James Graham, Marquess of Montrose (1612–50), who fought loyally for Charles I before his final defeat and execution. Britain's highest mountain, Ben Nevis (4,406 ft), lies a few miles to the south-east of the town and the summit can be reached by a well-marked path from Achintee in four or five hours. To the north of Fort William are the neglected remains of Inverlochy Castle (13c).

Alexandra Hotel, 89 rooms, T2241 (B)
Imperial Hotel, 36 rooms, T2040 (C)

Spean Bridge (Inverness-shire)

The Commando War Memorial stands on the left of the road shortly after leaving Spean Bridge and perhaps no other Memorial site in Great Britain can match this one for the sheer beauty of its surroundings. Three commandos in battle gear stare out across the magnificent Highland scenery that was their training ground.

Spean Bridge Hotel, 29 rooms, T250 (C)
Coire Glas Guest House, 15 rooms, T272 (D)

Invergarry (Inverness-shire)

Before reaching Invergarry, on the shore of Loch Oich, is a monument

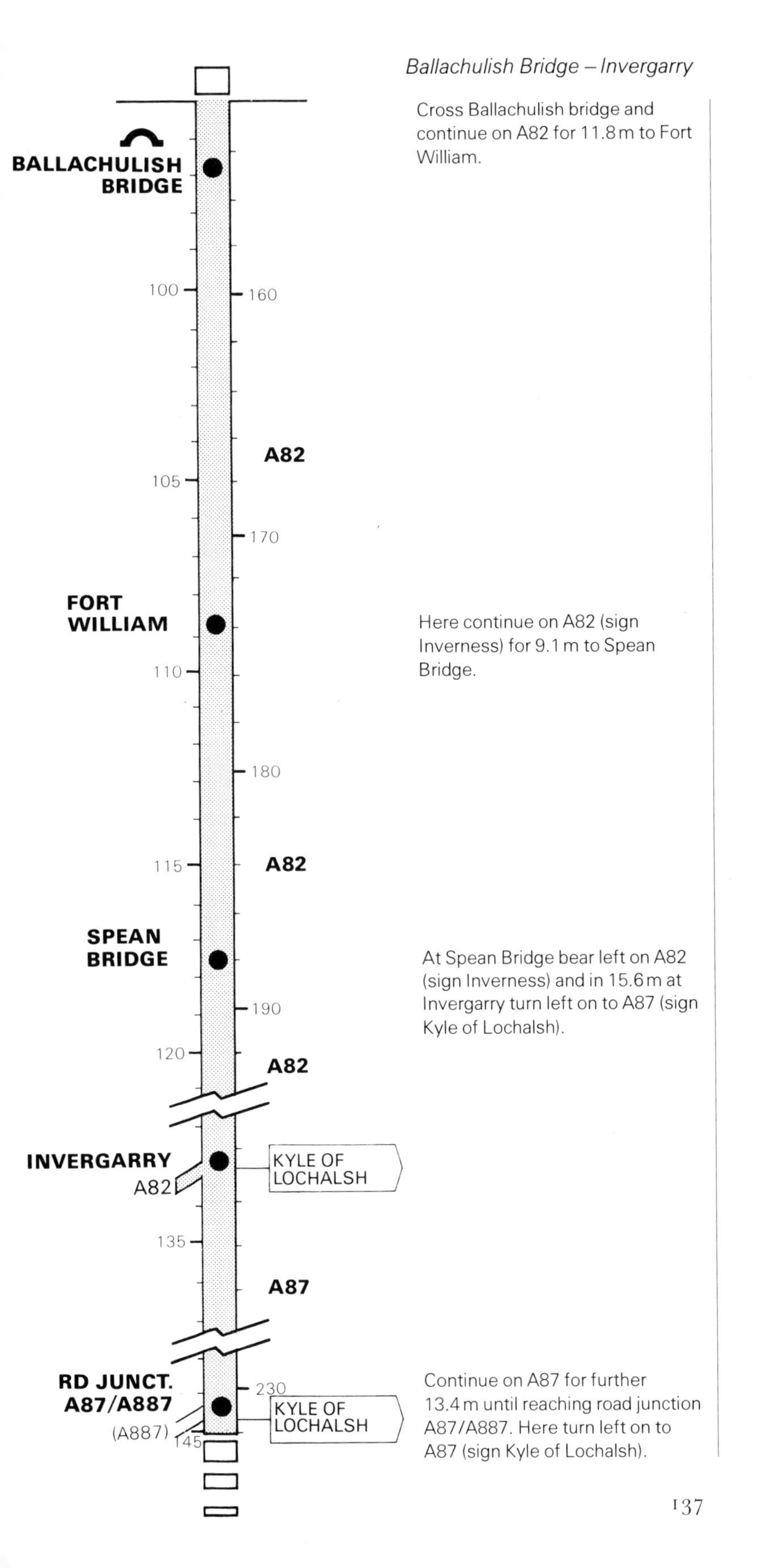

Cross Ballachulish bridge and continue on A82 for 11.8 m to Fort William.

Here continue on A82 (sign Inverness) for 9.1 m to Spean Bridge.

At Spean Bridge bear left on A82 (sign Inverness) and in 15.6 m at Invergarry turn left on to A87 (sign Kyle of Lochalsh).

Continue on A87 for further 13.4 m until reaching road junction A87/A887. Here turn left on to A87 (sign Kyle of Lochalsh).

with a gruesome history – a statue surmounted by seven engraved heads known as the Well of the Heads Monument. The inscription in English, French, Gaelic and Latin describes how two youths of the clan of MacDonnell were murdered by seven of their uncles. The murders were avenged by the family bard who slew the seven men, washing their severed heads in the well before presenting them to the chief of the clan at Glengarry.

Glengarry Castle Hotel, 30 rooms, T254 (C)
Craigard Private Hotel, 7 rooms, T258 (D)

Road Junction A87/A887 (Inverness-shire)

The A887 bears eastward towards Inverness. The A87 (chosen route) makes westward past Loch Cluanie and Glen Shiel. Much of the land to the north of the road is the National Trust property of Kintail that includes a line of the mountains known as the Five Sisters, the highest peak of which being 3,505 feet. In 1719 the glen formed the battleground for a skirmish between the Highlanders who supported the Old Pretender and the forces of George I. Other supporters of the Stuart cause were the Spaniards who managed to sail up Loch Duich in two ships with a force of soldiers and who, with the Highlanders, met defeat.

The Route

Spectacular Highland scenery throughout. There are fine views of Lochs Linnhe and Lochy, but perhaps the most breathtaking are those views of Lochs Garry and Loyne looking down upon them. After leaving Glengarry there is scarcely any habitation for miles.

Glencoe, a popular haunt of climbers.

Shiel Bridge, lying at the head of Loch Duich.

Shiel Bridge (Ross-shire)

Signed to the right is Morvich, where there is a National Trust camping site and information centre at the heart of the Kintail estate, where red deer and wild goats may be seen. From Morvich the road leads part of the way towards the Falls of Glomach, which can then only be reached after a stiff climb. These falls have a sheer drop of almost 400 feet.

Dornie (Ross-shire)

The village lies by a bridge that stretches across a point where Lochs Duich and Long converge, with Loch Alsh to the west. Dornie must be counted among the prettiest villages in West Scotland, its pride being the Eilean Donan castle that can be reached by crossing a footbridge off the old road which leads from the village to the loch. One of Scotland's most photographed buildings, the castle has for generations been the stronghold of the clan MacRea and now acts as a war memorial to them. Beneath the castle walls are inscribed the names of some five hundred MacReas from all over the world who died in the 1914–18 war, with this moving tribute from Lt Col. John MacRea: 'We are the Dead. Short days ago we lived, felt dawn, saw sunsets glow, loved and were loved and now we lie on Flanders fields.'

Among the most popular sports in these parts of the Highlands is shinty – a robust form of hockey. A large number of teams from outlandish places make up no less than four divisional leagues sponsored by well-known malt whisky distillers. Matches take place on Saturdays, when the pubs open early for the convenience of players and spectators.

Dornie Hotel, 17 rooms, T205 (C)
Loch Duich Hotel, 18 rooms, T213 (C)

The Route

Good views of Lochs Cluanie, Duich, Long and Alsh. On leaving Kyle of Lochalsh there are superb sea views. It will be noted that Plockton lies only two miles off the route (to the left). This is a pleasant remote village where yachting takes place and where there are hotels and guest houses.

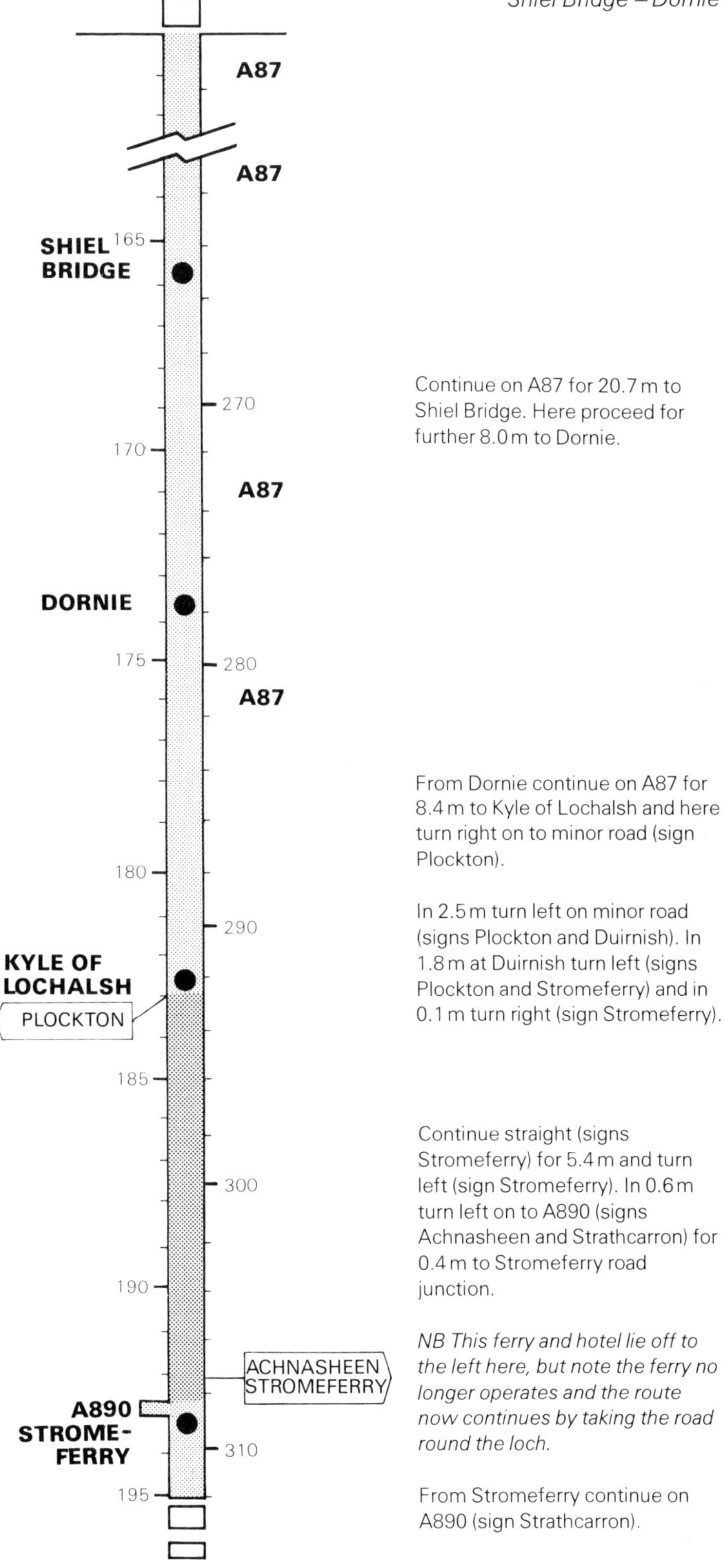

Continue on A87 for 20.7 m to Shiel Bridge. Here proceed for further 8.0 m to Dornie.

From Dornie continue on A87 for 8.4 m to Kyle of Lochalsh and here turn right on to minor road (sign Plockton).

In 2.5 m turn left on minor road (signs Plockton and Duirnish). In 1.8 m at Duirnish turn left (signs Plockton and Stromeferry) and in 0.1 m turn right (sign Stromeferry).

Continue straight (signs Stromeferry) for 5.4 m and turn left (sign Stromeferry). In 0.6 m turn left on to A890 (signs Achnasheen and Strathcarron) for 0.4 m to Stromeferry road junction.

NB This ferry and hotel lie off to the left here, but note the ferry no longer operates and the route now continues by taking the road round the loch.

From Stromeferry continue on A890 (sign Strathcarron).

The Lochalsh Hotel, Kyle of Lochalsh.

Opposite: *Salmon netting, Loch Duich.*

Kyle of Lochalsh (Ross-shire)

'Over the sea to Skye' runs the ballad, and indeed it is from here that the short and frequent ferry service to Kyleakin on that lovely island runs. But Kyle of Lochalsh tends to be a busy place in summer, and those wishing to cross to Skye after an overnight stop might find that Dornie is quieter and less expensive.

Lochalsh Hotel, 45 rooms, T 4202 (A)
Norwest Hotel, 8 rooms, T4204 (D)
Island View Guest House, Badicaul, 6 rooms, T4453 (D)
T.O. T4276

Stromeferry (Ross-shire)

The sea loch, Loch Carron, narrows at this point, and at one time, as the name of the village indicates, a ferry service operated, shortening the northern route and passing the ruined Strome Castle a former MacDonald stronghold. This service has now been abandoned and it is necessary to take the road which circumvents Loch Carron.

The Route

It will be noted that after leaving Lochcarron the most direct route to Shieldaig is taken (8 miles). At this point, however, a sign indicates an alternative route to Shieldaig (36 miles). This, the highest road in Britain, has been constructed recently – and one is warned that the road is not suitable for larger vehicles or for inexperienced drivers. Those taking this coastal route will be rewarded by superb panoramic scenery across to the island of Raasay and the mountains of Skye. The remote village of Applecross was once the centre for a monastery (AD 671), and among the remains of the old church, in the cemetery, is a Celtic cross nine feet high.

One of the most rewarding views along the chosen route is some three miles past Shieldaig where, from a parking-place on the left, one looks down upon Upper Loch Torridon and across to the mountains of Bhreac, Alligin and Eighe, the last two standing over 3,000 feet. Nearing Kinlochewe is the Beinn Eighe nature reserve — the first National Nature Reserve in Great Britain. The reserve covers more than 10,000 acres, with altitudes ranging from 30 to 3,000 feet. Here alpine growths are to be seen, as well as creatures such as red deer, wild cat, mountain goat and eagles.

A word of caution is necessary regarding some parts of the A roads on this section. Many miles of these are in fact single-track roads, unusual in that in other parts of Britain it is rare for such roads to get an A classification. These roads are, however, well surfaced and contain many passing-places that are clearly indicated.

Lochcarron (Ross-shire)

The village straggles for more than a mile along the north-western shore of the inland section of Loch Carron, and there is a good view across the loch from the hotel.

Lochcarron Hotel, 7 rooms, T226 (C)

Shieldaig (Ross-shire)

This is indeed a lovely spot – well worth taking the minor loop road to see. The hotel and fishermens' cottages with their colourful boats lie on the east shore of Loch Shieldag, from where there is an incomparable view of the loch and mountains beyond. The small offshore island was once barren; the trees that can now be seen there were planted for the convenience of the fishermen, giving them shelter and enabling them to dry their nets.

Tigh-an-Eilean Hotel, 10 rooms, T251 (C)

Kinlochewe (Ross-shire)

Lies on the edge of the Beinn Eighe National Nature reserve and is a familiar resort for climbers in the surrounding mountains. Stretching north-westward from here is one of Scotland's loveliest lochs – the 12-mile long Loch Maree, a favourite of Queen Victoria who once stayed at the well-known fishing hotel half-way along it. The loch, overlooked by spectacular mountains, is studded with islands and bordered by Scots pine, birch, oak and alder. Among the islands is Isle Maree, where a Celtic mission cell was established in the 7c. Loch Maree is famed for sea trout fishing, and occasional angling courses are held here.

Kinlochewe Hotel, 10 rooms, T253 (C)

Talladale (Ross-shire)

Loch Maree Hotel, 15 rooms, T Loch Maree 200 (B)

Gairloch (Ross-shire)

A seaside resort with some good sandy beaches and a golf course. The town is renowned for fine sunsets looking across the bay westward to Skye, but it does seem a pity that so many ugly houses have sprung up in a higgledy-piggledy fashion above the bay. A private road leads to Ru'Ro lighthouse, where visits can be arranged by appointment with the keeper. The museum houses exhibits illustrating life here from prehistoric to modern times.

Gairloch Hotel, 50 rooms, T2001 (B)
Myrtle Bank Hotel, 12 rooms, T2004 (D)
T.O. Achtercairn, T2130

Inverewe Gardens (Ross-shire)

The gardens lie on the left of the road just after passing the village of Poolewe and are in the care of the National Trust of Scotland. They stand on the edge of Loch Ewe and contain a wide variety of sub-tropical plants, growth made possible by the proximity of the Gulf Stream.

Pool House Hotel (Poolewe), 14 rooms, T272 (B)

The Route

From Kinlochewe a good straight road runs along the edge of Loch Maree before turning inland and climbing through forest and then descending to the shore of Loch Gairloch. This latter stretch of road is narrow with passing places. After leaving Poolewe there is scarcely any habitation for over twenty miles. There are good views of Loch Ewe and the Isle of Ewe, and later the road climbs for a rewarding view of the wide sandy beach of Gruinard Bay. Approaching Dundonnell are the spectacular Ardessie Falls and a fish farm that specializes in the culture of rainbow trout.

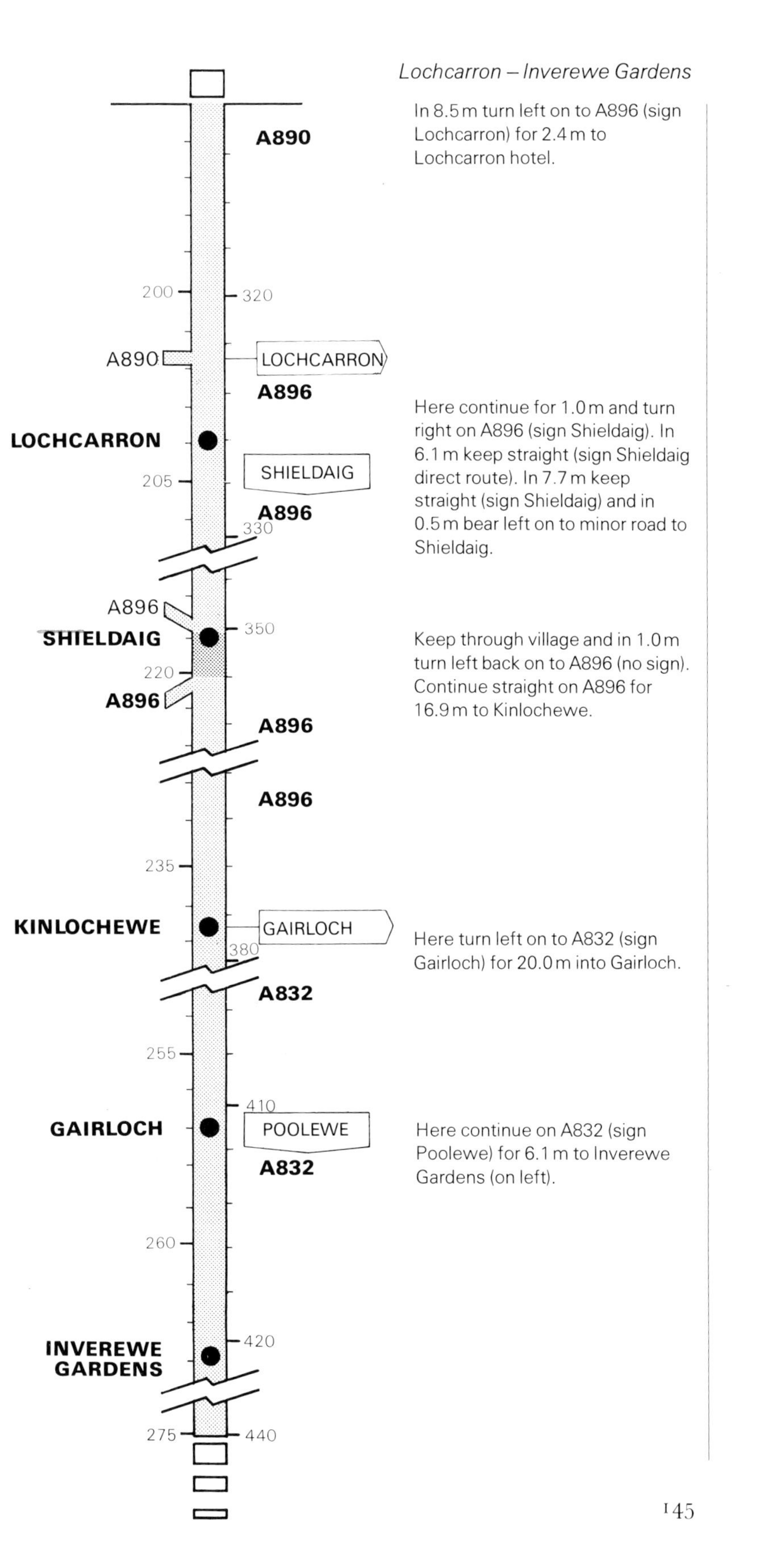

In 8.5 m turn left on to A896 (sign Lochcarron) for 2.4 m to Lochcarron hotel.

Here continue for 1.0 m and turn right on A896 (sign Shieldaig). In 6.1 m keep straight (sign Shieldaig direct route). In 7.7 m keep straight (sign Shieldaig) and in 0.5 m bear left on to minor road to Shieldaig.

Keep through village and in 1.0 m turn left back on to A896 (no sign). Continue straight on A896 for 16.9 m to Kinlochewe.

Here turn left on to A832 (sign Gairloch) for 20.0 m into Gairloch.

Here continue on A832 (sign Poolewe) for 6.1 m to Inverewe Gardens (on left).

Looking up the Corrieshalloch Gorge.

Dundonnell (Ross-shire)

There is little here other than the pleasant hotel that stands to the south-west of Little Loch Broom, a hotel popularized by ramblers and climbers in an area of forests and mountains, among them the nearby Mt Telleach (3,484 ft). At Dundonnell House, only occasionally open to the public, there are some fine gardens and an aviary. An interesting feature of this area is the village of Scoraig, which lies at the extreme western end of the peninsula to the north of Little Loch Broom. There is no road leading to Scoraig, and possibly this inaccessibility was the cause of the virtual extinction of the community there. Some years ago, however, new settlers took over to renovate the houses and take over the role of cattle and sheep farmers practised by earlier inhabitants. This growing community now has its own school but depends on boats for access to the mainland.

Dundonnell Hotel, 26 rooms, T204 (C)

Corrieshalloch Gorge
(Ross-shire)

Just before the A832 connects with the A835, a sign post to the left points to the gorge – a footpath leading down to the suspension bridge. Easier access to the gorge can be made, however, by diverting half a mile off the route along the A835 in the direction of Ullapool. The gorge is 200 feet deep and well worth stopping to see. The best view of the Measach Fall that thunders down into the ravine is from an overhanging platform, where only two people are permitted to stand at a time. The alternative view is from the suspension bridge spanning the gorge, on which only six people are allowed to stand.

Muir of Ord (Ross-shire)

A place of some importance due to the fact that a number of roads converge here. After so many miles of solitude Muir seems a busy place. Industry has sprung up here, and there is a golf course.

Ord House Hotel, 17 rooms, T492 (B)
Ord Arms Hotel, 12 rooms, T286 (B)

The Route

Initially the road runs past the Dundonnell and Braemore forests. There is scarcely any habitation for many miles, one of the first buildings encountered being the Aultguish Inn at the eastern edge of Loch Glascarnoch. This loch, four miles in length, was formed by damning the Glascarnoch river and connects by tunnel with Loch Vaich to the north. The final few miles into Beauly are more built up and less impressive than what came before.

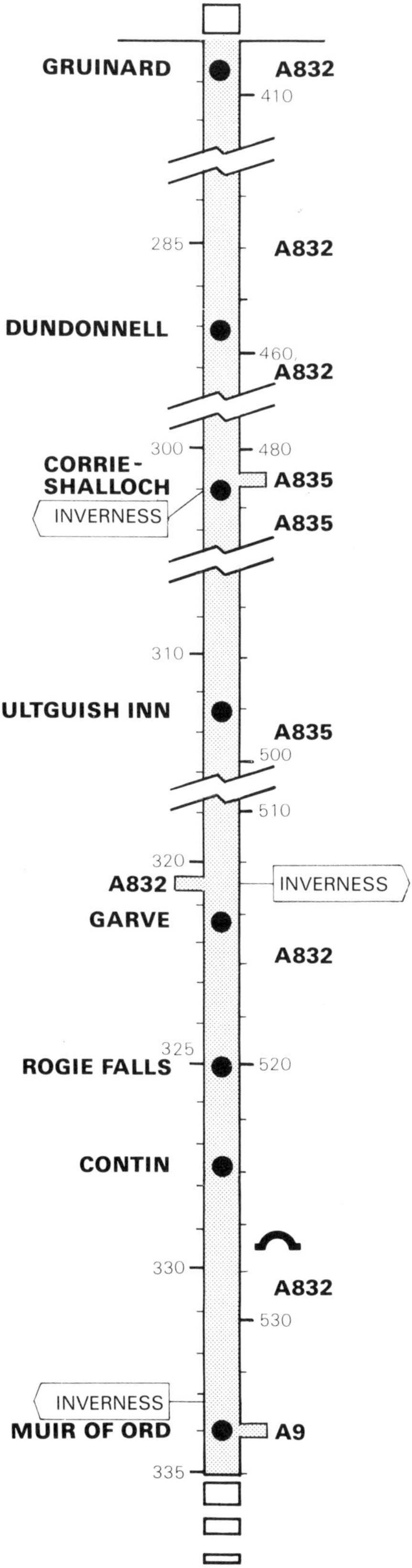

GRUINARD
A832
410
285
A832
DUNDONNELL
460
A832
300
480
CORRIE-
SHALLOCH
A835
INVERNESS
A835
310
AULTGUISH INN
A835
500
510
320
A832
INVERNESS
GARVE
A832
325
ROGIE FALLS
520
CONTIN
330
A832
530
INVERNESS
MUIR OF ORD
A9
335

Remain on A832 for 12.4 m to Gruinard Bay. Keep straight on A832 for further 11.3 m to Dundonnell.

From Dundonnell continue on A832 for 14.0 m and turn right on to A835 (sign Inverness). Keep straight on A835 for 10.4 m to Aultguish Inn and from here continue straight for 9.1 m.

Bear left on to A832 (sign Inverness) for 1.0 m to Garve.

Continue straight on A832 for 5.9 m and at Contin bear right on A832 (sign Inverness). In 1.7 m turn right on A832 over Moy bridge. In 0.7 m at Marybank turn left (sign Inverness) for 4.0 m to Muir of Ord.

Here turn right on to A9 (sign Inverness) for Beauly.

The 19c Inverness Castle, now housing law courts and offices.

Beauly (Inverness-shire)

Beaufort Castle, seat of the Frasers of Lovat, lies to the south of the town (A833). This family has featured prominently in Scottish history since Norman times, and possibly the town's name, Beauly (*beau lieu* – beautiful place), originates from the time of the arrival of the Frasers from France. In the broad main square is a striking war memorial and monument to mark the raising of the Lovat Scouts for service in the South African war by the 16th Lord Lovat who, the inscription explains, 'desired to show that the martial spirit of their forefathers still animates the Highlanders of today and whose confidence justified by the success in the field of the gallant corps whose existence was due to his loyalty and patriotism'. Beauly Priory, founded in 1230, is little more than a ruin, although some beautiful triangular windows are a notable feature of the south wall. Beauly Firth stretches from here to Inverness – and Moray Firth.

Lovat Arms Hotel, 20 rooms, T2313 (D)
Priory Hotel, 12 rooms, T2309 (C)

Inverness (Inverness-shire)

This busy town, capital of the Highlands, lies astride the R. Ness. It has a somewhat complicated one-way traffic system and at times considerable traffic congestion. Inverness Castle, a 19c building on the site of an older one, now houses the law courts and local government offices. At the base of the cross in front of the Town Hall, Bridge St, is a strange stone block known as the Clach-na-Cudainn ('stone of the tubs') – so called because this was where women collecting water from the river used to rest their tubs. The first British Cabinet meeting ever held in Scotland took place inside the Town Hall – an event remembered in the Council Chamber by the framed signatures of Lloyd George's Cabinet.

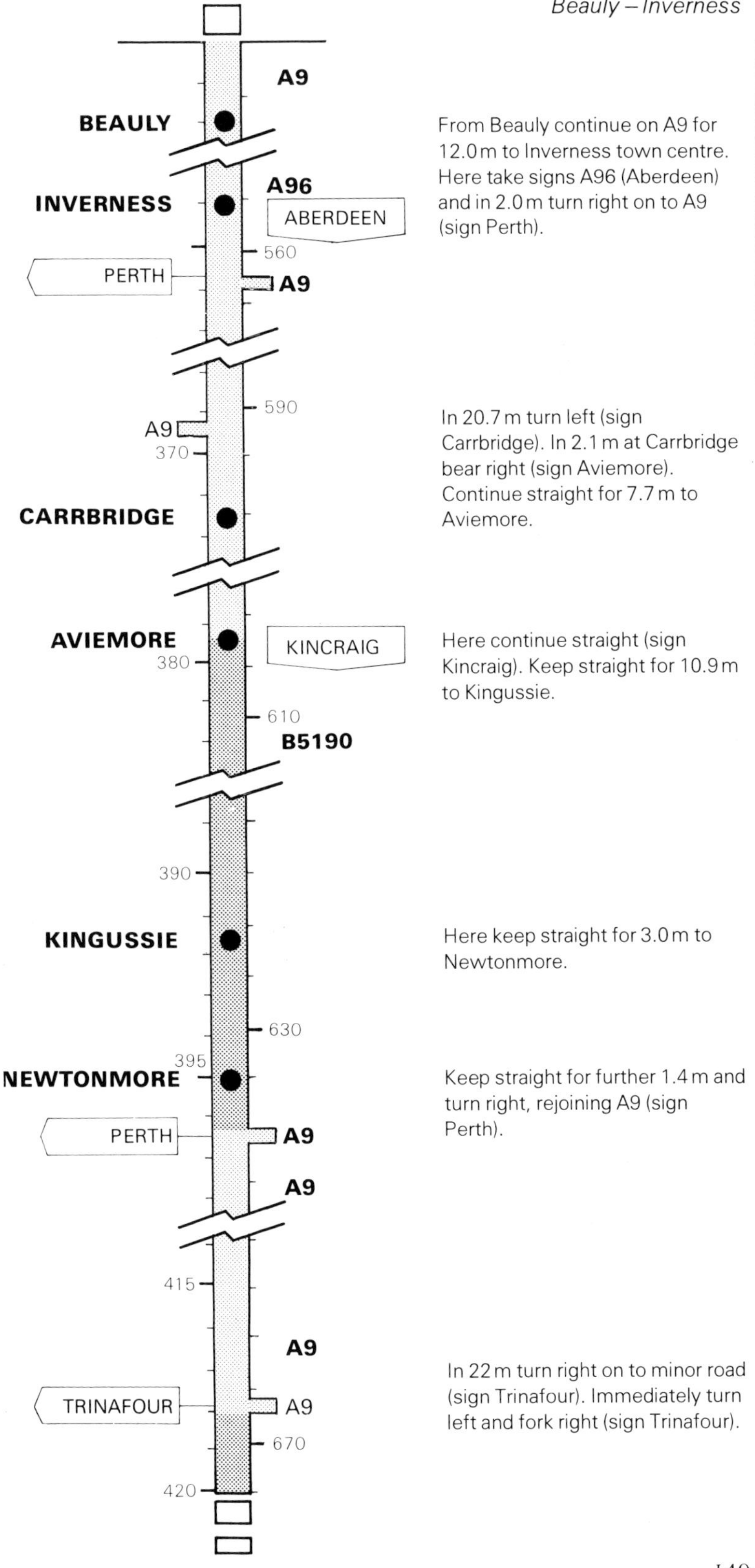

From Beauly continue on A9 for 12.0 m to Inverness town centre. Here take signs A96 (Aberdeen) and in 2.0 m turn right on to A9 (sign Perth).

In 20.7 m turn left (sign Carrbridge). In 2.1 m at Carrbridge bear right (sign Aviemore). Continue straight for 7.7 m to Aviemore.

Here continue straight (sign Kincraig). Keep straight for 10.9 m to Kingussie.

Here keep straight for 3.0 m to Newtonmore.

Keep straight for further 1.4 m and turn right, rejoining A9 (sign Perth).

In 22 m turn right on to minor road (sign Trinafour). Immediately turn left and fork right (sign Trinafour).

Inverness museum houses Jacobite and Highland material.

Caledonian Hotel, Church St, 120 rooms, T35181 (A)
Macdougall Clansman Hotel, Church St, 18 rooms, T31683 (D)
Glen Mhor Hotel, 10 Ness Bank, 32 rooms, T34308 (C)
T.O. 23 Church St, T34353

Carrbridge (Inverness-shire)

Hotels here cater, in the main, for winter skiers in the nearby Cairngorm mountains and for those who wish to explore the Spey valley in the summer. The original bridge across the R. Dulnain was built in 1775 – one of its arches remaining near the existing bridge. Beyond the town, in a pleasant setting of pine trees, is the Landmark Visitors Centre. This modern building includes a multi-vision theatre, where the history of the Highlands gets a frequent showing, and an environment exhibition. A nature trail leads through the pines, and there is a restaurant (specialities salmon and venison).

Carrbridge Hotel, 52 rooms, T202 (C)
Struan House Hotel, 26 rooms, T242 (D)
T.O. T630

The Route

The approaches to Inverness from Beauly are dull, and little is seen of Beauly Firth. on leaving Inverness it was felt best to start southwards for the initial miles on the A9, dual carriageway in some places but well landscaped giving pleasant views. The old road is taken through Carrbridge to Aviemore.

NB Since the completion of the A9 the road signs indicating the road numbers are often misleading.

Aviemore (Inverness-shire)

The town stands at the junction with the A895, which leads eastward to the Glen More Forest Park and the Cairngorm mountain range. The Forest Park, a 3,000-acre of pine and spruce woods together with over 9,000 acres of mountainside, has at its heart Loch Morlich, 1,000 feet above sea level with sandy beaches and bordered by Caledonian pine. The loch is now a water sports centre for sailing, windsurfing etc. Hides have been set up in the park for bird watching, and there is plenty of other wildlife, including reindeer. The Cairngorms make up the largest complex of mountains in the British Isles and include Cairn Gorm to the immediate south of Glen More (4,084 ft); still further south loom the even larger peaks of Ben Macdui (4,300 ft), Braeriach (4,248 ft) and Cairn Toul (4,241 ft). Only Ben Nevis (4,406 ft), near Fort William, is of greater altitude than the Cairngorm peaks, which attract rock and ice climbers, ramblers and winter sports enthusiasts. This area forms part of the Cairngorm Nature Reserve, where birds such as the golden eagle, dotterel and crested tit are to be seen together with wildlife that includes deer, mountain hare and wild cat.

The Aviemore Craft Centre, a new home for traditional Highland crafts.

Aviemore has grown rapidly as a tourist base from which to explore these areas. There are several hotels, and also a centre that includes facilities for skating, curling, ice hockey, dry skiing, squash and swimming in a heated pool. Santa Claus Land with his toy factory is of interest to children, and traditional Highland crafts can be seen at the Craft Centre.

Badenoch Hotel, 77 rooms, T810261 (C)
High Range Hotel, 22 rooms, T810636 (C)
T.O. Main Rd, T810363

Kincraig (Inverness-shire)

The Highland Wild Life Park is signed to the right – about half-way between Aviemore and Kingussie. On view here are animals and birds of the Highlands such as the roaring stag, black highland steer and black cock, together with other creatures, once habitants of the area but now extinct, such as wolf, bear, lynx and sea eagle.

Ossian Hotel, 9 rooms, T242 (C)

Kingussie (Inverness-shire)

Across the R. Spey from Kingussie are Ruthven Barracks, where Government Redcoats were once stationed to keep the Highlanders in check – before they were burned down by the retreating Jacobites prior to Culloden. The Highland Folk Museum includes an exhibition of farming as practised in the Highlands, craft displays, Highland costume and furniture.

Duke of Gordon Hotel, 47 rooms, T302 (C)
Scotts Hotel, 13 rooms, T351 (D)
T.O. King St, T297

Newtonmore (Inverness-shire)

The southernmost of the holiday resorts of Speyside, Newtonmore was once the home of the clan Macpherson. In the clan museum is the Black Chanter used by the piper who played the Macphersons into battle against the Davidsons in 1396, as well as other relics, portraits and documents from the clan's past.

T.O. Perth Rd, T253

The Route

After following the old road south from Aviemore, the A9 is rejoined just past Newtonmore. This road is followed for some 20 miles until the minor road to Trinafour is taken. The road is clearly signed to the right, but care needs to be taken at this point of diversion from the fast-moving traffic. There is a good view of Glen Errochty as the road descends to it from the high moorlands.

Tummel Bridge (Perthshire)

This is one of the forty bridges built by General George Wade (1673–1748), who came to Scotland in 1724 and built a network of roads and bridges in order to improve mobility and thereby contain the rebellious Highlanders. Wade's improvements in this respect are immortalized in the couplet:

Had you seen the roads before they were made
You would lift up your hands and bless General Wade.

The route makes southward across the bridge which crosses the river at the extreme western edge of Loch Tummel. Those with time to spare should note that from here a diversion can be taken along the northern shore of the loch to Pitlochry, returning by a minor road that skirts the southern edge of Loch Tummel. This would add some 30 miles to the route, making a pleasant drive and passing a well-known beauty spot, Queen's View, from where there is a good westward vista of the loch and of the conical peak, Schiehallion (3,547 ft), to the south of it. Some doubt exists as to the origin of the name, Queen's View, though it may spring from a visit made in 1564 by Mary Queen of Scots, who obtained the same panoramic view enjoyed by Queen Victoria almost exactly 300 years later. Nearby is a Forestry Commission information centre where information is provided about walks in the locality.

Coshieville (Perthshire)

There is little here other than the small hotel in pleasant surroundings. A sign from here points to the village of Fortingall – three miles off the route and a place of some interest, for in the churchyard there is a yew tree said to be 3,000 years old. According to legend Fortingall is the birthplace of Pontius Pilate, whose father was then in Scotland as ambassador.

Coshieville Hotel, 7 rooms, T Kenmore 319 (B)

Aberfeldy (Perthshire)

The bridge across the R. Tay is yet another of General Wade's bridges, and at its southern end is a monument to mark the raising of that famous Scottish regiment the Black Watch, so called because the clansmen who were the original members of the regiment wore a black tartan. Before reaching Aberfeldy, at Weem, is Castle Menzies, a huge fortified house which is being restored by the clan Menzies as a clan centre.

Palace Hotel, Breadalbane Terrace, 25 rooms, T359 (C)
Crown Hotel, Bank St, 20 rooms, T448 (D)

Ardeonaig (Perthshire)

Ardeonaig Hotel, 18 rooms, T400 (B)

The Route

Loch Tay, 14½ miles long and famed for its salmon, has parallel roads both to north and south. The chosen route runs along the southern shore — a quieter road than that to the north, with panoramic views of the loch from the wooded hill above it. There is a pleasant hotel at Ardeonaig along this stretch.

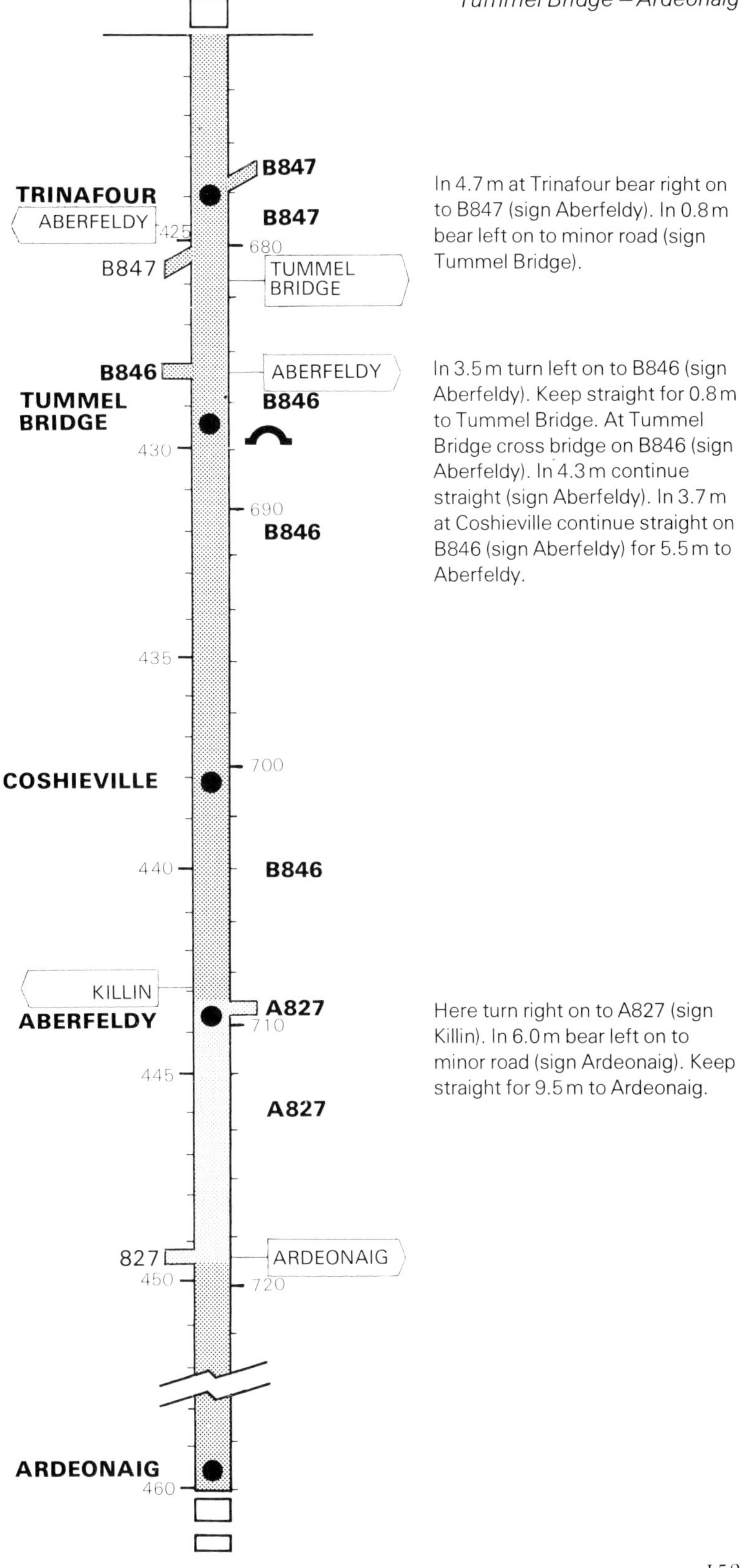

In 4.7 m at Trinafour bear right on to B847 (sign Aberfeldy). In 0.8 m bear left on to minor road (sign Tummel Bridge).

In 3.5 m turn left on to B846 (sign Aberfeldy). Keep straight for 0.8 m to Tummel Bridge. At Tummel Bridge cross bridge on B846 (sign Aberfeldy). In 4.3 m continue straight (sign Aberfeldy). In 3.7 m at Coshieville continue straight on B846 (sign Aberfeldy) for 5.5 m to Aberfeldy.

Here turn right on to A827 (sign Killin). In 6.0 m bear left on to minor road (sign Ardeonaig). Keep straight for 9.5 m to Ardeonaig.

Killin (Perthshire)

Lies at the extreme western end of Loch Tay with mountains in every direction, among them Ben Lawers (3,984 ft) to the north of the loch, with a mountain visitors centre nearby. The R. Dochart, renowned for salmon and trout fishing, cascades rapidly at the edge of the town to a point known as the Falls of Dochart.

Killin Hotel, 31 rooms, T296 (C)
Falls of Dochart Hotel, 8 rooms, T237 (D)

Crianlarich (Perthshire)

The village stands at an important road and rail junction.

Crianlarich Hotel, 31 rooms, T272 (D)

Ardlui (Dunbartonshire)

The hamlet lies at the northern tip of Loch Lomond, Britain's largest stretch of inland water where the 'bonny banks and braes' have been favourite subjects for poets and artists over centuries. Loch Lomond is twenty-four miles in length, north to south, and although at this point it is narrow (about ½ mile), it broadens further south to about five miles. The road follows the western shore of the loch, on the other side of which is the Queen Elizabeth Forest Park and Ben Lomond (3,192 ft). Another place of interest on the far shore at the northern end of Loch Lomond is Rob Roy's Cave – hideaway for Scott's hero. Spread around the southern part of the loch are some thirty islands, the largest of these being Inchmurrin (Isle of the Spears), where the Duchess of Albany retired to Lennox Castle after the execution of her husband by James I in 1425. A steamer can be taken from Balloch at the south of Loch Lomond for cruises around the islands.

Ardlui Hotel, ll rooms, T Inveruglas 243 (C)

Glen Falloch, on the road to Ardlui.

Tarbet (Dunbartonshire)

Good views of the loch from the village, where some of the houses are the property of those working on the Sloy hydro-electric scheme.

Tarbet Hotel, 81 rooms, T Arrochar 222 (B)

Luss (Dunbartonshire)

Has a picturesque setting at a broad point of Loch Lomond, with views of the wooded islands and Ben Lomond.

Colquhoun Arms, 23 rooms, T225 (C)

The Route

The road between Crianlarich and Ardlui runs through beautiful Glen Falloch, with Ben Glas (2,037 ft) and the Falls of Falloch to the east and Troisgeach (2,407 ft) to the west. After following Loch Lomond for the greater part of its length, the road turns westward towards Helensburgh, passing the entrance to Glen Fruin. It was in this glen in 1603 that 200 members of the Colquhoun clan were massacred by the MacGregors — resulting in the latter clan being outlawed by James VI, a state of affairs which subsequently formed the background for Scott's Rob Roy.

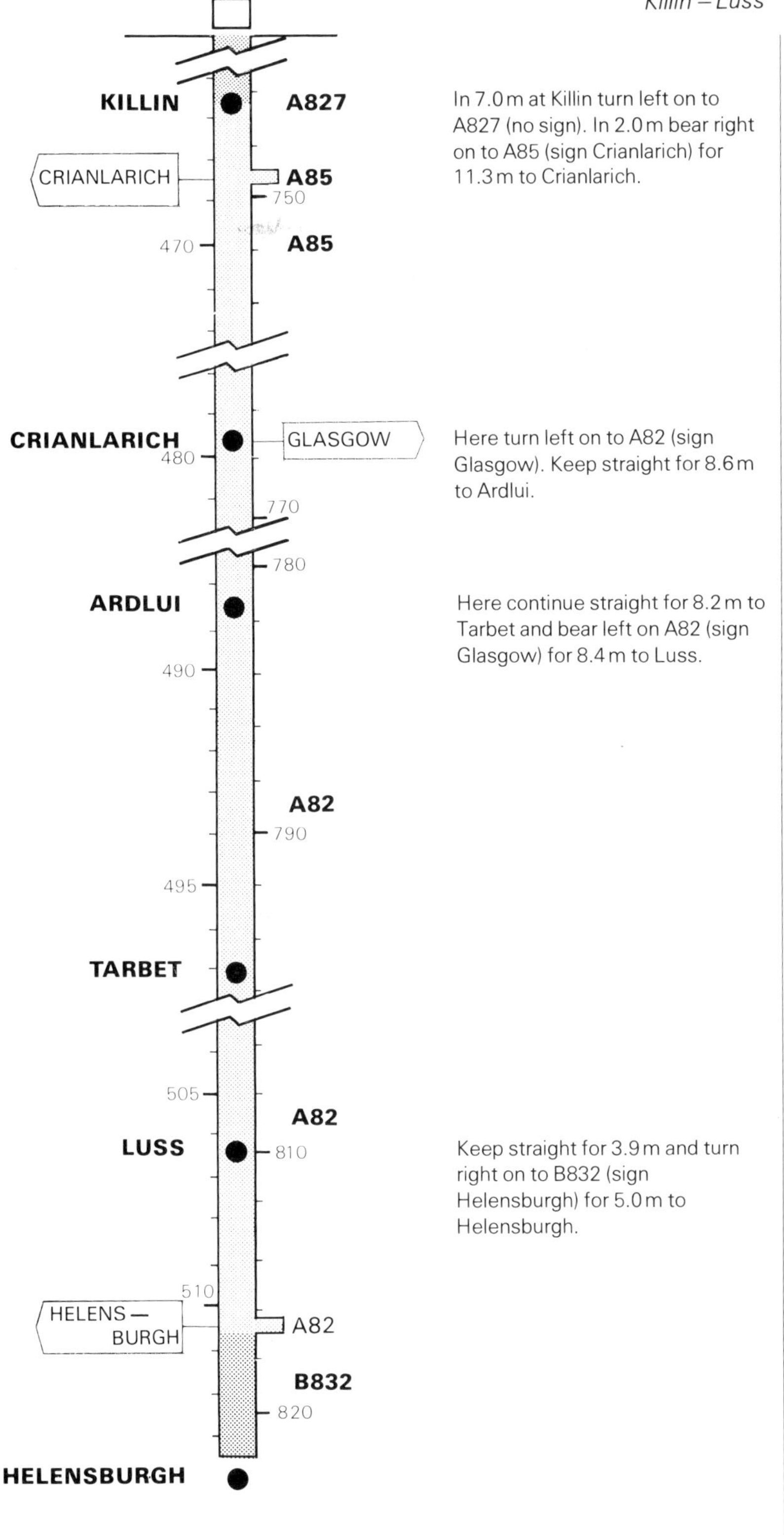

In 7.0 m at Killin turn left on to A827 (no sign). In 2.0 m bear right on to A85 (sign Crianlarich) for 11.3 m to Crianlarich.

Here turn left on to A82 (sign Glasgow). Keep straight for 8.6 m to Ardlui.

Here continue straight for 8.2 m to Tarbet and bear left on A82 (sign Glasgow) for 8.4 m to Luss.

Keep straight for 3.9 m and turn right on to B832 (sign Helensburgh) for 5.0 m to Helensburgh.

9 *Yorkshire: the Wolds, the Coast, the Moors*

THIS ROUTE, starting from the city of York, embraces country which, in the main, occupies the eastern part of the county of Yorkshire – as opposed to Route 2 which wends its way westward from York towards the Dales.

Until the Local Government Act of 1972 took effect Yorkshire was by far the largest county in England, covering some six thousand square miles where about one tenth of the total population of the country lived. Prior to the Act Yorkshire was split, quite simply, into the three Ridings – North, West and East, stretching from Middlesbrough in the north to Sheffield and Hull in the south. After the Act, however, parts of these areas were hived off into the new counties of Humberside and Cleveland, as well as into Lancashire and Cumbria.

York with its museums, churches, well preserved city walls and above all its Minster, the largest medieval church in Europe, makes a good starting-point. From the city the route runs south-eastward to Beverley, formerly capital of the East Riding but now part of Humberside. Its Minster is considered one of the finest churches in Europe and nearby is a church of almost equal splendour – St Mary's. From Beverley the route returns northwards through the rolling Wolds which two hundred years ago, as the name implies, consisted of uncultivated land supporting sheep and little else, but where subsequently, thanks to the Sykes family of Sledmere, huge areas were transformed to yield some of the most productive land in the county.

After passing through the beautiful Forge valley the road reaches the coast at Robin Hood's Bay and Whitby. At this point, if time permits, it would be worth diverting northward on the A174 to visit the attractive coastal villages of Runswick and Staithes. From the coast the road turns inland towards the North Yorkshire Moors, one of Yorkshire's two National Parks (for the Yorkshire Dales National Park see Route 2). The remote heather-clad moorlands contain many hidden valleys, the route passing through the area from east to west before turning southward and following the course of the rivers Seph and Rye to Rievaulx Abbey, set in an enchanting glen. From the Abbey the road continues southward towards the plains around York by way of one of the county's most beautiful towns, Helmsley, and the entrancing village of Hovingham.

Mention is made in the text of that famous explorer, Captain James Cook. But Yorkshire has claim to countless distinguished men and women in the widest variety of fields. No discussion of Yorkshire would be complete without reference to those whose writing has captured the scenery and lifestyle of the county – novelists from the Brontës to Winifred Holtby and J. B. Priestley. Nor should it be forgotten that cricket is Yorkshire's favourite traditional sport – a sport which conjures up the names of local heroes such as Rhodes, Sutcliffe, Verity, Hutton, Trueman and Boycott, to mention but a few.

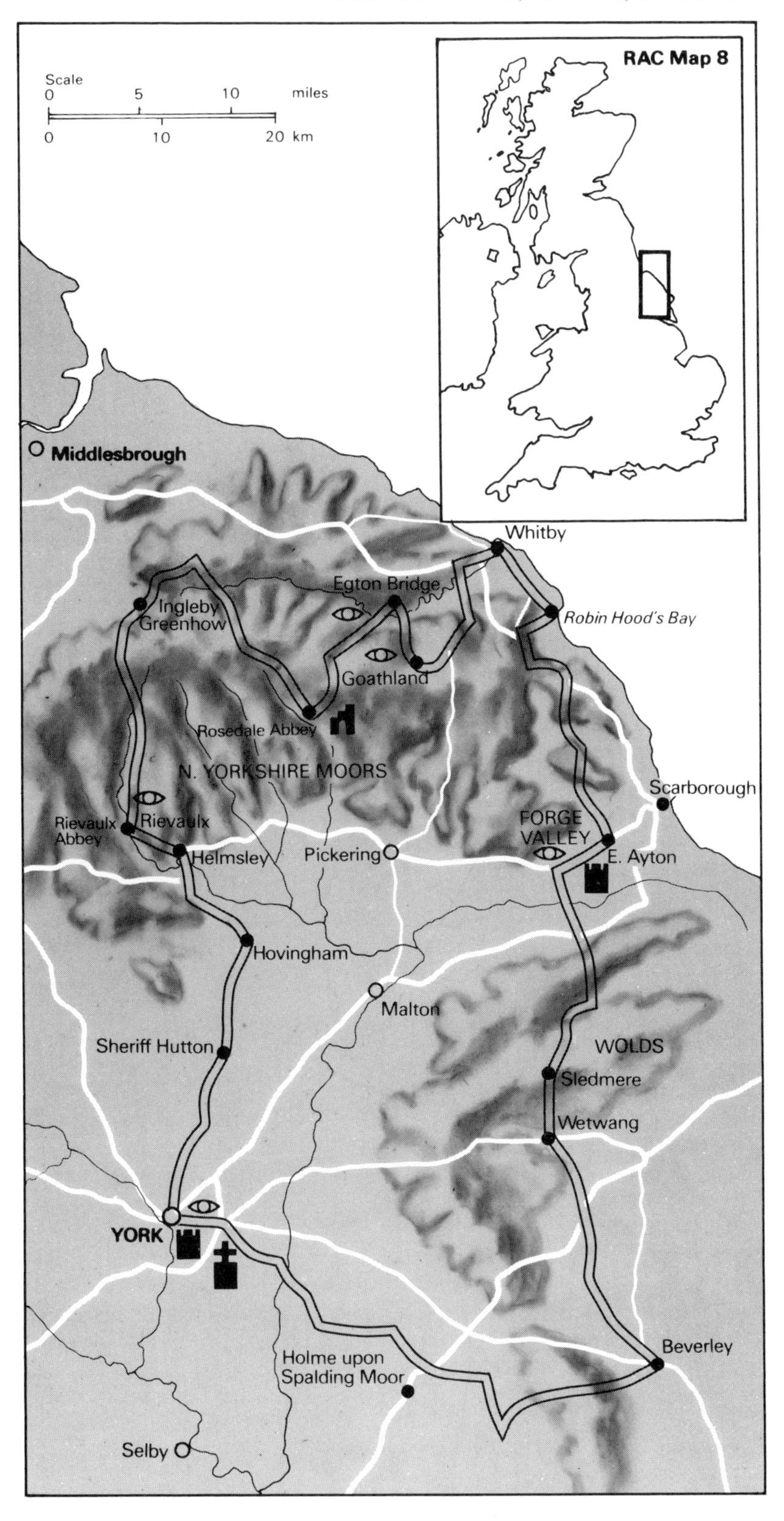
RAC Map 8
Scale
0 5 10 miles
0 10 20 km
Middlesbrough
Whitby
Egton Bridge
Robin Hood's Bay
Ingleby Greenhow
Goathland
Rosedale Abbey
N. YORKSHIRE MOORS
Scarborough
FORGE VALLEY
Rievaulx Abbey
Rievaulx
Helmsley
Pickering
E. Ayton
Hovingham
Malton
Sheriff Hutton
WOLDS
Sledmere
Wetwang
YORK
Beverley
Holme upon Spalding Moor
Selby

York (N. Yorks)

The city of York needs to be seen on foot, and there can be few better ways of getting an overall view than taking the 2½-mile walk along the top of the 14c city walls. In spring there is a dazzling display of tulips and daffodils beneath the walls, the ascent to which can be made at the various entrance gates or 'bars'. Among these are Micklegate Bar, the gruesome place where the heads of traitors used to be displayed after execution; and Bootham Bar, the northern gate, which once acted as the main defensive bulwark against attacks from the North.

York's prize possession is the Cathedral known as York Minster, where in 627 the first Christian king of Northumbria was baptized. The existing Cathedral, the fifth on the site, was reconsecrated in 1472 after 250 years of labour, and from that time few structural changes were necessary. No city in England can match the quantity of medieval stained glass that York possesses. In the Minster alone there are 128 windows which include the Great East Window and the Five Sisters Window, made of 100,000 pieces of glass.

Clifford's Tower, the remaining tower of the castle built by the Conqueror in 1068, stands on a green mound overlooking Castle Museum. This museum occupies what were once the female and the debtors' prisons, and in it can be seen three entire period streets lined with shops, inn, and fire station. Throughout the city there are fascinating narrow streets such as the Shambles and Stonegate with shops which have barely changed since medieval days; and near the Shambles is York's shortest street, Whip-Ma-Whop-Ma Gate, so called because it was here that delinquents were publicly flogged. York has more churches than anywhere in England apart from London and Norwich, and among other buildings of note are St William's College, Merchant Taylors' Hall and Merchant Adventurers' Hall.

Abbey Park Hotel, The Mount, 83 rooms, T25481 (B)
Beechwood Close Hotel, Shipton Rd, 12 rooms, T58378 (C)
Sheppard Hotel, 63 The Mount, 22 rooms, T20500 (C)
YHA, Haverford, Water End, Clifton, T53147.
'Tigga' Restaurant, 45 Goodramgate, T33787
(This specializes in the traditional Yorkshire Pudding.)
T.O. De Grey Rooms, Exhibition Square, T21756

Elvington (N. Yorks)

Although modern houses have sprung up around the approach to the village, there are pleasant old buildings near the R. Derwent where a narrow one-way bridge links Elvington with Sutton.

Everingham (N. Yorks)

This quiet village lies near the manor and wooded park, property of the Duke of Norfolk, which can be seen on the left as the road approaches the next village on the route, Harswell.

Hotham (N. Yorks)

Another fine wooded park lies to the south of the village. At the end of the village street, on the right, is the little red-roofed church fronted by some magnificent elm trees.

Walkington (N. Humberside)

The village is larger than any of those passed since leaving York and the cross-shaped church is signed off to the right (about ¼-mile and worth diverting to see) opposite an attractive old inn, The Dog and Duck. Further into the village, on the left, is a duck-pond shaded by colourful trees.

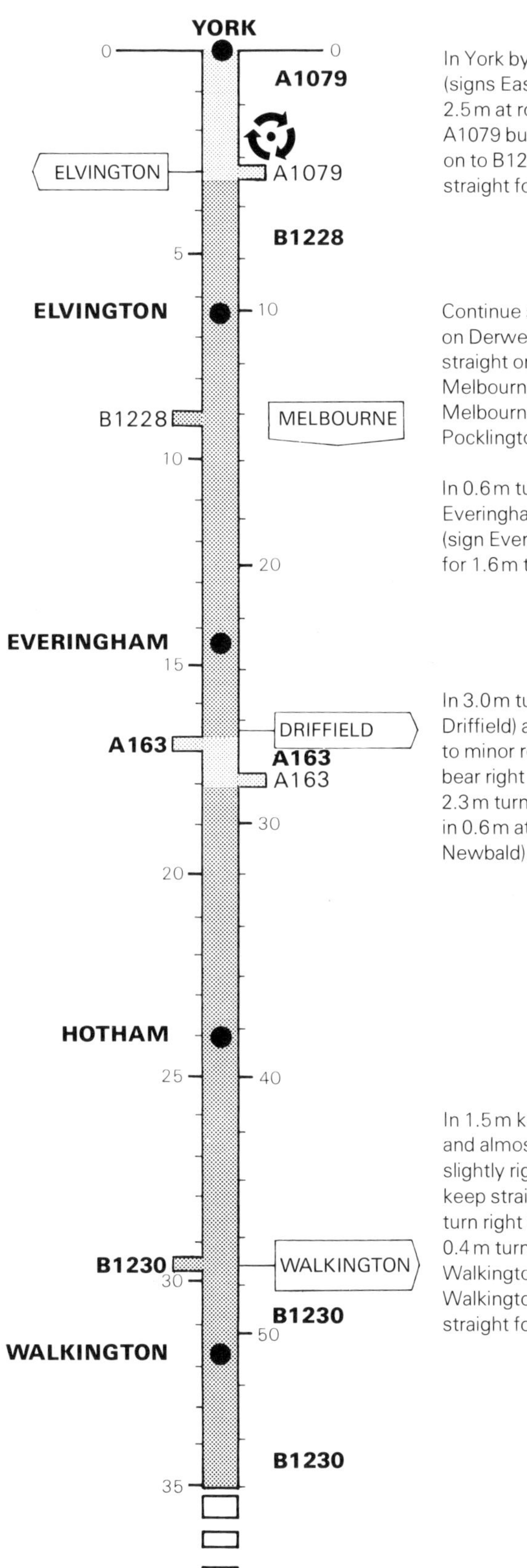

In York by City Wall take A1079 (signs East Coast and Hull). In 2.5 m at roundabout continue on A1079 but immediately turn right on to B1228 (sign Elvington). Keep straight for 4.2 m to Elvington.

Continue straight through Sutton on Derwent and in 2.2 m keep straight on to minor road (sign Melbourne). In 1.7 m at Melbourne keep straight (sign Pocklington).

In 0.6 m turn right (sign Everingham) and in 1.4 m bear left (sign Everingham). Keep straight for 1.6 m to Everingham.

In 3.0 m turn left on to A163 (sign Driffield) and in 0.6 m turn right on to minor road (no sign). In 3.1 m bear right (sign North Cave). In 2.3 m turn left (sign Hotham) and in 0.6 m at Hotham turn left (sign Newbald).

In 1.5 m keep straight (no sign) and almost immediately continue slightly right (no sign). In 2.2 m keep straight (no sign). In 1.9 m turn right (sign Walkington) and in 0.4 m turn left on to B1230 (sign Walkington) for 1.8 m to Walkington. Here continue straight for 4.0 m into Beverley.

The Route

One or two sections of the road between Hotham and Walkington are narrow and rough in parts. The final stretch from Beverley northward is straight, sparsely habitated and somewhat featureless. Very little traffic encountered throughout.

Beverley (N. Humberside)

A market town with many fine Georgian houses and a large market square known as Saturday Market, which is graced by a fine octagonal market cross (1714). Beverley is famed not only for the Minster, built between 1200 and 1400 and considered one of the most beautiful churches in Europe, but also for St Mary's Church which lies half a mile away. The pride of St Mary's is the West Front (15c), possibly the inspiration for King's College Chapel, Cambridge, erected some eighty years later.

Beverley Arms Hotel, North Bar Within, 61 rooms, T885241 (A)
T.O. The Hall, Lairgate, T882255

Wetwang (N. Humberside)

The route crosses the major road along which this bleak village of the Wolds straggles. Here Vikings once lived, and graves of Ancient Britons have also been discovered around the village.

Sledmere (N. Humberside)

The village lies in the heart of the Wolds, and the road has climbed sharply to enter it, for it lies 400 feet above sea level. Some of the best agricultural land in the country is to be found in these parts – and this reclamation of an area which at one time yielded little is to the credit of the Sykes family of Sledmere House. This Georgian manor, burnt in 1911 but rebuilt in the same style, lies in a beautiful park laid out by Capability Brown, and both park and house are open to the public on specified occasions. Sledmere, though a tiny place, is well endowed with monuments, notably the fascinating Waggoners' Monument, designed by Sir Mark Sykes, who had raised a company of 1,200 men of the Wolds for service in the First World War. The engraved figures of the volunteers, form a pictorial history.

Weaverthorpe (N. Humberside)

The village lies in a sheltered valley of the Wolds astride a little stream, the Gypsy Race. High on the hill, the church with its Norman tower overlooks the snug little village beneath.

Brompton (N. Yorks)

The church here was the marriage place of William Wordsworth and his bride, Mary Hutchinson. Sir George Cayley (1773–1857), who lived at Brompton Hall, is known as the 'father' of aeronautics. He built his first glider in 1804, and experimented with it on the Yorkshire moors – to the alarm of his valet, who was expected to accompany him.

Wykeham (N. Yorks)

The churchyard is entered by passing under a tower, formerly part of a much older chapel. Much of the wood carving in the church was undertaken by Robert Thompson, known as the 'mouseman' of Kilburn, whose work is identifiable because it always included the engraved figure of a mouse.

Downe Arms Hotel, 9 rooms, T Scarborough 862471 (C)

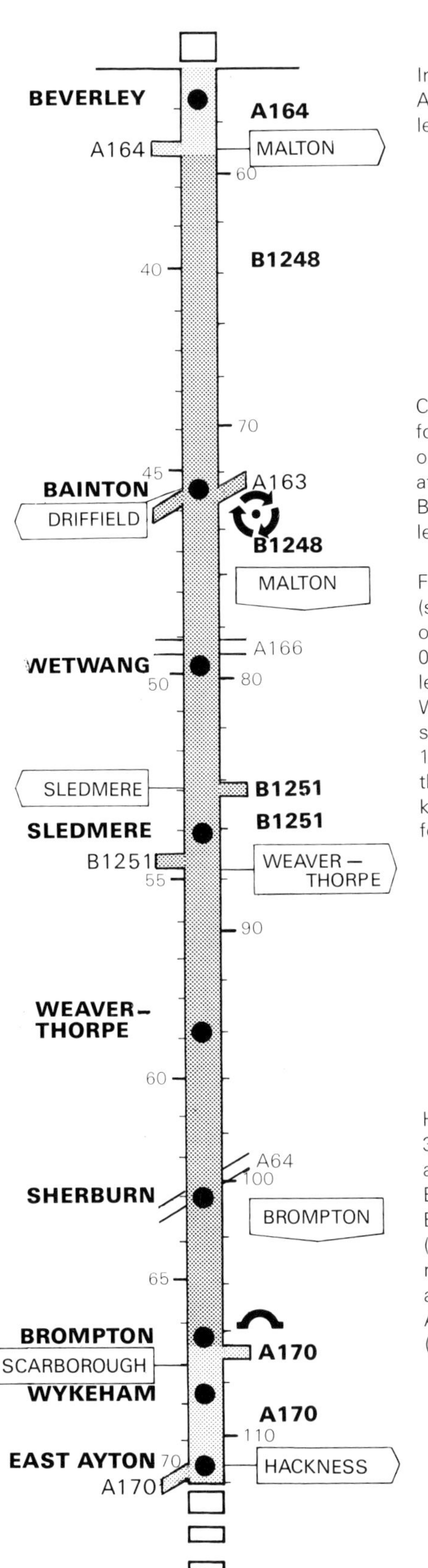

In Beverley town centre take A164 (sign Driffield). In 1.2 m bear left on to B1248 (sign Malton).

Continue on B1248 (signs Malton) for 8.7 m to Bainton and turn right on to A163 (sign Driffield). In 0.9 m at roundabout keep straight on B1248 (sign Malton). In 4.3 m turn left into Wetwang.

From Wetwang take minor road (sign Sledmere). In 3.1 m turn right on to B1251 (sign Sledmere for 0.9 m into Sledmere. Here turn left on to minor road (sign Weaverthorpe). In 2.2 m keep straight (sign Helperthorpe). In 1.2 m turn right (sign Helperthorpe). In 0.5 m at Helperthorpe keep straight (sign Weaverthorpe) for 0.7 m to Weaverthorpe.

Here turn left (sign Sherburn). In 3.9 m at Sherburn keep straight across A64 on to minor road (sign Brompton). In 3.4 m, entering Brompton, bear left across bridge (sign Scarborough). In 0.2 m turn right on to A170 (sign Scarborough) and continue for 3.4 m. At East Ayton turn left on to minor road (sign Hackness).

Above: *A roofscape at Robin Hood's Bay.*
Right: *The Cleveland Hills.*

East Ayton (N. Yorks)

The busy little villages of East and West Ayton are joined by a bridge across the R. Derwent. On a hill in the fields above West Ayton are the ruins of a 14c castle, once the home of the Evers family; while East Ayton can boast a 13c church.

Hackness (N. Yorks)

Occupies a beautiful position in the Forge valley to the east of the Derwent with forests on every side. Hackness Hall, seat of the Lord Derwent, was built in 1795 and lies in the midst of fine gardens and lake.

The Route

From Wetwang to Brompton the road undulates through the heart of the Wolds. On arrival at East Ayton the road turns due north by way of the beautiful Forge valley and through the Wykeham, Brosca and Harwood forests before reaching the moors above Robin Hood's Bay. The road down to the bay is as steep as 1 in 4 in places.

Robin Hood's Bay (N. Yorks)

Houses cling precariously to the cliffs over the bay. Until recently the chief occupation of this picturesque village, founded in the 15c, was fishing. Less than a century ago one of Yorkshire's largest fishing communities lived here, with 174 registered ships. Nobody knows the origin of the name, though some say that the Abbot of Whitby invited Robin to lend a hand in defence against the Danish pirates who constantly raided these shores.

Grosvenor Hotel, Station Rd, 15 rooms, T320 (C)
Victoria Hotel, Station Rd, 15 rooms, T205 (C)

Whitby (N. Yorks)

The ruins of the famous Whitby Abbey, standing high on the cliff-top and dominating the town, are signed off to the right before entering the town. 'The haven under the hill', as the town is sometimes called, is still a port and fishing town – though less important than formerly. (In 1828 it ranked as England's seventh port, with four hundred registered ships.) On West Cliff, connected to the harbour by a cutting through sheer rock known as the 'Khyber Pass', there is an impressive bronze statue of Captain James Cook (1728–79). Having lodged at Grape Lane, studying mathematics and navigation, in a house which can still be seen, Cook later took command of the Whitby ship *Endeavour*, in which he explored the New Zealand and Australian coasts as well as theSeas.

In recent years Whitby has become a popular tourist attraction and in the summer it might be best to seek accommodation inland.

Royal Hotel, West Cliff, 135 rooms, T2234 (B)
Marvic Hotel, White Point Rd, 29 rooms, T2400 (C)
YHA, East Cliff, T2878
T.O. New Quay Rd, T2674

The Route

After reaching Goathland the route runs through the heart of the North Yorkshire Moors, alternating between high remote moorland with fine views and peaceful valleys of the Esk and Severn.

Whitby Abbey, perched above the sea.

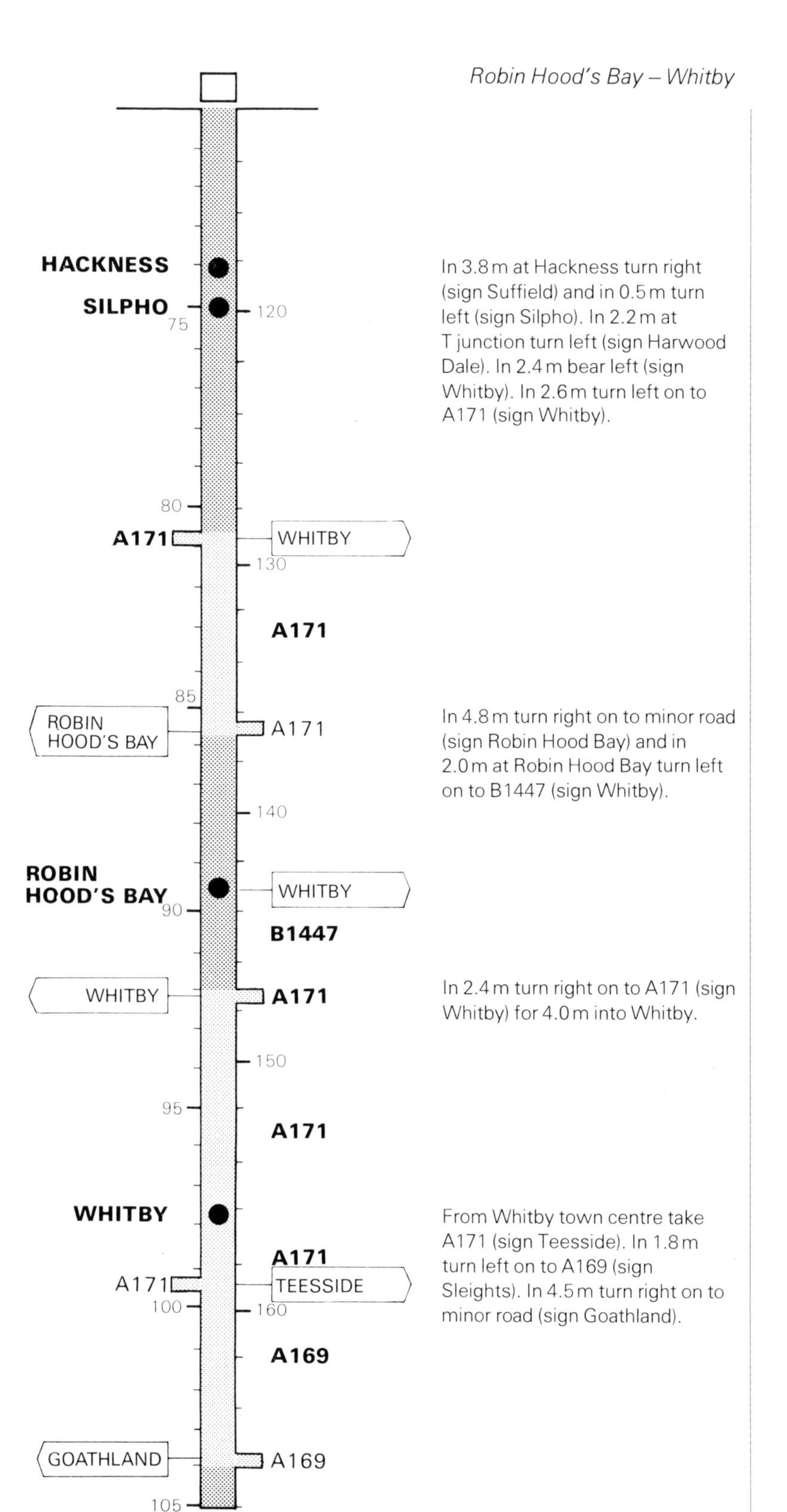

In 3.8 m at Hackness turn right (sign Suffield) and in 0.5 m turn left (sign Silpho). In 2.2 m at T junction turn left (sign Harwood Dale). In 2.4 m bear left (sign Whitby). In 2.6 m turn left on to A171 (sign Whitby).

In 4.8 m turn right on to minor road (sign Robin Hood Bay) and in 2.0 m at Robin Hood Bay turn left on to B1447 (sign Whitby).

In 2.4 m turn right on to A171 (sign Whitby) for 4.0 m into Whitby.

From Whitby town centre take A171 (sign Teesside). In 1.8 m turn left on to A169 (sign Sleights). In 4.5 m turn right on to minor road (sign Goathland).

Rosedale, seen from Blakey Ridge.

Goathland (N. Yorks)

The village lies high up in the moors, its buildings dotted around common land where sheep graze – and the church of St Mary, though comparatively modern, fits pleasantly into the scene. From Goathland there are fine moorland walks, and footpaths lead to a number of waterfalls with romantic names such as Mallyan Spout and Nelly Ayre Force.

Goathland Hydro, 33 rooms, T296 (B)
Mallyan Spout Hotel, 24 rooms, T206 (B)

Egton Bridge (N. Yorks)

The road just touches this leafy glade on the fringe of the Arncliffe woods. Near here lived the last of the English martyrs, Fr Nicholas Postgate, hanged in 1679 at the age of eighty-three for baptizing a child.

Rosedale Abbey (N. Yorks)

All that can be seen of the original Abbey (a Cistercian priory) is the tower to the west of the church. The village lies in a peaceful green valley – in contrast to the bleak moors to the north through which the route passes. High up on these moors, to the left of the road, is Ralph's Cross. It is said that Prioress Elizabeth of Rosedale set off for Westerdale to meet a delegation from that village, and both parties got lost in moorland fog – which in these parts comes as quickly as it goes. Suddenly the clouds lifted and the Prioress found the folk from Westerdale were standing nearby – at the point now marked by the cross. The village lies in the heart of the North Yorkshire Moors Park, a good place in which to stay and explore.

Milburn Arms Hotel, 8 rooms, T Lastingham 312 (C)
White Horse Hotel, 8 rooms, T Lastingham 239 (C)

Westerdale (N. Yorks)

Close to the village, near the R. Esk, is a pleasant youth hostel. Only a mile or two to the north (just off the route) is the pretty village of Castleton, with the Robin Hood Inn which dates from 1671.

YHA, Westerdale Hall, T469

Ingleby Greenhow (N. Yorks)

There is an inn but nowhere to stay in this small village which nestles in a valley by the R. Leven beneath the Cleveland Hills. High on Easby Moor, to the north-west, is an obelisk which can be seen from the village – another memorial to Captain James Cook. He was brought up by his mother and schooled at Great Ayton, a few miles away, where an obelisk marks the site of the family house – shipped brick by brick to Australia in 1934. In the churchyard Cook's mother and five of his brothers and sisters lie buried.

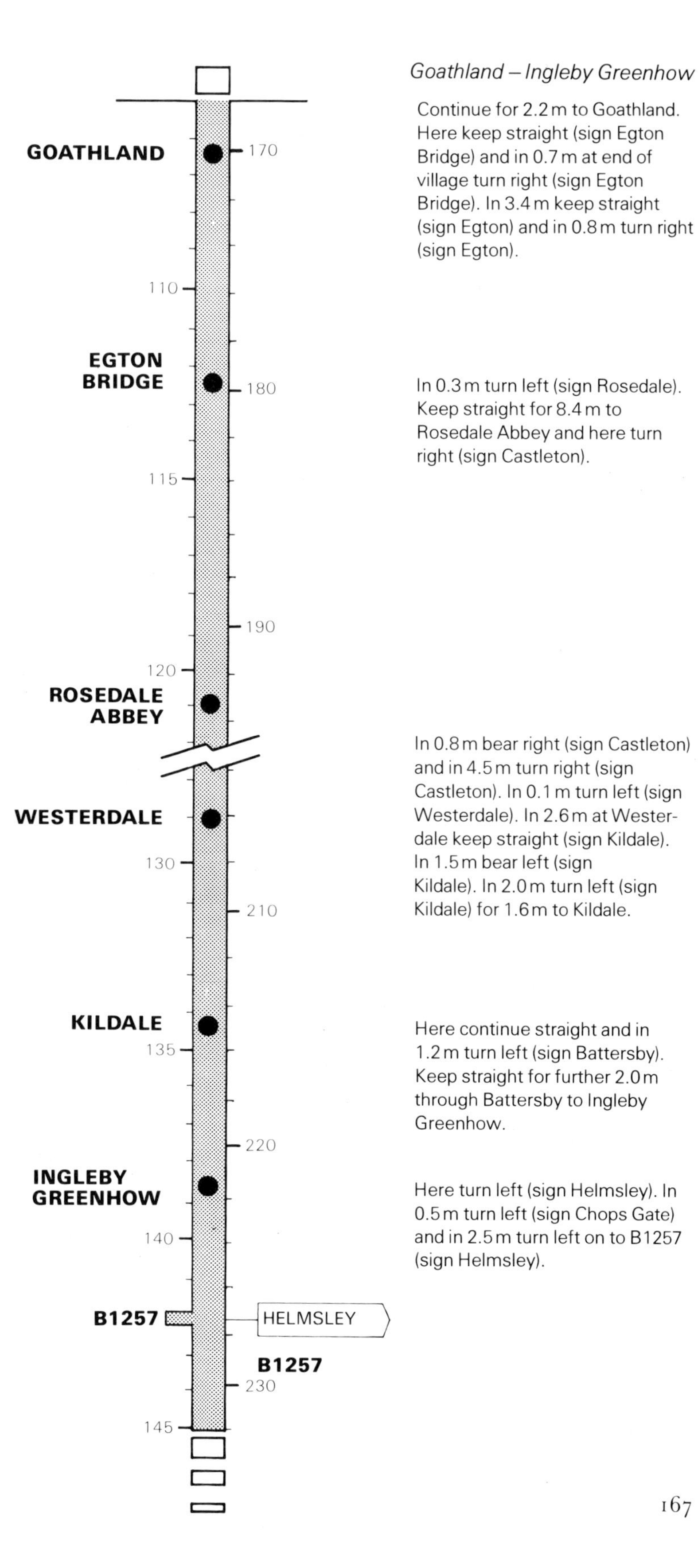

Continue for 2.2 m to Goathland. Here keep straight (sign Egton Bridge) and in 0.7 m at end of village turn right (sign Egton Bridge). In 3.4 m keep straight (sign Egton) and in 0.8 m turn right (sign Egton).

In 0.3 m turn left (sign Rosedale). Keep straight for 8.4 m to Rosedale Abbey and here turn right (sign Castleton).

In 0.8 m bear right (sign Castleton) and in 4.5 m turn right (sign Castleton). In 0.1 m turn left (sign Westerdale). In 2.6 m at Westerdale keep straight (sign Kildale). In 1.5 m bear left (sign Kildale). In 2.0 m turn left (sign Kildale) for 1.6 m to Kildale.

Here continue straight and in 1.2 m turn left (sign Battersby). Keep straight for further 2.0 m through Battersby to Ingleby Greenhow.

Here turn left (sign Helmsley). In 0.5 m turn left (sign Chops Gate) and in 2.5 m turn left on to B1257 (sign Helmsley).

Rievaulx (N. Yorks)

The ruins of the Cistercian Abbey, founded in 1131, stand just beyond the little village of stone houses in a beautiful tree-clad glen by the R. Rye. The narrowness of the valley site meant that it was found necessary to erect the Abbey lengthwise from north to south. Few abbeys in England occupy such a heavenly place and it is small wonder that artists like J. M. W. Turner painted it and that it was treasured by poets such as Cowper, who wished he could live there forever, 'just for the sight of it'. The finest view of the ruins as a whole is from the terrace above, half a mile long and with classic 18c temples at each end. The terrace stands high above the valley and is signed where the minor road descends from the B1257.

Helmsley (N. Yorks)

At the time of the Conqueror this was an area of dense forests where wild beasts roamed, and it was not until an enterprising soul named Helm uprooted a section of the trees that his clearing in the forest gave space for the market town named after him. Pleasant vine-clad buildings surround the square of this compact little town. The parish church is tucked back from one corner of the square with a black-and-white Tudor house at the church gate, once the vicarage but now part of the Black Swan Hotel. The Earls of Feversham are descended from the Duncombe family who in 1699 bought Helmsley and developed the park in which the ruins of Helmsley Castle stand. The castle ruins, entered by crossing wooden foot bridges over the two defensive ditches, surround well-tended lawns. The older parts of the castle are the keep (12c) and the west tower of the main building (14c). Unhappily the year 1644 marked the end of the castle as a defensive stronghold, for after Sir Thomas Fairfax had captured it from the Royalists it was demolished on the orders of Cromwell. Later in the century the Duke of Buckingham carried out some repairs, but on his death the building fell into disuse.

Black Swan Hotel, Market Place, 38 rooms, T557 (A)
Feathers Hotel, Market Place, 24 rooms, T275 (C)
YHA, Carlton Lane, T433

Hovingham (N. Yorks)

Hovingham Hall occupies a central position in this village of sturdy stone cottages with flower gardens which are a pleasure to behold. The Hall, built and designed in 1760 by Sir Thomas Worsley, friend of George III, is not open to the public and at present is the home of Sir William Worsley, father of the Duchess of Kent. Within the Hall boundaries, however, is a cricket ground used by the village cricket team, and musical festivals take place in a concert hall which forms part of the main entrance to the Hall. Important Roman remains including a bath house have been excavated in and around the grounds of the Hall.

Worsley Arms Hotel, 14 rooms, T234 (B)

Sheriff Hutton (N. Yorks)

The tall remnants of the castle stand in farm land and can be reached by footpaths on the left of the road through the village. The castle gets its name from a sheriff of Yorkshire who built it in the 12c. Two hundred years later the original building was replaced and was at one time the home of Warwick the King-Maker (1428–71).

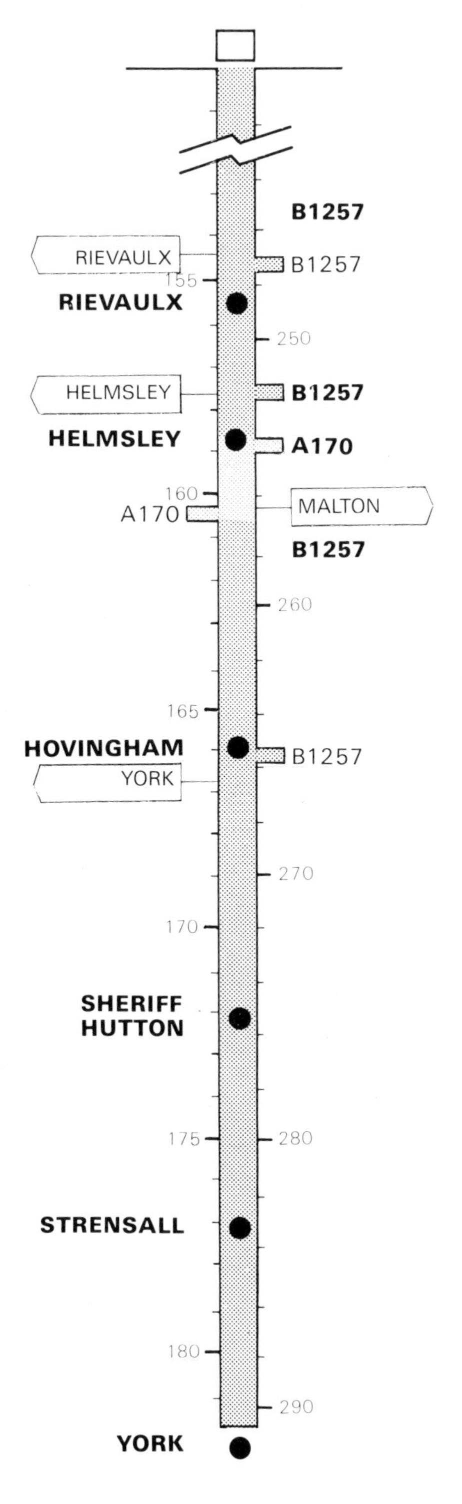

In 12.9 m turn right on to minor road (sign Rievaulx). In 0.6 m at Abbey car park continue straight and in 0.3 m turn left (sign Helmsley). In 1.3 m turn right on to B1257 (sign Helmsley) for further 1.3 m to Helmsley.

Here take A170 (sign York). In 1.4 m bear left on to B1257 (sign Malton). In 2.0 m keep straight on B1257 (sign Malton).

In 4.4 m at end of Hovingham turn right on to minor road (sign York). In 3.2 m turn right (sign York). In 3.0 m at Sheriff Hutton continue straight (sign York).

In 4.0 m at Strensall turn right (sign York). Continue on minor road (signs York) for further 6.0 m to York.

The Route

The road runs north to south through the North Yorkshire Moors National Park until it reaches Helmsley. Pleasant wooded country from Helmsley to Sheriff Hutton, but the last few miles into York are flat and featureless.

Top: *York Minster from the city walls.*
Above: *St William's College, York.*
Right: *Rievaulx Abbey.*

10 *The North-East: Durham, Northumberland*

The Pennine town of Alston, over a thousand feet above sea level.

THE GREATER PART of this 275-mile route is confined to the counties of Durham and Northumberland. However the starting town, Richmond, is in North Yorkshire, and because the Cheviot hills in the extreme northern section of the route form an east/west barrier it is necessary to circumvent them by passing through the southern fringe of Roxburghshire. Cumbria is entered around Brampton and Alston.

The county of Durham lies between Yorkshire and Northumberland, with the high ground of the Pennines to the west and the largely industrialized coastline of the North Sea to the east. This route is confined to the western, non-industrialized part of the county, which means unfortunately that the beautiful county town of Durham is not included. After leaving Richmond the road enters the county after crossing the River Tees at Winston. It then runs almost due north and crosses the River Wear at Stanhope before reaching Blanchland, the first village in Northumberland and considered by many to be one of that county's major beauty spots. The road now continues northward to Hexham and passes the line of Hadrian's Wall at Wall and Chollerford before arriving at Bellingham and veering north-east to Alnwick.

Although much of the south-eastern coastal area of Northumberland is industrialized this is not the case further north, where the coastline to the east of Alnwick as far north as the border town of Berwick-on-Tweed is known as the Northumbrian Riviera. It has been suggested in the text that Alnwick is both a pleasant place to stay and a suitable point from where a diversion might be made to explore this part of the coast.

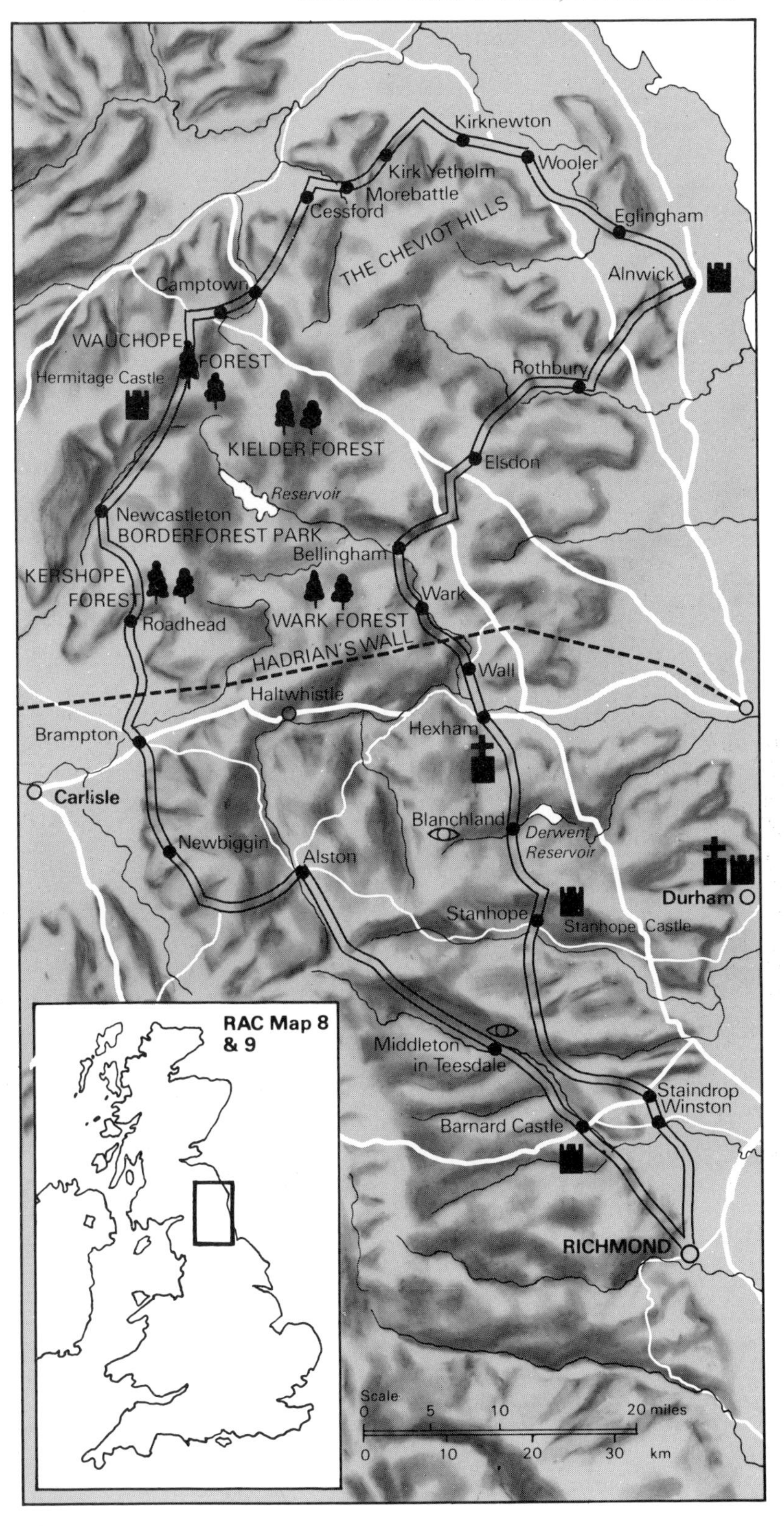
Kirknewton
Wooler
Kirk Yetholm
Morebattle
Cessford
THE CHEVIOT HILLS
Eglingham
Alnwick
Camptown
WAUCHOPE
FOREST
Hermitage Castle
Rothbury
KIELDER FOREST
Elsdon
Reservoir
Newcastleton
BORDERFOREST PARK
Bellingham
KERSHOPE
FOREST
Wark
Roadhead
WARK FOREST
HADRIAN'S WALL
Wall
Haltwhistle
Hexham
Brampton
Carlisle
Blanchland
Derwent
Reservoir
Newbiggin
Alston
Durham
Stanhope
Stanhope Castle
RAC Map 8
& 9
Middleton
in Teesdale
Staindrop
Winston
Barnard Castle
RICHMOND
Scale
0
5
10
20 miles
0
10
20
30
km

Richmond, Yorkshire, dominated by the castle keep.

From Alnwick the route turns north-eastward towards the Scottish border – an interesting feature of the border counties of both England and Scotland being the small square Pele towers, often part of the larger country houses, where villagers used to congregate for protection against border forays. At its most northern point the route runs through the southern edge of Roxburgh in Scotland and then makes southward, leaving the Cheviots to the east and the towns of Jedburgh and Hawick to the west. Either of these historic towns can be visited easily by diverting from Chesters.

Shortly after leaving Newcastleton in the extreme south of Scotland, the road reaches the Cumbrian towns of Brampton and Alston, the latter being England's highest market town.

The return route to the starting-point, Richmond, is by way of Teesdale, passing one of England's highest waterfalls, High Force, and the pleasant market town of Barnard Castle.

The countryside of these northern counties cannot be said to resemble the more picturesque scenic beauty of the Lake District (Route 3). The attraction of this part of Britain is the spaciousness of hills and moorland, where cattle graze in an environment that has hardly changed at all over the centuries.

The castle from the river.

Richmond (N. Yorks)

The town, in the extreme north of Yorkshire, is built on a hill above the R. Swale, and although the huge Norman castle which dominates it was allowed to fall into decay centuries ago, the tower remains intact and can be climbed for superb views. Beneath the castle is a large market square, surrounded by shops and hotels, where an obelisk (1771) has replaced the market cross. In the centre of the square a building of particular interest is the Chapel of the Holy Trinity, founded in 1135, used over the years as an assize court, a prison and a school but today being the home of the regimental museum of the Green Howards. From the square a narrow path leads down to the river, passing under the Bar – a postern gate which once formed part of the town wall. Other interesting features are the Georgian theatre, recently restored, and the tall 15c tower, Greyfriars, which lies in the public gardens and is all that remains of the Franciscan church.

Kings Head Hotel, Market Square, 23 rooms, T53168 (B)

Frenchgate Hotel, 59 Frenchgate, 12 rooms, T2087 (C)

T.O. Friary Gardens, Queens Rd, T3525

Winston (Durham)

The village lies immediately across the Durham border, high above the R. Tees, which is crossed by a stone bridge built in 1763 with a span of 37 yards – reputed to be the largest single span in Europe at that time. Above the village is the 13c church of St Andrews where, from the churchyard, there is a fine view of the river.

Staindrop (Durham)

A pretty little town where the stone houses stand back from the main street alongside a large green. The place to visit here is Raby Castle – about a mile from the town on the A688 (Bishop Auckland road). This well-preserved castle (seat of the Lord Barnard) dates from the 14c and is fully furnished in mainly Victorian style, with medieval Kitchen and Servants' Hall. Also on view is a collection of carriages and other horse-drawn vehicles and the ten-acre garden.

Stanhope (Durham)

The little town is known as the capital of Weardale. Facing each other across the small square are Stanhope Castle (not on view to the public as it is now a boarding school) and the parish church, where a fossilized tree stump, said to be 250 million years old, can be seen just across the wall of the churchyard. To the west of the town a path leads to Heathery Burn where, in 1843, workmen discovered a remarkable collection of bronze-age tools, which are now to be seen in the British Museum.

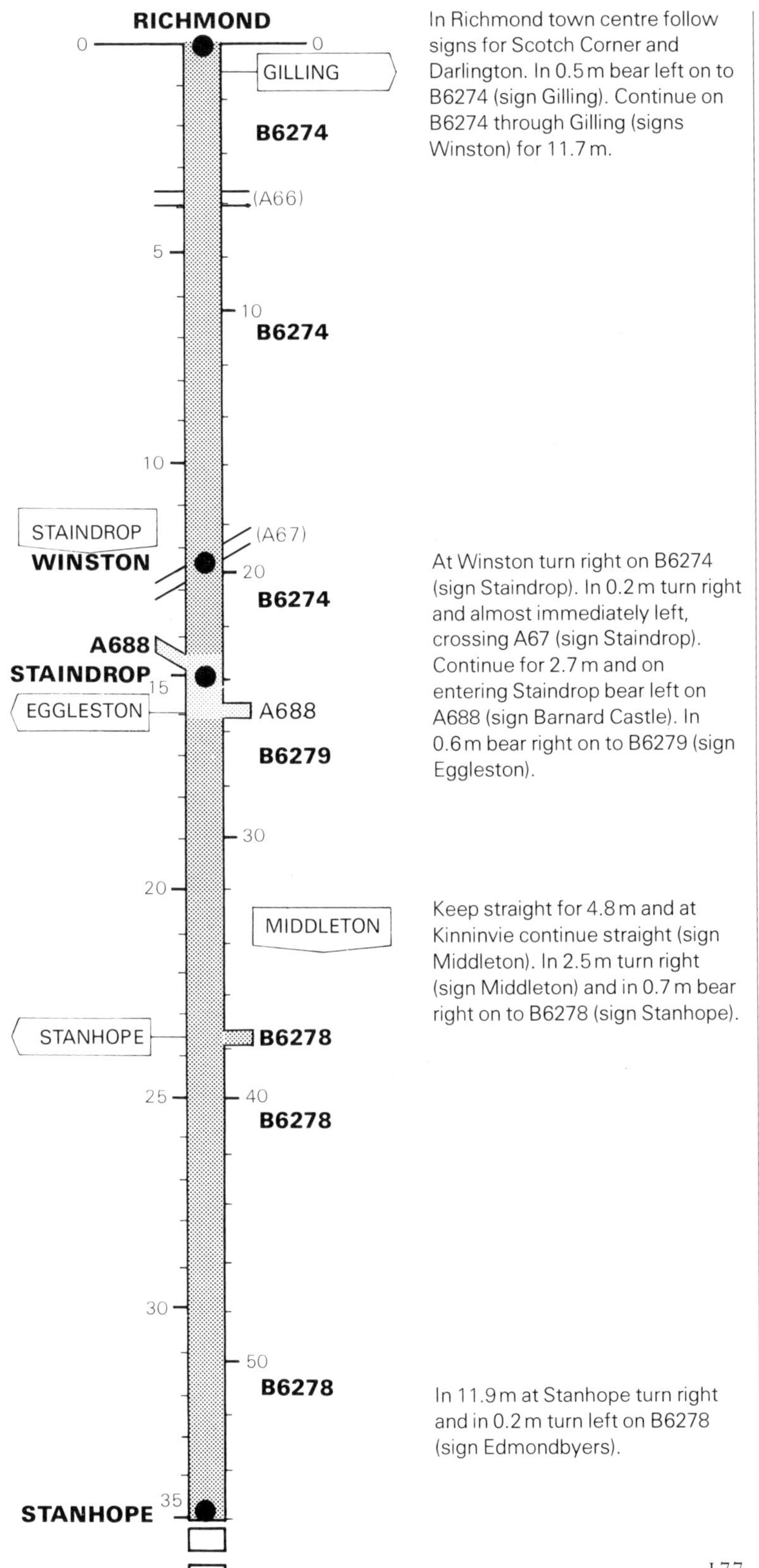

In Richmond town centre follow signs for Scotch Corner and Darlington. In 0.5 m bear left on to B6274 (sign Gilling). Continue on B6274 through Gilling (signs Winston) for 11.7 m.

At Winston turn right on B6274 (sign Staindrop). In 0.2 m turn right and almost immediately left, crossing A67 (sign Staindrop). Continue for 2.7 m and on entering Staindrop bear left on A688 (sign Barnard Castle). In 0.6 m bear right on to B6279 (sign Eggleston).

Keep straight for 4.8 m and at Kinninvie continue straight (sign Middleton). In 2.5 m turn right (sign Middleton) and in 0.7 m bear right on to B6278 (sign Stanhope).

In 11.9 m at Stanhope turn right and in 0.2 m turn left on B6278 (sign Edmondbyers).

The Route

Shortly after leaving Richmond the road crosses into Durham through pasture land, but after Staindrop the road winds ahead like a ribbon through the browns and the reds of the moors, dropping sharply into the valley of the Wear at Stanhope and that of the Derwent at Blanchland. On leaving Blanchland, the road ascends once more to grant a good view of the Derwent reservoir.

Blanchland (Northumberland)

The road descends sharply from the moors, entering a village which many people believe to be the most beautiful in Northumberland. It lies in a wooded glen on the R. Derwent, complete with church, inn and delightful stone houses surrounding the square. These houses were rebuilt 200 years ago out of the estate of Lord Crewe, one-time Bishop of Durham, for the miners who worked on the moors. The Lord Crewe Arms hotel was once the home of the Prior of the Abbey. This was burned down by the Scots, but what was once the Abbey crypt has been retained as a bar.

Lord Crewe Arms, 14 rooms, T251 (B)

Hexham (Northumberland)

The crypt of Hexham Abbey on the west side of the market-place dates from AD 674, although the greater part of the Abbey was constructed between 1180 and 1250. On the opposite side of the square is the Moot Hall, once the gatehouse of the Castle, while the manor house in which the tourist office is located was probably the castle keep. Hexham is a popular resting-place for tourists who wish to explore the surrounding countryside and Hadrian's Wall a few miles to the north. Two miles out of the town is a fine National Hunt racecourse.

Royal Hotel, Priestpopple, T2270 (C)
County Hotel, Priestpopple, T2030 (C)
T.O. Manor House, Hallgates, T605225

Hadrian's Wall.

Wall (Northumberland)

Hadrian Hotel, 8 rooms, T Humshaugh 232 (C)

Chollerford (Northumberland)

The road crosses the R. Tyne near to one of the best preserved of the seventeen forts which were strung along Hadrian's Wall. Chesters (Cilernum) stood on the bank of the river, and there is a sign to the remains (off to the left after crossing the bridge). Just *before* crossing the bridge there is another sign to a footpath running for half a mile along the river to an abutment of the old Roman bridge.

George Hotel, 55 rooms, T Humshaugh 205 (A)

Wark (Northumberland)

The centre of the village green is graced by an enormous chestnut tree. Wark was the scene of the murder in AD 788 of Alfwaid of Northumbria, a 'just and pious king' who had tried to preserve the Christian way of life in the area.

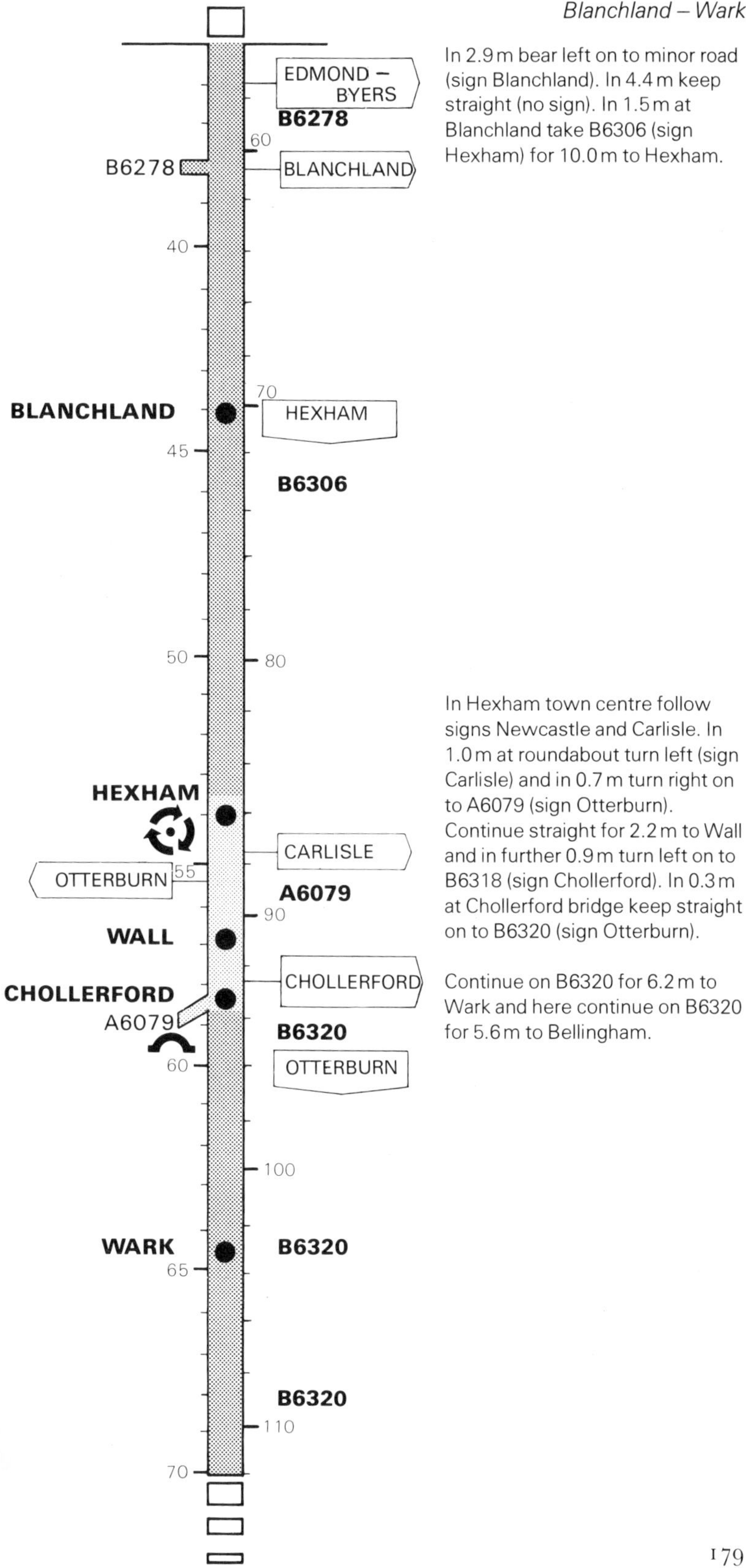

In 2.9 m bear left on to minor road (sign Blanchland). In 4.4 m keep straight (no sign). In 1.5 m at Blanchland take B6306 (sign Hexham) for 10.0 m to Hexham.

In Hexham town centre follow signs Newcastle and Carlisle. In 1.0 m at roundabout turn left (sign Carlisle) and in 0.7 m turn right on to A6079 (sign Otterburn). Continue straight for 2.2 m to Wall and in further 0.9 m turn left on to B6318 (sign Chollerford). In 0.3 m at Chollerford bridge keep straight on to B6320 (sign Otterburn).

Continue on B6320 for 6.2 m to Wark and here continue on B6320 for 5.6 m to Bellingham.

Bellingham (Northumberland)

A number of pleasant inns are grouped in the centre of this small town where there are glimpses of the green hills which surround it in every direction. Among these inns is the Rose and Crown in the sunken square, where there also stands a monument in memory of the Yeomen and Volunteers who fell in the Boer War. The church of St Cuthbert occupies a fine position above the river – and on entering the churchyard a sign directs to the 'Pack Grave', about which there is a macabre tale.

Elsdon (Northumberland)

A moorland village with a large expanse of green where cattle from the surrounding moors used to be herded in harsh weather. In olden days this isolated village was the scene of much lawlessness and cattle raiding. Two miles to the east, at Steng Cross, is Winter's Gibbet – where one William Winter was hanged for murder.

Rothbury (Northumberland)

The broad main street is flanked by old stone houses and a green which is adorned by sycamore trees. The town, on the R. Coquet, is known as the capital of Coquetdale.

Coquet Vale Hotel, Station Rd, 9 rooms, T20305 (C)
Queens Head Hotel, Town Foot, 11 rooms, T20470 (C)
T.O. United Auto Services Ltd, Front St, T20358

Alnwick (Northumberland)

The ancient town grew up around Alnwick Castle, home of the Percy family in the 14c when it was in use, primarily, as a fortress for protection from the Scots. Much of the castle was restored in the 18c, an interesting feature being the carved figures which stand looking down from the ramparts as if repelling attack. Inside the castle can be seen the Keep, Armoury, Library and Dungeon, as well as furnished rooms with pictures by Titian, Van Dyck and other famous artists. The High Street, flanked by a tree-shaded cobbled parking area, narrows as it passes under the medieval arch of Hotspur tower, built around 1450 and named after the father of the second Earl of Northumberland, Harry Hotspur. A column, 84 feet high, was built in 1816 by local tenants, grateful that the Duke of the day had reduced their rents during a period of depression. The town only lies a few miles from the coast, and those with the time to spend a night or two here would be well advised to divert from the route and visit places of interest such as Holy Island, the birthplace of English Christianity – connected to the mainland by a causeway during low tides; Bamburgh Castle, towering above the sea and the little town, and frequently used as a film set; Seahouses, with its colourful fishing harbour; and Craster, famed for its kippers.

Hotspur Hotel, Bondgate Without, 29 rooms, T2924 (C)
White Swan Hotel, Bondgate Within, 40 rooms, T2109 (A)
T.O. The Shambles, T603120

The Route

Between Hexham and Rothbury the road undulates – crossing high moorlands before dipping into wooded valleys such as those of the North Tyne, the Rede and the Coquet. The minor road between Woodburn and Elsdon is gated (two gates). After leaving the woods around Rothbury the road rises again across moorland which stretches all the way to Alnwick.

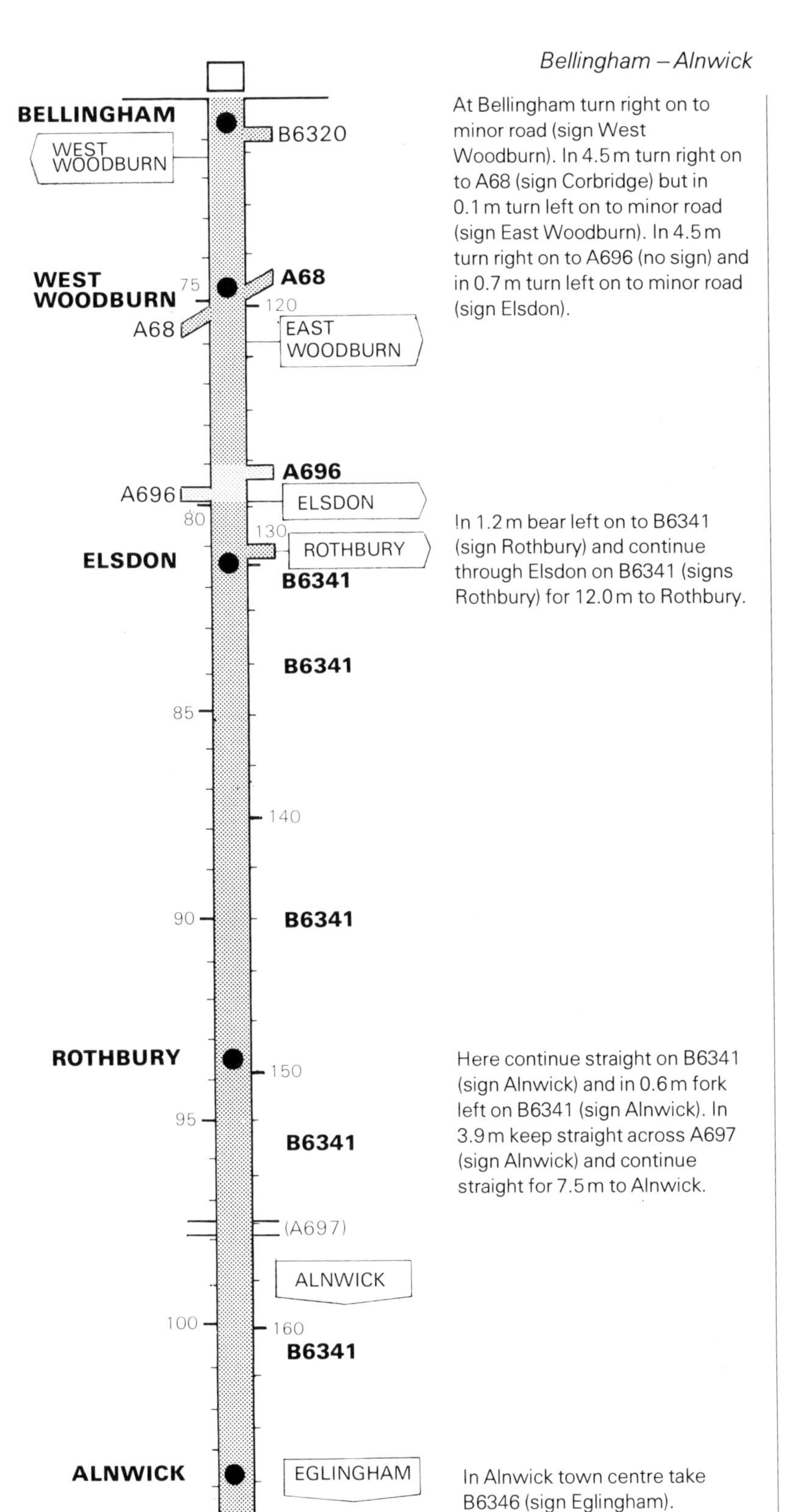

At Bellingham turn right on to minor road (sign West Woodburn). In 4.5 m turn right on to A68 (sign Corbridge) but in 0.1 m turn left on to minor road (sign East Woodburn). In 4.5 m turn right on to A696 (no sign) and in 0.7 m turn left on to minor road (sign Elsdon).

In 1.2 m bear left on to B6341 (sign Rothbury) and continue through Elsdon on B6341 (signs Rothbury) for 12.0 m to Rothbury.

Here continue straight on B6341 (sign Alnwick) and in 0.6 m fork left on B6341 (sign Alnwick). In 3.9 m keep straight across A697 (sign Alnwick) and continue straight for 7.5 m to Alnwick.

In Alnwick town centre take B6346 (sign Eglingham).

A shepherd and some of his flock, near Kirk Yetholm.

Eglingham (Northumberland)

Pretty rock plants are inset in the cottage walls. Eglingham Hall, privately owned and not on view to the public, used to be the home of Colonel Henry Ogle, who entertained Cromwell here and who was much respected for his exposure of the local witchfinder, saving many women from a horrible death.

Wooler (Northumberland)

A market town, bypassed by the main road, Wooler makes a good centre for exploring the Cheviot Hills to the south-west.

Tankerville Arms Hotel, Cottage Rd, 20 rooms, T581 (C)
YHA, 30 Cheviot St, T365

Kirknewton (Northumberland)

Just before arriving at the little village, on the right, a raised wall is inscribed with a notice announcing that this place was 'GETHRIN, Royal Township of the 7th century Anglo-Saxon Kings of Northumbria.' The R. Glen flows nearby, and it was in this river in AD 627 that the missionary Paulinus baptized people into the Christian faith. To the left of the road is a hill known as the Yeavering Bell (1,182 ft), where there are traces of a prehistoric camp. In a nearby field is the Battle Stone, commemorating the victory of the English over the Scots here in 1415. At the foot of the west tower of the village church is the grave of Josephine Butler, the great social reformer who died at Wooler in 1906.

Kirk Yetholm (Roxburghshire)

The first village across the Scottish border – a delightful one with an old inn, timbered and partially thatched, on a large village green. The village was once the headquarters of the Scottish gipsies, and the gipsy 'Palace' to the left of the road was once the home of the Blythe family, the gipsy Kings and Queens.

YHA. No phone.

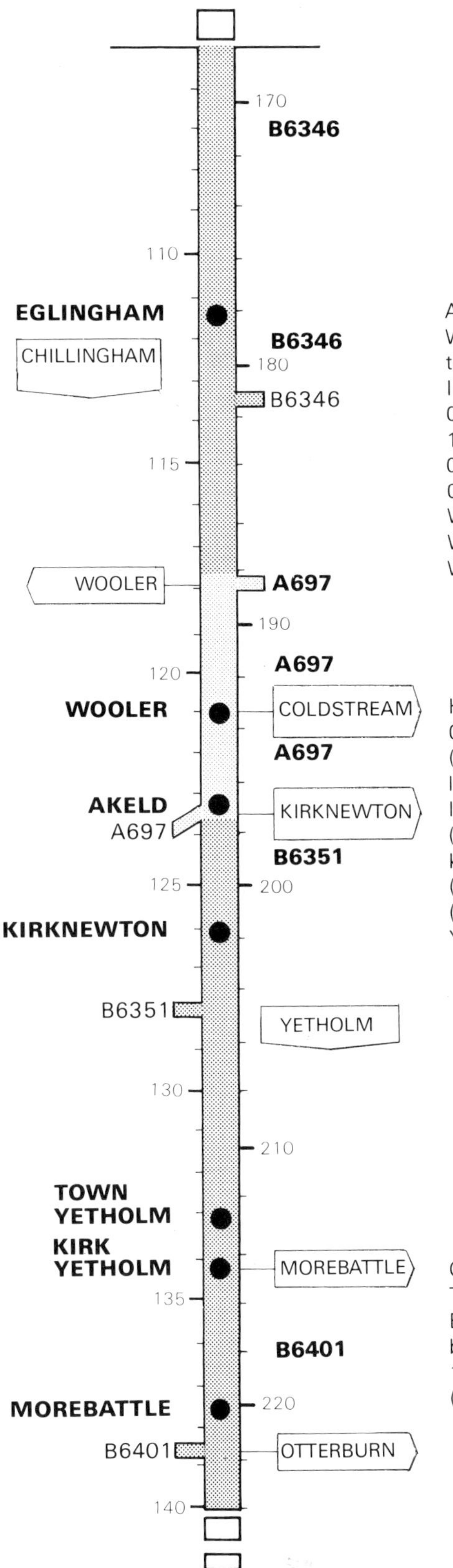

After 7.3 m continue straight (sign Wooler). In 1.8 m keep straight on to minor road (sign Chillingham). In 1.3 m bear left (sign Wooler). In 0.7 m bear right (sign Wooler). In 1.8 m bear right (sign Wooler). In 0.4 m turn left (sign Wooler) and in 0.6 m turn right on to A697 (sign Wooler). In 3.0 m bear left (sign Wooler town centre) for 0.2 m to Wooler town centre.

Here continue straight and in 0.4 m turn left, rejoining A697 (sign Coldstream). In 2.4 m bear left on to B6351 (sign Kirknewton). In 2.7 m at Kirknewton bear right (sign Yetholm) and in further 2.7 m keep straight on to minor road (sign Yetholm). Continue straight (signs Yetholm) for 5.6 m to Kirk Yetholm.

Continue straight and in 0.5 m at Town Yetholm turn left on to B6401 (sign Morebattle). In 3.3 m bear right (sign Morebattle). In 1.7 m turn left on to minor road (sign Otterburn).

Cessford (Roxburghshire)

Just before reaching the farm buildings at Cessford the ruins of the ancient castle lie forlornly on the hill to the left.

Chesters (Roxburghshire)

Consisting only of a handful of houses at a remote road junction, Chester lies equidistant from Hawick and Jedburgh. Either of these Border towns can be reached quite quickly by diverting from here. There is a little guest house (below) which specializes in home-baked bread and cakes.

Steppin' Stane, Southdean, Chesters, T Bonchester Bridge 253 (D)

Jedburgh Abbey can be reached from Chesters.

Hermitage Castle (Roxburghshire)

The vast ruins of the castle are signed to the right, lying some four miles to the west. Legend has it that Hermitage Castle was 'ruled by the devil', and it was to here that Mary Queen of Scots made her perilous night ride from distant Jedburgh to meet her lover, Bothwell, after he had been wounded by a local rival. Mary's journey resulted in a fever which nearly proved fatal, but on recovery she married Lord Bothwell, who in 1561 had been acquitted of the murder of her husband, Darnley. Mary was later to declare that all her troubles began at Hermitage – and it certainly seems that the devil did rule the castle, for she was subsequently executed and her husband died insane as a result of his close confinement in a Danish dungeon.

Newcastleton (Roxburghshire)

Perhaps the most isolated town in the Border region, Newcastleton runs astride a long drab street with a small bleak square on either side of it. Set in the heart of Liddesdale, with the Northumbrian forest only a few miles to the east, the place is rich in legends concerning the reivers who crossed the borders to fight and plunder their rivals. The townsmen prefer to call their town by a nickname, *Copshieholme* – a name almost impossible for outsiders to pronounce and the origin of which is obscure.

Grapes Hotel, T Liddesdale 245 (D)
Liddesdale Hotel, T Liddesdale 255 (D)

The Route

From Alnwick the route heads north-west in the direction of the Northumbrian National Park which is entered after leaving Wooler. From here the road runs through the valley of the R. Glen, with the Cheviots to the south. After crossing the Scottish border at Kirk Yetholm the road heads southward, running between Kelso and Jedburgh to the west and the Cheviots to the east. The route climbs through the heart of the Wauchope Forest before descending and following the R. Liddle into Newcastleton.

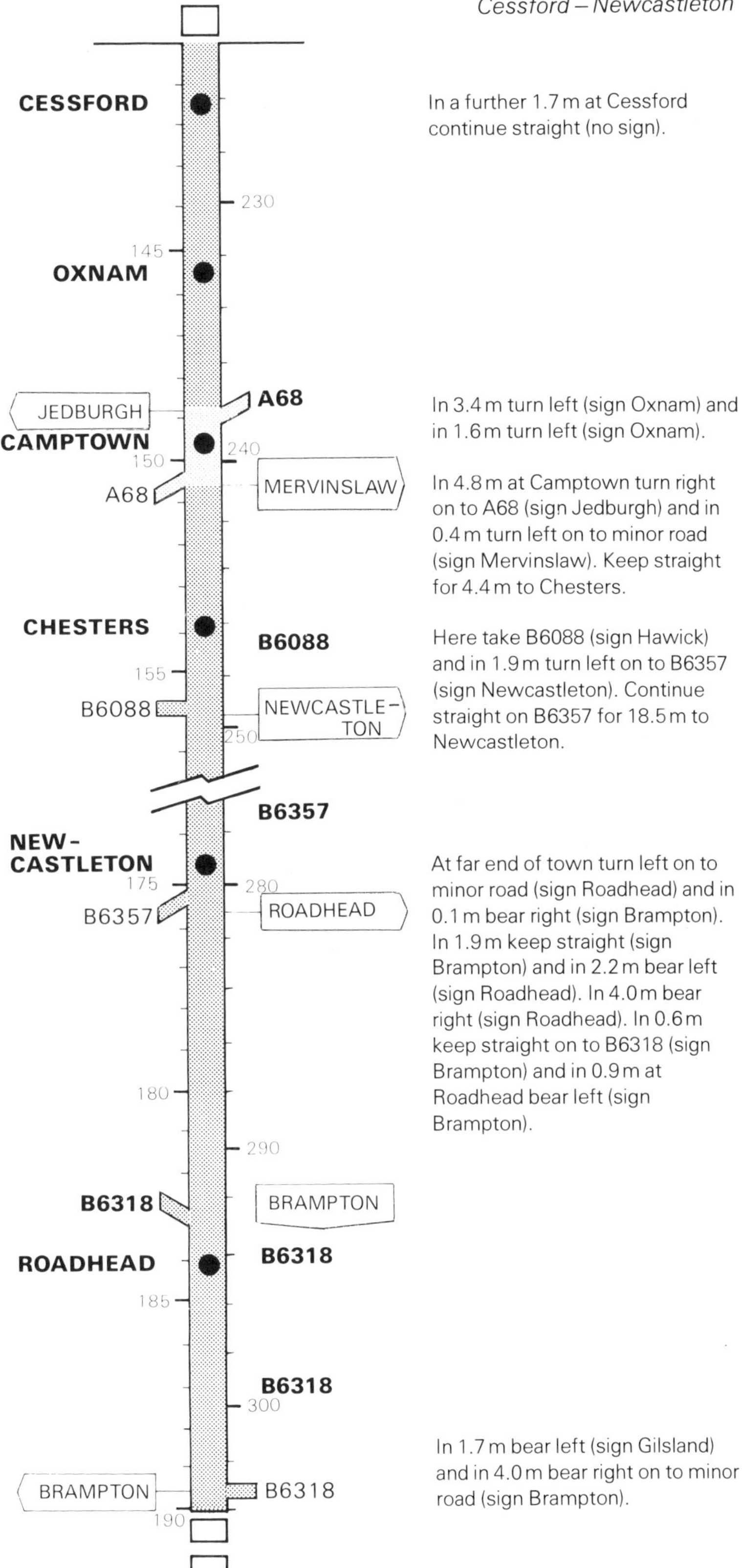

In a further 1.7 m at Cessford continue straight (no sign).

In 3.4 m turn left (sign Oxnam) and in 1.6 m turn left (sign Oxnam).

In 4.8 m at Camptown turn right on to A68 (sign Jedburgh) and in 0.4 m turn left on to minor road (sign Mervinslaw). Keep straight for 4.4 m to Chesters.

Here take B6088 (sign Hawick) and in 1.9 m turn left on to B6357 (sign Newcastleton). Continue straight on B6357 for 18.5 m to Newcastleton.

At far end of town turn left on to minor road (sign Roadhead) and in 0.1 m bear right (sign Brampton). In 1.9 m keep straight (sign Brampton) and in 2.2 m bear left (sign Roadhead). In 4.0 m bear right (sign Roadhead). In 0.6 m keep straight on to B6318 (sign Brampton) and in 0.9 m at Roadhead bear left (sign Brampton).

In 1.7 m bear left (sign Gilsland) and in 4.0 m bear right on to minor road (sign Brampton).

The Route

From Newcastleton the minor road at first runs through the Kershope Forest before heading through pleasant, sparsely populated countryside towards Brampton and Newbiggin.

Brampton (Cumbria)

In this compact market town most of the more interesting buildings cluster round the Moot Hall, a place where Cromwell held forty prisoners in 1648. In fact the existing structure dates only from 1817, and additions were made to it as recently as 1896. In front of the Moot Hall, set in the cobblestones, is a ring used for tethering the bulls when bull baiting was in vogue, and nearby are the town stocks. Peter Burn, a local poet whose house is now a laundry near the Moot Hall, recalled seeing the last use of the stocks in 1836. Among other old buildings is Prince Charlie's house, now a shoeshop, where the Young Pretender stayed in 1745, being presented with the keys of Carlisle in the front of the house after his troops had successfully besieged the town. After the defeat of Charles at Culloden a number of his supporters were hanged on the Capon tree near the town – a monument marks the spot. A century ago Brampton boasted no less than forty-five inns, their reduction to the mere seven which remain being due to the influence of Lady Carlisle, a radical and social reformer. Among the nice old inns that do remain are the White Lion and the Nag's Head.

White Lion Hotel, High Cross St, 7 rooms, T2338 (D)
T.O. T2685

Newbiggin (Cumbria)

According to the map there are a number of places that go by this name in the area. This village must certainly be the smallest, consisting of an inn and a few scattered farm-houses with a population in 1980 of only thirty-eight. The Blue Bell Inn provides food at the bar and the barn next door to it has been converted into a restaurant, open at weekends only.

Croglin (Cumbria)

The village is a little larger than Newbiggin. The church is faced by a 14c house, once the rectory but now the post office, with a Pele tower where centuries ago the villagers would congregate for protection at the time of border raids. The Croglin vampire was recently the subject of a television film.

Robin Hood Inn, 3 rooms, T227 (D)

Alston (Cumbria)

The town lies at the heart of the northern Pennines, and at more than 1,000 feet above sea level is claimed to be the highest market town in England. Cross Fell (2,930 ft), to the south of the town, is England's highest mountain outside the Lake District. The town is built on a slope, and it is quite a stiff climb from the disused railway station, now the tourist office, to the top of the town. The church is comparatively modern (1869), but the present building is the third on a site where records date back to 1184. There are a number of old houses and inns in the town, among them 'Church Gaytes' (1681) and the Quaker Meeting House (1732).

Hillcrest Hotel, Townfoot, 12 rooms, T251 (C)
Lowbyer Manor Hotel, 11 rooms, T230 (B)
T.O. The Railway Station, T696

Langdon Beck (Durham)

YHA. T Forest in Teesdale 228

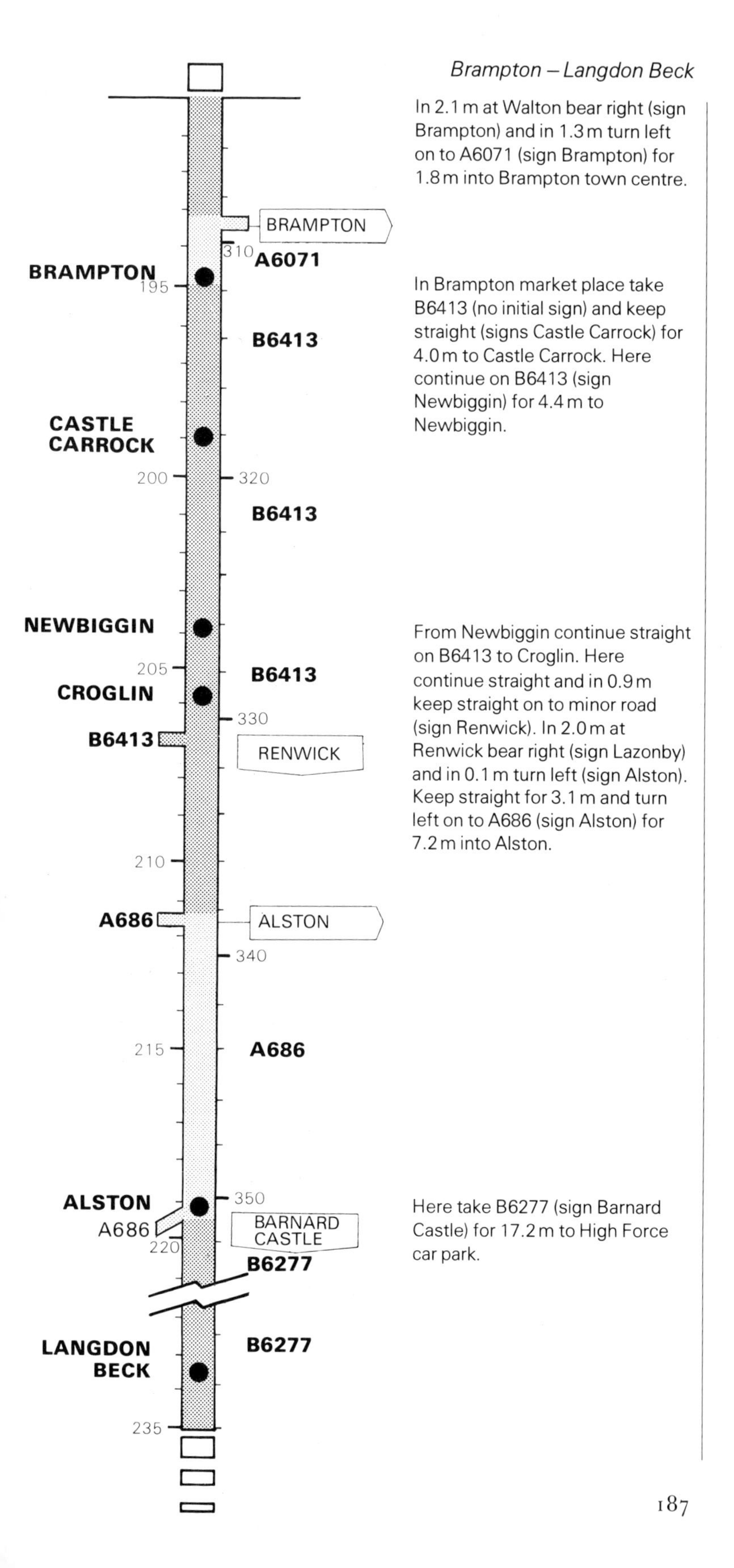

In 2.1 m at Walton bear right (sign Brampton) and in 1.3 m turn left on to A6071 (sign Brampton) for 1.8 m into Brampton town centre.

In Brampton market place take B6413 (no initial sign) and keep straight (signs Castle Carrock) for 4.0 m to Castle Carrock. Here continue on B6413 (sign Newbiggin) for 4.4 m to Newbiggin.

From Newbiggin continue straight on B6413 to Croglin. Here continue straight and in 0.9 m keep straight on to minor road (sign Renwick). In 2.0 m at Renwick bear right (sign Lazonby) and in 0.1 m turn left (sign Alston). Keep straight for 3.1 m and turn left on to A686 (sign Alston) for 7.2 m into Alston.

Here take B6277 (sign Barnard Castle) for 17.2 m to High Force car park.

The Route

The minor road joined just past Croglin rises to Hartside Height where there is a cafe and a panoramic view. There is a warning notice that this road can be treacherous in winter – under icy conditions it would be necessary to go round by the major roads to Alston. After Alston the road rises again to afford views of the Pennine fells before it descends to the river. From Middleton there are two roads to Barnard Castle. The distance is the same by each, but the one chosen is more attractive and less busy.

High Force (Durham)

The High Force Car Park and Picnic Area lies on the left of the road beyond the High Force Hotel. A pleasant wooded footpath opposite leads for half a mile to England's highest waterfall, where the Tees drops seventy feet down the side of a huge black rock to the deep pool beneath. Another impressive waterfall along the Tees is known as the Cauldron Snout. It lies further from the road than High Force and entails a longer walk – but it can be seen by diverting right at Langdon.

High Force Hotel, 9 rooms, T Forest in Teesdale 264 (C)

Middleton in Teesdale
(Durham)

Known as the capital of Upper Teesdale, the town lies by a beautiful wooded valley on the north bank of the Tees. The town prospered in the 19c with the arrival of the Quaker-owned London lead mining company – employers with a social conscience who erected a number

Right: *England's highest waterfall.*

of sturdy buildings for the use of their employees. A century later mining ceased in the area, but Middleton remains a good place from which to explore the beautiful country around it. Teesdale has been acclaimed in the poetry of Sir Walter Scott and William Wordsworth – but Teesdale's own poet is Richard Watson (1833–91). Watson, who started work in the lead mines at the age of ten, was born in Middleton and now lies buried there. His poetry proclaimed his love of Teesdale.

The rolling hills of the Cheviots.

Romaldkirk (Durham)

The village used to be part of Yorkshire before county boundaries were changed. Yorkshire's loss is Durham's gain, because Romaldkirk must number among the county's most beautiful villages. The church, the two inns and the houses, all in grey stone, cluster around a number of greens which the villagers tend with pride.

Rose and Crown Hotel, 11 rooms,
T Cotherstone 213 (C)

Barnard Castle (Durham)

The ruins of the castle, after which the town is called, can be seen on the edge of the steep seventy-foot cliff before entering the town. Originally the town was named Bernard's Castle after Bernard de Baliol, son of Guy de Baliol who founded the castle, which Bernard improved around AD1100. Bernard's son, John, was the founder of the Oxford college. The town's most renowned building is the Bowes Museum (19c), named after John Bowes, 10th Earl of Strathmore. This is a massive building with works of art that include masterpieces by El Greco and Goya as well as a great variety of continental and English porcelain. There are many furnished rooms, among them the Childrens' Room with a delightful collection of dolls' houses and dolls in national costume. The many old buildings scattered around the town include the Golden Lion Inn (1679), the King's Head Hotel, where Charles Dickens lived while writing *Nicholas Nickleby*, and the 16c Blagraves House, where Oliver Cromwell rested in 1648.

Kings Head Hotel, 12 Market Place, 16 rooms, T38356 (C)
YHA, 91, Galgate, T2127
T.O. 43 Galgate, T38481

Kirby Hill (Durham)

From the car park of the Shoulder of Mutton Inn, on the left of the road, is a magnificent view over mile upon mile of country to the north.

The Route

These last few miles from Barnard Castle to Richmond could be taken along the A68 and B6274. This minor road from Greta Bridge is a short cut which winds past some pleasant little villages, and then rises sharply before dropping down into Richmond.

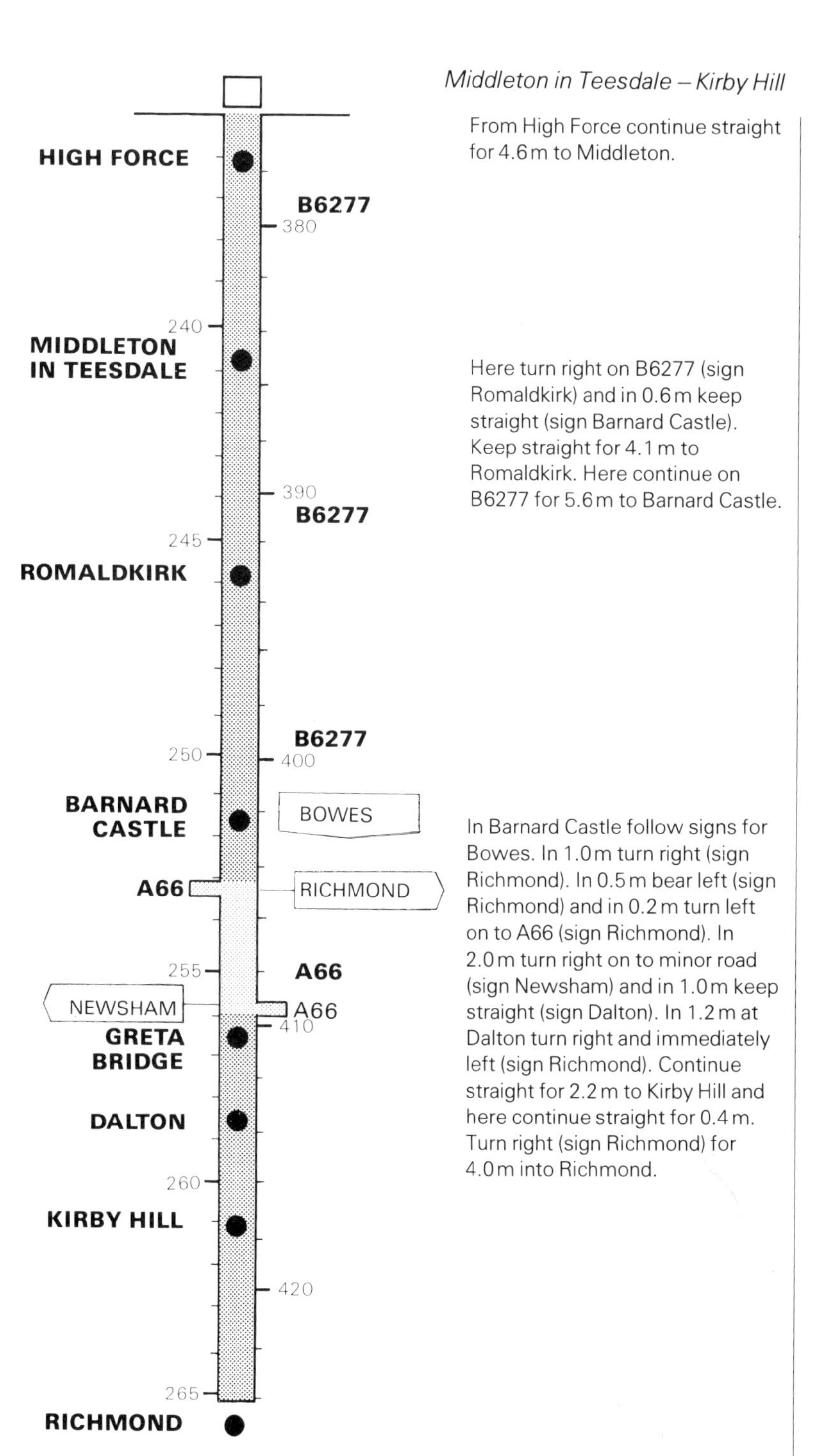

From High Force continue straight for 4.6 m to Middleton.

Here turn right on B6277 (sign Romaldkirk) and in 0.6 m keep straight (sign Barnard Castle). Keep straight for 4.1 m to Romaldkirk. Here continue on B6277 for 5.6 m to Barnard Castle.

In Barnard Castle follow signs for Bowes. In 1.0 m turn right (sign Richmond). In 0.5 m bear left (sign Richmond) and in 0.2 m turn left on to A66 (sign Richmond). In 2.0 m turn right on to minor road (sign Newsham) and in 1.0 m keep straight (sign Dalton). In 1.2 m at Dalton turn right and immediately left (sign Richmond). Continue straight for 2.2 m to Kirby Hill and here continue straight for 0.4 m. Turn right (sign Richmond) for 4.0 m into Richmond.

11 *West Surrey, West Sussex, Hampshire (New Forest)*

FROM GUILDFORD, SURREY'S CAPITAL, the route makes in the direction of West Sussex. Shortly after leaving Godalming the main roads are left behind, the next forty miles to Petersfield running through such tranquil and unspoilt countryside that it is hard to believe that London lies a mere fifty miles away. This tranquillity is largely due to the various town and country planning acts which prevent London encroaching too far into the home counties. Many of the smaller villages passed in Surrey, Sussex and Hampshire consist of little more than a church, a pub and a handful of cottages. Travelling in these parts one is reminded of the French born author Hilaire Belloc (1870–1953) whose love of the south of England, and Sussex in particular, is reflected in the lines:

> If I ever become a rich man,
> Or if I ever grow to be old,
> I will build a house with deep thatch
> To shelter me from the cold,
> And there shall the Sussex songs be sung
> And the story of Sussex told.

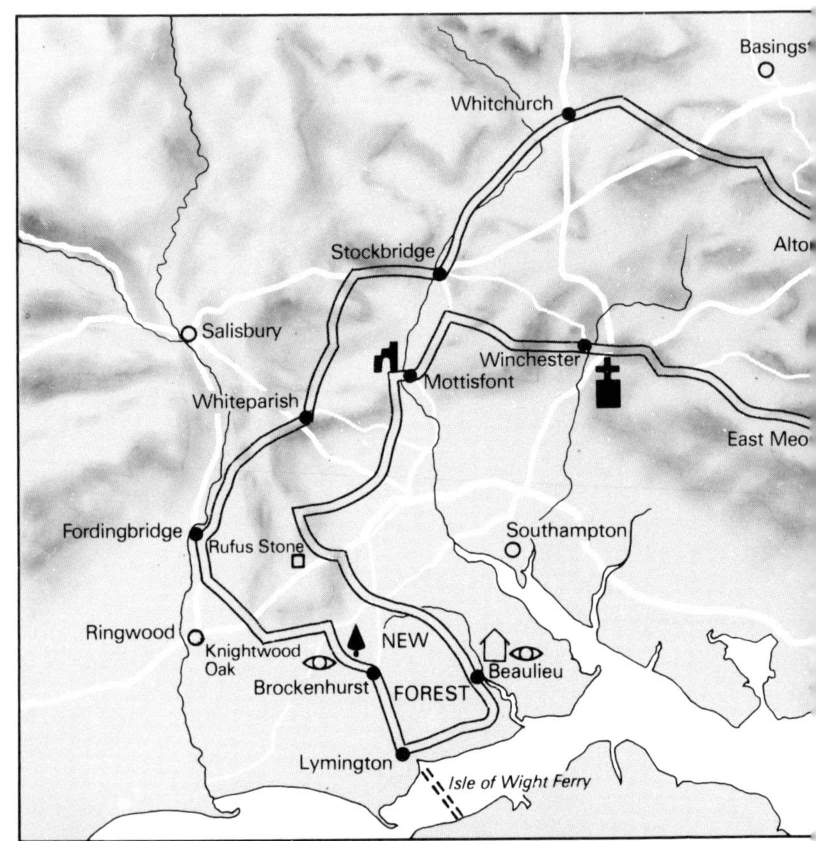

After leaving Sussex the route continues into Hampshire, passing directly through Winchester, a cathedral city where the reader must decide whether to linger or push on towards the New Forest.

It was in 1079 that William the Conqueror ordered the afforestation of the New Forest which today covers ninety thousand acres, an area that varies from dense woodland to wide expanses of heathery moors across which some five thousand ponies, said to be the descendants of the jennets that swam ashore from the wrecks of the Armada, graze. The New Forest is an ideal place for a walking holiday – but for the less energetic there is much to see, whether by visiting the various churches, gardens and museums or simply by gazing across the water at Beaulieu.

After leaving the New Forest the route passes the Wiltshire villages of Woodfalls, Whiteparish and West Dean. The road then runs through wooded country back into Hampshire and the valley of the Test, with the lovely villages of Longstock and Wherwell.

Whitchurch and Andover are Hampshire towns of reasonable size, and Surrey is re-entered on arrival at Frensham with a pleasant hotel on the banks of what perhaps deserves the title of lake rather than pond. The last few miles back to Guildford are by way of the busy A3 – but before reaching the main road it is worth pausing at Tilford, one of Surrey's prettiest villages, where the vast oak on the green was described by William Cobbett, born a few miles away at Farnham, as the most beautiful oak he had ever seen.

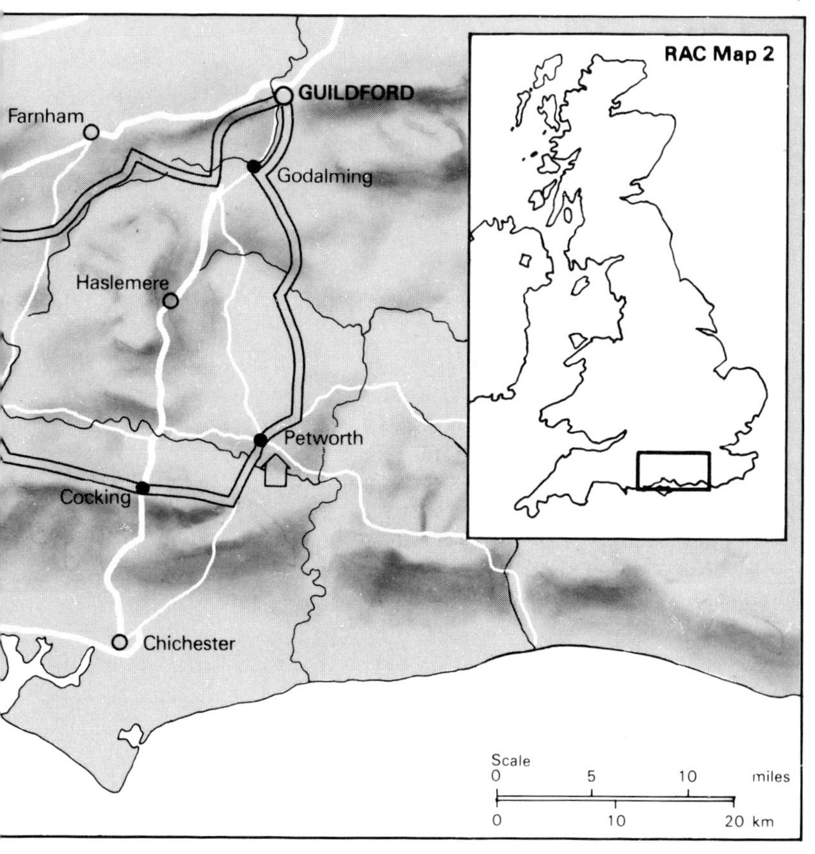

Guildford (Surrey)

The novelist, Charles Dickens (1812–70), referred to the High Street as 'the most beautiful in England' and William Cobbett (1763–1835), in his 'Rural Rides', described Guildford as 'the most agreeable and happy looking town that I ever saw in my life'. The cobbled High Street descends sharply past many fine buildings – among them the 16c Royal Grammar School, the 17c Guildhall with huge gilded clock, and an old coaching inn, The Angel. The more modern buildings include the 20c Cathedral and the Yvonne Arnaud Theatre, delightfully situated on the banks of the R. Wey. Near to the remains of the old castle is a museum where items are displayed in connection with Lewis Carroll (1832–98), author of *The Adventures of Alice in Wonderland*, who often stayed with his six unmarried sisters in a nearby house, The Chestnuts.

Angel Hotel, High St, 25 rooms, T64555 (A)
T.O. Civic Hall, London Rd, T67314

Godalming (Surrey)

Among several old coaching inns dotted around the congested streets of the town is the Kings Arms Royal Hotel, where there is a record of the visit of Tsar Peter the Great of Russia who, in 1689, consumed a gargantuan meal washed down by thirty bottles of sack and twelve of claret. The famous public school, Charterhouse, moved here from London a century ago, numbering among its ex-pupils many literary figures, including Crashaw, Lovelace, Steele, Addison, Thackeray and Max Beerbohm.

Kings Arms Royal Hotel, 12 rooms,

Hascombe (Surrey)

Winkworth Arboretum (National Trust) lies to the left of the road before it reaches Hascombe. This woodland garden, which includes numerous species of tree, notably cherries, maples, oaks, and magnolias, covers 96 acres of hillside that slope down to two lakes. The pleasant White Horse Inn in the tiny village is embellished by the charming painting of a white horse on the inn sign – done more than 50 years ago by a local artist, Gertrude Jekyll.

Dunsfold (Surrey)

The houses of this spacious village are separated from the road by a huge green. The Sun Inn has a restaurant.

Petworth (Sussex)

An attractive town of narrow streets and timber-framed houses where, as a centrepiece, stands Petworth House (National Trust) in a 2,000-acre park. Among outstanding features of this huge mansion are the Carved Room, said to be the finest work of Grinling Gibbons (1648–1721); the Grand Staircase; and the State Rooms with paintings by Van Dyck, Holbein, Rembrandt, and Reynolds.

Petworth Park Hotel, 19 rooms, T43030 (D)

Cocking (Sussex)

The Richard Cobden Inn (T Midhurst 2974) prides itself on its real ale and has a good small restaurant.

The Route

After leaving Godalming the route passes wooded countryside and a number of isolated villages. The road is very narrow between Cocking and Elsted.

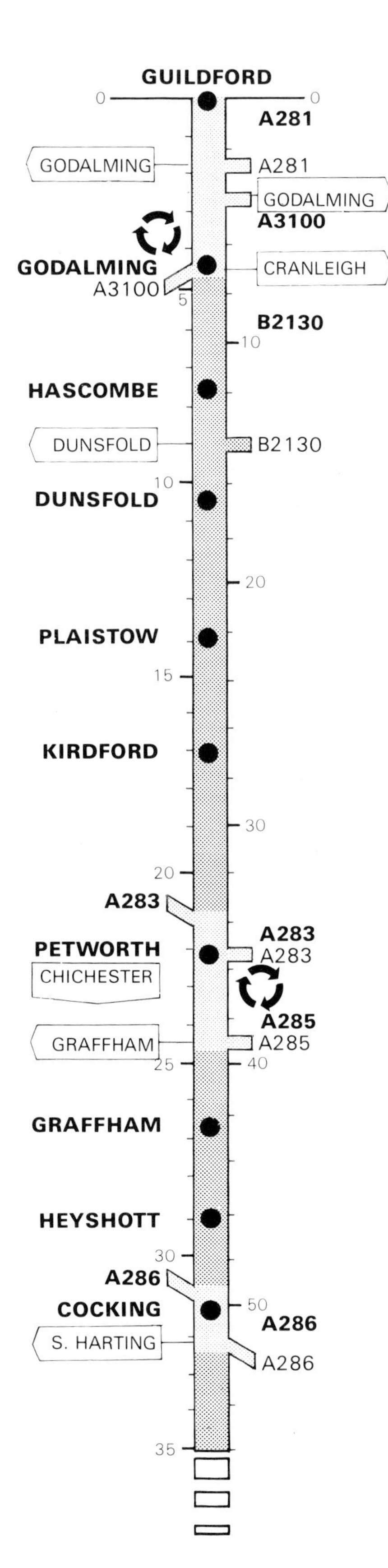

In Guildford proceed down High St and almost at foot of High St turn left at compulsory one-way street until reaching traffic lights. Here turn left on to A281 (sign Godalming). In 1.5 m turn right (sign Godalming) and in 0.7 m turn left on to A3100 (sign Godalming).

Arriving at Godalming follow one-way system and turn left on to B2130 (sign Cranleigh). In 0.8 m keep straight (sign Hascombe) for 2.5 m to Hascombe. Here continue straight and in 1.6 m turn right on to minor road (sign Dunsfold) for 1.0 m to Dunsfold. Here keep straight and in 0.7 m bear left (sign Plaistow).

In 3.3 m at Plaistow bear right (sign Kirdford) and in 3.1 m at Kirdford T junction turn right (sign Petworth). In 4.4 m bear left on to A283 into Petworth.

At Petworth follow one-way system through town and take A285 (sign Chichester). In 2.3 m turn right on to minor road (sign Graffham). In 1.4 m turn left (sign Graffham) and in 1.5 m at Graffham turn right (sign Heyshott).

In 1.7 m turn left (sign Heyshott) and in further 1.7 m after passing Heyshott turn left (sign Cocking). In 1.0 m turn left on A286 into Cocking.

Here turn right on to minor road (sign S. Harting). Keep straight (signs S. Harting) and in 4.0 m turn left (sign S. Harting).

South Harting (Sussex)

A number of famous people lived in or around S. Harting, among them the novelist Anthony Trollope (1815–82), Lady Emma Hamilton (1765–1815), mistress of Nelson, and the writer H. G. Wells (1866–1946). Trollope lived at Harting Grange and both Lady Hamilton and H. G. Wells at Uppark (National Trust), where the latter's mother was a housekeeper when he worked as a chemist's assistant in Midhurst – an experience which formed the basis for his novel, *Kipps.* Two very old inns, The White Hart (T355) and The Ship (T302), serve meals and bar snacks.

Petersfield (Hampshire)

A statue of William III stands in the main square from which Sheep Street leads into 'The Spain', where a number of elegant houses cluster round a small green. 'The Spain' is so called because it was here in this once prosperous wool town that Spanish merchants used to congregate to make their purchases. An impressive modern addition to the town is the Folly Market, completed in 1978, consisting of a dozen or so small arcaded shops.

Red Lion Hotel, 3 College St, 12 rooms, T3025 (B)

East Meon (Hampshire)

First glimpse of this delightful village is the Norman church on the lower slopes of a hill – worth a visit if only to admire the marble font with carvings of doves, dragons and scenes from the life of Adam and Eve. A stream flows alongside the main village street.

Warnford (Hampshire)

The minor road to Winchester leads off from the village – but a diversion of half a mile to Warnford Park (signed further up the main road on the left) is recommended. Here, in the heart of the park, is a remote little Saxon church. Engraved on a tomb-stone, by a holly tree near the porch, is a tree and skeleton depicting how an estate carpenter had been struck by lightning after ignoring warnings not to work on Sundays.

Izaak Walton window in Winchester Cathedral.

Winchester (Hampshire)

Much time is needed to admire the beauty of the cathedral city, a city that was fortified in Roman times and was later to become the capital of Wessex. The Cathedral, started in 1079 and the longest in Britain, provides a burial place for many kings as well as famous figures of more recent days that include the novelist Jane Austen (1775–1817) and Izaak Walton (1593–1683), author of *The Compleat Angler.*

Royal Hotel, Saint Peter St, 30 rooms, T3468 (B)
Stanmore Hotel, Romsey Rd, 10 rooms, T2720 (C)
YHA, The City Mill, 1 Water Lane, T3273
T.O. Guildhall, The Broadway, T68166

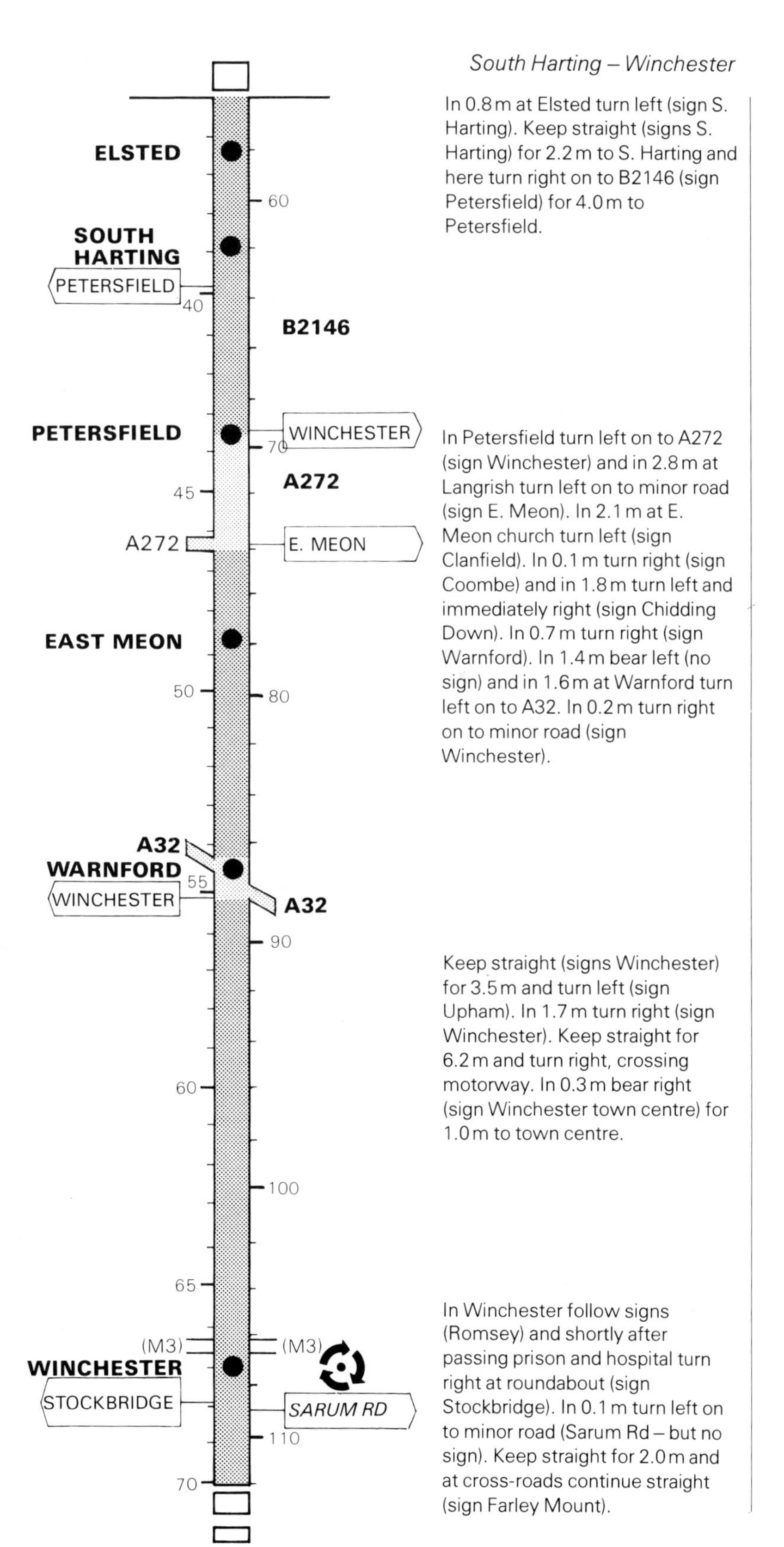

In 0.8 m at Elsted turn left (sign S. Harting). Keep straight (signs S. Harting) for 2.2 m to S. Harting and here turn right on to B2146 (sign Petersfield) for 4.0 m to Petersfield.

In Petersfield turn left on to A272 (sign Winchester) and in 2.8 m at Langrish turn left on to minor road (sign E. Meon). In 2.1 m at E. Meon church turn left (sign Clanfield). In 0.1 m turn right (sign Coombe) and in 1.8 m turn left and immediately right (sign Chidding Down). In 0.7 m turn right (sign Warnford). In 1.4 m bear left (no sign) and in 1.6 m at Warnford turn left on to A32. In 0.2 m turn right on to minor road (sign Winchester).

Keep straight (signs Winchester) for 3.5 m and turn left (sign Upham). In 1.7 m turn right (sign Winchester). Keep straight for 6.2 m and turn right, crossing motorway. In 0.3 m bear right (sign Winchester town centre) for 1.0 m to town centre.

In Winchester follow signs (Romsey) and shortly after passing prison and hospital turn right at roundabout (sign Stockbridge). In 0.1 m turn left on to minor road (Sarum Rd – but no sign). Keep straight for 2.0 m and at cross-roads continue straight (sign Farley Mount).

Kings Somborne (Hampshire)

The R. Test runs through this quiet little village, to the west of which the maps show the position of the deer park where John of Gaunt (1340–99), fourth son of Edward III, once hunted. The deer park has now become agricultural land but the banks enclosing it can still be seen in places.

Mottisfont (Hampshire)

Mottisfont Abbey (National Trust) enjoys a peaceful setting on lawns that are shaded by huge plane, cedar, oak and beech trees. Once a 13c priory, the building has been transformed over the centuries, and today an outstanding feature is the room decorated in 1938 by Rex Whistler (1905–44), killed in Normandy a few years later.

Mottisfont Abbey.

Bramshaw (Hampshire)

In the church of this pretty village is a memorial to seven men of the parish who were drowned in 1912 when the White Star liner, *Titanic*, collided with an iceberg. The hotel (below) lies outside the village – further along the route on the right.

Bramble Hill Hotel, 16 rooms, T Cadnam 3165 (C)

Stoney Cross (Hampshire)

The minor road across the A31 has recently been closed for reasons of safety – thus, as the route instructions indicate, it is necessary to cross the main road further along it. To the left of the A31 a sign points to the Rufus Stone, a monument originally placed in 1745 to mark the spot where William Rufus (William II, 1056–1100) met his death while hunting in the New Forest.

The Rufus Stone, a New Forest landmark.

Lyndhurst (Hampshire)

A busy tourist centre, known as the capital of the New Forest. Alice Liddell, model for *Alice in Wonderland*, is buried in the churchyard of St Michael's Church.

Lyndhurst Park Hotel, High St, 68 rooms, T2824 (A)
Forest Gardens Hotel, Romsey Rd, 13 rooms, T2367 (C)
T.O. Main Car Park, T2269

The Route

Confined almost entirely to minor roads, at first through wooded countryside and later through more open landscape with fine views. The New Forest is entered after leaving W. Wellow, a particularly fine stretch lying between Bramshaw and Fritham.

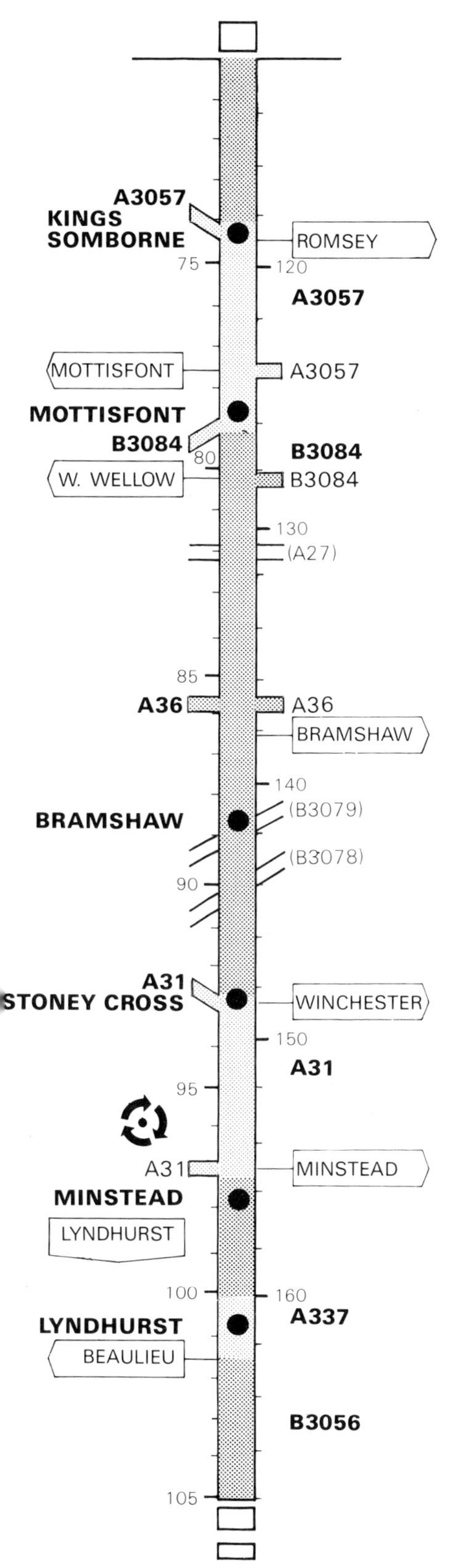

In 1.0 m bear right (no sign) and in 3.3 m bear left (no sign). In 0.6 m bear left (sign Kings Somborne). In 0.7 m turn right (sign Romsey) and in 0.1 m at Kings Somborne turn left on to A3057 (sign Romsey).

In 3.5 m turn right on to minor road (sign Mottisfont) for 0.6 m to Mottisfont. Here at post office bear left (no sign) and in 0.4 m turn left on to B3084 (no sign). In 0.3 m at Dunbridge bear left (sign Romsey). In 0.7 m turn right on to minor road (sign W. Wellow).

In 0.6 m turn left and immediately right (sign W. Wellow) and in 1.2 m keep straight (sign The Wellows). Continue straight for 2.7 m and turn right on to A36 (sign Salisbury). In 0.1 m turn left on to minor road (sign Bramshaw). Continue straight for 2.9 m to Bramshaw and here keep straight (sign Fritham). In 1.2 m keep straight across B3078 (sign Fritham). In 0.8 m bear left (sign Stoney Cross) for 1.9 m to Stoney Cross.

NB at Stoney cross the gap has now been closed.

Turn left on to A31 (sign Winchester) and in 2.3 m bear left (sign non-motorway traffic). In 0.4 m at roundabout keep right, returning on A31, and in 1.3 m turn left on to minor road (sign Minstead). In 0.3 m keep straight (sign Lyndhurst). Continue straight (signs Lyndhurst) for 1.5 m and turn right on to A337 into Lyndhurst.

Here keep straight (sign Southampton) but before leaving town turn right on to B3056 (sign Beaulieu) and continue straight for 7.3 m.

Beaulieu (Hampshire)

Here are the beautiful ruins of the Abbey founded in 1204 by King John, once a place of sanctuary where Perkin Warbeck (1474–99) sought protection after his failure to dethrone Henry VII. The National Motor Museum, in the Abbey grounds, was founded in 1952 by the third Baron Montagu of Beaulieu with a collection of vintage vehicles that include world speed record holders, trams, and bicycles used by Edward VII and George V.

Montagu Arms, 26 rooms, T61234 (B)

Bucklers Hard (Hampshire)

New Forest oaks were used here for the building of ships for Nelson's navy – ships that included the *Agamemnon*, a model of which can be seen at the Maritime Museum. The Master Builder's House is now an hotel with a bar and restaurant overlooking the river. A little further along the minor road, on the right, are the ancient granaries of St Leonards where one barn is believed to be the largest in England.

Lymington (Hampshire)

The car ferry to the Isle of Wight leaves from here. Georgian and Victorian houses flank the broad High Street, at the top of which is the square-towered church with strangely shaped cupola where the poet Coventry Patmore (1823–96) is buried.

Angel Hotel, 108 High St, 16 rooms, T72050 (C)
Stanwell House, High St, 17 rooms, T77123 (C)

Brockenhurst (Hampshire)

The route turns westward on reaching the town, the most notable building being the parish church (Norman and Early English) where in the churchyard is an interesting headstone portraying 'Brusher' Mills, snake catcher. After leaving the town the road runs through the heart of the New Forest by way of the Rhinefield Ornamental Drive and the Bolderwood Arboretum Ornamental Drive. Entering the latter Drive, a sign to the right indicates the Knightwood Oak – the largest oak in the forest with a girth, at 4 feet above the ground, of 22 feet. An interesting short walk from here is signed by yellow markers past a variety of trees that include a rare fused oak and beech tree and the Queen's Oak, planted on 12 April 1979 by H.M. the Queen to mark the ninth centenary of the New Forest founded by William the Conqueror in 1079.

Forest Park Hotel, Rhinefield Rd, 40 rooms, T2095 (B)

Moyles Court (Hampshire)

The restored manor house, now a school, was once the home of the Lisle family, and it was here that the 70-year-old Dame Alicia gave refuge to fugitives from Monmouth's army after the battle of Sedgemoor. For this deed she was acquitted by two juries – but the infamous Judge Jeffreys bullied a third jury into condemning the old lady to death at his 'Bloody Assizes' in Winchester.

Fordingbridge (Hampshire)

The route only touches the fringe of this pleasant town on the R. Avon.

Albany Hotel, Bridge St, 10 rooms, T52237 (C)

The Route

The entire section runs through the New Forest. There are many well sited car parks that give access to forest walks.

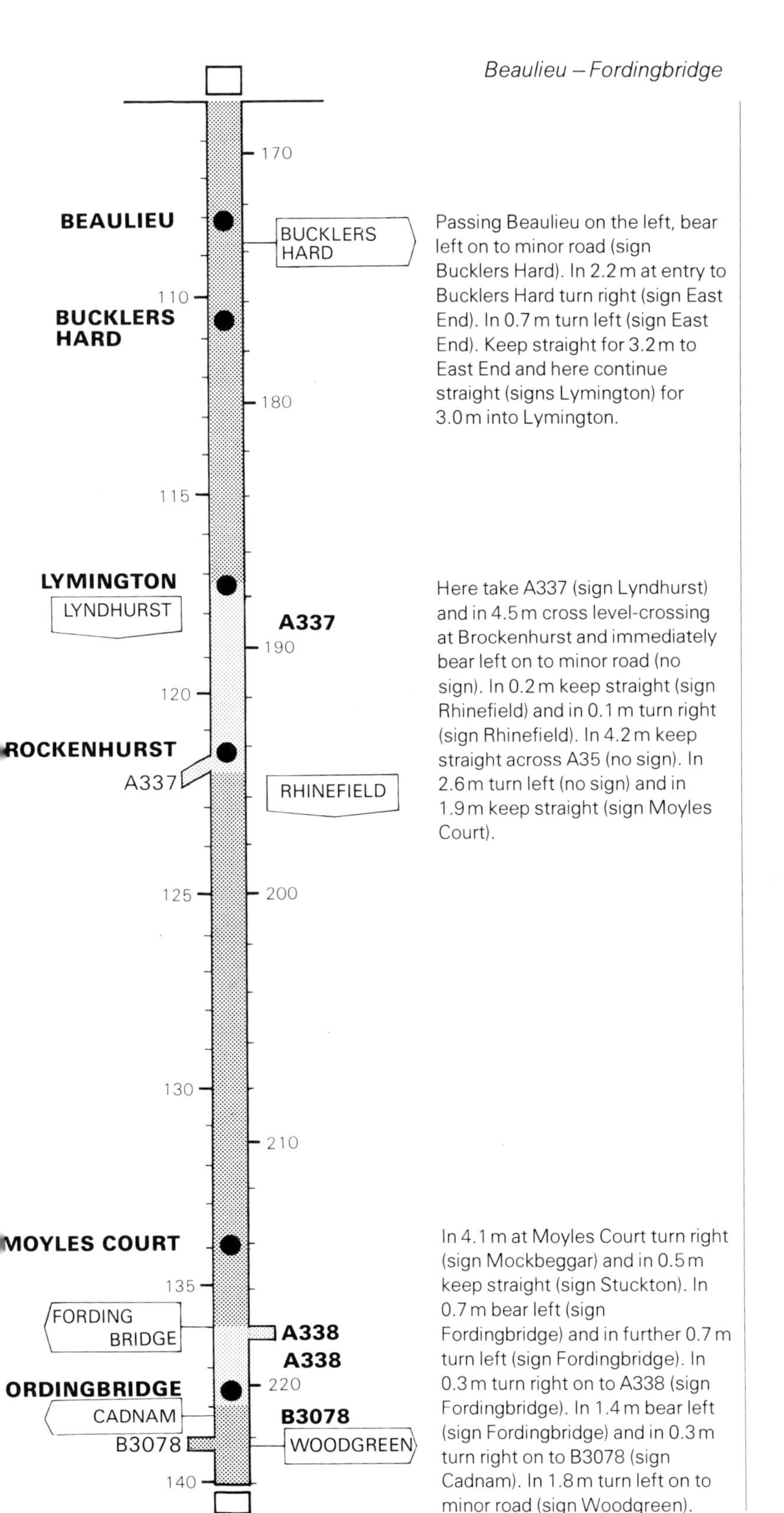

Passing Beaulieu on the left, bear left on to minor road (sign Bucklers Hard). In 2.2 m at entry to Bucklers Hard turn right (sign East End). In 0.7 m turn left (sign East End). Keep straight for 3.2 m to East End and here continue straight (signs Lymington) for 3.0 m into Lymington.

Here take A337 (sign Lyndhurst) and in 4.5 m cross level-crossing at Brockenhurst and immediately bear left on to minor road (no sign). In 0.2 m keep straight (sign Rhinefield) and in 0.1 m turn right (sign Rhinefield). In 4.2 m keep straight across A35 (no sign). In 2.6 m turn left (no sign) and in 1.9 m keep straight (sign Moyles Court).

In 4.1 m at Moyles Court turn right (sign Mockbeggar) and in 0.5 m keep straight (sign Stuckton). In 0.7 m bear left (sign Fordingbridge) and in further 0.7 m turn left (sign Fordingbridge). In 0.3 m turn right on to A338 (sign Fordingbridge). In 1.4 m bear left (sign Fordingbridge) and in 0.3 m turn right on to B3078 (sign Cadnam). In 1.8 m turn left on to minor road (sign Woodgreen).

Whiteparish (Wiltshire)

The Anglo-Saxon name for the village was Frustfeld, though around AD 1200 the colour of the new church resulted in the adoption of the name Whitechurch, later adapted to Whiteparish. The church has a beautiful setting in the middle of this small village which also boasts no less than three pubs, almost cheek by jowl. One of these, the White Hart (T323), has accommodation and serves meals.

West Dean (Wiltshire)

The Wilts/Hants border runs through the village, where the Red Lion Inn occupies a pleasant position on the green above the river. Excavations from Roman villas in the locality have been removed to the Salisbury museum.

The River Test at Stockbridge.

Stockbridge (Hampshire)

The main road turns northward on reaching the edge of Stockbridge, a centre for fishing on the nearby R. Test. The town consists almost entirely of one long broad main street where the hotel (below) gets a special recommendation for comfort and friendly service.

Grosvenor Hotel, 12 rooms, T606 (B)

Longstock (Hampshire)

The village of picturesque thatched cottages lies above lush meadows on the banks of the R. Test, renowned for trout fishing. There is a pleasant inn with an unusual name, The Peat Spade, which offers rooms and serves real ale.

Wherwell (Hampshire)

A tributary of the R. Test runs through this village of entrancing thatched and timbered cottages.

Longparish (Hampshire)

The village is appropriately named, for it is spread out for a mile or more. Outside the lychgate of the 12c church of St Nicholas are the remains of the village stocks, and the parish registers include entries such as the burial in 1731 of 'a travailing old woman, nicknamed Mother Stump'.

Whitchurch (Hampshire)

The 15c White Hart Hotel was the fishing headquarters of the Anglican divine and author, Charles Kingsley (1819–75), who, in a letter on view there, extols the virtues of the hotel but regrets that his fishing was spoilt by rain. Another feature of this pleasant hotel is a bedhead in one of the rooms, once the property of Benjamin Disraeli.

White Hart Hotel, Newbury St, 15 rooms, T2900 (B)

The Route

Large sections of the route run through wooded countryside, passing isolated villages with picturesque thatched and timbered cottages that are washed in pink, green or white.

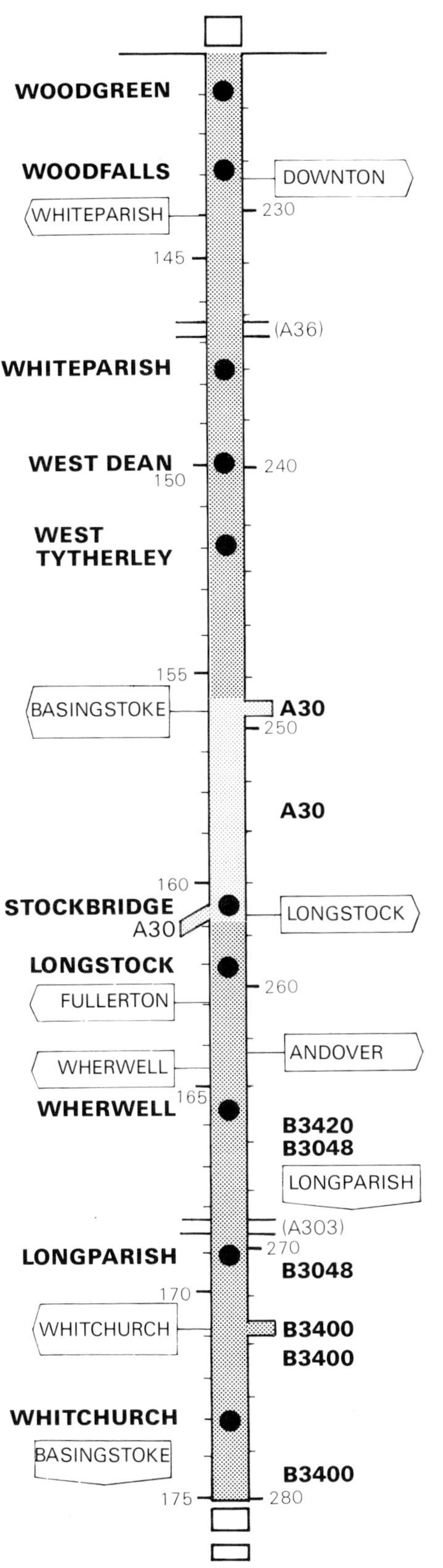

Keep straight (signs Woodgreen) for 1.8 m to Woodgreen. Here turn right (sign Woodgreen Common) and in 0.5 m keep straight (sign Redlynch). Keep straight for further 1.9 m to Woodfalls. On entering Woodfalls turn left (sign Downton) and in 1.0 m turn right on to minor road (sign Whiteparish). In 0.8 m bear left (sign Whiteparish) and in 2.0 m keep straight across A36 (sign Whiteparish). In 0.6 m turn right (no sign) and in 0.3 m at Whiteparish turn left (sign West Dean).

Keep straight for 2.2 m, turn right and shortly right again (no initial sign) into West Dean. Here continue straight (sign Tytherley) for 1.2 m and fork right (sign Tytherley) for 1.0 m to W. Tytherley. Here bear left (sign Winterslow) and in 1.6 m turn right (sign The Wallops). Keep straight (signs Stockbridge) and in 2.5 m turn right on to A30 (sign Basingstoke).

In 4.4 m, entering Stockbridge, turn left on to minor road (sign Longstock) for 1.3 m to Longstock. In 0.7 m turn right (sign Fullerton) and in further 1.4 m bear right (no sign). In 0.1 m turn left on to A3057 (sign Andover) and in 0.2 m turn right on to minor road (sign Wherwell). In 1.0 m at Wherwell keep straight on B3420 (no sign) and in 0.3 m keep straight on to B3048 (sign Longparish).

In 2.0 m turn right and immediately left across A303 (sign Longparish) for 1.0 m to Longparish. Here continue straight on B3048 for 2.2 m and turn right on to B3400 (sign Whitchurch) for 2.0 m into Whitchurch.

Overton (Hampshire)

A 'sleepy' little town with a broad main street; less busy, perhaps, than in olden times when coaches passed through and there was a market and silk mill.

YHA, Red Lion Lane, No phone

Alton (Hampshire)

Although hops for the brewing of beer are most prolific in Kent, many hopfields are to be seen around Alton for the supply of local brewers. This market town has some Georgian houses and a museum named after William Curtis, the 18c botanist, where there is a fine collection of pottery, porcelain and old farming equipment.

Swan Hotel, High St, 25 rooms, T82369 (B)

Frensham (Surrey)

Frensham Ponds spread across more than 100 acres amidst the gorse and heather of Frensham Common. The comfortable hotel (below) stands at the water's edge, near the Yacht club.

Frensham Pond Hotel, 15 rooms, T3175 (A)

Tilford (Surrey)

Central feature of the village is the huge green with the immense Tilford Oak, more than 26 feet in girth, and other oak trees that commemorate events such as the Diamond Jubilee of Queen Victoria and the crowning of George VI. Cricket is played in the midst of this splendour, and Tilford's green and adjoining pub provided an excellent setting for the filming of A. G. MacDonnell's classic story *England their England* – village cricket seen through the eyes of a Scotsman. Philip Snowden (1864–1937), the prominent Labour politician, spent the last years of his life in this lovely village, where the R. Wey is spanned by two medieval bridges.

Elstead (Surrey)

Unlike Tilford the village has grown recently – but the central part of Elstead lies round a green where there is a pleasant inn, The Woolpack. A five-arch medieval bridge crosses the Wey near an 18c rambling mill.

Guildford's 17c Guildhall.

The Route

The road is particularly narrow between Kingsley and Tilford. Quiet country roads apart from the final seven miles on the A3 back to Guildford. On the way to Guildford (on the A3 between Milford and Guildford) a short diversion to the right by way of the B3000 and minor road leads to the Watts Gallery (well signed). Many of the paintings of George Frederick Watts (1817–1904) are to be seen here, and the artist and his wife are buried in the Mortuary Chapel.

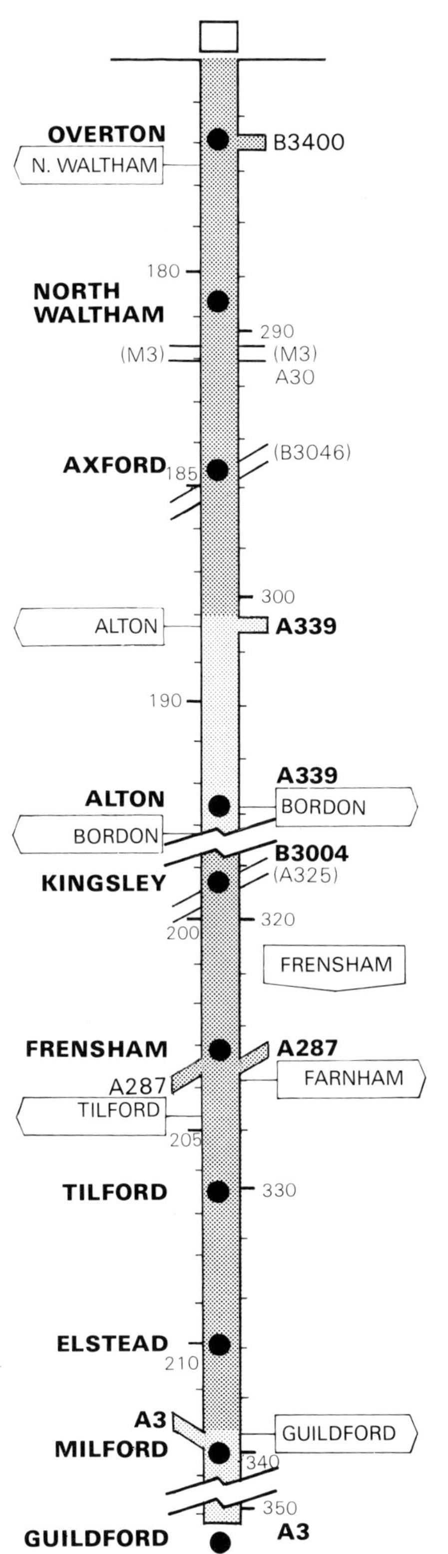

Continue straight on B3400 (sign Basingstoke) for 3.8 m to Overton and turn right on to minor road (sign N. Waltham).

Keep straight for further 3.8 m to N. Waltham and here continue straight (sign Axford). In 0.7 m turn left and immediately right, crossing A30 and M3 (sign Axford) for 3.1 m to Axford. Here turn right and immediately left (sign Herriard). In 1.7 m keep straight (sign Herriard) and in 0.8 m turn right (sign Bradley). In 0.3 m turn left (sign Alton). Keep straight (signs Alton) and in 1.2 m turn right on to A339 for 5.0 m into Alton.

On entering Alton turn left (sign Bordon) and in 0.3 m turn right on to B3004 (sign Bordon). Keep straight for 5.8 m past Worldham and Kingsley and bear left, crossing A325 on to minor road (sign Frensham). In 1.0 m turn left (sign Frensham) and in further 0.5 m turn left (sign Frensham). Keep straight (signs Frensham) for 1.5 m to Frensham Pond Hotel.

Here continue straight and in 1.1 m turn left on to A287 (sign Farnham). In 0.4 m turn right on to minor road (sign Tilford). In 1.7 m at T junction turn right (no sign) for 0.2 m to Tilford. Here turn left (sign Elstead) and in 0.8 m turn right (sign Elstead). In 1.7 m at Elstead keep straight (sign Milford). In 2.6 m at Milford turn left on to A3 (sign Guildford) for 7.0 m into Guildford.

12 *East Anglia (North): Norfolk*

THE CHOSEN ROUTE is confined almost entirely to the county of Norfolk, the largest of the eastern counties, extending over some two thousand square miles. This route of rather under two hundred miles is an attempt to embrace some of the more beautiful inland areas as well as visit points along the coast.

After leaving the lively city of Norwich the road runs southwards until reaching Pulham Market, a particularly attractive village, where an easterly course is set which runs roughly parallel to the River Waveney. The town of Beccles lies on the Waveney which connects with the most southerly of the Broads – Oulton.

The Broads are reed-bordered lakes, many of which are linked by rivers or connected to them by narrow channels. Most of them can only be seen by boat, for they lie tucked away out of sight of the roads. They offer a wide variety of wildlife, including the great crested grebe, bittern (a relation of the heron), bearded tit, Canada geese and several species of duck.

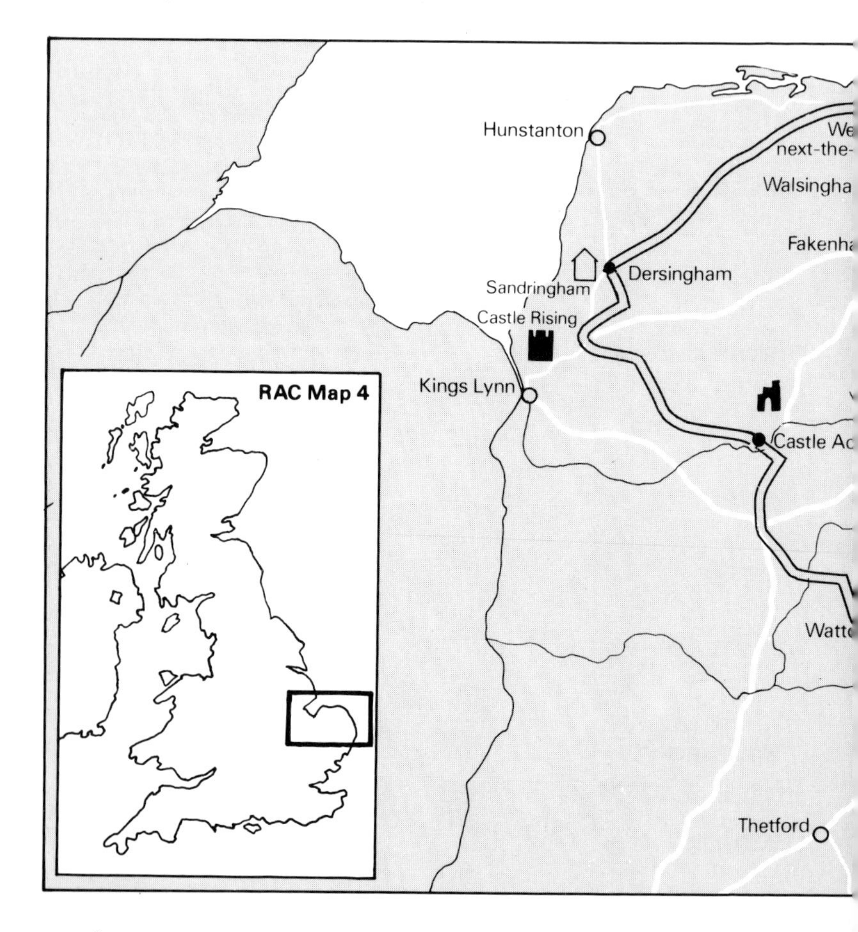

After striking north from Beccles there is a glimpse of Filby and Rollesby Broads which are part of a complex of Broads, the others being Lily, Little and Ormesby Broads. At Horsey, further north, Horsey Mere lies to the west and connects with Hickling, the largest of the Broads. Thus, along this coastal road, many of the Broads lie to the west with numerous sandy seaside resorts to the east.

The most northerly part of the route is the big resort of Cromer, which lies only four miles from another popular seaside resort, Sheringham. From Cromer, however, the road avoids Sheringham as it runs westward through pleasant enclosed countryside before returning to the coast once more at Blakeney. From here the route loops inland for a view of the beautiful and historic village of Little Walsingham. Then, after visiting Wells-next-the-sea, Holkham and Burnham Overy the road leads in the general direction of Sandringham, holiday residence of the Royal Family. The picturesque village of Castle Rising is the most westerly point, and from here the road returns eastward to Norwich by way of enchanting Castle Acre and many other pretty villages.

Norfolk would not claim to be England's fairest county. But it has a healthy climate with below average rainfall, fine beaches, a great variety of scenery, excellent sailing and fishing, and more species of waterfowl than can be found in any other part of the country.

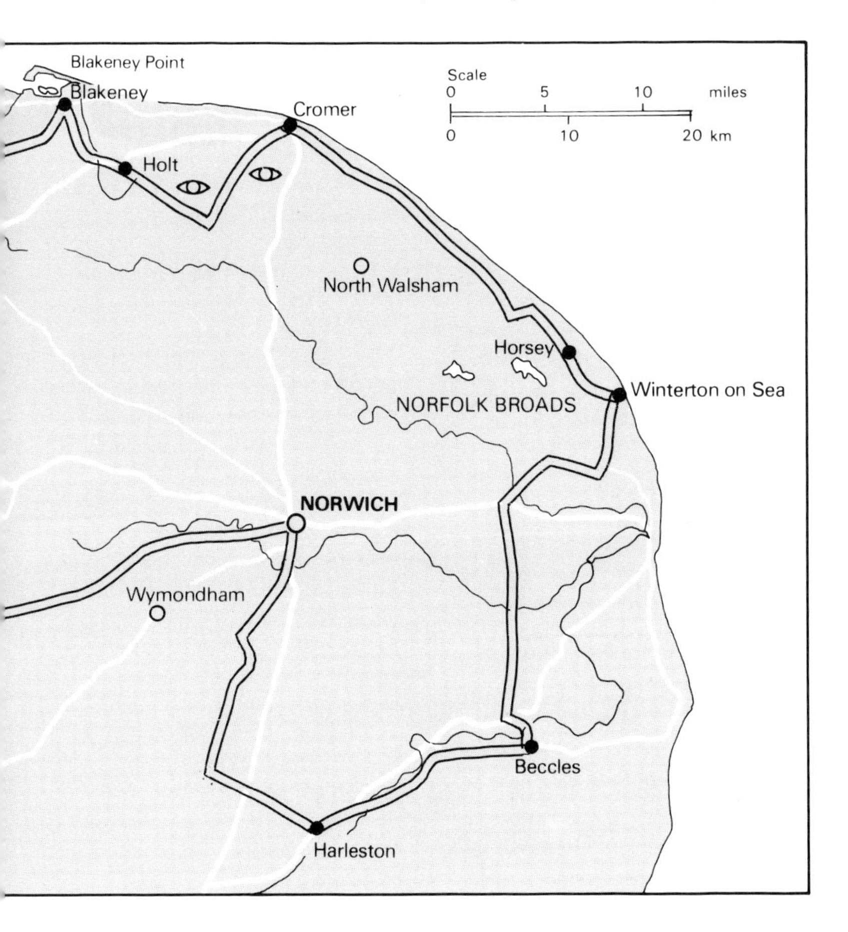

Norwich (Norfolk)

In order to explore the maze of narrow streets which run between the Cathedral, the castle, the market place, and the old Guildhall it is best to be equipped with a street plan, obtainable from the tourist office. The Cathedral can be approached by way of a picturesque cobbled street, Elm Hill, Wensum St and Tombland, through either of two huge medieval archways, the Ethelbert Gate (1316) or the Erpingham Gate (1420). The Cathedral spire (315 ft) stands second only to that of Salisbury Cathedral (404 ft) and alongside the cathedral walls is the grave of Edith Cavell (1865–1915), the nurse who was executed by the Germans for assisting allied prisoners to escape. The stone keep of the castle on the hill dates from 1120. The castle, which acted as the town prison until less than a hundred years ago, has since been converted into a museum of great variety – including a particularly fine collection of stuffed birds – and an art gallery.

Castle Hotel, Castle Meadow, 78 rooms, T611511 (A)
Beeches Hotel, 2 Earlham Road, 33 rooms, T21167 (D)
Earlham Guest House, 147 Earlham Road, 7 rooms, T54169 (D)
YHA, 9 Earlham Road, T27647.
T.O. Augustine Steward House, 14 Tombland, T20679

Swardeston (Norfolk)

In the church there are two photographs of Edith Cavell (see Norwich). Her father was rector here for 46 years. The church lies peacefully off the road in a village which has now become little more than a modern suburb of Norwich.

Mulbarton (Norfolk)

The huge fifty-acre green is the feature of this village. It is possibly the biggest green in the county.

Pulham Market (Norfolk)

A particularly attractive village where the thatched Crown Inn is among a number of old whitewashed houses surrounding the village green. A licensed restaurant, the Old Bakery, is tucked away to the left of the road near the green.

Harleston (Norfolk)

This old town is bisected by a long narrow High Street which tends to get congested with traffic, reminding one that this is the first A road the route has touched since leaving Norwich. Two inns stand close together with attractive wrought iron signs.

Swan Hotel, The Thoroughfare, 12 rooms, T852221 (B)

Flixton (Suffolk)

The Buck Inn Free House (T2382) serves good meals. Immediately behind it is the Norfolk and Suffolk Aero Museum, where there is a small collection of historic aircraft. Entry is free.

Bungay (Suffolk)

The Three Tuns, a 17c coaching inn, is said to be haunted by quite a variety of ghosts, and in 1969 a committee actually came here to investigate them. There is no accommodation, but excellent bar food is available, and the enterprising landlord now organizes medieval banquets each Friday and Saturday. Outside the inn the Black Dog of Bungay is carved on a lamp standard – a reminder of the legend that in 1577, during a thunderstorm, a fearsome beast entered the church and attacked the congregation. Tucked away on the other side of the road are the ruins of Bungay Castle.

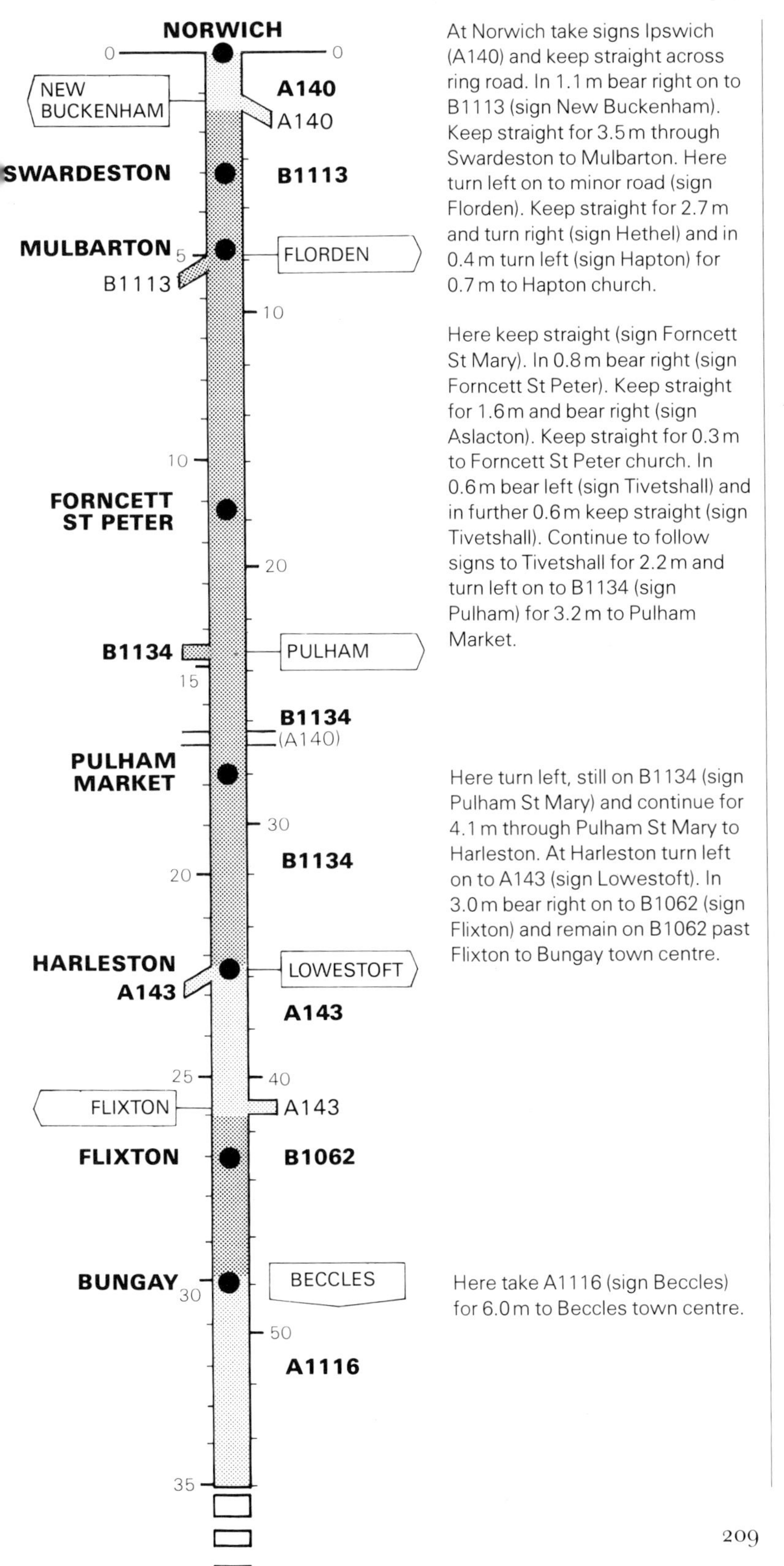

At Norwich take signs Ipswich (A140) and keep straight across ring road. In 1.1 m bear right on to B1113 (sign New Buckenham). Keep straight for 3.5 m through Swardeston to Mulbarton. Here turn left on to minor road (sign Florden). Keep straight for 2.7 m and turn right (sign Hethel) and in 0.4 m turn left (sign Hapton) for 0.7 m to Hapton church.

Here keep straight (sign Forncett St Mary). In 0.8 m bear right (sign Forncett St Peter). Keep straight for 1.6 m and bear right (sign Aslacton). Keep straight for 0.3 m to Forncett St Peter church. In 0.6 m bear left (sign Tivetshall) and in further 0.6 m keep straight (sign Tivetshall). Continue to follow signs to Tivetshall for 2.2 m and turn left on to B1134 (sign Pulham) for 3.2 m to Pulham Market.

Here turn left, still on B1134 (sign Pulham St Mary) and continue for 4.1 m through Pulham St Mary to Harleston. At Harleston turn left on to A143 (sign Lowestoft). In 3.0 m bear right on to B1062 (sign Flixton) and remain on B1062 past Flixton to Bungay town centre.

Here take A1116 (sign Beccles) for 6.0 m to Beccles town centre.

Beccles (Suffolk)

The bulk of the town, including the church and huge tower, lies high above the river Waveney. The Waveney House Hotel, however, stands right on the river at a point where it is particularly broad and pleasant. At the quay there are a multitude of boats, either privately owned or for hire for use on the broads.

Waveney House Hotel, Puddingmoor, 14 rooms, T712270 (B)

Reedham (Norfolk)

At one time ferry boats crossed the R. Yare at a number of points between Norwich and Yarmouth, but Reedham ferry is the sole survivor. It is available from 8 a.m. to 10 p.m. and there is a charge of 60p a car for this short crossing. On the other side of the river the Ferryboat Inn occupies a good position to overlook the various small craft which moor here.

The Route

Quiet traffic-free roads except where it was found necessary to take the A road between Bungay and Beccles. Although almost this entire route is confined to Norfolk, the northern edge of Suffolk is skirted from around Flixton to Beccles.

Filby (Norfolk)

Filby Broad and Rollesby Broad lie astride the road before it enters the village. In the village there is a sign to the right which directs to Thrigby Hall Wild Life Gardens, a diversion of less than a mile which is well worth taking. In 1979 the Hall's lake and gardens were converted into a home for mammals, birds and reptiles (Asian varieties). The gardens are open every day of the year, and among the wildlife to be seen are leopard, monkeys, otters, antelope and wild fowl. Thrigby Hall was built in 1876 on the remains of a much older building, and there is supposed to be a secret tunnel from the hall to the summer house, but the new owners have yet to discover it.

Ormesby St Margaret (Norfolk)

The Top House Inn stands on a pleasant village green. Although this is an attractive village it must be rather noisy as the busy A149, which the route crosses, runs through the heart of it.

Winterton on Sea (Norfolk)

The beach can be reached by turning right off the route by the church. Bathers are warned that a section of this beach is dangerous. The church is particularly beautiful and is noted for the tall tower, which is locally claimed to be a 'herring and a half' higher than Cromer. Many of these church towers were designed as landmarks for sailors, and there is another imposing tower further along the route at Happisburgh. The church has a Fisherman's Corner where almost everything, including the memorial cross to drowned sailors, has been constructed from materials salvaged from ships.

Horsey (Norfolk)

The village lies in secluded woodland a mile from the sand dunes, across which the sea has encroached and flooded the area on a number of occasions. The little church occupies a particularly peaceful woodland glade not far from Horsey Mere, a reed-fringed lake which provides a home for a variety of wildlife.

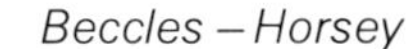

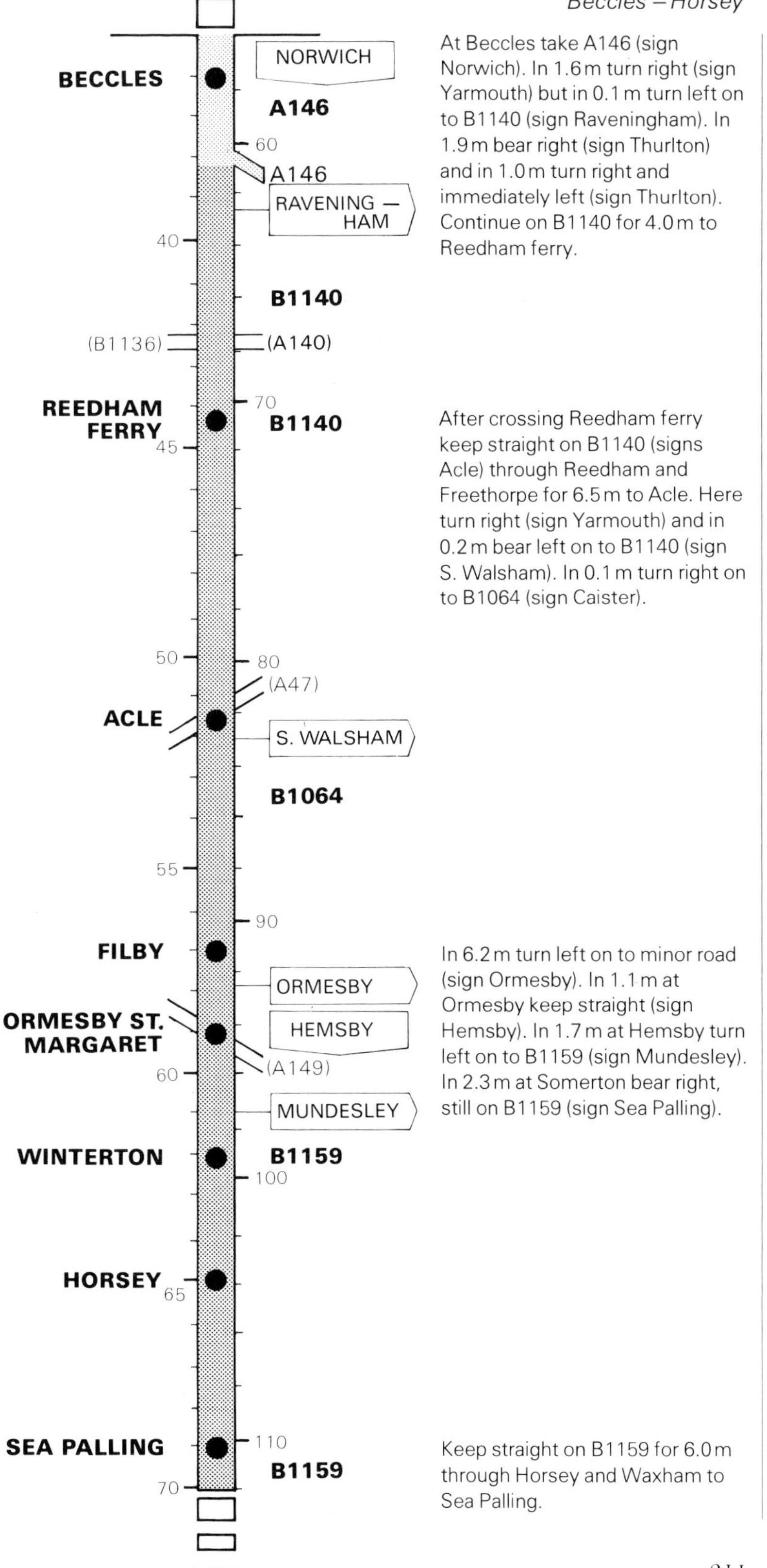

At Beccles take A146 (sign Norwich). In 1.6 m turn right (sign Yarmouth) but in 0.1 m turn left on to B1140 (sign Raveningham). In 1.9 m bear right (sign Thurlton) and in 1.0 m turn right and immediately left (sign Thurlton). Continue on B1140 for 4.0 m to Reedham ferry.

After crossing Reedham ferry keep straight on B1140 (signs Acle) through Reedham and Freethorpe for 6.5 m to Acle. Here turn right (sign Yarmouth) and in 0.2 m bear left on to B1140 (sign S. Walsham). In 0.1 m turn right on to B1064 (sign Caister).

In 6.2 m turn left on to minor road (sign Ormesby). In 1.1 m at Ormesby keep straight (sign Hemsby). In 1.7 m at Hemsby turn left on to B1159 (sign Mundesley). In 2.3 m at Somerton bear right, still on B1159 (sign Sea Palling).

Keep straight on B1159 for 6.0 m through Horsey and Waxham to Sea Palling.

Happisburgh (Norfolk)

Its name pronounced 'Hazeboro', this village stands on a cliff overlooking a treacherous sandy shore where many ships have foundered. In the churchyard there are memorials and graves of shipwrecked seamen.

Mundesley (Norfolk)

There is a huge sandy beach in this resort which is the largest on the north-east coast of Norfolk. The poet William Cowper (1731–1800) stayed in a large Georgian house here which is named after him.

Hotel Continental, Cromer Road, 55 rooms, T720271 (C)
Manor Hotel, Cromer Road, 25 rooms, T720309 (D)
Seaview Hotel, Paston Road, 12 rooms, T720252 (D)

Cromer (Norfolk)

The seaside town of Cromer.

Once a small fishing port, Cromer began to be popular as a seaside resort a century ago. Fishermen still bring in quantities of the renowned Cromer crabs which are sold not only here but also in stalls along many of the major roads. A number of hotels have good sea views across the grassy cliffs, where there are pleasant sunken gardens and paths which lead to the beach and pier. After leaving Cromer but before arriving at Holt there are two particular places of interest in the beautiful remote countryside along the minor road. The first is Felbrigg Hall (National Trust), which lies on the left of the road in the Great Wood (600 acres) and where, on the first floor, there is a library in Gothic style as well as a number of Georgian rooms and furniture. The Hall and surrounding park and woods are open to the public. A little further along the route, signed to the right, is Baconsthorpe Castle. The remains of the 15c manor house are in the care of the Department of Environment and consist principally of the outer gate-house, later converted into a dwelling, and a moat which can be crossed for entry into the inner gatehouse and hall. Open to the public daily.

Hotel de Paris, Jetty Cliff, 60 rooms, T513141 (C)
Cliftonville Hotel, Runton Road, 42 rooms, T512543 (C)
Ship Hotel, Church Street, 8 rooms, T2461 (D)
T.O. North Lodge Park, T512497

Holt (Norfolk)

A pleasant market town with a particularly impressive war memorial cross in the market square. To the east of the town is the well-known public school, Greshams, founded in 1555 by Sir John Gresham, a native of Holt.

Feathers Hotel, 6 Market Place, 22 rooms, T2318 (C)

The Route

There are numerous points of interest along the route, some of which have been emphasized. Unhappily, much of the coastal road from Sea Palling to Mundesley has now become grossly overcrowded with bungalows and caravan sites. Nevertheless there are many fine sandy beaches.

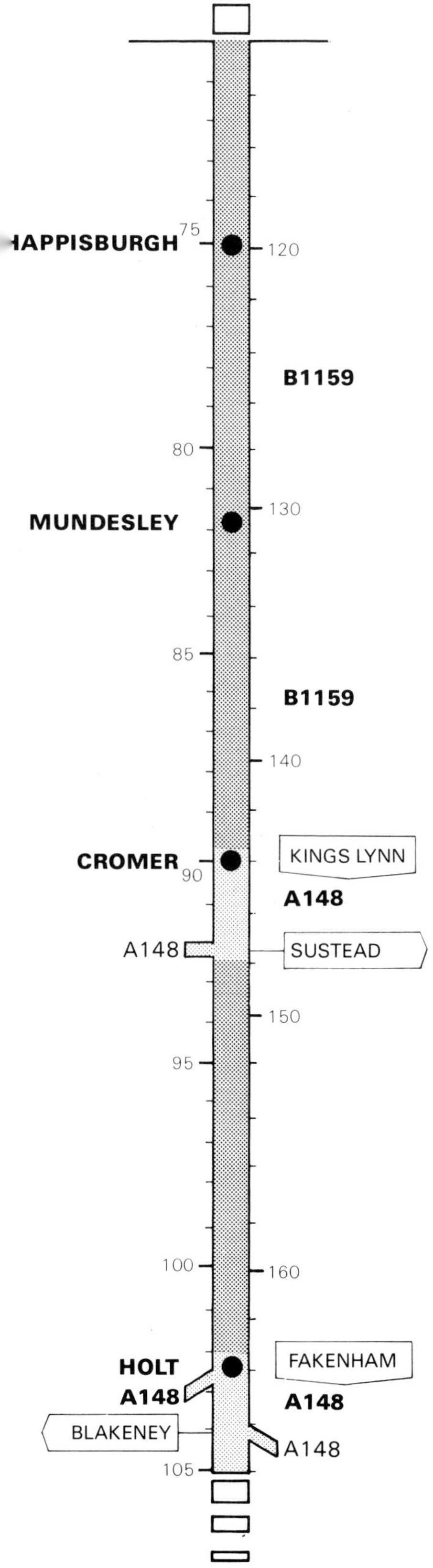

HAPPISBURGH 75 120
B1159
80
MUNDESLEY 130
85
B1159
140
CROMER 90
KINGS LYNN
A148
A148 SUSTEAD
150
95
100 160
HOLT FAKENHAM
A148 A148
BLAKENEY A148
105

Continue on B1159 for 5.8 m to Happisburgh.

In 1.3 m turn right, still on B1159 (sign Cromer) and in further 2.1 m turn right (sign Cromer). Keep straight on B1159 for 11.0 m through Mundesley to Cromer.

In Cromer take A148 (sign Kings Lynn) and in 2.2 m turn left on to minor road (sign Sustead). In 0.8 m keep straight (no sign) and in 0.5 m turn right (no sign). In 0.3 m turn left (sign Gresham) and in 0.5 m keep straight (sign W. Beckham).

In 0.4 m turn left (sign Bessingham) and in 1.0 m bear right (sign Holt). In 0.2 m keep straight (sign Baconsthorpe). In 1.6 m keep straight (sign Matlaske) but in 0.1 m bear right (sign Baconsthorpe). In 0.8 m turn left (sign Baconsthorpe) and in 0.6 m turn right (sign Holt). Keep straight for 3.5 m to Holt. Here take A148 (sign Fakenham) and in 1.4 m turn right on to B1156 (sign Blakeney).

Fishing boats at Blakeney.

Blakeney (Norfolk)

A narrow street of fishermen's cottages leads down to an estuary from where launch trips can be taken to Blakeney Point (National Trust), a sanctuary where no less than 256 different species of bird have been sighted and a part of the coast which is often visited by seals. The recommended hotel enjoys a fine position overlooking the quay and the colourful boats.

Blakeney Hotel, 54 rooms, T797 (C)

Binham (Norfolk)

Binham Priory is signed to the right, just outside the village. The Priory was founded by a nephew of William the Conqueror at the end of the 12c.

Little Walsingham (Norfolk)

A delightful village, full of old buildings. In the village there is a sign to the 'Slipper Chapel' at Houghton St Giles, a mile away. It was from here that pilgrims in pre-Reformation days used to leave their footgear in order to walk barefoot to worship at the shrine of Our Lady of Walsingham. The shrine is said to have been built in 1061, and pilgrims in their thousands flocked to Walsingham until the shrine was removed and burned by Henry VIII. Both Catholics and Anglicans recommenced pilgrimages in this century. The ruins of the 12c Augustinian priory and the Franciscan friary should be visited.

Black Lion Hotel, Friday Market, 12 rooms, T235 (D)
YHA, Friday Market, T459

Wells-next-the-Sea (Norfolk)

Inappropriately named, this town of narrow streets lies a good mile from the sea. The pine-fringed beach can be reached by a road which leads from the quay. At Holkham, just after leaving Wells, Holkham Hall is signed to the left. This imposing stately home, seat of the Earl of Leicester, can be visited on certain days in the summer, as can the extensive grounds.

Crown Hotel, 12 rooms, T Fakenham 71209 (C)

Burnham Overy (Norfolk)

The water-mill (National Trust) lies among a cluster of charming cottages.

Dersingham (Norfolk)

This large village straggles along the main road. The quieter part of the village lies along the minor road to Sandringham, and it is along this road that the recommended hotel is to be found.

Feathers Hotel, 6 rooms, T40207 (D)

The Route

The more open countryside has been left behind, and this section of the route is by way of a number of narrow winding roads which wend through woods and small villages.

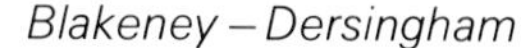

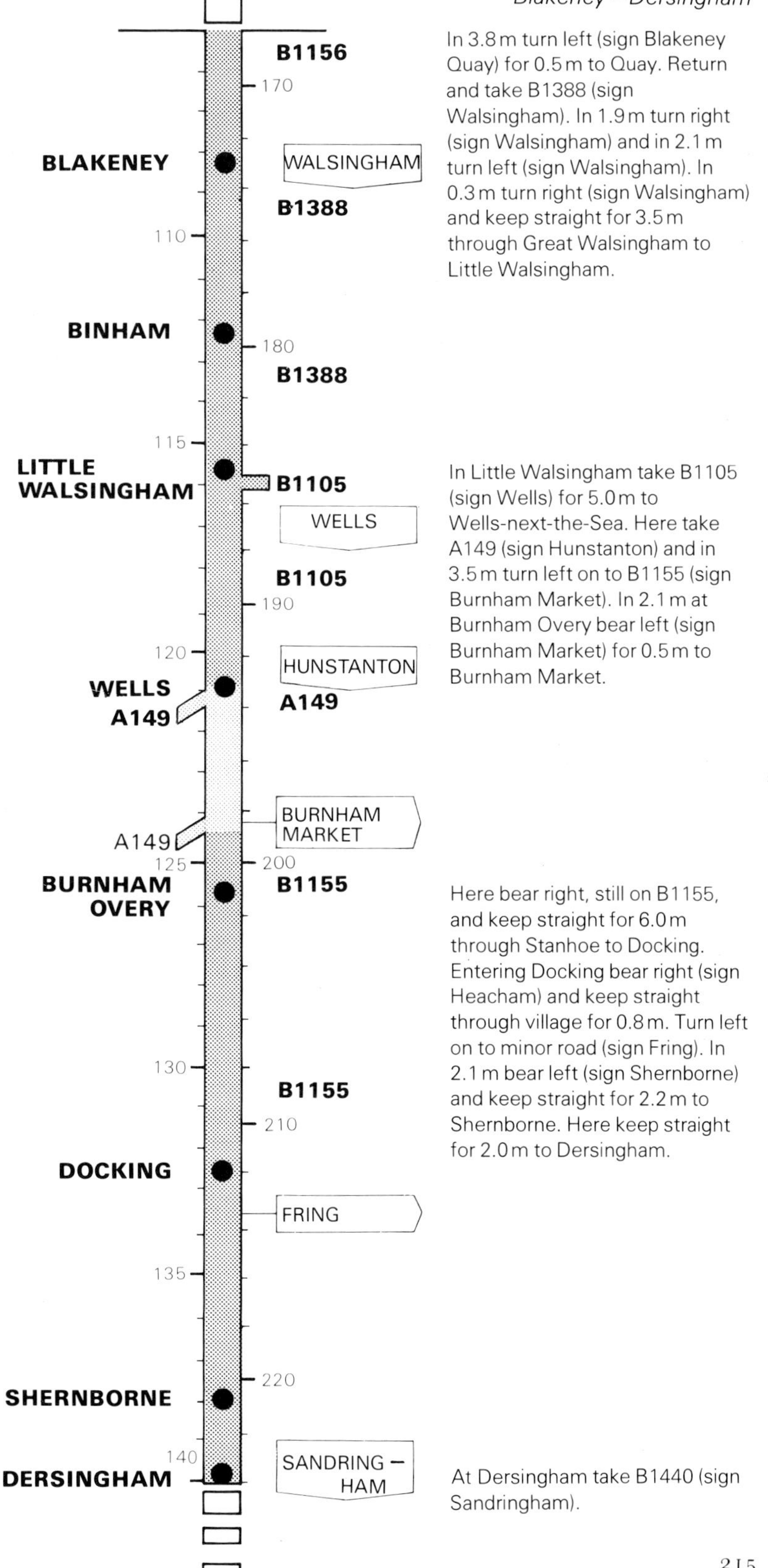

In 3.8 m turn left (sign Blakeney Quay) for 0.5 m to Quay. Return and take B1388 (sign Walsingham). In 1.9 m turn right (sign Walsingham) and in 2.1 m turn left (sign Walsingham). In 0.3 m turn right (sign Walsingham) and keep straight for 3.5 m through Great Walsingham to Little Walsingham.

In Little Walsingham take B1105 (sign Wells) for 5.0 m to Wells-next-the-Sea. Here take A149 (sign Hunstanton) and in 3.5 m turn left on to B1155 (sign Burnham Market). In 2.1 m at Burnham Overy bear left (sign Burnham Market) for 0.5 m to Burnham Market.

Here bear right, still on B1155, and keep straight for 6.0 m through Stanhoe to Docking. Entering Docking bear right (sign Heacham) and keep straight through village for 0.8 m. Turn left on to minor road (sign Fring). In 2.1 m bear left (sign Shernborne) and keep straight for 2.2 m to Shernborne. Here keep straight for 2.0 m to Dersingham.

At Dersingham take B1440 (sign Sandringham).

Above the village of Castle Rising stands the Norman Castle.

Sandringham (Norfolk)

The road runs alongside the walls and entrances of Sandringham House. The Sandringham Estate was bought in 1861 by Queen Victoria for King Edward VII, then Prince of Wales, and Sandringham House was built almost ten years later. The estate as a whole covers some 20,000 acres, of which 15,000 are occupied by tenant farmers. The park of Sandringham House which includes shrubberies, flower, fruit and vegetable gardens can be visited by the public when no member of the Royal Family is in residence. The little church, restored in the 19c, stands just inside the west entrance.

Castle Rising (Norfolk)

To the east of the Norman church in this beautiful little village is an almshouse presented by the Earl of Northampton, Henry Howard, in 1622. This red-brick house, containing rooms with their original Jacobean furniture, stands round a well-tended lawn. The original requirements for the occupation of the house, as laid down by Howard, were that the governess and eleven inmates should be 'of honest life and conversation, religious, grave and discreet, able to read if such a one may be had . . .' To this day the house remains occupied, and the inhabitants comply with tradition by attending services at the church, dressed in red cloaks adorned with the Howard badge and cone-shaped hats. The ruins of the Norman castle stand proudly above the village, and it was here that Isabella, mother of Edward III, was imprisoned for complicity in the murder of her husband. The R. Babingley was once tidal and navigable, and the village was once a thriving port.

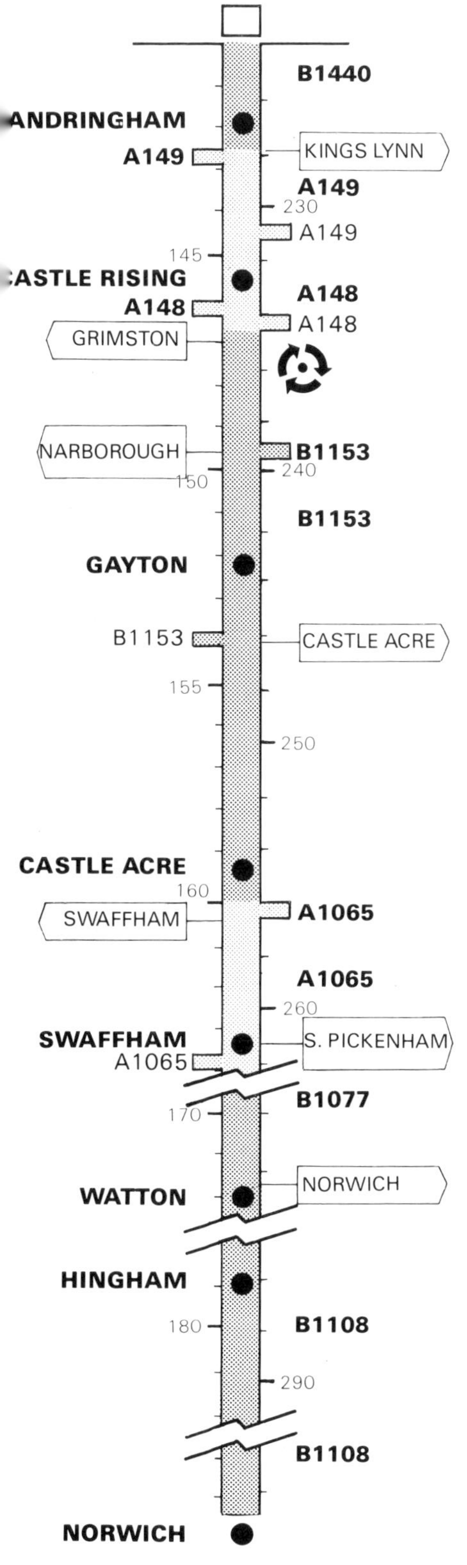

In 2.0 m at W. Newton turn right (no sign). In 1.8 m turn left on to A149 (sign Kings Lynn) and in 1.1 m turn right (sign Castle Rising) for 0.4 m into Castle Rising.

Leave Castle Rising by castle car park (no sign) and in 0.8 m turn left on to A148. Keep straight across roundabout (sign Cromer) and in 0.3 m turn right on to minor road (sign Grimston). Keep straight for 3.2 m and turn right on to B1153 (sign Narborough). In 2.2 m at Gayton keep straight (sign Narborough). In 2.1 m bear left on to minor road (sign Castle Acre). In 4.5 m turn right (sign Castle Acre) for 0.4 m into Castle Acre.

In Castle Acre pass through Bailey Bridge (sign Swaffham) and in 0.4 m bear right (sign Swaffham). In 1.0 m turn right on to A1065 (sign Swaffham) for 2.6 m into Swaffham. Here continue on A1065 (sign Thetford) and in 0.4 m turn left on to B1077 (sign S. Pickenham). In 8.2 m entering Watton turn left on to B1108 (sign Norwich). Keep on B1108 for 7.0 m into Hingham. Here continue on B1108 for 12.0 m to Norwich.

The majestic ruins of Castle Acre Priory.

The picturesque Elm Hill (right), *one of Norwich's many cobbled streets, leads to the Cathedral* (above).

Castle Acre (Norfolk)

The main street of the village is approached by passing through the 11c gateway which is all that remains of what was once a vast Norman castle. The houses in the attractive square above the gateway are flint-walled to blend with it. But, tragically, some modern houses have been built right along the other side of the gate, where they make an unpleasant contrast. Castle Acre Priory is signed from the square and has been preserved by the Dept. of the Environment. This is an extensive ruin with clearly defined foundations which have been well mapped within the Prior's lodge, the upper floor of which can be reached by a rather narrow, dark and steep stairway.

Swaffham (Norfolk)

A large town with spacious market place. A bypass is being built – and is much needed, for at present there can be considerable traffic congestion in and around the town.

George Hotel, Station Road, 17 rooms, T21238 (C)

Hingham (Norfolk)

Attractive Georgian houses are grouped around the market-place. In the north aisle of the church is a bust of Abraham Lincoln, who was descended from the Lincolns of Hingham.

The Route

Initially narrow roads through much wooded country. After Swaffham the road is straighter, broader and almost traffic-free as it runs through flat and sparsely populated countryside back to Norwich.

13 *Oxfordshire, Buckinghamshire, Gloucestershire, Berkshire*

THIS ROUTE COVERS a distance of about 244 miles through the counties of Oxfordshire, Berkshire, Gloucestershire, Northamptonshire, Buckinghamshire, Bedfordshire and Hertfordshire.

From Oxford, described by Matthew Arnold as 'that sweet city with her dreaming spires', the road runs southward through the fascinating village of Ewelme until crossing into Berkshire at Streatley on Thames. It is worth pausing at Newbury, if only to see the fine museum, before reaching the horse-racing centre of Lambourn and the lovely church of St Michael and All Angels. It was at this church, incidentally, that a certain William Bush made history in 1607 when he travelled by air, land and water from the church to London. He

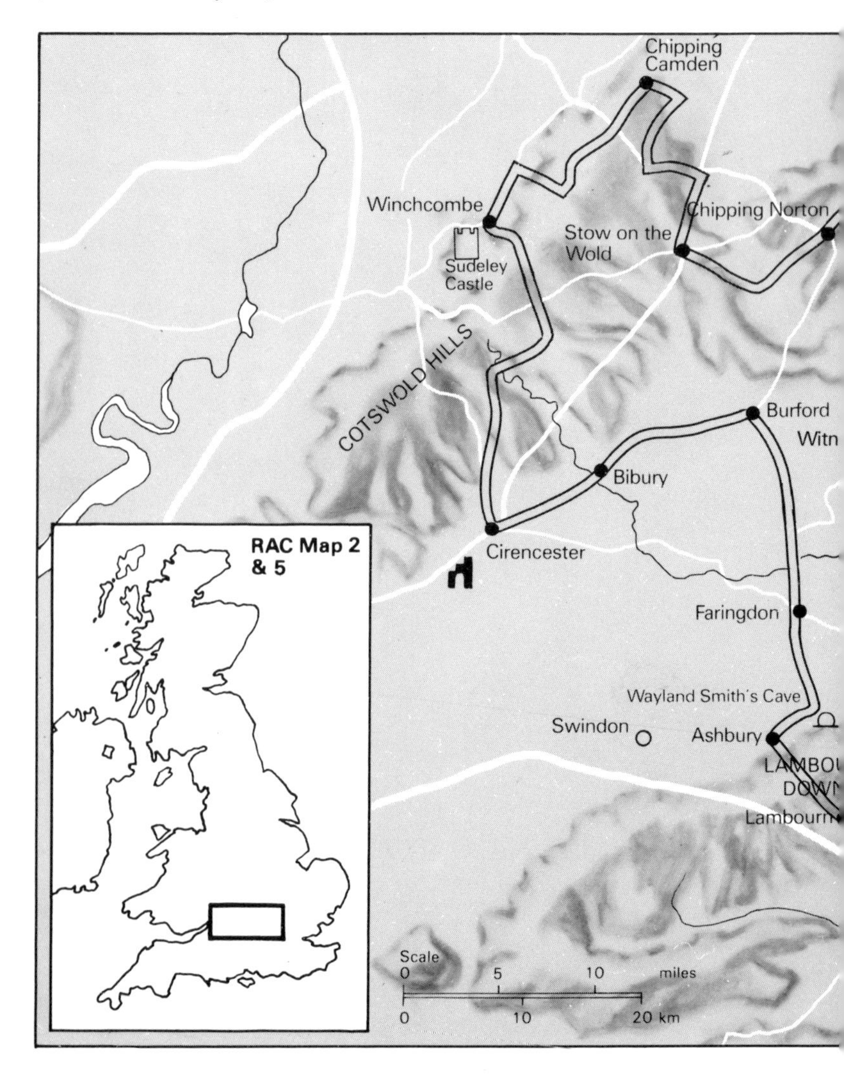

had invented an amphibious machine which was lowered by ropes from the church tower and which he then propelled on land to Streatley and, from there, by river to London.

Between Lambourn and Ashbury (left of road) is Ashdown House, a three-storey building surmounted by a golden cupola in a forty-acre park that is owned by the National Trust and open to the public on specified occasions. Beyond Ashbury is the Vale of the White Horse, an area made famous by Thomas Hughes in his novel, *Tom Brown's Schooldays*, where features of interest include White Horse Hill, Dragon's Hill, a prehistoric fort – Uffington Castle, and a place known as Wayland's Smithy, where according to myth a ghostly blacksmith shod horses overnight.

Burford marks the entry to the Cotswolds, where the stone-built towns and villages nestle near the fifty-mile-long range of hills that stretch from Bristol to Chipping Campden. After leaving the old Roman town of Cirencester it is worth noting that one of Britain's best preserved Roman villas, Chedworth, is signed off to the right of the

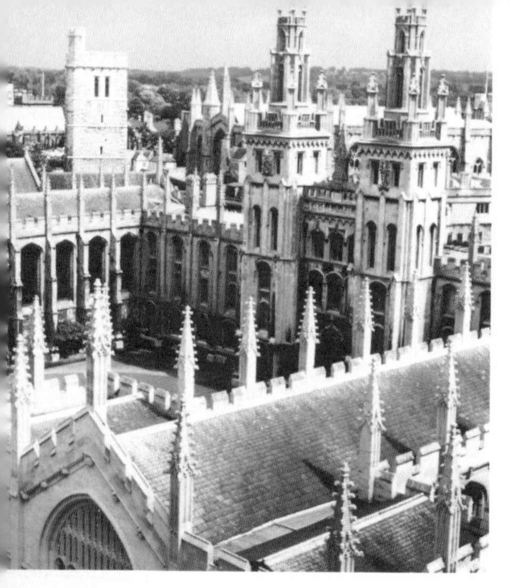

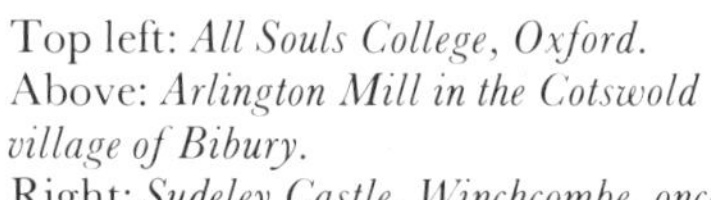

Top left: *All Souls College, Oxford.*
Above: *Arlington Mill in the Cotswold village of Bibury.*
Right: *Sudeley Castle, Winchcombe, once the home of Katherine Parr.*

road before it reaches the tiny village of Withington with its cathedral-like church. Sudeley Castle at Winchcombe ought to be visited and there is much to see in and around Chipping Norton with the Jacobean Chastleton House close at hand and with Blenheim Palace, home of the Duke of Marlborough and birthplace of Winston Churchill, only ten miles away.

Chipping Norton lies on the fringe of the Cotswolds and the route now runs eastward towards Buckingham through Aynho, Northamptonshire's southernmost village, with the 17th century mansion Aynho Park (National Trust) to the south of the village. From Buckingham, a typical market town of steep narrow streets and many old buildings, the road continues eastward through Winslow, home of the

Florence Nightingale Museum, as far as Leighton Buzzard.

Soon after leaving Leighton Buzzard the road reaches the eastern edge of the Chilterns, passing Dagnall (Whipsnade Park Zoo a mile away), Ashridge Park, and the pretty village of Aldbury before arriving at Wendover, a town of many old inns that include the half-timbered Red Lion where Oliver Cromwell rested in 1642. The final place of interest before returning to Oxford is Thame, an ancient market town where the annual Thame Show takes place in the broad High Street.

Oxford

Britain's oldest university town, named after the 'ford for oxen' that once permitted the Thames to be crossed at nearby Hinksey. Carfax is the name given to the central crossroads where the 14c tower can be climbed for a good overall view of the city. At nearby Christ Church (1525), Tom Tower stands above the main gate, and the huge bell, Great Tom, tolls 101 times at 9.05 p.m. as a reminder that this was the signal for the original 101 students that the gates were about to be closed. Apart from Oxford's colleges, of which the oldest are University College (1249), Balliol (1263) and Merton (1264), the city abounds with museums, libraries, gardens, art galleries and theatres. Places of interest include the Cathedral (12c); the Botanic Gardens (1621); the Bodleian Library, founded in 1602 by Sir Thomas Bodley and now containing some 2,500,000 books; the Ashmolean Museum, paintings and ceramics; and the Sheldonian theatre, built by Sir Christopher Wren, where university ceremonies and concerts take place. Oxford, of course, is more than an ancient university city, for it has now become an important industrial centre where car manufacturing predominates.

Randolph Hotel, Beaumont St, 115 rooms, T47481 (A)
Isis Hotel, 45 Iffley Rd, 33 rooms, T48894 (C)
Windsor Guest House, 226 Iffley Rd, 7 rooms, T48649 (D)
YHA, Jack Straw's Lane, T62997
T.O. St Aldates T48707

Watlington (Oxfordshire)

John Hampden (1594–1643), whose refusal to pay 'ship money' led up to the Civil War, was mortally wounded at Chalgrove after a skirmish with the Cavaliers, and the obelisk marking the spot lies to the left of the road before reaching Watlington. This is an attractive old town on the edge of the Chilterns with narrow streets, half-timbered 17c houses, and a gabled town hall dating from 1644.

Ewelme (Oxfordshire)

The small Chiltern village is famed for the church, almshouse and school which lie placidly in a group to the right of the road. Within the Church of St Mary are the tombs of Alice, Duchess of Suffolk (d. 1475), and her parents Thomas and Matilda Chaucer, son and daughter-in-law of the poet Geoffrey Chaucer. The adjacent school, founded in 1437 and claiming to be the oldest of our church schools, was set up with the proviso that a grammar school master should be appointed to teach the children of Ewelme 'freely without exaccion of any Schole hire'. This school still provides grammar school education for local children.

Streatley on Thames (Berks)

Entering Streatley there is a fine view of the river and old water-mill from the 19c bridge which connects Berkshire and Oxfordshire. Prior to the building of the bridge the Thames was crossed by ferry boat – a hazardous arrangement, for on one occasion fifty people were drowned while returning from Goring to Streatley.

YHA, Hill House, Reading Rd, T Goring 2278

Hampstead Norreys (Berks)

The earliest parts of St Mary's Church date from the 11c. The church stands next to the manor house in woods and pasture land.

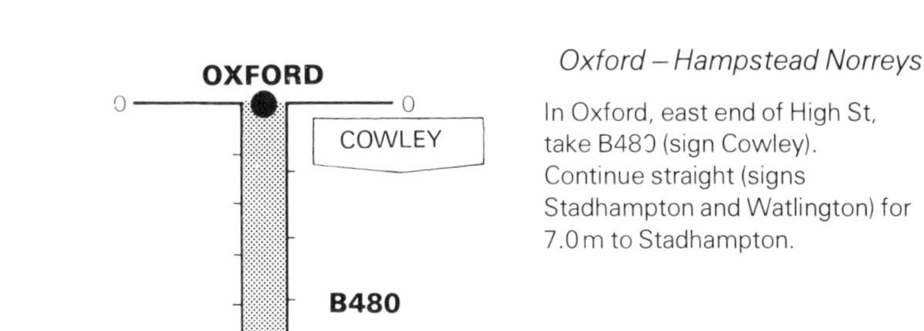

In Oxford, east end of High St, take B480 (sign Cowley). Continue straight (signs Stadhampton and Watlington) for 7.0 m to Stadhampton.

Here turn left and almost immediately right, still on B480, for 6.4 m to Watlington.

Here turn right on to B4009 (sign Brightwell) and in 2.4 m turn left (sign Ewelme). In 1.0 m at Ewelme turn left past church (sign Swyncombe) and in 0.3 m turn right (no sign). In 0.2 m turn left (sign Crowmarsh) and in 0.9 m turn right and immediately left (sign Crowmarsh).

At Crowmarsh Giffard turn right (sign Wallingford) and in 0.2 m turn left on to A4074 (sign Goring). In 0.9 m bear right on to B4009 (sign Goring). Continue straight for 4.7 m and turn right, still on B4009, into Streatley on Thames.

Here keep straight on B4009 for 6.9 m to Hampstead Norrys and bear left, still on B4009. Continue on B4009 for 7.0 m to Newbury.

The Route

Quiet traffic-free roads soon after leaving the outskirts of Oxford and Cowley.

Newbury (Berks)

A narrow balustraded bridge crosses the R. Kennet in this old cloth-making town. The District Museum is of interest and features include the Civil War battles that took place here as well as the evolution of photography. There is a fine racecourse to the east of the town.

Chequers Hotel, Oxford St, 64 rooms, T43666 (A)
Brooklyn Lodge Hotel, London Rd, 15 rooms, T47358 (C)
T.O. Council Offices, Wharf Rd, T42400

Lambourn (Berks)

Racehorse stables surround this small town, an intimate version of Newmarket, where many a tip for a 'good thing' can be heard in the local inns. In fact it was a Newmarket trainer, William Jousiffe, who set up the first training establishment here in 1878, and the lych gate of the parish church is the memorial to him. King Charles II once lodged at the Red Lion opposite the church.

Red Lion Hotel, Market Place, 12 rooms, T71406 (B)

Ashbury (Oxfordshire)

Most of the older buildings lie to the left of the road in a village which has the distinction of being the home of the first Sunday School ever to be held in England (1777). A number of interesting features are to be found after leaving Ashbury on the way to Uffington. High up on the right of the road is England's largest and possibly oldest 'White Horse', a hillside carving 374 feet in length and known to have existed for at least 700 years, that gives its name to the vale beneath. Near to the White Horse is Dragon's Hill where, according to legend, St George slew the dragon.

Rose and Crown Hotel, 8 rooms, T222 (D)

Uffington (Oxfordshire)

Thomas Hughes (1822–96), author of *Tom Brown's Schooldays*, the novel about life under Arnold at Rugby College, was born in Uffington and describes the area vividly in his famous book: 'I pity people who weren't born in a Vale. I don't mean a flat country bounded by hills. The having your hill always in view if you choose to turn towards him, that's the essence of a vale.' This little village of the White Horse Vale, well removed from the main road, cannot have changed much since Hughes wrote about it.

Folly Hill, outside Faringdon.

Faringdon (Oxfordshire)

A market town noted for its dairy produce with a number of pleasant old inns. Just to the east of the town is Folly Hill, where in 1935 Lord Berners built his famous tower.

Bell Hotel, Market Place, 9 rooms, T20534 (C)

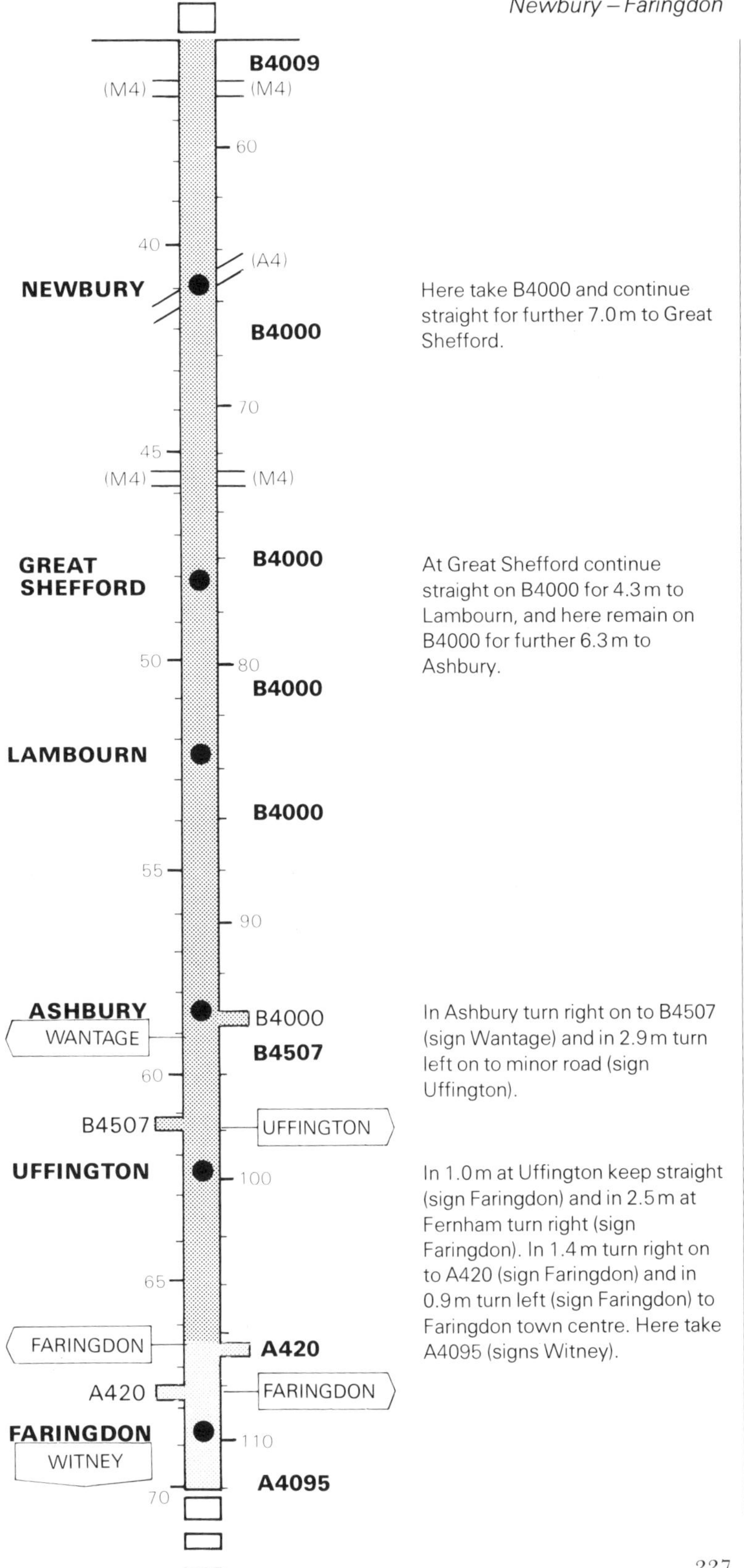

Here take B4000 and continue straight for further 7.0 m to Great Shefford.

At Great Shefford continue straight on B4000 for 4.3 m to Lambourn, and here remain on B4000 for further 6.3 m to Ashbury.

In Ashbury turn right on to B4507 (sign Wantage) and in 2.9 m turn left on to minor road (sign Uffington).

In 1.0 m at Uffington keep straight (sign Faringdon) and in 2.5 m at Fernham turn right (sign Faringdon). In 1.4 m turn right on to A420 (sign Faringdon) and in 0.9 m turn left (sign Faringdon) to Faringdon town centre. Here take A4095 (signs Witney).

The High Street, Burford.

Burford (Oxfordshire)

Known as the 'Gateway' to the Cotswolds, this small town lies astride a steep high street which descends to the R. Windrush. The town is close to the main A40 and does tend to get overcrowded in high season.

T.O. High St, T2168

Bibury (Glos)

Attractive stone-built cottages nestle on either side of the R. Coln and these include Arlington Row, cottages that were converted in the 17c from a 14c wool factory. Arlington Row (*below*), preserved by the National Trust, is reached by a footbridge across the river.

Swan Hotel, 24 rooms, T204 (A)

Cirencester (Glos)

Known as the 'Capital of the Cotswolds', Cirencester was once the second largest town in Roman Britain (Corinium) and the Corinium Museum reconstructs the life of the town in Roman times. Cirencester Park extends from the town for some five miles of park and woodland and is open to the public (cyclists and pedestrians only) by permission of the owner, Lord Bathurst. The 400-year-old Black Horse Inn was previously a monastery, which perhaps accounts for the ghost of the elderly lady and the monks which earlier in this century were said to have been seen on the premises. Today, however, the proprietors appear to be getting no visitations but they certainly provide a warm welcome in this pleasant well preserved old inn.

Kings Head Hotel, Market Place, 73 rooms, T3322 (A)
Black Horse Hotel, Castle St, 4 rooms, T3094 (D)

T.O. Corn Hall, Market Place, T4180

The Route

Of particular interest are the stone-built houses and cottages of the Cotswolds which the route reaches at Burford – buildings which have been planned to harmonize with the landscape.

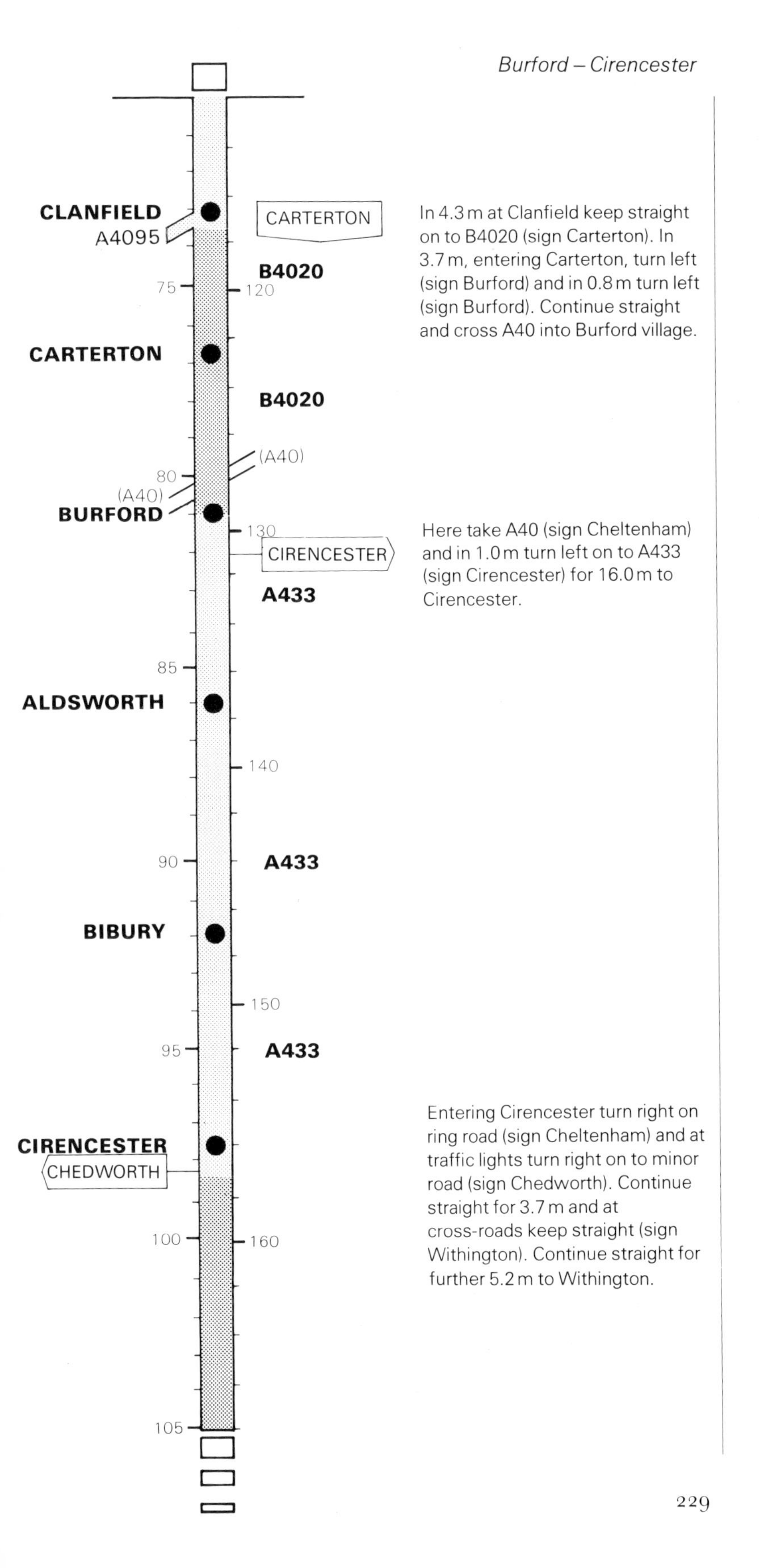

In 4.3 m at Clanfield keep straight on to B4020 (sign Carterton). In 3.7 m, entering Carterton, turn left (sign Burford) and in 0.8 m turn left (sign Burford). Continue straight and cross A40 into Burford village.

Here take A40 (sign Cheltenham) and in 1.0 m turn left on to A433 (sign Cirencester) for 16.0 m to Cirencester.

Entering Cirencester turn right on ring road (sign Cheltenham) and at traffic lights turn right on to minor road (sign Chedworth). Continue straight for 3.7 m and at cross-roads keep straight (sign Withington). Continue straight for further 5.2 m to Withington.

Three Cotswold villages
Top: *Snowshill.*
Above: *Withington.*
Right: *Chipping Campden.*

Withington (Glos)

'The village of Withington has a Church like a small Cathedral which is as sound as it was 800 years ago' wrote William Cobbett when he visited in 1826. And St Michael's Church is indeed huge for a tiny village which cannot even boast a shop. On leaving the village

A peaceful, shady lane, with its wall of Cotswold stone.

the road drops to the river where in a secluded valley is the fascinating Mill Inn, partitioned into a variety of bars. Several signs to the right show the way to Chedworth Villa, well-preserved remains of a Roman-British villa that was excavated in the last century and is maintained by the National Trust.

Compton Abdale (Glos)

This remote little Cotswold village is distinguished by the medieval church perched on the tree-clad hill above the village, as if guarding it.

Winchcombe (Glos)

Katherine Parr, sixth wife of Henry VIII, lies buried in the chapel of Sudeley Castle, a castle with more than 1,000 years of history, for in the 10c King Ethelred the Unready had his deer park here. Katherine Parr's prayer book can be seen in the castle, where there are also paintings by Constable, Turner, Reynolds and Rubens.

George Hotel, High St, 17 rooms, T602331 (C)
White Hart Hotel, High St, T602359 (C)

Snowshill (Glos)

Snowshill Manor is a Tudor house with a unique collection of musical instruments, clocks and toys, etc. Opening times are variable – for latest details phone Broadway 2410.

Chipping Campden (Glos)

The largest town on the road since leaving Cirencester with a number of good hotels and shops. There are impressive stone-built houses in the broad High Street, where the town hall and market hall were once the homes of prosperous wool merchants when Chipping Campden was capital of the Cotswold wool trade.

Noel Arms Hotel, High St, 21 rooms, T840317 (B)

The Route

Narrow but fairly straight minor roads that run from south to north across the Cotswold hills.

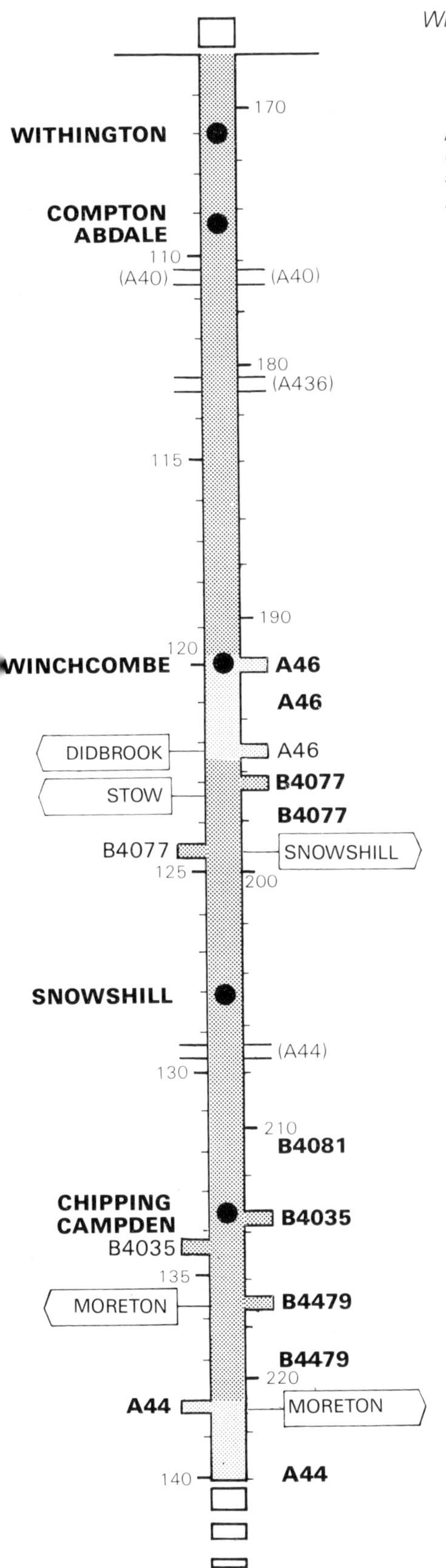

At Withington turn right (sign Compton Abdale), keep straight for 2.4 m to Compton Abdale and turn left (sign Salperton). In 0.9 m keep straight across A40 (sign Salperton). Keep straight for 1.4 m and here continue straight (sign Winchcombe). In further 0.8 m keep straight across A436 (sign Brockhampton) and in 1.0 m turn right (sign Winchcombe).

Keep straight for 1.0 m and turn left (sign Winchcombe). Continue straight for 3.0 m and turn left (sign Winchcombe). Continue straight for 2.0 m into Winchcombe. Entering Winchcombe turn right on to A46 (no sign) and in 2.1 m turn right on to minor road (sign Didbrook).

Keep straight for 1.5 m and turn right on to B4077 (sign Stow). In 1.7 m turn left on to minor road (sign Snowshill). In 0.9 m turn right (sign Snowshill) and in 0.3 m turn left (sign Snowshill). In 1.1 m turn left (sign Snowshill) to Snowshill. Here turn right and almost immediately left (signs Chipping Campden).

Keep straight across A44 and join B4081 (sign Chipping Campden) for 5.0 m into Chipping Campden. Here take B4035 (sign Ebrington) and in 0.5 m keep straight on to minor road (sign Paxford). In 0.9 m turn right (sign Paxford).

In 0.8 m turn right on to B4479 (sign Moreton) and keep straight for 4.0 m. Turn left on to A44 (signs Moreton) for 2.5 m into Moreton in Marsh.

The square, Stow on the Wold.

Stow on the Wold (Glos)

A number of old inns surround the large square in the centre of the town – but the oldest building of all is possibly the King Edward's Cafe (16c) where home-made cakes and jams are a speciality. The 14c market cross and the village stocks stand at either end of the square, in the middle of which is a prominent building, once the town hall but now in use as a social centre and library, where portraits of both Royalist and Commonwealth leaders remind one that Stow and the surrounding countryside was the scene of much activity in the Civil War.

Parkdene Hotel, Sheep St, 9 rooms, T30344 (C)
Limes Guest House, Tewkesbury Rd, 4 rooms, T30034 (D)
YHA, Market Square, T30497

Bledington (Glos)

The Norman church lies off to the right of the road and is faced by a number of well preserved old terraced cottages. Warren Hastings (1732–1818), the controversial Governor-General of India who was impeached on grounds of corruption and later pardoned, was born at Churchill, a little further along the route. His father, Penniston Hastings, is listed among the vicars of Bledington church.

Chipping Norton (Oxfordshire)

The name 'Chipping' means 'market' – and permission to hold fairs and markets at Chipping Norton, the highest town in Oxfordshire, was first granted by King John in 1205. St Mary's Church (12c) is the town's oldest building and close to it are an attractive row of almshouses bequeathed to the town in 1646.

White Hart Hotel, High St, 22 rooms, T2572 (A)

Deddington (Oxfordshire)

In 1635 the tower of the church collapsed, bringing down the massive church bells. These were sold to Charles I, who needed the metal for munitions – the money raised going towards replacements. Deddington Castle, place of the arrest of Piers Gaveston, favourite of King Edward II, is shown prominently on the maps. Today, however, the ruins are not evident, although it is understood that excavations are planned on the site of the castle which lies beyond the sports field across the road from the church.

The Route

The hills of the Cotswolds are left behind on reaching Chipping Norton, the road thereafter running eastward through flatter agricultural land.

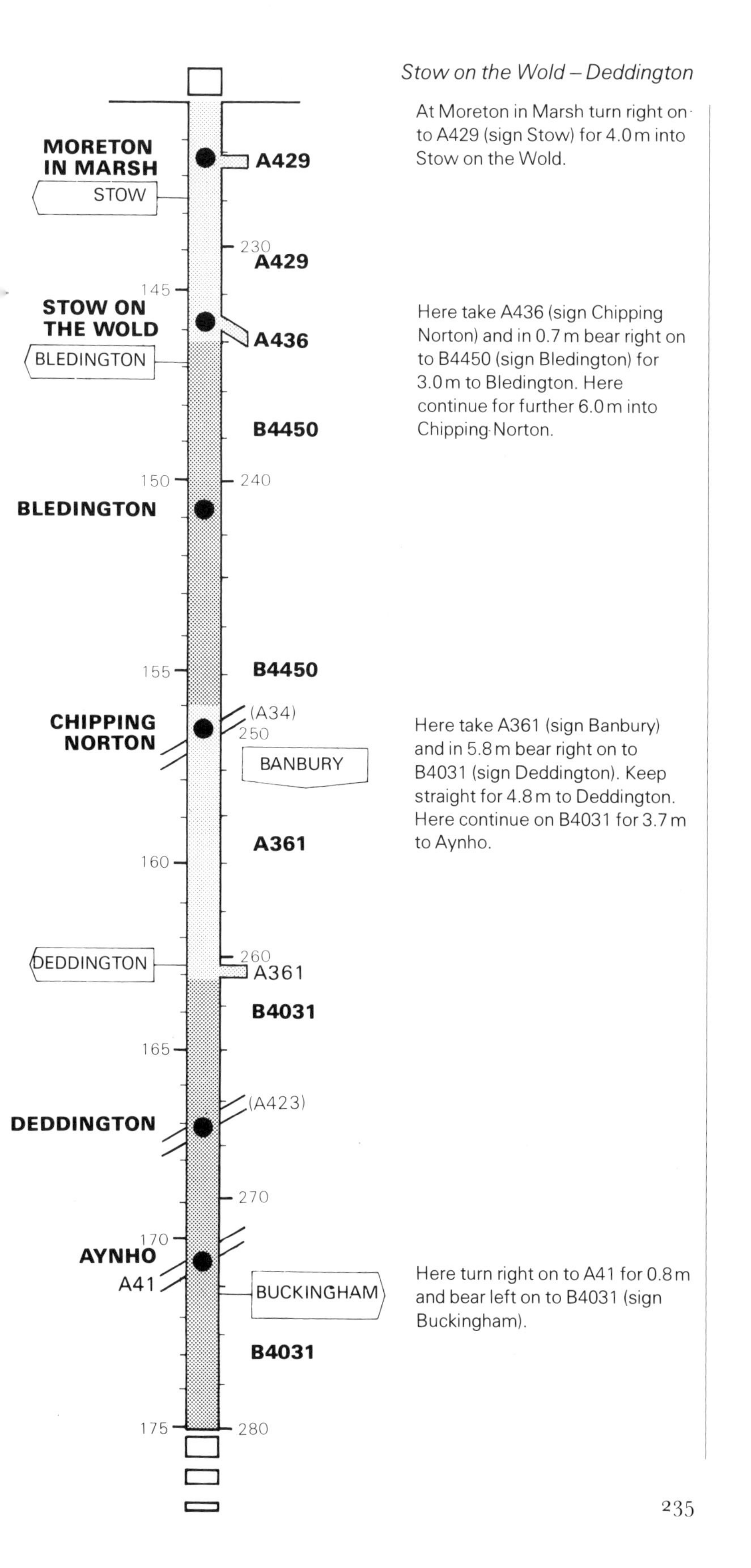

At Moreton in Marsh turn right on to A429 (sign Stow) for 4.0 m into Stow on the Wold.

Here take A436 (sign Chipping Norton) and in 0.7 m bear right on to B4450 (sign Bledington) for 3.0 m to Bledington. Here continue for further 6.0 m into Chipping Norton.

Here take A361 (sign Banbury) and in 5.8 m bear right on to B4031 (sign Deddington). Keep straight for 4.8 m to Deddington. Here continue on B4031 for 3.7 m to Aynho.

Here turn right on to A41 for 0.8 m and bear left on to B4031 (sign Buckingham).

Buckingham (Bucks)

A great part of the old town was destroyed by fire in 1725. One of the interesting relics is the gaol house in the middle of the main street, now in use as an antique shop where, upstairs, a line of the old cells has been preserved.

White Hart Hotel, Market Place, 21 rooms, T2131 (A)
Swan and Castle Hotel, Castle St, 7 rooms, T3082 (C)

Stewkley (Bucks)

In contrast to many of the villages passed earlier that lie compactly around broad market squares, Stewkley is a long straggling place covering some two miles. The church history of St Michael and All Angels, left of road, informs that this is one of only three Norman churches (out of a total of about 6,000 built), that have survived without the original plan having been altered.

Leighton Buzzard (Beds)

The town, now incorporated with Linslade, straddles the Grand Union Canal. Much industry has sprung up – but fortunately ring roads protect the town centre, a pleasant, spacious area, where traffic is prohibited.

Hunt Hotel, 19 Church Rd, 18 rooms, T4962 (B)

Dagnall (Beds)

Whipsnade Park Zoo lies a mile away. Here wild animals are not caged but allowed to roam within large enclosures and paddocks. After leaving Dagnall, before turning off to Aldbury, the huge Ashridge Park is entered. The golf course lies to the left of the road, and on the right there is parking space by an information office that provides plans for nature trail walks through the 4,000-acre deer forest, Most of this area is owned by the National Trust.

The Old Gaol at Buckingham, taken when it was still covered in creeper.

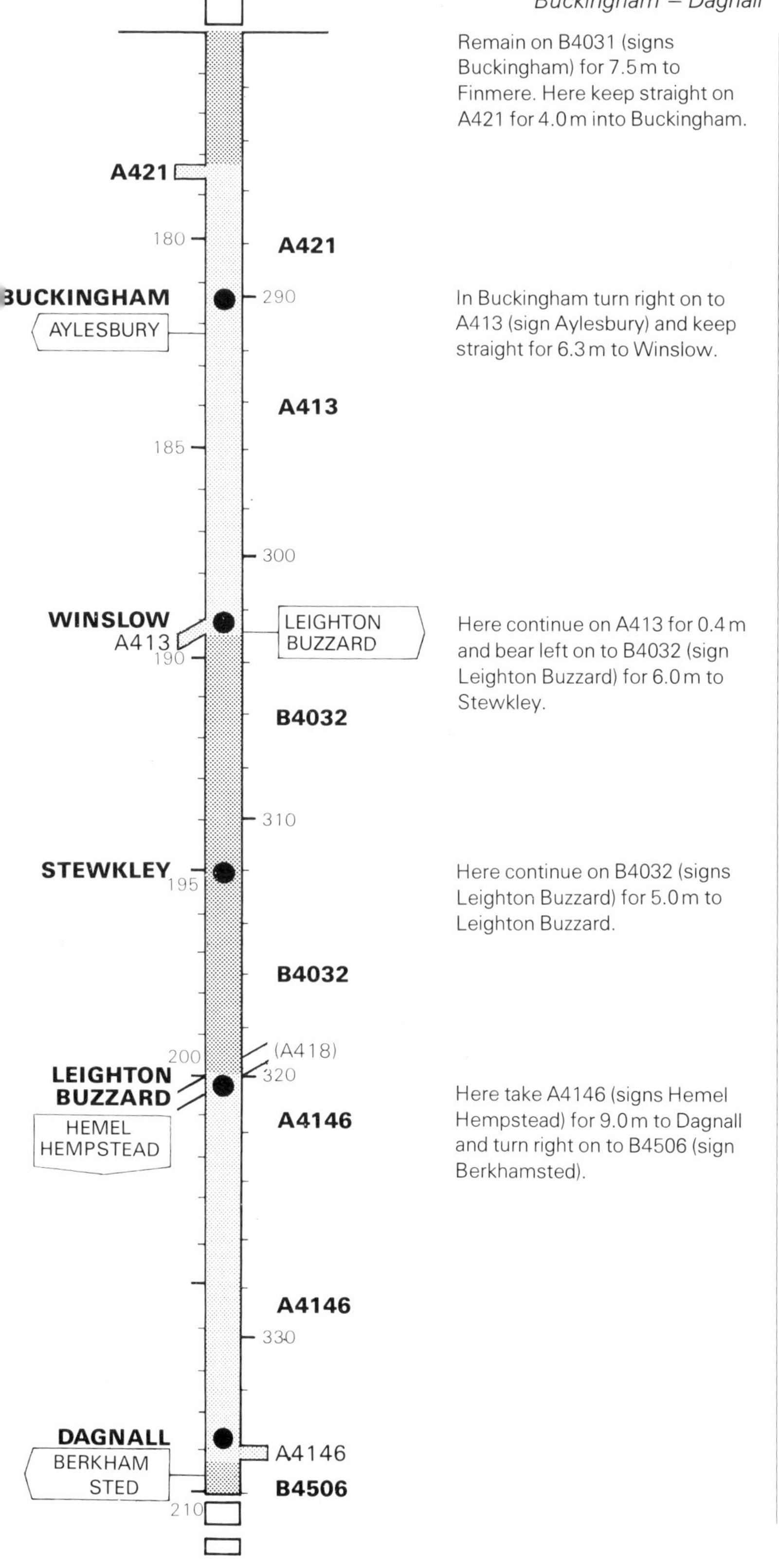

Remain on B4031 (signs Buckingham) for 7.5 m to Finmere. Here keep straight on A421 for 4.0 m into Buckingham.

In Buckingham turn right on to A413 (sign Aylesbury) and keep straight for 6.3 m to Winslow.

Here continue on A413 for 0.4 m and bear left on to B4032 (sign Leighton Buzzard) for 6.0 m to Stewkley.

Here continue on B4032 (signs Leighton Buzzard) for 5.0 m to Leighton Buzzard.

Here take A4146 (signs Hemel Hempstead) for 9.0 m to Dagnall and turn right on to B4506 (sign Berkhamsted).

Wendover, where the route crosses the Chilterns.

Aldbury (Herts)

A quiet little village with green and duck-pond beneath the Chiltern hills.

Tring (Herts)

The Rothschild family once lived here, and the late Lord Rothschild built the Zoological Museum, bequeathing it to the British Museum. Exhibits include rare birds, fish, reptiles etc.

Rose and Crown Hotel, High St, 16 rooms, T4071 (A)
Royal Hotel, Tring Station, 11 rooms, T2169 (B)

Wendover (Bucks)

Coombe Hill, National Trust property and the highest point of the Chilterns, lies to the left of the road as it leaves Wendover – a town which has grown considerably in recent years but where the centre retains an old-world charm.

Shoulder of Mutton Hotel, 20 Pound St, 9 rooms, T623223 (D)

Thame (Oxfordshire)

A market town with broad High Street and many old houses and inns, including one of particular note, the Spread Eagle. A building in the High Sreet was once the grammar school, which numbered Milton and John Hampden among its pupils – Hampden dying in a nearby house after the battle at Chalgrove.

Spread Eagle Hotel, Cornmarket, 29 rooms, T3661 (A)
Star and Garter Inn, Wellington St, 3 rooms, T2166 (D)

The Route

Rather flat featureless country from Stewkley to Leighton Buzzard. Soon afterwards the road runs through the Chiltern hills and woods. The final stretch is by way of flat open countryside and for this reason the A40 was taken to complete the last seven miles to Oxford.

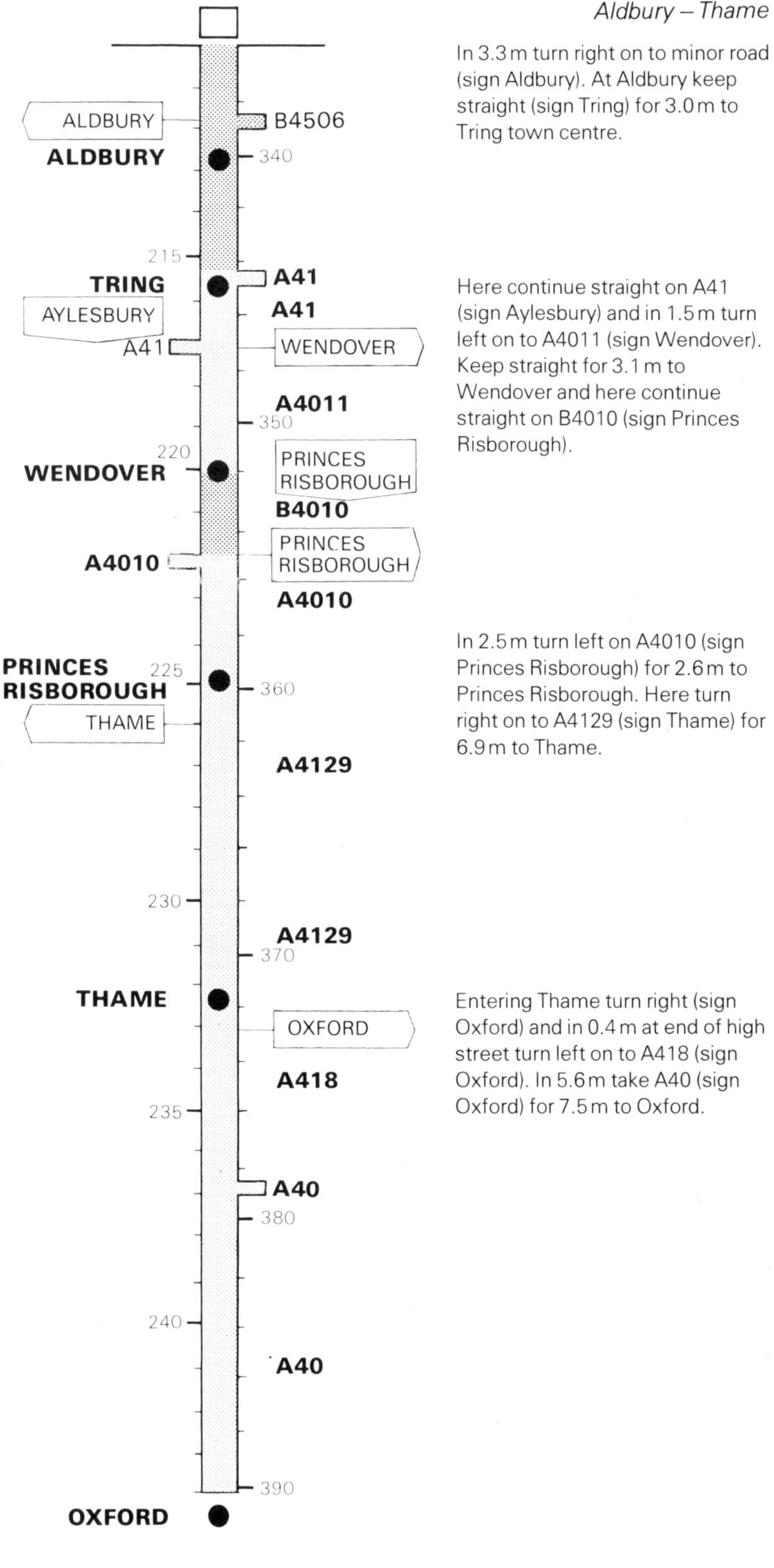

In 3.3 m turn right on to minor road (sign Aldbury). At Aldbury keep straight (sign Tring) for 3.0 m to Tring town centre.

Here continue straight on A41 (sign Aylesbury) and in 1.5 m turn left on to A4011 (sign Wendover). Keep straight for 3.1 m to Wendover and here continue straight on B4010 (sign Princes Risborough).

In 2.5 m turn left on A4010 (sign Princes Risborough) for 2.6 m to Princes Risborough. Here turn right on to A4129 (sign Thame) for 6.9 m to Thame.

Entering Thame turn right (sign Oxford) and in 0.4 m at end of high street turn left on to A418 (sign Oxford). In 5.6 m take A40 (sign Oxford) for 7.5 m to Oxford.

14 *South Wales*

SOUTH WALES is blessed with such a wide variety of unspoilt, sparsely populated countryside that a single tour of some three hundred miles on minor roads is bound to have many omissions. This route was chosen because it embodies some of the more beautiful inland areas, only touching the coast at the attractive little fishing port of New Quay. One obvious omission is the Gower Peninsular – best approached by diverting from the route at Llandeilo (page 246). Another omission is the Pembrokeshire coast – but this is an area which really needs to be explored on foot by way of the Pembrokeshire Coast Path, which extends from Cardigan southwards, rounding St David's Peninsular to a point beyond Tenby.

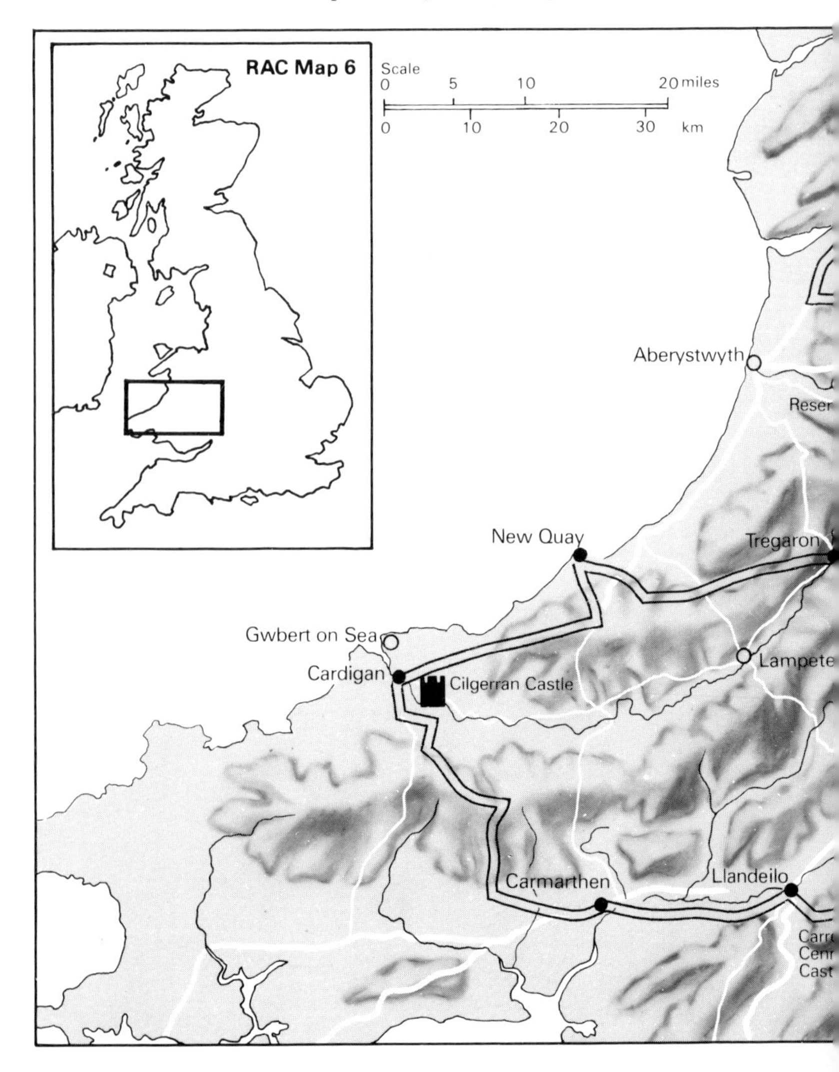

Leaving Abergavenny the road runs in the general direction of Carmarthen, following the valleys of the Usk and Tywi. Throughout much of this stretch the Brecon Beacons are in sight, but between Carmarthen and Cardigan the road follows hills rather than mountains through rich agricultural land and small villages. The rugged area around Devil's Bridge was described by George Borrow in his *Wild Wales* (published 1862) as being 'one of the most remarkable localities in the world' – a superlative which deserves respect in view of the fact that before Borrow journeyed through Wales he had travelled through most of Europe and the Balkans. From Devil's Bridge the route progresses to Machynlleth and then through the lovely Dovey valley to its northernmost point at Mallwyd, before turning south to Llandrindod Wells via remote moorlands where sheep and Welsh ponies graze. The final stretch is by way of the Llanthony valley, home of the poet Walter Savage Landor, who later expressed his love of the valley from the 'distant streams' of Italy.

Some confusion may still exist with regard to the regrouping and

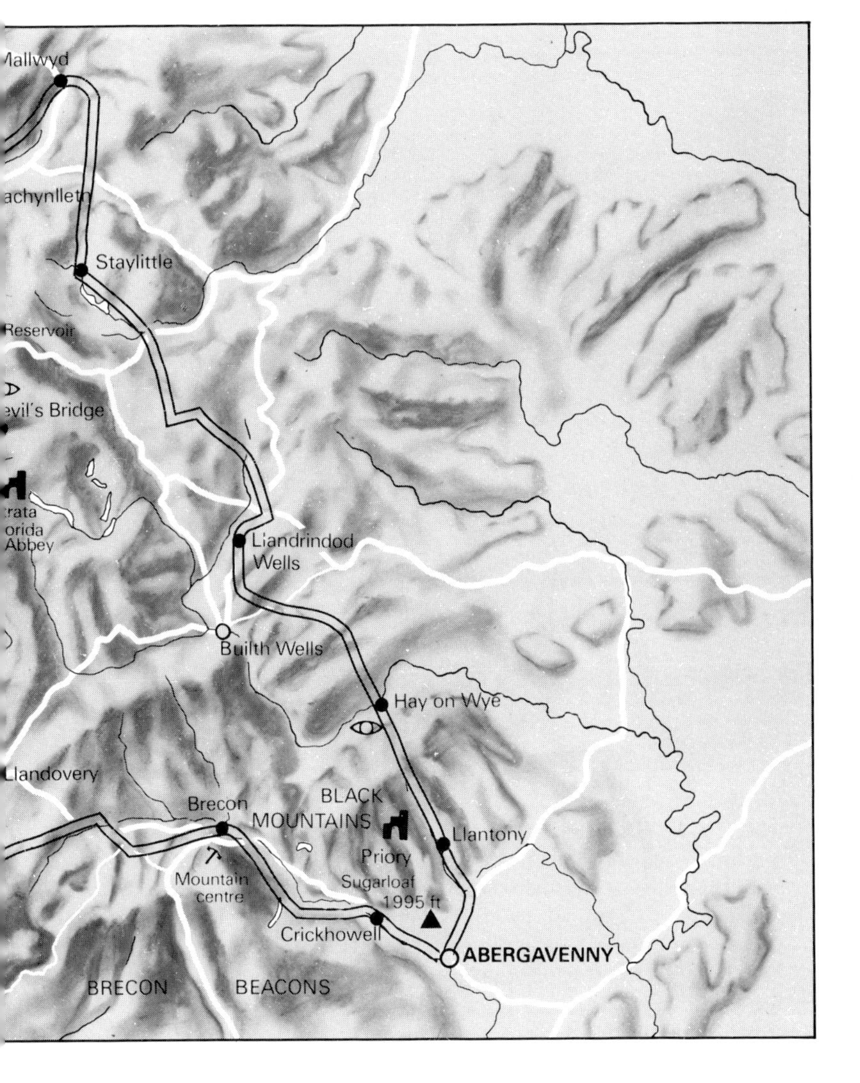

The evocative ruins of Llanthony Priory, in its unrivalled setting.

renaming of the Welsh counties. Thus although reference has just been made to the Pembrokeshire coast it needs to be remembered that the county of Pembrokeshire together with those of Cardiganshire and Carmarthenshire have now been renamed to form the single county of Dyfed. Other counties visited are Powys (formerly Montgomeryshire, Radnorshire and Breconshire), Gwynedd (Caernarvonshire, Merionethshire and Anglesey) and Gwent (Monmouth-

shire). The new names are in fact those of the ancient Welsh kingdoms.

Although many of the minor roads in Wales are narrow, they are well surfaced and normally endowed with well marked passing-places. There is a wide range of accommodation, from luxurious hotels to farm-houses. Prices, generally, tend to be lower than those found in the south of England.

A short glossary of the meaning of some Welsh place names is to be found in the introduction to North Wales (page 13).

Abergavenny (Gwent)

This flourishing market town, known as the 'Gateway to Wales', is overlooked by the Black Mountains to the north and the Brecon Beacons to the west. The Beacons, stretching for more than 10 miles from east to west, include Pen-y-Fan (2,907 ft), the highest point in South Wales. The ruins of the castle, which was founded soon after the Norman conquest, stand on high ground at the back of the Angel Hotel, a former coaching inn. The ruins consist of little more than two towers, the gateway and walls overgrown with creeper – but within the ruins there is a small museum (furniture, pottery and domestic items which have been arranged as a typical Welsh kitchen) and the surrounds have been laid out as a public park with flower beds and tennis courts. There are two markets: the General Market, a huge Victorian structure, and the Cattle Market, one of the largest in Wales.

Angel Hotel, Cross St, 31 rooms, T2613 (B)
Swan Hotel, Cross St, 12 rooms, T2829 (C)
Belgrave Guest House, Brecon Rd, 5 rooms, T2691 (D)
T.O. 2 Lower Monk St, T3254

Crickhowell (Powys)

The 13-arch bridge across the R. Usk dates from 1358, although it has been rebuilt on several occasions, notably in 1706 at a cost of only £400. Little remains of the Norman castle, one of the many destroyed by Owen Glendower, the rebel Welsh prince, but there are numerous old buildings – among them the Bear Hotel, a coaching hostelry with cobbled forecourt, and the Bridge End Inn, formerly a toll-house.

Dragon Guest House, High St, 9 rooms, T810362 (D)
YHA, Ivy Towers, Tower St, T810295

Llandetty (Powys)

Llandetty Church is to be found on the right of the road between Crickhowell and Talybont in a beautiful situation on the banks of the Usk. A little further along the road, on the left, is Llandetty Hall, once the property of a Cromwellian officer, Col. Jenkin Jones, about whom there is an amusing legend. At the time of the Commonwealth the Colonel was in the church when, on hearing of the landing of Charles II, he mounted his horse, fired his pistol at the church, and rode off exclaiming, 'Ah, thou old whore of Babylon, thou'll have it all thy own way now.' Nothing more was ever heard of Col. Jones – but his manor house remains, as well as a bullet hole in the church wall to mark this strange event.

Llandetty Hall Farm, 3 rooms, T Talybont 267 (D)

Brecon (Powys)

The town lies at a point where the Rivers Usk and Honddu meet – hence the town's Welsh name Aber-Honddu. The ruins of the Norman castle can be seen on application to the Castle Hotel which adjoins it. The Cathedral, damaged by Owen Glendower and later at the time of the Civil War, was restored in the 19c. Among other buildings of interest is the birthplace of the actress Sarah Siddons (1755–1831), now a wine vault, and Boleyn House, which is still owned by descendants of Anne Boleyn. The museum contains an interesting natural history and archaeology collection.

Castle of Brecon Hotel, The Avenue, 18 rooms, T2551 (B)
Coach House Guest House, 13 Orchard St, 4 rooms, T3803 (D)
T.O. 7 Glamorgan St, T2763

Trescastle (Powys)

Castle Hotel, 8 rooms, T Sennybridge 354 (D)

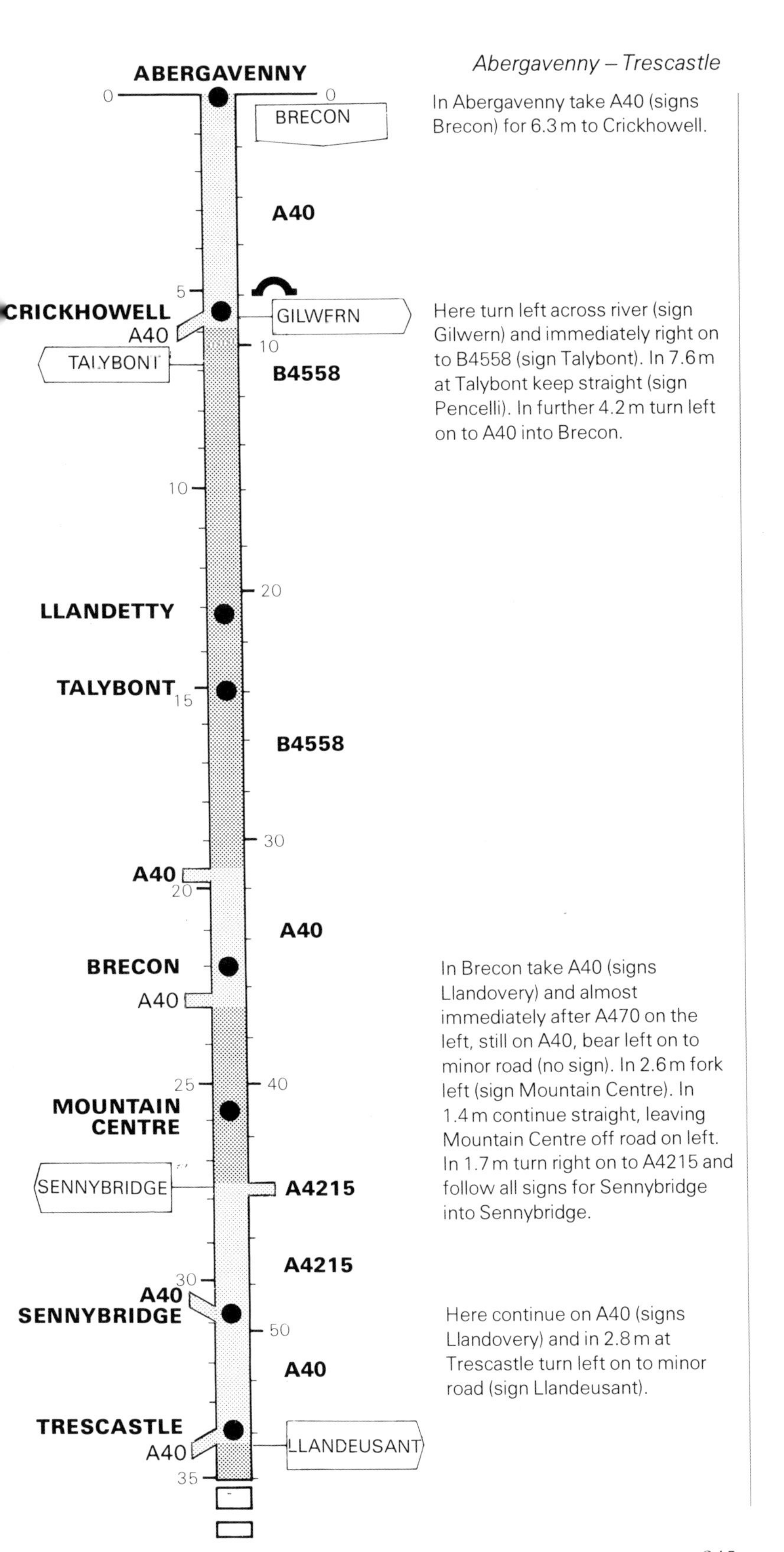

In Abergavenny take A40 (signs Brecon) for 6.3 m to Crickhowell.

Here turn left across river (sign Gilwern) and immediately right on to B4558 (sign Talybont). In 7.6 m at Talybont keep straight (sign Pencelli). In further 4.2 m turn left on to A40 into Brecon.

In Brecon take A40 (signs Llandovery) and almost immediately after A470 on the left, still on A40, bear left on to minor road (no sign). In 2.6 m fork left (sign Mountain Centre). In 1.4 m continue straight, leaving Mountain Centre off road on left. In 1.7 m turn right on to A4215 and follow all signs for Sennybridge into Sennybridge.

Here continue on A40 (signs Llandovery) and in 2.8 m at Trescastle turn left on to minor road (sign Llandeusant).

The Usk bridge at Crickhowell.

The Route

Quiet motoring by the R. Usk and the canal between Abergavenny and Brecon. Throughout this section the Brecon Beacons and later the Black Mountain – not to be confused with the Black Mountains north of Abergavenny – are prominent. The road is very narrow for one mile just before reaching Capel Gwynfe.

Trapp (Dyfed)

Before entering this small village, signed to the left and only 400 yards off the route, is Carreg Cennan Castle. One of the most spectacular castle ruins in this part of Wales, it is perched on a limestone crag, separated from the Black Mountain by the R. Cennan. The south face of the rock on which the castle stands rises perpendicularly for 300 feet – but a car park has been provided by the farm to the north, and the castle can be visited by a footpath from there. The castle, first mentioned in 1248, passed through numerous hands: in 1362 it was the possession of John of Gaunt, and shortly afterwards of Henry IV. Later, during the wars of the Roses, it was surrendered by the Lancastrians to the Yorkists. An interesting feature of the castle is the long tunnel leading to a cave in the rock where water constantly drips into a natural basin.

Llandeilo (Dyfed)

Beautifully situated on the slope of a hill above the Tywy valley. The ruins of the 13c castle lie to the west of the town in the grounds of the modern castle, which is now occupied by a school.

Cawdor Arms Hotel, 20 rooms, T3500 (A)
Brynywawr Guest House, Penybanc, 4 rooms, T2419 (D). This small guest house is in the quiet village of Penybanc, north of Llandeilo off the A40. Particularly recommended for those who want a quiet stay near the edge of the town.

Carmarthen (Dyfed)

Stands on the north side of the R. Tywy – a town of narrow, busy streets with a pleasant footpath along the river. About all that remains of the old Carmarthen Castle are two towers and the gatehouse.

Ivy Bush Royal Hotel, 100 rooms, T5111 (B)
Boars Head, 10 rooms, T6043 (C)

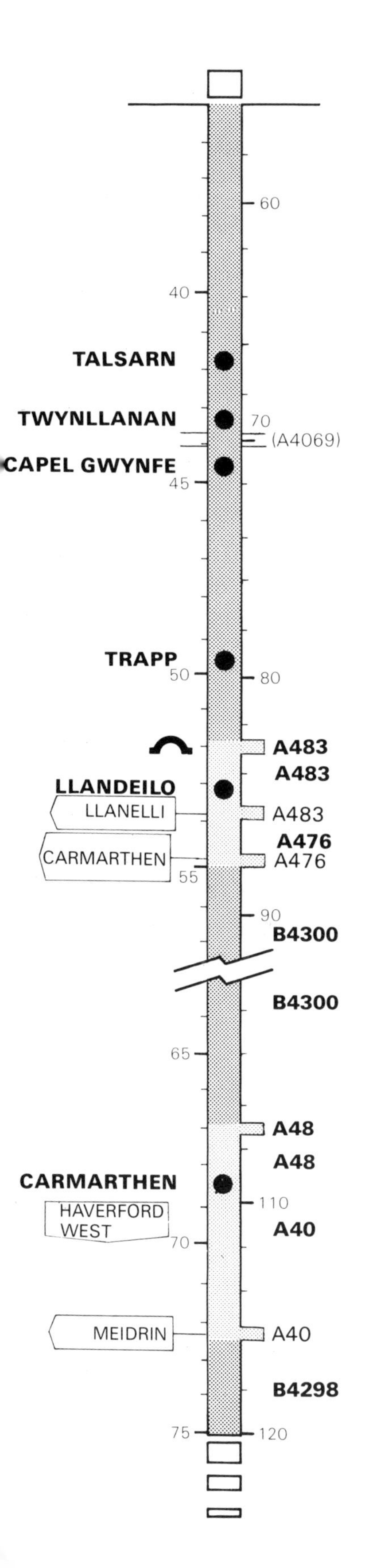

Keep straight for 7.8 m to Talsarn (Cross Inn). Here continue straight (sign Llangadog). In 1.5 m at Twynllanan turn left (sign Gwynfe). Keep straight across A4069 to Capel Gwynfe. In 0.7 m turn right (sign Trapp) and in 1.1 m turn left and immediately right (signs Trapp). Keep straight into Trapp.

NB Sign to Carreg Cennen Castle is to left just before reaching Trapp.

In Trapp follow signs Landeilo for 3.0 m, crossing bridge on A483 into town. In Llandeilo re-cross bridge on A483 (sign Swansea) and in 1.0 m turn right on to A476 (sign Llanelli). In 0.8 m bear right on to B4300 (sign Carmarthen).

In 13.0 m turn right on to A48 into Carmarthen. Here take A40 (sign Haverfordwest) and in 4.0 m turn right on to B4298 (sign Meidrin) for 4.2 m.

Meidrin (Dyfed)

A small hillside village in the midst of rich agricultural land.

Tegryn (Dyfed)

This small village occupies one of the highest points in the area with fine views across rolling country-side from the bar of the 18c inn, the Butcher's Arms (T Llwyndrain 680). This inn, named after a butcher who once owned it and dabbled in amateur wine-making, has recently opened a restaurant that serves excellent food. No accommodation.

Cilgerran (Dyfed)

The 13c castle, preserved by the National Trust, has a commanding position above the gorge of the river. The castle is hidden from view in the village, but is clearly signed to the right of the route and can only be approached on foot. The modern gateway leading into the castle is the village War Memorial, inscribed with the moving lines of Ezekiel XXXVII: 'Come from the four winds, Oh breath, and breathe upon those slain that they may live.'

Wenallt Guest House, Church Rd, 4 rooms, T Lechryd 569 (D)

The lofty ruins of Cilgerran Castle.

Cardigan (Dyfed)

The town stands at the northern extremity of spectacular coast land, preserved as the Pembrokeshire Coast National Park, which extends by way of rocky headlands and secluded coves as far as Amroth in Carmarthen Bay. This coastal path begins at St Dogmaels, south of Cardigan on the estuary of the R. Teifi, and runs southwards round Cemaes Head to Fishguard. This means that Cardigan is an ideal setting-off point for those who wish to leave the route and drive or ramble along the lengthy Pembrokeshire coastline. The Cardigan Wild Life Park at Cilgerran contains some of the animals that roam, or used to roam, freely in Wales – among them deer, bison, wild board, wolves and wild cats. Cardigan, an old market town and once a flourishing port, might be a noisy place to spend a night and consequently the recommended hotels are at Gwbert on Sea, an attractive little resort only two miles from the town on the mouth of the river. Gwbert is clearly signed on the left of the route as it leaves Cardigan.

Anchor Hotel, 13 rooms, T2368 (D)
Cliff Hotel, 70 rooms, T3241 (A)
YHA, Sea View, Poppit, T2963
T.O. The Market Place, T3230

The Route

Between Llandeilo and Carmarthen the road runs through the beautiful Tywy valley. Thereafter the road climbs, though not steeply, through agricultural land and small villages by quiet traffic-free roads before emerging at Cardigan. The Cardigan Wildlife Park is passed at Cilgerran – for details see Cardigan.

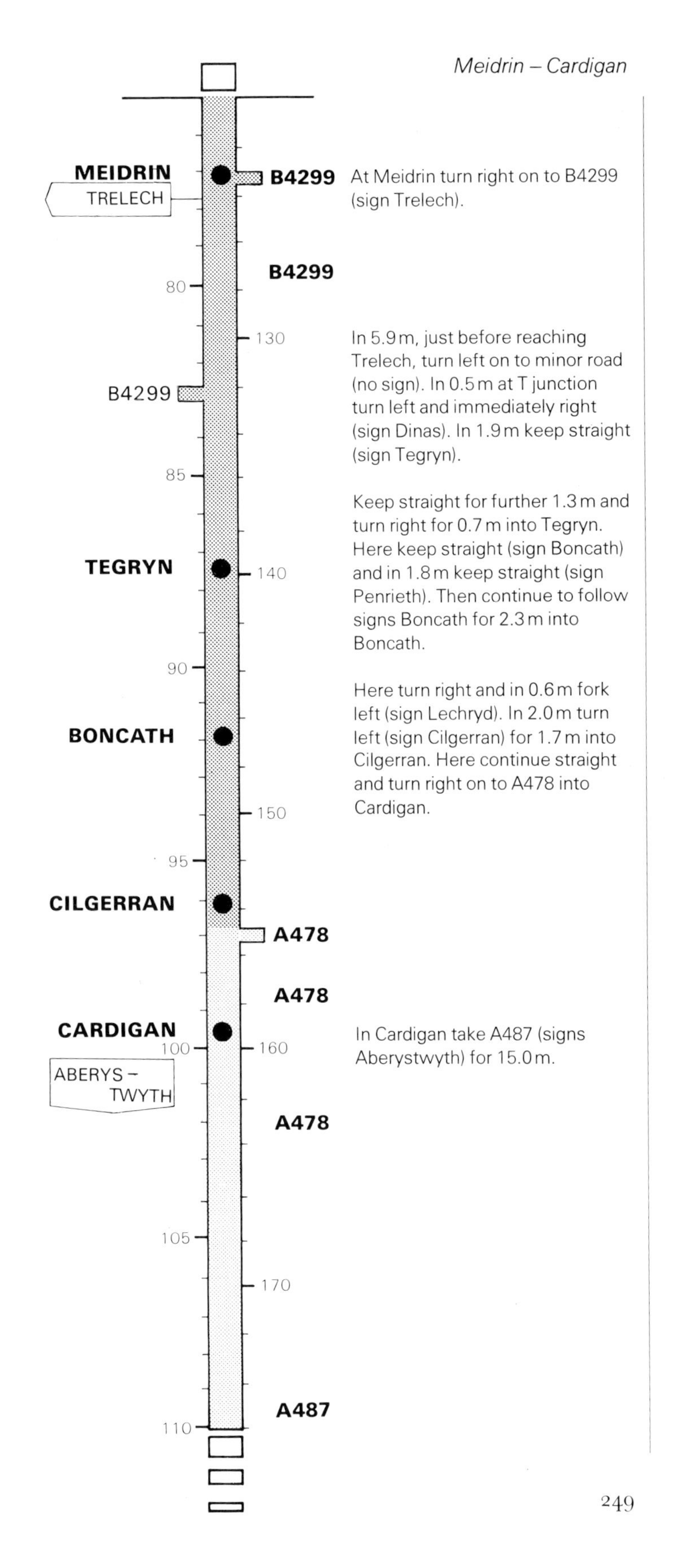

At Meidrin turn right on to B4299 (sign Trelech).

In 5.9 m, just before reaching Trelech, turn left on to minor road (no sign). In 0.5 m at T junction turn left and immediately right (sign Dinas). In 1.9 m keep straight (sign Tegryn).

Keep straight for further 1.3 m and turn right for 0.7 m into Tegryn. Here keep straight (sign Boncath) and in 1.8 m keep straight (sign Penrieth). Then continue to follow signs Boncath for 2.3 m into Boncath.

Here turn right and in 0.6 m fork left (sign Lechryd). In 2.0 m turn left (sign Cilgerran) for 1.7 m into Cilgerran. Here continue straight and turn right on to A478 into Cardigan.

In Cardigan take A487 (signs Aberystwyth) for 15.0 m.

The Talbot Hotel in Tregaron, with the statue of Henry Richard.

New Quay (Dyfed)

This is in every way a delightful holiday resort, lying above a sheltered sandy bay and quay from where fishing boats ply, exporting lobsters to France and providing plaice and sole for local consumption. The bar of the Black Lion Hotel dates from the 15c and was a favourite haunt of the Welsh poet, Dylan Thomas, in the 1940s. A few years ago the Black Lion was bought by the former boxing champion, Steve Donohue, who not only furnished it in impeccable taste but also extended the hotel, making it a really comfortable place in which to stay or dine. Mr Donohue has now handed over the results of his labours to his son, but he still likes to welcome visitors and show them his varied collections which range from antique furniture to ancient bottles of scotch whisky.

Black Lion Hotel, 10 rooms, T560209 (C)
YHA, The Glyn, Church St, T560337

Llangeitho (Dyfed)

Daniel Rowland (1713–90), a great Methodist leader, once drew crowds in thousands to hear him preach in this quiet remote little village. His statue is just off the route (on the Aberystwith road), and he lies buried in the parish church.

Tregaron (Dyfed)

This small town is the headquarters of the Welsh pony trekking organization. Focal point of the town is the black and white Talbot Hotel, named after a breed of dog known as the 'talbot' but now extinct. Opposite the hotel is the statue of Henry Richard (1812–88), one-time liberal MP and secretary of an international peace movement, whom today's politicians might do well to heed: 'My hope for the abatement of the war system lies in the permanent conviction of the people rather than the policies of cabinets or the discussions of parliament.'

Talbot Hotel, 14 rooms, T208 (C)

The Route

It was found necessary to travel 19 miles on an A road in order to get from Cardigan to New Quay through somewhat bare country. Thereafter the road undulates through pleasant countryside in the valleys of the Aeron and Teifi.

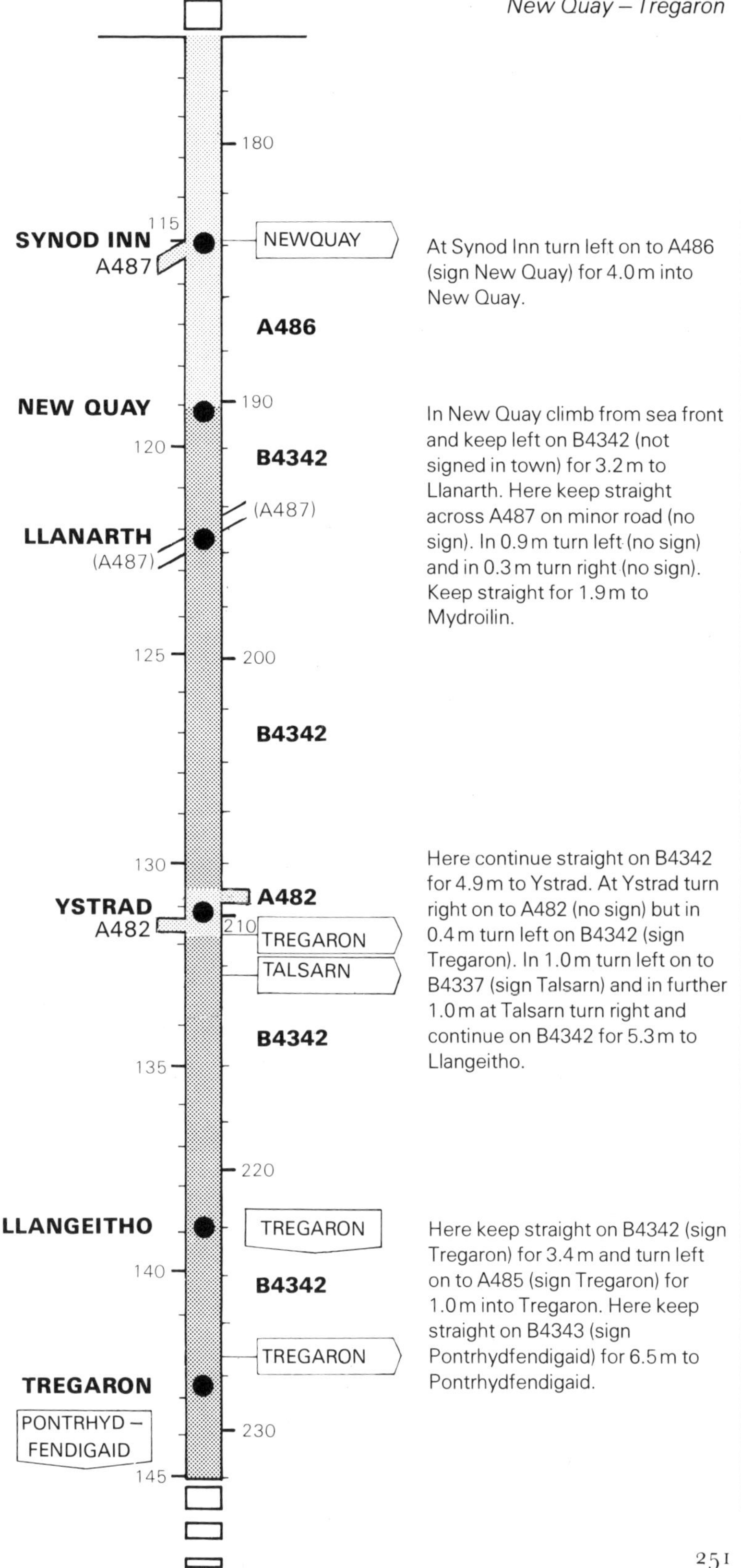

At Synod Inn turn left on to A486 (sign New Quay) for 4.0 m into New Quay.

In New Quay climb from sea front and keep left on B4342 (not signed in town) for 3.2 m to Llanarth. Here keep straight across A487 on minor road (no sign). In 0.9 m turn left (no sign) and in 0.3 m turn right (no sign). Keep straight for 1.9 m to Mydroilin.

Here continue straight on B4342 for 4.9 m to Ystrad. At Ystrad turn right on to A482 (no sign) but in 0.4 m turn left on B4342 (sign Tregaron). In 1.0 m turn left on to B4337 (sign Talsarn) and in further 1.0 m at Talsarn turn right and continue on B4342 for 5.3 m to Llangeitho.

Here keep straight on B4342 (sign Tregaron) for 3.4 m and turn left on to A485 (sign Tregaron) for 1.0 m into Tregaron. Here keep straight on B4343 (sign Pontrhydfendigaid) for 6.5 m to Pontrhydfendigaid.

Pontrhydfendigaid (Dyfed)

At the entry to the village, on the right, is the sign to Strata Florida Abbey, which lies a mile away, beautifully situated on well tended lawns on the bank of the R. Teifi. The Abbey was built for Cistercian monks in 1164, and though now in ruins it contains many interesting relics, such as tombstones marking the burial places of the early Welsh princes, and a Norman arch at the west entry. The parish church stands next to the Abbey, and in the huge graveyard the celebrated Welsh poet, Dafydd ap Gwilym (1340–70), lies buried.

Strata Florida Abbey.

Devil's Bridge (Dyfed)

The existing bridge which crosses high above the R. Mynach is superimposed above two earlier bridges. The middle bridge was built in 1709 and the lowest, 'Devil's Bridge', is said to have been built by the monks from Strata Abbey centuries earlier. The lower bridges and waterfalls can be seen by descending steps which lead from the upper bridge to the ravine some 300 feet below. *The Devil's Bridge Nature Trail*, a small pamphlet published by the Best Western Hotels Group, can be obtained from the Hafod Arms Hotel and indicates numerous points of interest. Why Devil's Bridge? According to legend an old woman's cow crossed the ravine, and she was approached by a monk who offered to build her a bridge if she gave him the first living creature to cross it. The woman agreed and the bridge was built. When the monk beckoned her to cross, she noticed the cloven hoof under his cloak, and instead of crossing the bridge she drove her dog across it – telling the devil to keep it.

Hafod Arms Hotel, 21 rooms, T Ponterwyd 232 (B)

Talybont (Dyfed)

On entering the village from the mountain road the two hotels both stand near the woollen mill.

Black Lion Hotel, 5 rooms, T335 (D)
White Lion Hotel, 6 rooms, T245 (D)

Machynlleth (Powys)

This attractive old town of broad main streets nestles in the Dovey valley at the head of the river estuary, with the Snowdonia National Park to the north. Owen Glendower lived and held parliament here in 1404, possibly on the site of the house which now accommodates the tourist office.

White Lion Hotel, Pentrerhedyn St, 20 rooms, T2048 (C)
T.O. Owain Glyndwr Centre, T2401

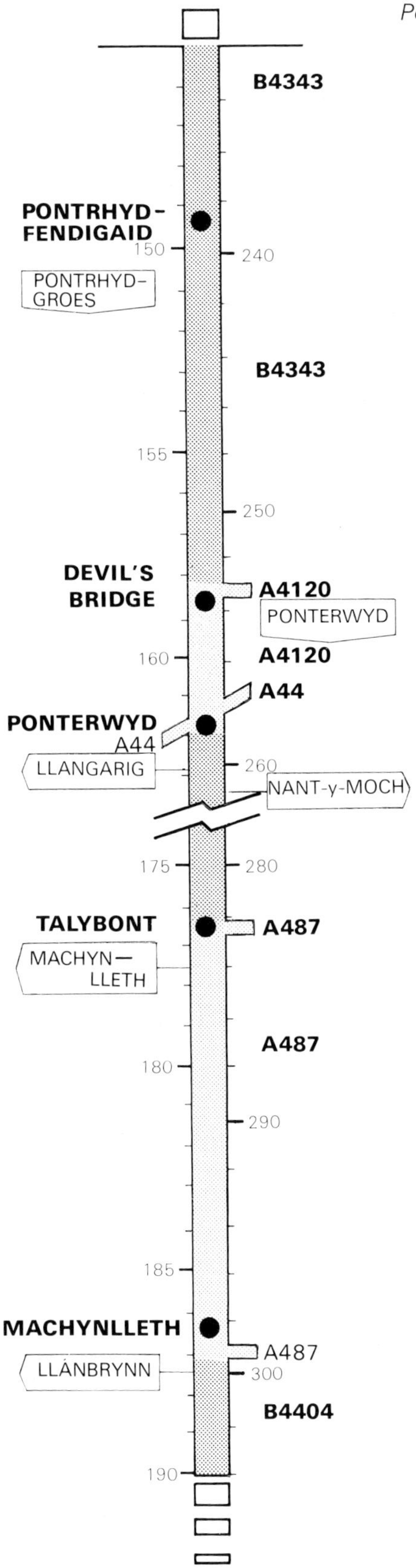

B4343

PONTRHYD-FENDIGAID

150 240

PONTRHYD-GROES

B4343

155

250

DEVIL'S BRIDGE

A4120

PONTERWYD

160

A4120

A44

PONTERWYD

A44

LLANGARIG

260

NANT-y-MOCH

175 280

TALYBONT

A487

MACHYN-LLETH

A487

180

290

185

MACHYNLLETH

A487

LLANBRYNN

300

B4404

190

In Pontrhydfendigaid turn right on to B4343 (sign Pontrhydgroes) and remain on B4343 (signs Pontrhydgroes, later Devil's Bridge) for 8.7 m to Devil's Bridge.

Here take A4120 (sign Ponterwyd) for 3.0 m to Ponterwyd. Turn right on A44 (sign Llangarig) and in 0.1 m turn left on to minor road (sign Nant-y-Moch, scenic road) and continue to follow minor road signs (Nant-y-Moch) and later signs (Talybont) for 14.7 m to Talybont.

At Talybont turn right on to A487 (sign Machynlleth) and keep straight for 10.6 m into Machynlleth. Here take A487 for further 1.3 m and turn right on to B4404 (sign Llanbrynn).

Top: *A farm near Llanidloes.*
Above: *Devil's Bridge.*
Right: *The Cader Idris range.*

The Route

Shortly after Devil's Bridge the mountain road is taken, passing the huge Nant-y-Moch reservoir. On these uplands, above the tree-line, sheep graze and there are numerous cattle grids. After passing the reservoir the road bears west to give a marvellous view over Cardigan Bay and from Machynlleth the road passes through the lovely Dovey valley.

Mallwyd (Gwynedd)

The village lies at the extreme northern point of this route, and those wishing to connect with Route 1 (N. Wales) should note that Dolgellau lies only 11 miles away (A470). Mallwyd consists of only a handful of cottages and an inn that look across the Dovey valley and forest, with views of Cader Idris (2,927 ft), the mountain that towers above Tal-y-llyn in the south of Snowdonia. Centuries ago this wild and remote countryside was a lawless area – famed, in particular, for a gang known as the Red-Headed Brigands of Mawddwy, who used the 15c Brigands Inn as their headquarters. According to legend, Queen Mary decided to put a stop to the gang's activities and ordered Lewis Owen, a baron from Caernarvon, to wipe them out. Owen captured eighty of the bandits and hanged them in the nearby woods, despite the pleas of an old woman to spare the life of her son. She was to have her revenge. A year later the brothers of the executed man waylaid the baron, hacking him to death at a point two miles from Brigands Inn known as Baron's bridge, where, it is said, his ghost still roams. Today a huge log fire burns in the timbered lounge of the inn where once the red-headed brigands planned their escapades, but which now makes a good centre for salmon and trout fishing or for rambling in the Snowdonia National Park.

Brigands Inn, 13 rooms, T Dinas Mawddwy 208 (C)

Staylittle (Powys)

Lies at the northern tip of the six-mile-long Llyn Clywedog, a reservoir formed by a dam 214 feet in height. The Welsh name for the village is Penffordlas ('head of the green roads') – for the few metalled roads that converge here were formerly nothing more than grass tracks. An interesting story explains the origin of the English name. A century ago the builder who was constructing the Baptist chapel on the hill was short of labour and asked a stranger who wandered into the valley to stop and help him. This the visitor agreed to do, assisting the builder to complete the chapel – despite the proviso that he could only 'stay a little'.

Llanidloes (Powys)

The old Market Hall, a small Tudor half-timbered building stands in the middle of the main street, the traffic flowing either side of it. At one time it contained the court-house and cell, but it now houses a museum of local interest, open from Easter until the end of September.

Red Lion Hotel, 9 rooms, T2270 (D)
Lloyds Hotel, 10 rooms, T2284 (D)

The Route

By way of almost traffic-free minor roads, some across high moorlands and others through wooded valleys. The road from Mallwyd is particularly steep and narrow for the first three or four miles.

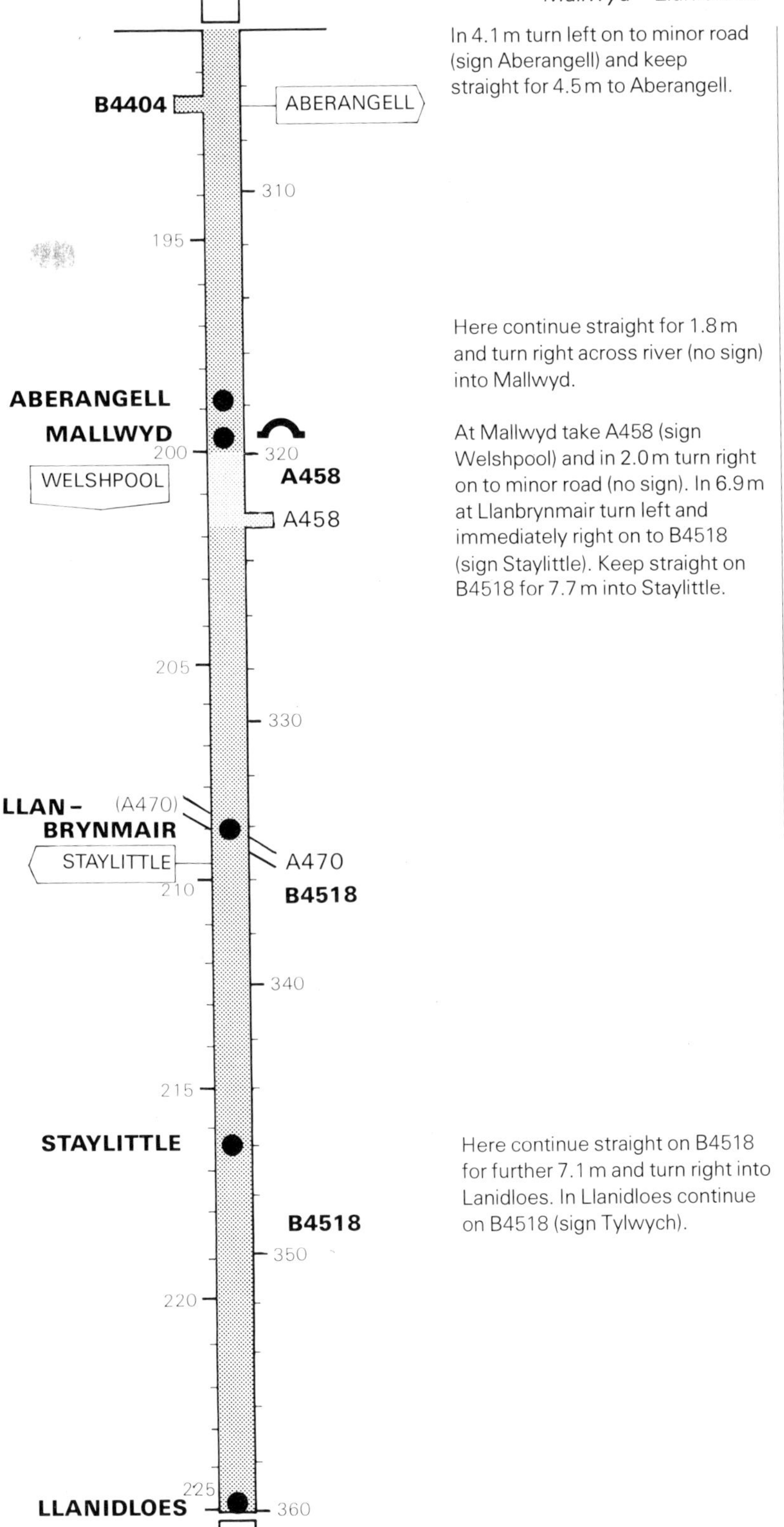

In 4.1 m turn left on to minor road (sign Aberangell) and keep straight for 4.5 m to Aberangell.

Here continue straight for 1.8 m and turn right across river (no sign) into Mallwyd.

At Mallwyd take A458 (sign Welshpool) and in 2.0 m turn right on to minor road (no sign). In 6.9 m at Llanbrynmair turn left and immediately right on to B4518 (sign Staylittle). Keep straight on B4518 for 7.7 m into Staylittle.

Here continue straight on B4518 for further 7.1 m and turn right into Lanidloes. In Llanidloes continue on B4518 (sign Tylwych).

The spa town of Llandrindod Wells.

Abbeycwmhir (Powys)

The small village in a wooded valley is entered with the church on the left and the pub opposite. Just past the village, on the right, are the ruins of the Cistercian abbey (1143), another of the many buildings destroyed by Owen Glendower. Little more than the foundations remain.

Llandrindod Wells (Powys)

Lies on a plateau above the valley of the R. Ithon, beneath the Cambrian hills. Mineral springs were first found here by the Romans – but this spa town was not really developed until a century ago, at a time when 'taking the waters' was becoming the fashion. Today spa waters can be sampled at Rock Park from a spring which trickles from the walled area by the wooden bridge. The location of one particular spring in Rock Park is said to have been pinpointed by a certain Mr Pilot who dreamed of its existence – a dream which came true. Originally the town was named Ffynnen-llwyn-gog ('the well in the cuckoo's grove') after one of the springs. The modern name means the Church of the Trinity, referring to the parish church by the lake.

Glen Usk Hotel, 79 rooms, T2085 (B)
Hampton Hotel, 29 rooms, T2585 (C)
T.O. Town Hall Gardens, T2600

Glascwm (Powys)

Apart from the YHA, only a post office and a few cottages make up this village, beautifully situated near Gwaunceste Hill (1,778 ft).

YHA, The School,
T Hundred House 367

The Route

The road is particularly narrow and gated (2 gates) between Glascwm and the B4594. It is also narrow as it runs through the Llanthony valley, but there are numerous well-marked passing-places.

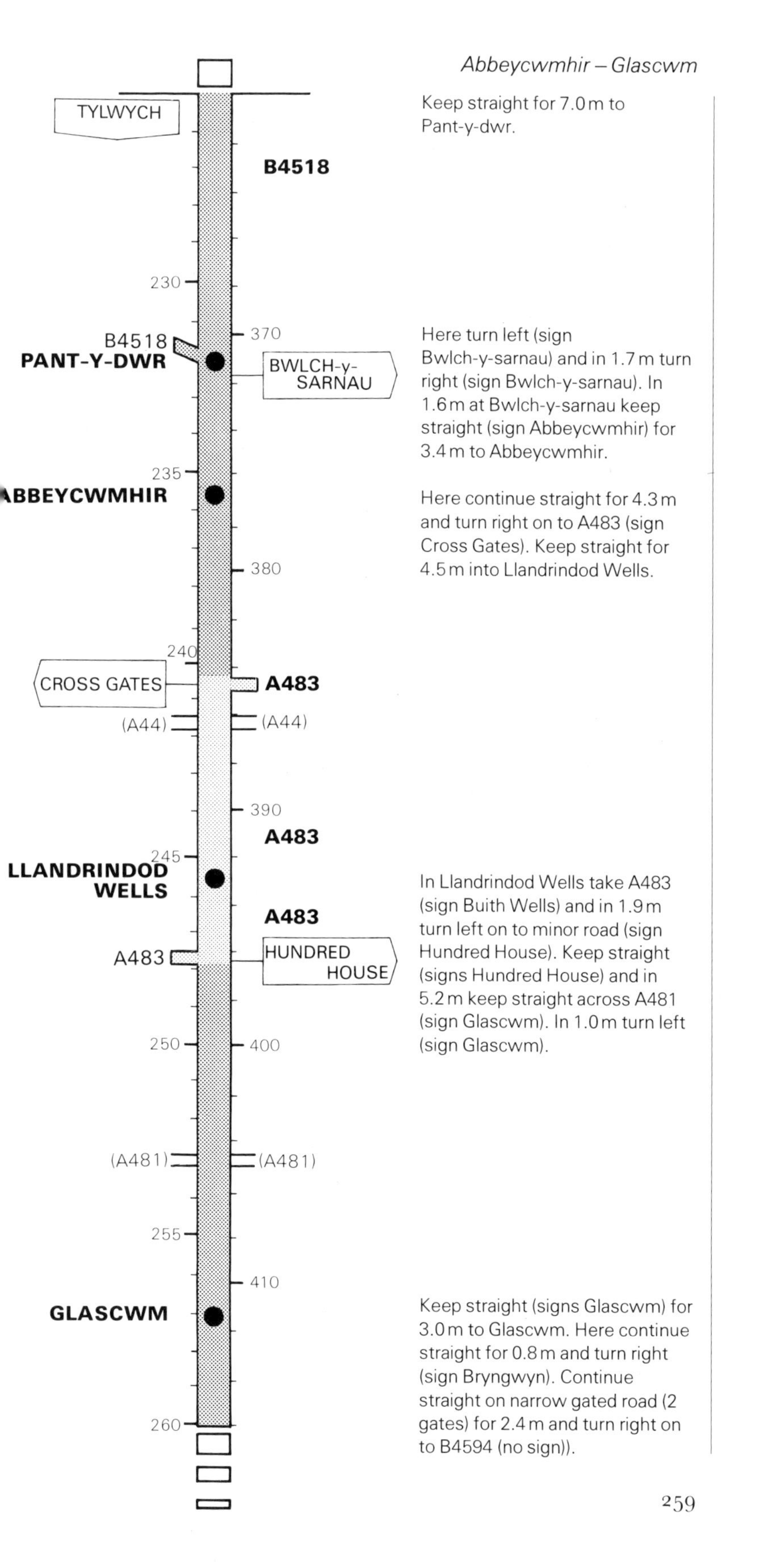

Keep straight for 7.0 m to Pant-y-dwr.

Here turn left (sign Bwlch-y-sarnau) and in 1.7 m turn right (sign Bwlch-y-sarnau). In 1.6 m at Bwlch-y-sarnau keep straight (sign Abbeycwmhir) for 3.4 m to Abbeycwmhir.

Here continue straight for 4.3 m and turn right on to A483 (sign Cross Gates). Keep straight for 4.5 m into Llandrindod Wells.

In Llandrindod Wells take A483 (sign Buith Wells) and in 1.9 m turn left on to minor road (sign Hundred House). Keep straight (signs Hundred House) and in 5.2 m keep straight across A481 (sign Glascwm). In 1.0 m turn left (sign Glascwm).

Keep straight (signs Glascwm) for 3.0 m to Glascwm. Here continue straight for 0.8 m and turn right (sign Bryngwyn). Continue straight on narrow gated road (2 gates) for 2.4 m and turn right on to B4594 (no sign)).

Hay on Wye, now a paradise for book collectors.

Hay on Wye (Powys)

Hay stands just inside the Welsh border, the ruins of the 11c castle occupying the centre of the town. Almost every other shop in this attractive little town appears to stock second-hand books. The man who made Hay a book collectors' paradise is Richard Booth, reputed to be the world's largest seller of second-hand and antiquarian books. Booth has a number of shops dotted around the town – his largest collection taking up the entire area of what was once the cinema.

Crown Hotel, 14 rooms, T435 (C)
Brooklands Guest House, 4 rooms, T445 (D)

Capel-y-Ffynn (Powys)

All that can be seen on arrival here is the tiny box-shaped church on the left, opposite a cottage. Along a narrow lane just past this cottage the remains of the monastery lie abandoned. In 1880 a variety of witnesses testified to seeing the Virgin Mary appear in the field next to the monastery.

YHA, T Crucornery 373

Llanthony (Powys)

The ruins of the Priory, once a 12c Augustinian monastery, lie on the left of the road by the Abbey Hotel – a conversion of the old prior's lodge and west tower. This beautiful part of Wales was the home of the poet Walter Savage Landor, who lived here from 1809 to 1814 before he departed to Italy. From there he was to remember Llanthony in these nostalgic lines:

Llanthony! an ungenial clime,
And the broad wings of restless time,
Have rudely swept thy mossy walls,
And rocked thy abbots in their palls.
I loved thee by the streams of yore,
By distant streams I love thee more.

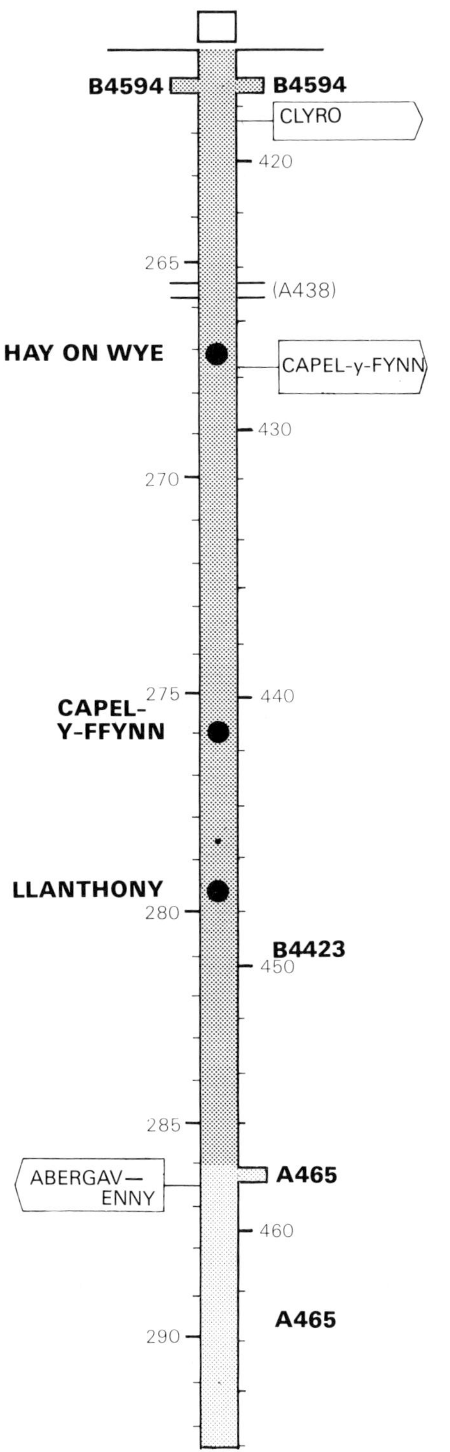

In 0.4 m turn left on to minor road (sign Clyro). Keep straight for 3.8 m to Clyro. Here cross A438 (sign Hay on Wye) and continue straight for 1.0 m into Hay on Wye.

In Hay town centre take B4350 (sign Brecon) but before leaving town turn left on to minor road (sign Capel-y-Fynn).

Keep straight (signs Capel and Abergavenny) for 8.1 m to Capel-y-Fynn and here continue straight for 3.1 m to Llanthony. Keep straight, road now designated B4423, for 6.2 m and turn right on to A465 (sign Abergavenny) for 6.5 m into Abergavenny.

15 *Heart of England (West)*

THIS ROUTE of approximately 185 miles starts at the cathedral city of Worcester and runs through an area which lies entirely to the west of the city. Like Route 5, its title is somewhat arbitrary, and it might equally well be described as the South-West Midlands, the route being confined to the counties of Hereford and Worcester (a county formed on 1 April 1974 as a result of the merger of the independent counties of Herefordshire and Worcestershire), Salop, and a small part of Gloucestershire.

Initially the route sets off in a north-westerly direction through the lovely towns of Bewdley and Bridgnorth, passing the Wyre forest which lies between them. Bridgnorth occupies the extreme northern tip of the route which from here travels in a southerly direction, parallel and often close to the Welsh border, as far south as St Briavels in the Forest of Dean.

Perhaps it would be fair to say that the hilltop town of Ludlow with its famous castle and medieval buildings which lie compactly above the river is the most beautiful town encountered throughout this route. The country around the city of Hereford is renowned for the quality of its livestock – in particular the 'white-faced' Hereford cattle which are world-famous. No less than six thousand acres of the county consist of cider fruit orchards, so it is not surprising that the city is one of the largest cider producers in the world. As the road continues south from Hereford in the direction of the Forest of Dean, it runs through the Wye valley by way of another market town, Ross on Wye.

The Forest of Dean lies in the extreme north-west corner of Gloucestershire. More than two thousand woodland paths run through this huge forest of oaks, ash, conifers, etc, and although this route runs through the heart of the forest it is essentially a place for the rambler rather than the motorist. Those wishing to spend some time in the area will find that the Speech House Hotel (page 270) stands in the centre of the forest. This hotel (price grade A) is among the more expensive of the listed hotels but there are more modestly priced establishments around Ross and Symonds Yat in addition to the two nearby YHAs (at Ross and Mitcheldean).

After leaving the forest the route returns northward by way of Ledbury and Bromyard as far as Tenbury Wells, from where it returns to Worcester and the beautiful cathedral in its midst, the resting-place of a king of England (King John, 1167–1216) and a boy of fifteen who died too young to be king (Prince Arthur, eldest son of Henry VII, 1487–1502).

This is an area rich in fruit orchards and hopfields, like the Vale of Evesham, which can be reached by diverting from Newent or Ledbury. The Malvern Hills, too, can be reached easily from Ledbury.

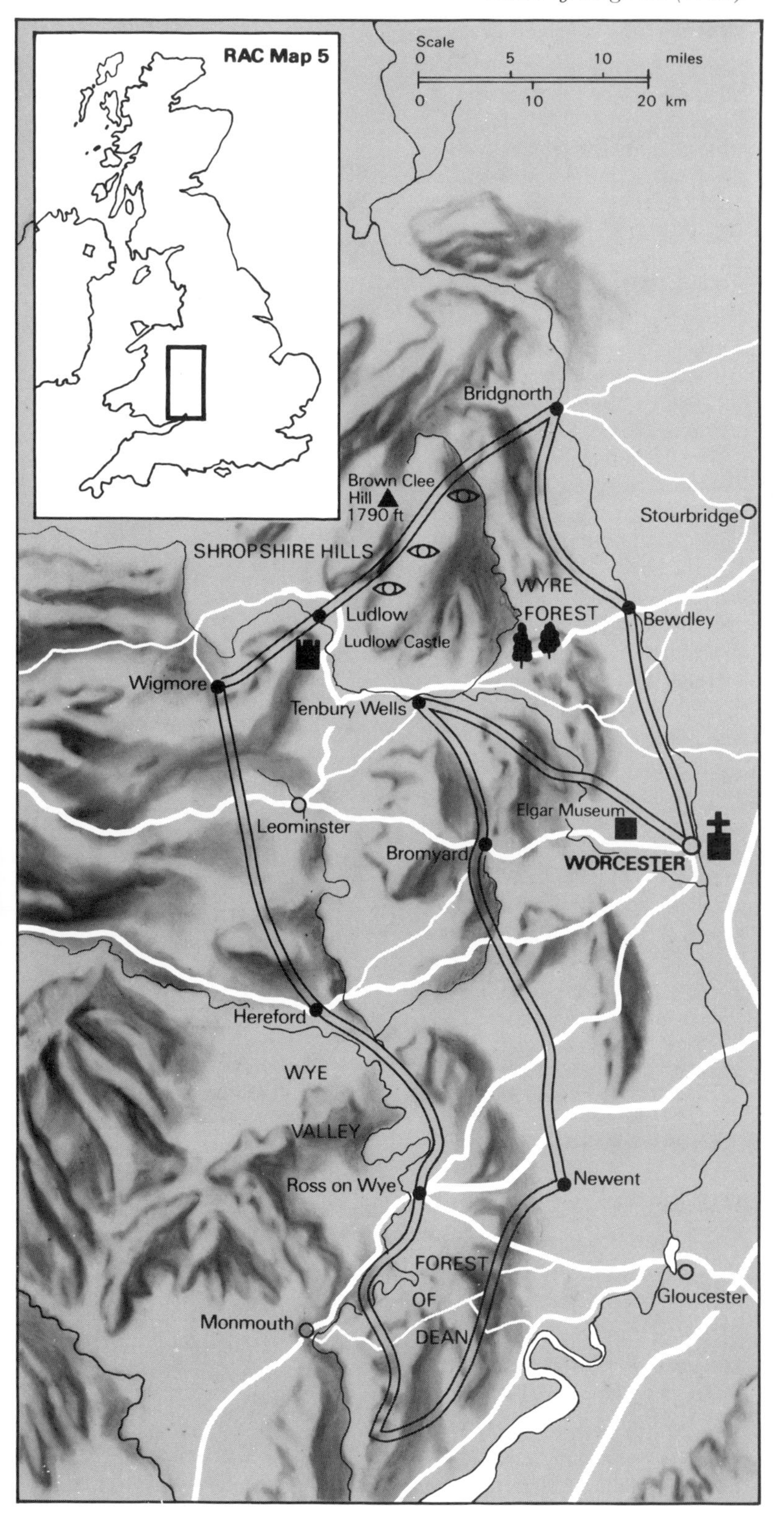
RAC Map 5
Scale
0 5 10 miles
0 10 20 km
Bridgnorth
Brown Clee Hill 1790 ft
Stourbridge
SHROPSHIRE HILLS
WYRE FOREST
Ludlow
Bewdley
Ludlow Castle
Wigmore
Tenbury Wells
Leominster
Elgar Museum
Bromyard
WORCESTER
Hereford
WYE VALLEY
Ross on Wye
Newent
FOREST OF DEAN
Gloucester
Monmouth

Worcester (Hereford & Worcs)

There are many reminders that this beautiful city on the R. Severn is known as the 'faithful city'. Worcester was the last city to capitulate to the Roundheads in 1646, and over the doorway of the Guildhall are statues of Charles I and Charles II with the head of Cromwell, nailed by the ears, above them. A house in New Street, now a restaurant, harboured Charles II before he fled for his life after his defeat at the battle of Worcester in 1651.

The Cathedral, begun in 1062 but much restored, occupies a fine position high above the river and although numerous buildings of historic interest lie near it there is also some modern development in the shape of a good shopping precinct and hotel.

Today Worcester is renowned for such diverse products as sauce and porcelain – the Royal Worcester porcelain works and museum being open to the public. The county cricket ground, across the river, is considered to be among the most beautiful in England, and just outside the town, at Broadheath, is the house where the composer Sir Edward Elgar (1857–1934) was born and which is now a museum.

Star Hotel, Foregate St, 36 rooms, T24308 (C)
St Lawrence Hotel, Bath Rd, 15 rooms, T351383 (D)
T.O. Guildhall, High St, T23471

Hallow (Hereford & Worcs)

This village straggles for about a mile along the road with a large village green on the right.

Bewdley (Hereford & Worcs)

The original name was Beaulieu (beautiful place) and the town certainly does enjoy a beautiful position on the R. Severn, where there are some gracious houses along the waterfront. A mile or so before arriving at Bewdley, on the right, is a memorial stone to Stanley Baldwin, (1867–1947). Immediately upon entering the town, on the right of the very narrow street, is the tall, grim terraced house where Baldwin was born – a striking contrast to his later residence, Astley Hall. There are, however, many fine old houses in the town, among them the Angel Inn, where Charles I sheltered in 1645.

Black Boy Hotel, Kidderminster Rd, 20 rooms T402119 (C)

Buttonoak (Hereford & Worcs)

This small village lies in the heart of the beautiful Wyre forest.

Bridgnorth (Salop)

A delightful town built on both sides of the R. Severn in the form of the 'high town', which grew around the castle, and the 'low town' on the other side of the river. A little railway with the steepest gradient in England connects the two areas of the town and the return fare of 10p is certainly a boon to the foot-weary. The 12c castle was destroyed by the Parliamentarians but the tower remains, standing at a grotesque angle of 17 degrees. The town hall (1652) is built on arches through which the High Street runs. There are some fascinating walks along narrow lanes past cave dwellings, now bricked up, which were occupied little more than a hundred years ago. Fine views of the river can be seen from Castle Walk.

Falcon Hotel, St John's St, Low Town, 14 rooms, T3134 (B)
Severn Arms Hotel, Underhill St, 10 rooms, T4616 (D)
Ball Hotel, East Castle St, 5 rooms, T2478 (D)
T.O. The Library, Listley St, T3358

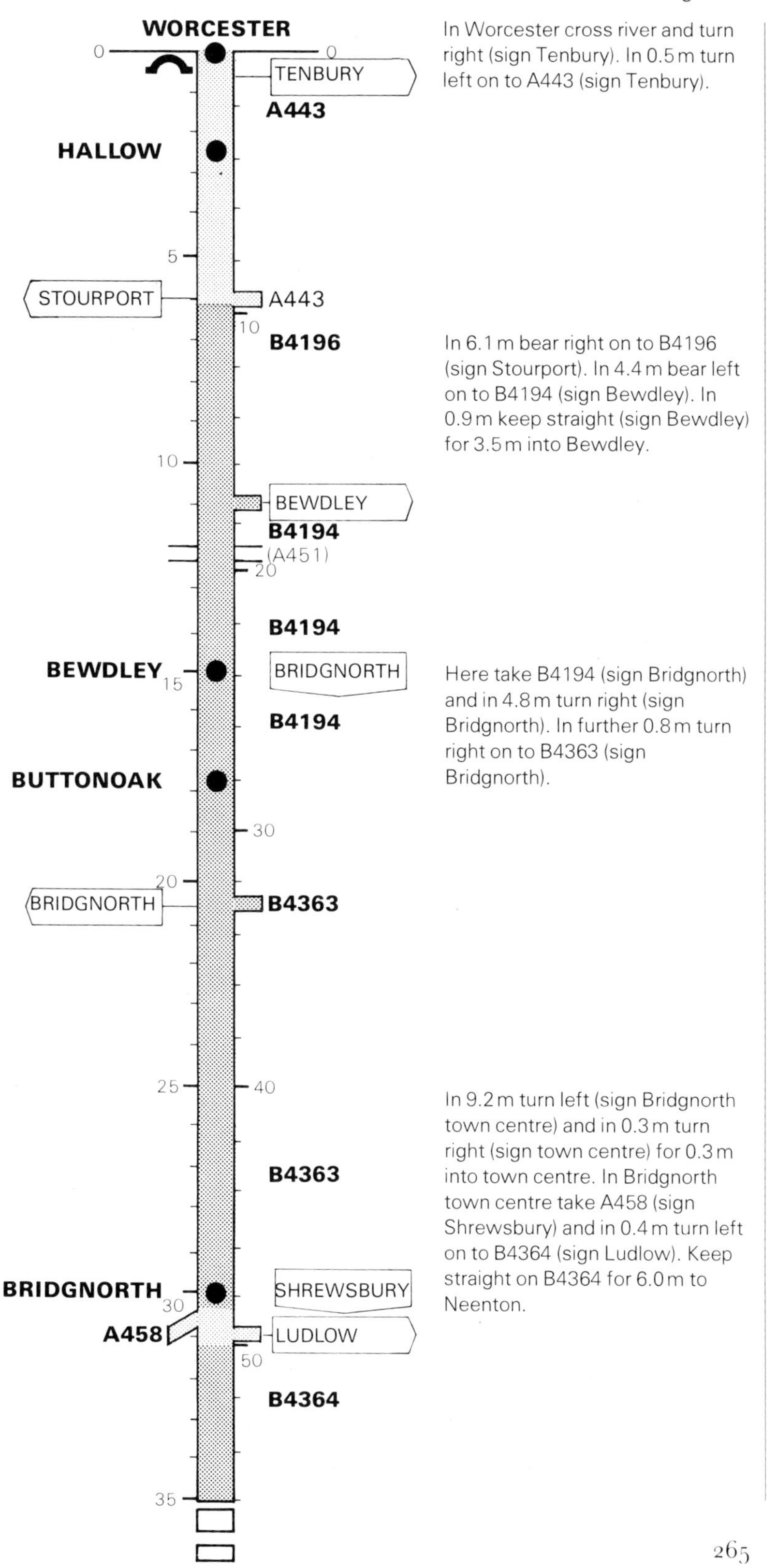

In Worcester cross river and turn right (sign Tenbury). In 0.5 m turn left on to A443 (sign Tenbury).

In 6.1 m bear right on to B4196 (sign Stourport). In 4.4 m bear left on to B4194 (sign Bewdley). In 0.9 m keep straight (sign Bewdley) for 3.5 m into Bewdley.

Here take B4194 (sign Bridgnorth) and in 4.8 m turn right (sign Bridgnorth). In further 0.8 m turn right on to B4363 (sign Bridgnorth).

In 9.2 m turn left (sign Bridgnorth town centre) and in 0.3 m turn right (sign town centre) for 0.3 m into town centre. In Bridgnorth town centre take A458 (sign Shrewsbury) and in 0.4 m turn left on to B4364 (sign Ludlow). Keep straight on B4364 for 6.0 m to Neenton.

Neenton & Burwarton (Salop)

Both are tiny, remote villages set in beautiful countryside but consisting of little more than church, pub and manor house. Neenton boasts the Pheasant Inn and Burwarton the Boyne Arms.

Ludlow Castle.

Ludlow (Salop)

Focal point of this hilltop town which is crammed with medieval hotels, shops and houses is, perhaps, the castle. Today, during the annual summer festival, plays are staged in the castle where John Milton's *Comus* was performed in 1634 and where the satirist Samuel Butler (1612–80) wrote his *Hudibras*. From the Butter Cross at the top of Broad Street the road descends sharply through the sole remaining gate of this fortified town to a lovely point of the R. Teme, where the Charlton Arms hotel and the YHA occupy fine positions. Among a number of ancient hotels are the Bull, the Angel, and the Feathers, opened as an inn in 1521, which is entered by the original door embossed with 350 studs. 17c fare at this hotel included 'Whyte Bredde for Gentylfolke and browne for Churles', as well as 'Suculente hares guaranteyed not to cause the Shropshire melancholiye.' The poet A. E. Houseman (1859–1936) is buried in the parish church here, and reflects on the beauty of the town in his most famous work 'A Shropshire Lad'.

Feathers Hotel, Bull Ring, 31 rooms, T2919 (A)
Angel Hotel, Broad St, 19 rooms, T2531 (B)
Charlton Arms Hotel, Ludford Bridge, 6 rooms, T2813 (D)
YHA, Ludford Bridge, T2472.
T.O. Castle St, T3857

Wigmore (Hereford & Worcs)

A quiet village with a 16c Hall, some 17c houses near the church, and the overgrown ruins of a 13c castle.

Compasses Hotel, Ford St, 4 rooms T203 (D)

Aymestrey
(Hereford & Worcs)

The Crown Inn (T Kingsland 440) lies right on the R. Lugg and serves bar snacks.

Mortimers Cross
(Hereford & Worcs)

The sign outside the inn here depicts a solemn knight surrendering his sword to a cheerful one. It was on this spot that the decisive battle of the Wars of the Roses was fought, which led to the crowning of Edward Mortimer as King Edward IV. A mile along the road is the Monument Inn, outside which is a monument raised by public subscription in 1799 as a reminder of the battle in which some four thousand men were slain.

The Route

Rather dull for the first few miles out of Worcester. The road then runs through the Wyre forest towards undulating countryside which becomes progressively more beautiful and remote.

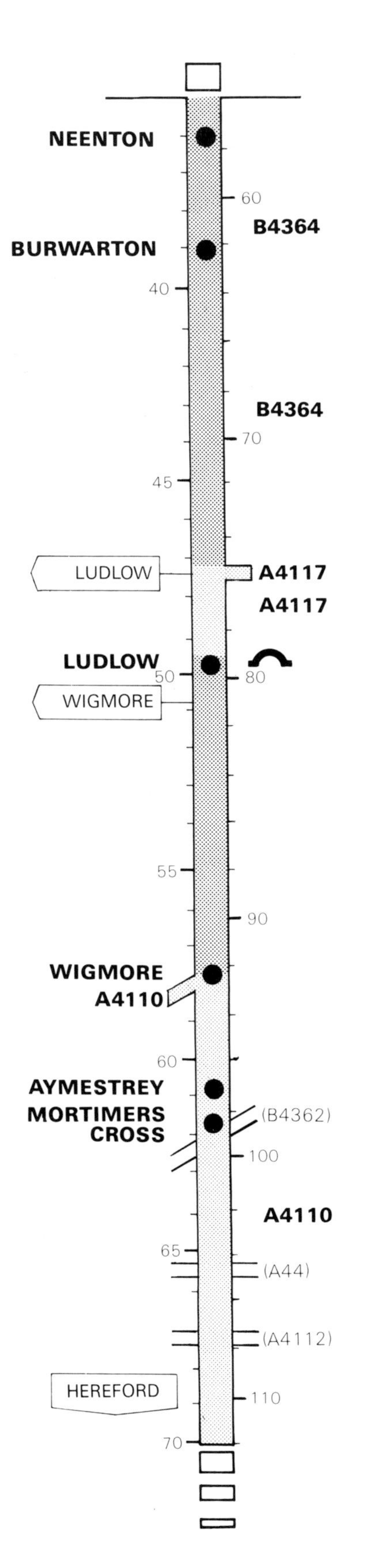

Continue on B4364 to Burwarton. Here continue straight for further 8.3 m and turn right on to A4117 (sign Ludlow). Follow signs Ludlow town centre for 2.3 m into Ludlow town centre.

In Ludlow follow signs Leominster and cross river. Immediately turn right on to minor road (sign Wigmore). Keep straight on minor road (signs Wigmore) for 7.8 m and turn left on to A4110 (no sign).

Keep straight for 3.7 m through Aymestrey to Mortimer's Cross.

Here keep straight for 3.2 m and keep straight across A44 (sign Hereford). In 1.4 m keep straight across A4112 (sign Hereford). Continue straight for further 5.0 m to Canon Pyon.

The Route

A pleasant minor road between Ludlow and Wigmore. From here it was found necessary to follow a road which although categorized A is in fact reasonably quiet and traffic-free. After Hereford the road runs through the Wye valley with some superb views of the river.

Hereford (Hereford & Worcs)

This is much the largest town through which the route passes and needs to be explored on foot. The 11c Cathedral has a famous chained library of some 1,400 volumes and a map of the world as seen in 1305. A black-and-white building (1621) near the High Street, known as the Old House, is now a museum with contemporary Jacobean furniture. Near the Wye bridge is a stone which marks the birthplace of Nell Gwyn (1651–87), the actress and favourite mistress of Charles II.

Green Dragon Hotel, Broad St, 93 rooms, T35491 (A)
Graftonbury Hotel, Grafton Lane, 45 rooms, T56411 (C)
Booth Hall Hotel, East St, 11 rooms, T2898 (D)
T.O. Shirehall, St Owen's St, T68430

Mordiford (Hereford & Worcs)

Nestles in a valley beneath wooded hills. It was from these hills, according to legend, that the green dragon descended to kill the villagers, until it was eventually slain by a convict who had been offered his freedom for doing so. The village is reached by a bridge over the rivers Wye and Lugg.

Fownhope (Hereford & Worcs)

Lies in the heart of the Wye valley. Much history is attached to the 15c Inn, the Green Man, which back in 1485 was known as the 'Naked Boy'. In the 18c the Petty Sessional Court was held here, and the iron bars to which the prisoners were chained, the cell, and the Judge's bedroom with four poster bed can all be seen.

Green Man Inn, 7 rooms, T243 (D)

Ross on Wye
(Hereford & Worcs)

From the Prospect, a public garden near the church, there are fine views of the river. In the churchyard of the parish church of St Mary is the Plague Cross – in memory of 315 townsfolk who were victims of the 'black death' in 1637.

Royal Hotel, Palace Pound, 32 rooms, T2769 (A)
Swan Hotel, Edde Cross St, 19 rooms T2169 (C)
T.O. 20 Broad St, T2768

Goodrich (Hereford & Worcs)

The ruins of Goodrich Castle can be seen high up on a spur above the Wye on the right of the road between Walford and Symonds Yat. It was while wandering among the evocative ruins of this 12c castle in 1793 that William Wordsworth met the little girl who features in his poem 'We are Seven'.

Symonds Yat
(Hereford & Worcs)

The word yat means gate or pass – and a half-mile diversion to the right of the route leads to a well-known beauty spot where the Wye twists through a steep and narrow gorge. There are several hotels by the river and a motel further along the road, which rises sharply to Yat Rock from where there are good views.

Royal Hotel, Symonds Yat East, 23 rooms, T238 (C)
Symonds Yat Rock Motel, 4 rooms, T Coleford 3015 (C)

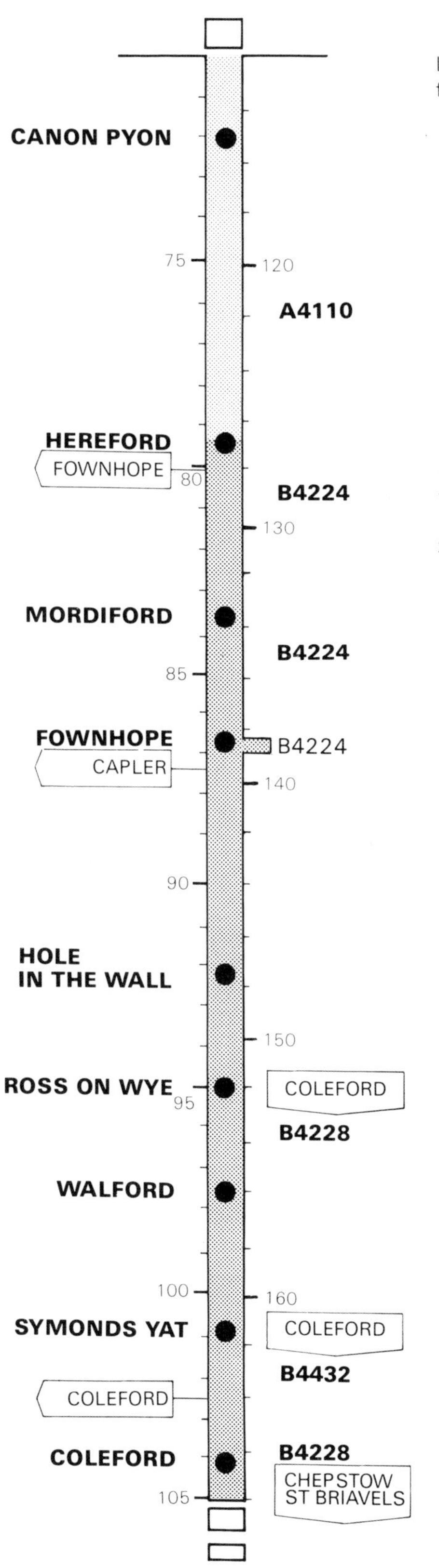

In Canon Pyon continue straight for 7.3 m to Hereford.

Here follow signs A438 (Tewkesbury) but before leaving town bear right on to B4224 (sign Fownhope). Keep straight for 3.8 m to Mordiford and here bear right (sign Fownhope). In 2.3 m at Fownhope turn right on to minor road (sign Capler).

In 1.7 m keep straight (sign How Caple) and in 1.5 m continue straight (no sign). Keep straight for 5.0 m (signs Ross), and turn right for 0.3 m into Ross on Wye town centre.

In Ross on Wye take B4228 (sign Coleford). In 3.7 m turn right (sign Symonds Yat). In 0.9 m turn left (sign Symonds Yat East). In 1.2 m keep straight (sign Yat Rock) to hill top car park. Here continue straight on B4432 (sign Coleford). In 1.8 m turn right on to B4228 (sign Coleford). In 0.7 m keep straight (sign Coleford) and in further 0.6 m turn left (sign Coleford).

Keep straight through Coleford (signs Chepstow and St Briavels), on B4228.

The Route

Fine views of the Wye around Symonds Yat. Later the road runs through the heart of the Forest of Dean. Fruit orchards and hopfields abound as Ledbury is neared.

St Briavels (Glos)

The remains of the medieval castle stand at a high point above the Wye. The gatehouse and two round towers (13c) lead through to what is now the YHA.

YHA, The Castle, T272

Forest of Dean (Glos)

The forest occupies some 20,000 acres in an area which lies in a triangular shape bounded by Ross, Chepstow and Gloucester, and there are hundreds of footpaths, which make it an ideal centre for rambling. The most central point of the forest is marked by a stone opposite the Speech House Hotel – built on the site of the headquarters of the Court of Verderers, who administered the forest laws. Many of the small towns and villages within the forest boundaries are centres for privately owned coal mines.

Speech House Hotel, Forest of Dean, 14 rooms, T Cinderford 22607 (A)

Mitcheldean (Glos)

YHA, Lion House, High St, T Drybrook 542366

Newent (Glos)

This pleasant little town is less busy than at one time as the main road now bypasses it. To visit the town centre it is necessary to divert from the route half a mile to the right. The George Hotel, a 17c coaching inn, was recently the scene of the discovery of a trove of golden guineas, unearthed from the fireplace. In the church opposite the hotel is a glass case which displays the Newent Stone, excavated in 1912 and believed to date back to the 11c.

George Hotel, Church St, 10 rooms, T820203 (D)

Ledbury (Hereford & Worcs)

Birthplace of one-time Poet Laureate John Masefield (1878–1967), the town lies close to the Gloucestershire border. It is surrounded by beautiful country, much of which consists of hopfields and apple orchards. At a central point of the broad main street is the market house – a larger version than that found at Newent but also, coincidentally, supported by sixteen pillars of oak. This mid-17c building was constructed by the king's carpenter, John Abel, as a cornmarket. Today the ground floor is in use as an open market, while the upper floor serves as a meeting-place and library.

From the market-place there is a fascinating walk along the cobbled Church Lane to the huge church of St Michael and All Angels. On the left of the lane is a pleasant little 15c inn, the Prince of Wales, alongside which, with an overhanging first floor, is a larger building known as the Old Grammar School, also 15c and now in use as a heritage museum. The church, mainly 14c, has a monument to Edward Moulton Barrett who is buried here and is remembered as the overbearing parent of the poetess Elizabeth Browning (1806–61), who spent much of her unhappy childhood near the town. Back in the main street is the Feathers Hotel, once an important post and coaching house on the Cheltenham–Hereford–Aberystwith route.

Feathers Hotel, High St, 13 rooms, T2600 (B)

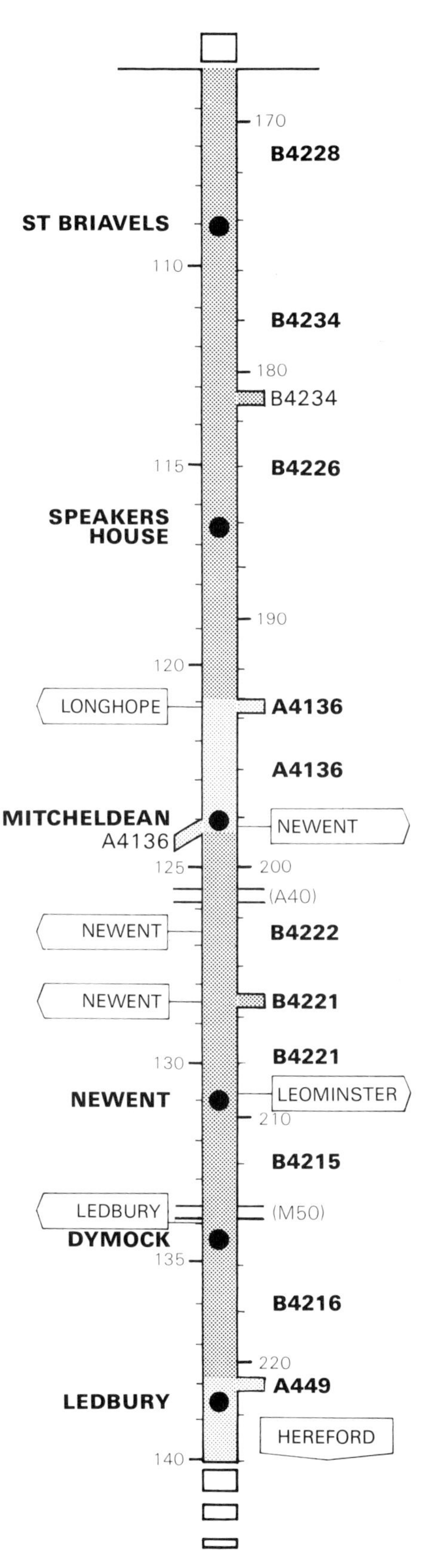

Continue on B4228 for 4.8 m to St Briavels. Here turn left on to minor road (no sign). In 2.0 m turn left (sign Bream) and in 0.2 m turn right (sign Bream). In 0.5 m turn right (sign Lydney) but in 0.1 m turn left (sign Parkend).

In 1.6 m turn right (sign Parkend) and in 0.5 m turn left (sign Lydbrook). In 2.1 m turn right (sign Cinderford). In 0.8 m keep straight (sign Cinderford). In 2.0 m turn left (sign Cinderford). In 1.4 m turn left (sign Drybrook). In 1.0 m turn right on to A4136 (sign Longhope) and in 2.2 m at Mitcheldean) bear left on to minor road (sign Newent).

In 1.8 m keep straight across A40 (sign Newent). In 1.3 m turn right on to B4222 (sign Newent). In 2.2 m turn right on to B4221 (sign Newent). In 1.7 m at entry to Newent turn left on to B4215 (sign Leominster). In 3.5 m at Dymock turn right on to B4216 (sign Ledbury). In further 3.7 m turn right on to A449 for 0.7 m into Ledbury. Here take A438 (sign Hereford) and in 0.6 m keep straight on to B4214 (sign Bromyard).

The view of Worcester Cathedral from across the River Severn.

Bromyard (Hereford & Worcs)

Those wishing to visit the town centre would only need to divert from the described route by less than a mile. Bromyard is a quiet market town with a number of half-timbered houses – among them the Falcon Inn.

Hop Pole Hotel, The Square, II rooms, T2449 (C)
Park House, 28 Sherford St, 5 rooms, T2294 (D)

Tenbury Wells
(Hereford & Worcs)

This little market town on the banks of the R. Teme once took on the dignity of a spa town when saline springs were discovered here in 1839. Pump rooms were constructed and although they now lie derelict behind the Crow Inn, there has been recent debate as to whether they should be restored and put to some practical use. The Royal Oak Hotel in Market Street makes a pleasant rendez-vous and distinguishes itself for the excellent lunches served at reasonable prices.

Royal Oak Hotel, Market St, 6 rooms, T810417 (C)
Swan Hotel, 12 rooms, T810422 (D)
T.O. Teme St, T810465

Clifton upon Teme
(Hereford & Worcs)

The name is misleading because this charming village lies high above the river, which is in fact bridged almost two miles further along the route. The 12c Lion Hotel lies next to the church and possessed a delightful saloon bar, which was once the banqueting hall of a private house and where good bar snacks and excellent evening meals are served. This room is separated into two parts by a magnificent log fireplace, open on all sides. A pillar in St Kenelm's Church details at length the fascinating legend of St Kenelm, who as a Saxon king of Mercia was reputed to have been murdered at the instigation of his sister when he was only seven years old. Also in the church is the recumbent figure of a knight. Out in the churchyard is a huge yew tree, in the hollow of which it would be possible to hide a man.

The Route

Quiet traffic-free motoring throughout – by way of many hopfields and orchards of fruit.

Bromyard – Clifton upon Teme

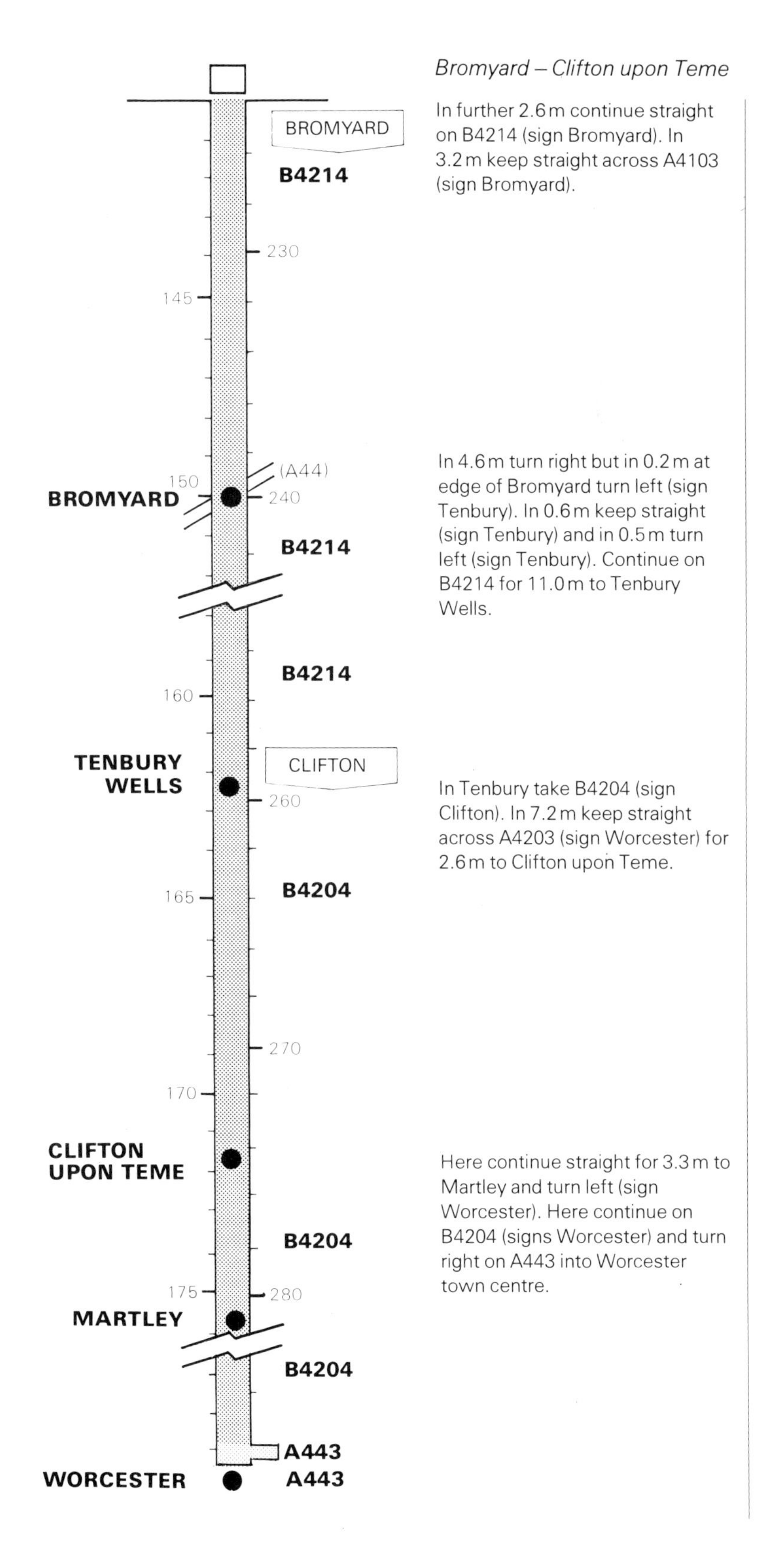

In further 2.6 m continue straight on B4214 (sign Bromyard). In 3.2 m keep straight across A4103 (sign Bromyard).

In 4.6 m turn right but in 0.2 m at edge of Bromyard turn left (sign Tenbury). In 0.6 m keep straight (sign Tenbury) and in 0.5 m turn left (sign Tenbury). Continue on B4214 for 11.0 m to Tenbury Wells.

In Tenbury take B4204 (sign Clifton). In 7.2 m keep straight across A4203 (sign Worcester) for 2.6 m to Clifton upon Teme.

Here continue straight for 3.3 m to Martley and turn left (sign Worcester). Here continue on B4204 (signs Worcester) and turn right on A443 into Worcester town centre.

16 *East Surrey, Sussex, Kent*

AFTER LEAVING GUILDFORD the route soon diverts from the main road by way of country lanes past one of Surrey's prettiest villages, Shere, before climbing to the county's highest vantage point, Leith Hill. Surrey has been called the 'Cockneys' Back Yard' and parts of the county are known as the 'Stockbroker Belt'. But although the main roads to the south coast do tend to get overcrowded, and some of the newer villages do contain much that is garish and 'mock tudor', many quiet unspoilt villages remain.

Very shortly, at Rudgwick, the road enters Sussex, and between Ditchling and Lewes runs eastward directly in line with and alongside the South Downs. South coast seaside resorts such as Worthing,

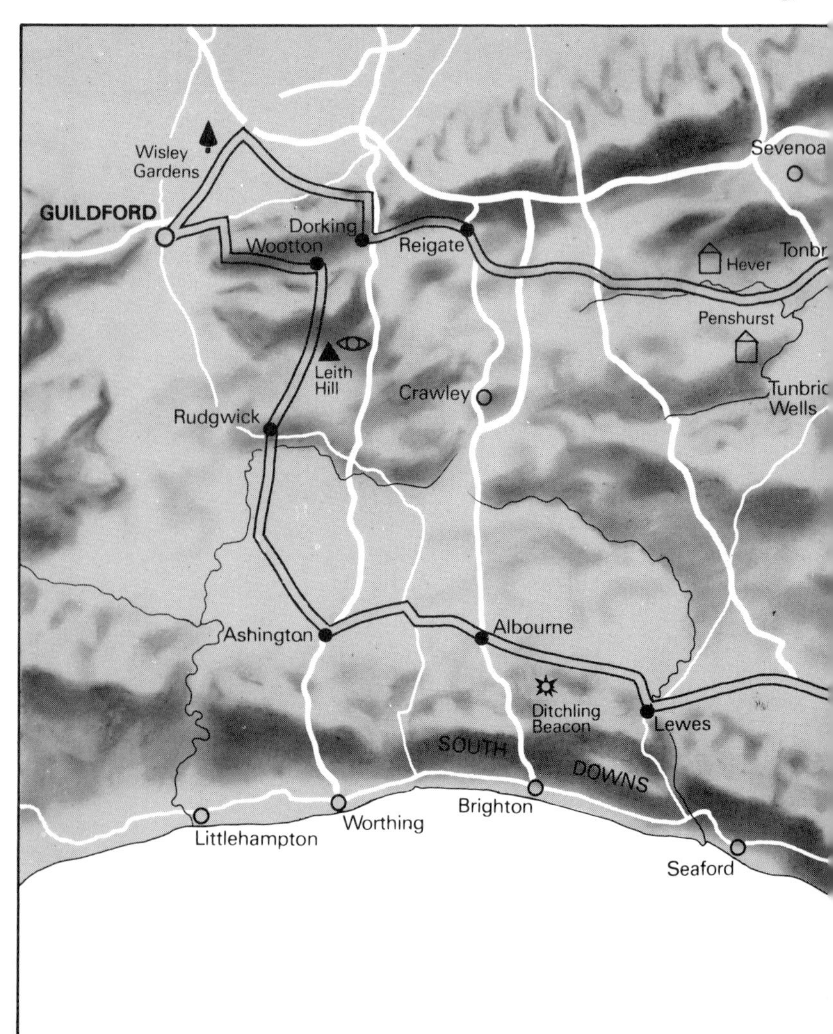

Brighton, Seaford and Eastbourne, while not lying along the route are easily accessible from Albourne or Lewes, and there can be no better overall view of the downs than from Ditchling Beacon.

Around Battle and Rye there are constant historical reminders. It was at Battle that the course of history was changed with the Norman invasion, while the picture-book town of Rye is numbered among the Cinque Ports. The term Cinque Ports (Cinque is pronounced Sink) is misleading, as in fact there are not five but seven towns in a confederation which since 1336 has been known as the Confederation of the Cinque Ports and the Two Ancient Towns. It was Edward the Confessor who decreed that five south-coast ports should take on the responsibility of guarding the straits between England and the Continent – these original five being Sandwich, Dover, Hythe, Romney and Hastings. Thus it was not until almost 300 years later that Rye and nearby Winchelsea joined the confederation.

This coastal area of Sussex and Kent later became a smugglers' paradise, and in his novel, *The Smuggler*, G. P. R. James wrote: 'Of all

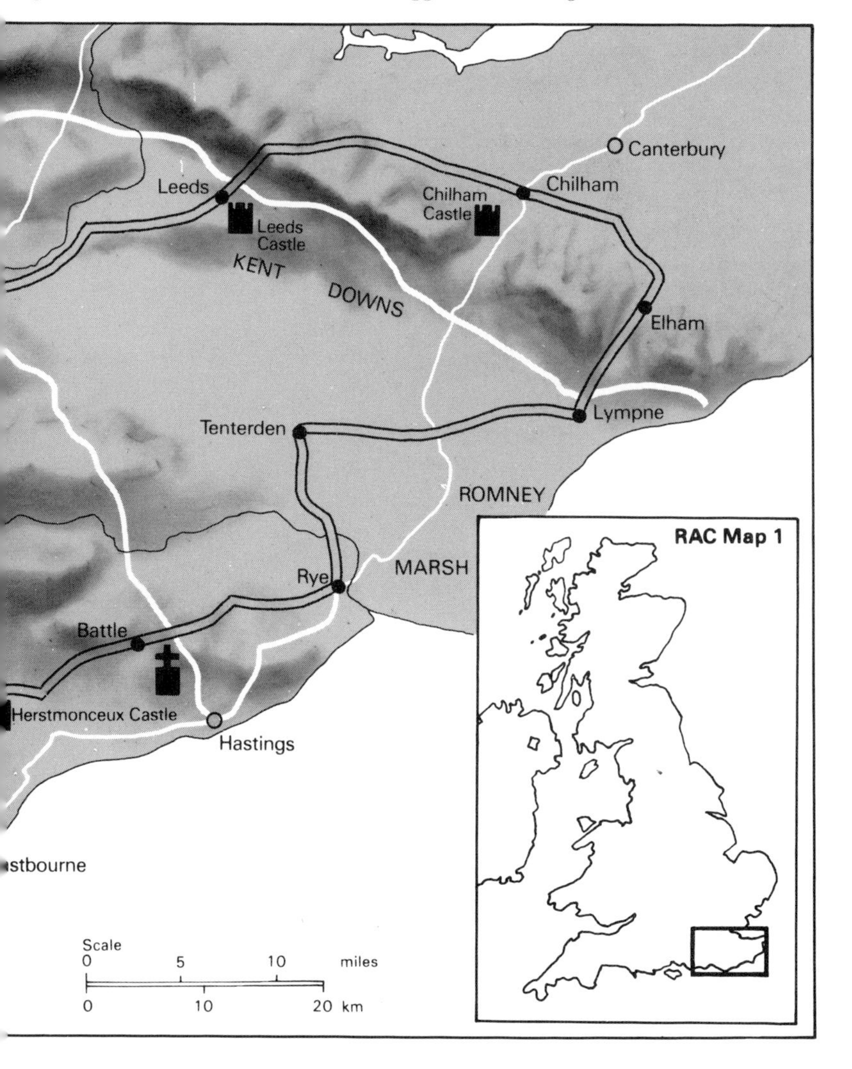

The fortified manor house of Hurstmonceux, surrounded by its wide moat.

counties the most favoured by nature and by art for the very pleasant sport of smuggling is the county of Kent.' To this day many subterranean passages, cellars and caves are to be found in villages around the Romney marshes – reminders of the Hawkhurst gang who terrorized the area in the 18th century and Russell Thorndike's fictional Dr Syn.

From Rye the road runs northward into Kent, through attractive towns and villages such as Tenterden, Lympne, Elham and Barham before veering westward to Chilham and onward through the heart of the Kent Downs by way of narrow traffic-free roads and remote villages. This part of the route bypasses Canterbury, which can, however, be visited if a two-mile diversion is taken at Street End. After leaving Maidstone to the north the road runs through Tonbridge and

thence through the entrancing villages of Leigh (pronounced Lie), Penshurst, Chiddingstone and Hever – the last three being tiny feudal villages alongside castles that are open to the public on specified occasions. The route leaves Kent at Edenbridge and returns once more to Surrey. It has passed through a variety of the countryside of a county which has been termed the 'Garden of Eden' – a county rich in fruit orchards, hop-gardens, and attractive cone-shaped oast-houses.

Re-entering Surrey it was found necessary to keep to the rather crowded major road between Reigate and Dorking before making for Polesden Lacey and the little village of Bookham. The woods on the right of the road near Effingham junction were once the home of the Effingham witches – and covens of witches are reputed to meet there even today! From Effingham a quiet country road leads to Wisley lake with the famous Wisley gardens near at hand. From here it seemed pointless to avoid the A3 for the last few miles back to Guildford.

Guildford (Surrey)

See Route 11, page 194.

Angel Hotel, High St, 24 rooms, T64555 (A)
T.O. Civic Hall, London Rd, T67314

Clandon Park (Surrey)

The road passes the fringe of Clandon Park, but the entrance to Clandon Park House is signed off to the left of the route. This square red brick Elizabethan house, redesigned in about 1730, is celebrated for its huge marble hall, rising through two storeys, and for the famous collection of antique furniture and Chinese porcelain bequeathed by the late Mrs David Gubbay.

Clandon Park House.

Leith Hill.

Shere (Surrey)

The route runs by way of Shere bypass, but it is worth taking the short diversion to visit this old-world village of narrow streets that is entered by passing beneath a quaint footbridge straddling the road. The White Horse Inn, partly constructed of ships' timbers, lies near a little willow-fringed stream that bisects the High Street.

Leith Hill (Surrey)

The road rises beneath the summit of Leith Hill, which at 965 feet is the highest point in Surrey. From the tower at the summit, built in 1766 by Richard Hull of Leith Hill Place, there are magnificent views that stretch as far as St Paul's in London and the Chiltern Hills 50 miles away. Leith Hill was a scene of battle in 851, for it was here that King Ethelwulf, father of Alfred the Great, defeated the invading Danish army after they had sacked London and Canterbury.

Forest Green (Surrey)

The village is scattered round a huge green, where cricket is a popular pastime in summer. Good bar snacks complement the real ale served at the Parrot Inn.

Walliswood (Surrey)

The local pub, Scarlett Arms, is a building that dates from the 16c, being a conversion of what were formerly agricultural cottages.

Rudgwick (Sussex)

Lies immediately across the Sussex border, stretching down a hill at the top of which is the Holy Trinity Church where the West Tower dates from the 13c.

Bucks Green (Sussex)

The Goblins Pool Hotel lies in a pleasant garden where excellent cream teas are served in summer.

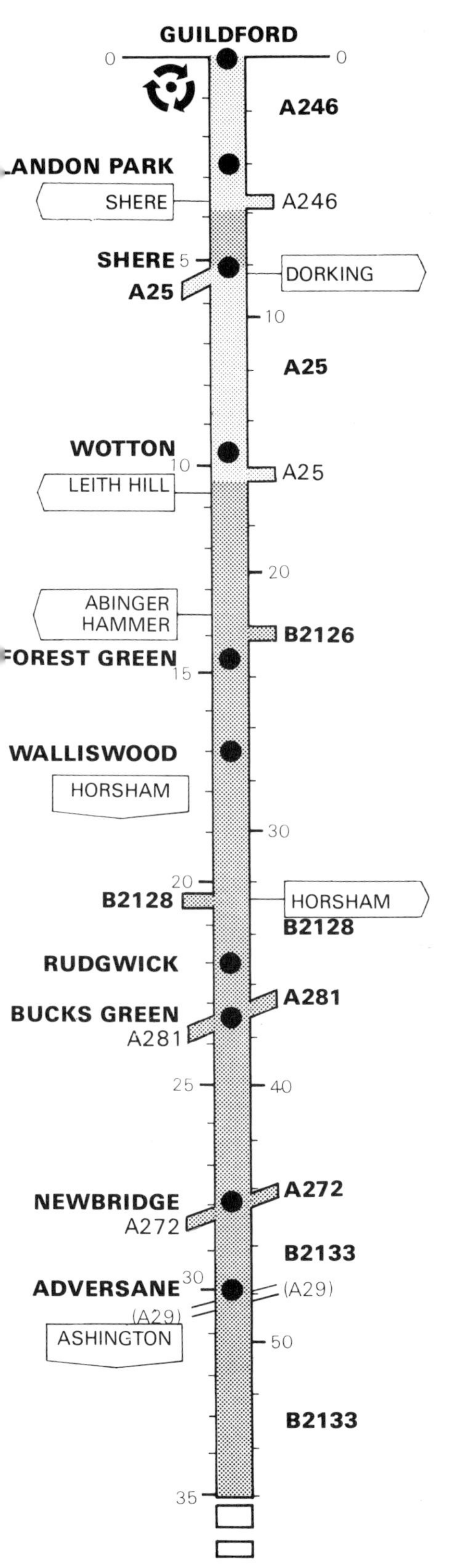

At the top of Guildford High St, by Odeon cinema, bear right at roundabout on to A246 (sign Leatherhead) and keep straight on A246 for 3.8 m. Here turn right on to minor road (sign Shere). Continue for 2.5 m on minor road (signs Shere) and turn left on to A25 (signs Gomshall and Dorking).

In 3.3 m at Wotton turn right on to minor road (sign Leith Hill). Keep straight for 4.2 m following signs Leith Hill and later Ockley. Turn right on to B2126 (sign Abinger Hammer) and in 0.6 m at Forest Green bear left on to B2127 (sign Cranleigh). In 0.1 m bear left on to minor roads (sign Horsham).

Continue straight for 2.1 m to Walliswood. Here keep straight (signs Horsham) and in 1.6 m turn right (sign Ellens Green). In 1.3 m turn left on to B2128 (sign Horsham) and in 1.9 m turn right on to A281 (sign Guildford). In 0.1 m turn left on to minor road (sign The Haven).

In 1.5 m turn right (sign Okehurst) and in 0.3 m turn left (sign Okehurst). In 2.1 m keep straight (sign Newbridge). In 1.3 m turn left on to A272 and immediately right on to B2133 (sign Ashington).

In 1.6 m at Adversane keep straight across A29 (sign Ashington). In 3.6 m keep straight (sign Ashington).

The Route

Initially by way of narrow Surrey roads through hilly wooded countryside. After entering Sussex the minor roads continue to be relatively free of traffic as they progress south-eastward, crossing the main roads to the south coast.

Hurstpierpoint (Sussex)

The narrow High Street contains many old houses – but a number of new estates have 'mushroomed' nearby. The church in the High Street was demolished in 1843 to make way for a larger one after complaints made at that time that there was room for 'only 500 sittings, none of them free'.

Ditchling (Sussex)

A mile to the south, on the South Downs Way, a fine view is obtained from Ditchling Beacon, one of many beacons sited, originally, to give warning of the coming of the Spanish Armada. The village is graced by many old timbered cottages.

The Downs from Ditchling Beacon.

Lewes (Sussex)

A town of steep narrow streets with a High Street of many Georgian buildings and a castle keep near the centre from where there is a good view of the town

The Keep, Lewes Castle.

and surrounds. A popular restaurant, the Old Bull, was formerly the home of Thomas Paine (1737–1809), who lodged here when an excise officer before writing such influential works as *Common Sense*, *The Rights of Man*, and *Age of Reason.* Anne of Cleves House, bequeathed by Henry VIII to his divorced wife, is now a museum where a number of rooms exhibit a variety of local arts and crafts as well as items of historical interest and wild life. Lewes is renowned for its torchlight procession on 5 November, when participants in medieval dress parade through the town amidst a spectacular display of fireworks and blazing bonfires. Plumpton racecourse, north-west of Lewes, holds regular National Hunt meetings.

Shelleys Hotel, High St, 21 rooms, T2361 (A)
White Hart Hotel, High Street, 18 rooms, T4676 (B)
T.O. 187 High St, T6151

Laughton (Sussex)

Only a tiny village – but the 15c Roebuck Inn deserves a visit for the good food served in the large timbered banqueting hall.

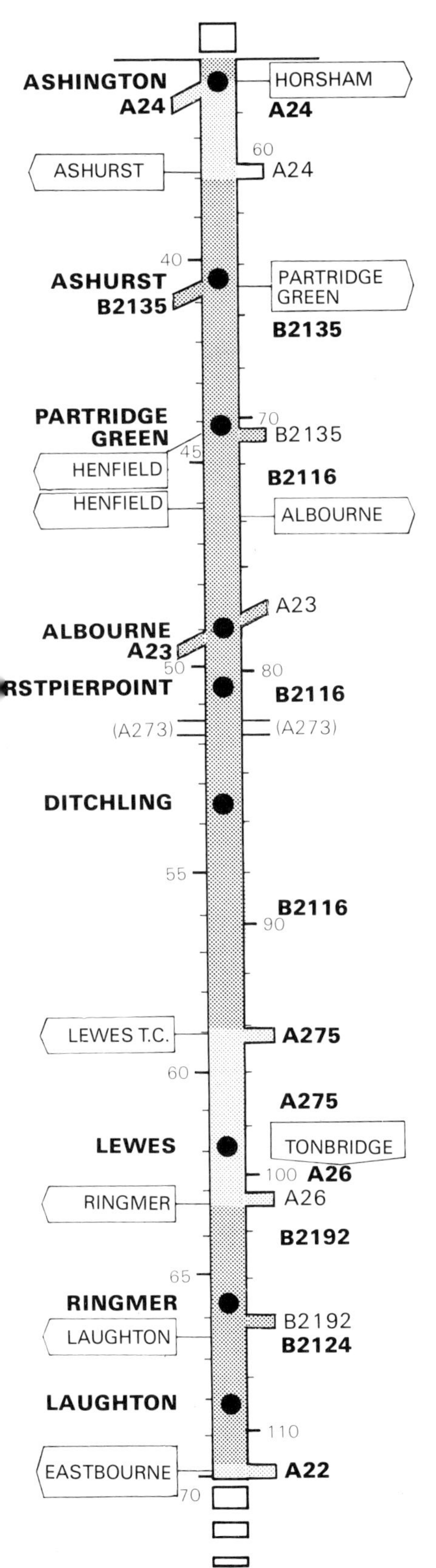

In 2.5 m at Ashington turn left on to A24 (sign Horsham). In 2.0 m turn right on to minor road (sign Ashurst). In 2.8 m turn right (no sign) and in 0.3 m at Ashurst turn left on to B2135 (sign Partridge Green).

In 2.2 m at Partridge Green turn right on to B2116 (sign Henfield). In 1.0 m turn right on to A281 (sign Henfield) and in further 1.4 m turn left on to B2116 (sign Albourne). Keep straight for 3.6 m to Albourne cross-roads.

At Albourne turn right on A23 and almost immediately left on to B2116 for 1.3 m to Hurstpierpoint. Here continue straight on B2116 for 2.7 m to Ditchling. Remain on B2116 for further 5.6 m and turn right on to A275 (sign Lewes) for 2.3 m to Lewes town centre.

In Lewes take A26 (signs Tonbridge) and in 1.2 m bear right on to B2192 (sign Ringmer) into Ringmer. Here bear right on B2124 (sign Laughton) to Laughton. In 2.0 m bear right on to A22 (sign Eastbourne).

Herstmonceux (Sussex)

This fortified manor house, originally built in the 15c, lies two miles to the south of the main road and is clearly signed. The castle, surrounded by a wide moat, is now the home of the Royal Greenwich Observatory and only the grounds are open to the public.

Battle (Sussex)

Before the Battle of Hastings (1066), Duke William of Normandy vowed that if he was the conqueror he would build an Abbey on the battlefield – a pledge he fulfilled as after his victory William the Conqueror commanded that the altar of the Abbey Church should be placed over the spot where King Harold had been slain. The buildings have seen many changes over the centuries – but the gatehouse and vaulted rooms beneath the monks dormitory retain much of their original splendour.

George Hotel, High St, 17 rooms, T2844 (B)
T.O. High St, T3721

Sedlescombe (Sussex)

The street of attractive old timbered houses broadens into a village green with a pump and fountain. Outside the village is one of the Pestalozzi Childrens' Villages, named after the Swiss educationist Johann Pestalozzi (1746–1827). The aim of the Childrens' Village is to provide children from abroad with a wide range of education which will be of use to their fellow countrymen when they return home.

Brickwall Hotel, 16 rooms, T202 (C)

Rye (Sussex)

This fascinating town of narrow cobbled streets stands above cliffs which were once washed by the sea. (The name Rye means 'island'.) In the impressive courtyard entrance to the Mermaid Hotel, its history is recorded. It was once a 'haunt' of smugglers, who terrorized the neighbourhood, drinking freely at the Mermaid bar with their pistols at the ready. At the top of Mermaid St is Lamb House, once the home of the American author Henry James (1843–1916). The house is preserved by the National Trust and the white panelled Henry James room contains some of the writer's furniture and library as well as original paintings of him by his compatriot John Sargent. Entry to the High Street is beneath the arch of Landgate, constructed in 1340 and the sole survivor of the four gates to this fortified town.

Old harbour warehouses, Rye.

Saltings Hotel, Hilders Cliff, 18 rooms, T3838 (C)
Hope Anchor Hotel, Watchbull St, 15 rooms, T2216 (C)
T.O. Cinque Ports St, T2480

The Route

Good views of the Sussex Downs around Ditchling, Plumpton and Lewes.

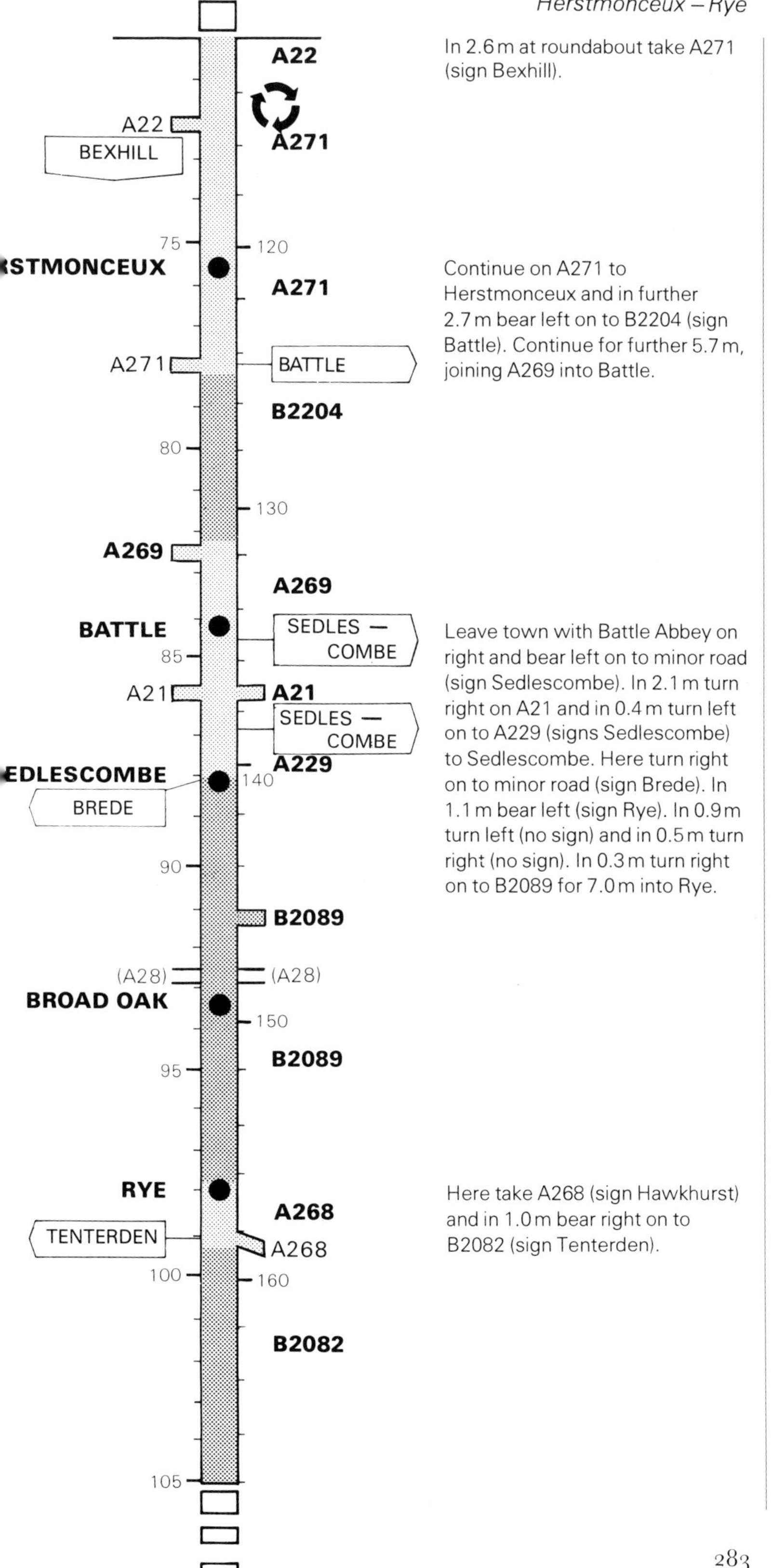

In 2.6 m at roundabout take A271 (sign Bexhill).

Continue on A271 to Herstmonceux and in further 2.7 m bear left on to B2204 (sign Battle). Continue for further 5.7 m, joining A269 into Battle.

Leave town with Battle Abbey on right and bear left on to minor road (sign Sedlescombe). In 2.1 m turn right on A21 and in 0.4 m turn left on to A229 (signs Sedlescombe) to Sedlescombe. Here turn right on to minor road (sign Brede). In 1.1 m bear left (sign Rye). In 0.9 m turn left (no sign) and in 0.5 m turn right (no sign). In 0.3 m turn right on to B2089 for 7.0 m into Rye.

Here take A268 (sign Hawkhurst) and in 1.0 m bear right on to B2082 (sign Tenterden).

Small Hythe (Kent)

The actress Dame Ellen Terry (1848–1928) lived for 29 years in the 15c half-timbered Small Hythe Place, which is now a museum with a collection of her personal and theatrical momentos.

Tenterden (Kent)

The town's long broad High Street contains many old buildings and inns of note. Among these are the William Caxton Inn, named after England's first printer (1422–91) who was reputedly born here, and the Tudor Rose – a restaurant within a house which has scarcely altered since the 16c.

White Lion Hotel, High St, 12 rooms, T2921 (C)

Ruckinge (Kent)

The village was once very much a centre for smugglers, and a macabre reminder of them is to be found in the porch of the Norman church, where a chart indicates the grave of the Ransley brothers – hanged 150 years ago and buried in the churchyard in a grave marked only by a wooden plank supported by rusty iron framework. The Ransleys, it is said, lived in a cottage with an underground escape tunnel not far from the Blue Anchor Inn, where, incidentally, good bar snacks are available.

Lympne (Kent)

Some 400 yards off to the right of the road is Lympne Castle (signed), majestically situated to overlook Romney Marsh above the ruins of a Roman fortress.

Mockbeggar (Kent)

The Gate Inn stands above a duck pond in this remote village.

Lympne Castle, high above the Marsh.

Elham (Kent)

Among the many interesting buildings in this lovely village is the 15c Abbots Fireside, now a good restaurant but formerly an inn, which faces the Rose and Crown in the main street. It is worth wandering into the placid square at the back of the Rose and Crown for a view of the church and several other attractive old buildings that surround the square.

Pett Bottom (Kent)

The little Duck Inn appears to be the only building here. Despite its size and remoteness the inn has enjoyed a reputation over many years for excellent food, and it offers a highly unusual *à la carte* menu.

Duck Inn, T Canterbury 830354

The Route

The minor roads between Lympne and Street End are narrow but easy to negotiate, though there is a particularly narrow stretch for about a mile between Pett Bottom and Street End.

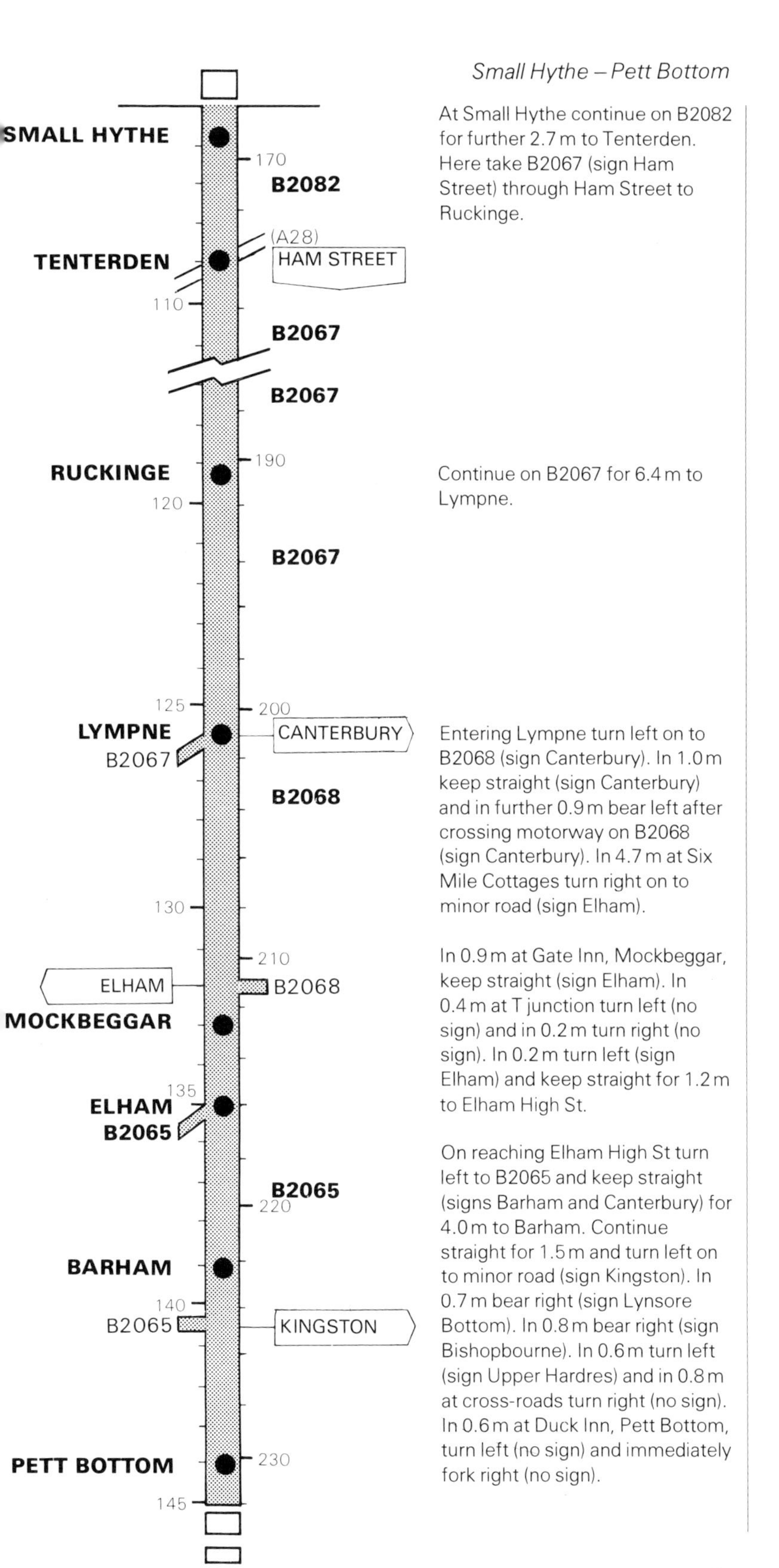

At Small Hythe continue on B2082 for further 2.7 m to Tenterden. Here take B2067 (sign Ham Street) through Ham Street to Ruckinge.

Continue on B2067 for 6.4 m to Lympne.

Entering Lympne turn left on to B2068 (sign Canterbury). In 1.0 m keep straight (sign Canterbury) and in further 0.9 m bear left after crossing motorway on B2068 (sign Canterbury). In 4.7 m at Six Mile Cottages turn right on to minor road (sign Elham).

In 0.9 m at Gate Inn, Mockbeggar, keep straight (sign Elham). In 0.4 m at T junction turn left (no sign) and in 0.2 m turn right (no sign). In 0.2 m turn left (sign Elham) and keep straight for 1.2 m to Elham High St.

On reaching Elham High St turn left to B2065 and keep straight (signs Barham and Canterbury) for 4.0 m to Barham. Continue straight for 1.5 m and turn left on to minor road (sign Kingston). In 0.7 m bear right (sign Lynsore Bottom). In 0.8 m bear right (sign Bishopbourne). In 0.6 m turn left (sign Upper Hardres) and in 0.8 m at cross-roads turn right (no sign). In 0.6 m at Duck Inn, Pett Bottom, turn left (no sign) and immediately fork right (no sign).

Street End (Kent)

There is little here apart from another pleasant inn, the Granville, with restaurant and bar snacks. Those wishing to visit Canterbury should note that the cathedral city lies only 2 miles to the north of this point along the B2068.

Granville Inn, T Petham 402

Chilham (Kent)

Considered by many to be Kent's prettiest village, Chilham is perched on a hill and isolated from the traffic that speeds along the two major roads beneath. Chilham Castle, St Mary's Church and the White Horse Inn, as well as numerous other medieval buildings, surround Chilham's square. The latter is probably best seen off season, as during summer weekends the village tends to get over-run with tourists. Displays of jousting and falconry take place within the castle grounds, where there are Jacobean terraces, rose gardens and tea rooms.

Eastling (Kent)

The village stands high on the north downs with a church surrounded by yew trees, among them a vast yew at the porch believed to be older than the church itself.

Doddington (Kent)

YHA, Ellenscourt, Lady Margaret Manor, T220

Ringlestone Inn (Kent)

'Is there anybody there?' said the traveller, knocking at the old inn door. Not the precise words of the de la Mare poem – but apt ones to describe the feeling of surprise upon arriving at this remote inn at an isolated point along the way between Doddington and Hollingbourne. The two bars, separated by a strange swing gate, contain much antique furniture and can have altered little in appearance over several centuries.

Hollingbourne (Kent)

Situated below the 'famous chalk ridge' from which Cobbett admired the view in 1823, Hollingbourne is today divided by the railway and some new buildings. In the church are many monuments to the Culpeper family, including a fine white marble monument in the Culpeper chapel to Elizabeth (died 1638).

Great Danes Hotel, Ashford Rd, 78 rooms, T381 (A)

Leeds Castle, one of the glories of Kent.

Leeds Castle (Kent)

The castle, originally built in wood and standing on two islands in the middle of a lake, is named after Led, Chief Minister of Ethelbert IV, King of Kent in AD 857. Points of particular interest within the castle are the Norman cellar, the chapel, and King Henry VIII's banqueting hall. Outside the castle is a duckery with rare swans, geese and ducks, as well as a nine-hole golf course and restaurant.

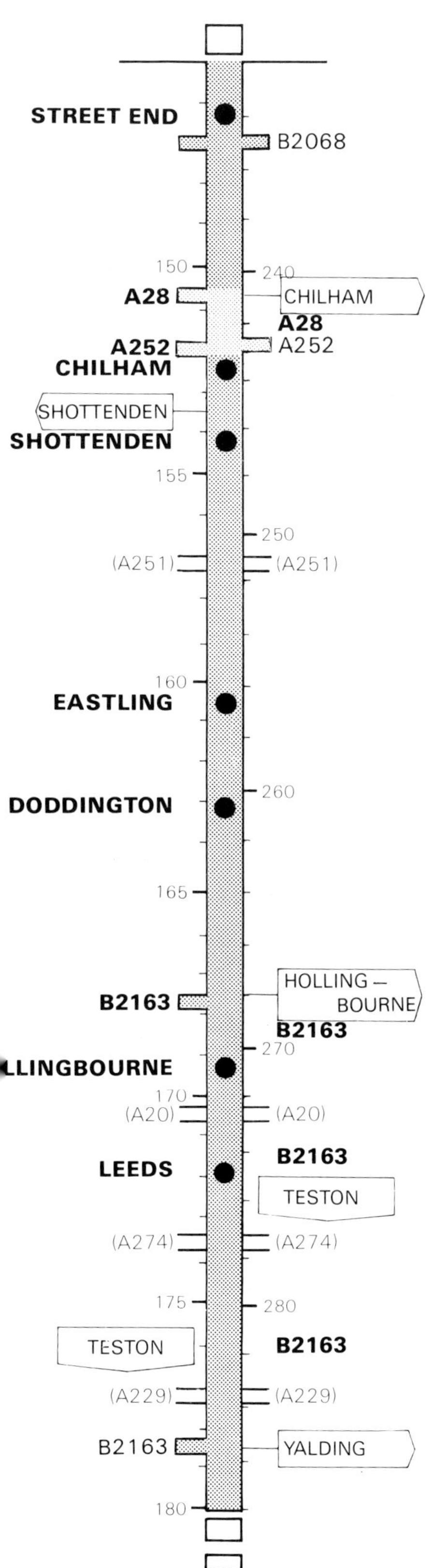

In 1.1 m turn right (sign Street End) for 0.3 m to Street End. Here, at Granville Inn, turn left (sign Folkstone) and immediately right on to minor road (sign Chartham). Keep straight (signs Chartham and Ashford) for 3.8 m and turn left on to A28 (sign Chilham). In 1.1 m bear right on A252 (sign Chilham) and immediately bear left on to minor road (sign Chilham Village) for 0.4 m to Chilham.

Here continue straight and turn left, rejoining A252, and immediately turn right on to minor road (sign Shottenden). In 1.4 m at Shottenden turn right (sign Badlesmere) and in 0.3 m turn left (sign Badlesmere). Keep straight (signs Badlesmere) and in 1.2 m bear left (no sign). In 1.0 m turn left and almost immediately right across A251 on to minor road (sign Eastling).

Keep straight and in 1.1 m turn right (no sign). In 0.2 m keep straight (sign Eastling) and in 0.4 m turn left (sign Eastling). In 0.2 m turn right (sign Eastling) and keep straight for 1.7 m to Eastling. Here turn right (sign Ospringe) and almost immediately turn left (sign Newnham). Keep straight for 0.8 m to Newnham and here turn left (sign Doddington).

Keep straight and in 1.7 m at far end of Doddington bear right (sign Hollingbourne). Keep straight (signs Hollingbourne) and in 5.0 m turn left on to B2163 (sign Hollingbourne) to Hollingbourne. Here keep straight through village and turn left and almost immediately right, crossing A20, on to B2162 (sign Leeds).

In 2.7 m keep straight across A274 (sign Teston). Keep straight (signs Coxheath and Linton) and in 3.4 m keep straight across A229 (sign Teston). In 1.4 m turn left on to minor road (sign Yalding) and keep straight for further 3.2 m to Yalding.

Yalding (Kent)

The poet Edmund Blunden spent much of his boyhood in this beautiful village set among the hop-gardens of Kent.

Tonbridge (Kent)

The most impressive feature of Tonbridge is the substantial ruin of the Norman castle that dominates the centre of the ancient town and overlooks the R. Medway. The town is also the home of the famous public school founded in 1553.

Rose and Crown Hotel, High St, 44 rooms, T357966 (A)
Postern Forge, Postern Lane, 4 rooms, T352206 (D)

Leigh (Kent)

St Mary's Church, rebuilt in the 13c, stands at the highest point of the village across from the huge green where there are many pleasant period houses. An interesting feature of this lovely church is a 16c hour-glass on the pulpit.

Penshurst (Kent)

Penshurst Place, ancestral home of the soldier-poet Sir Philip Sidney (1554–86), stands near the centre of the village, screened by tall trees. There is a delightful entry to the parish church beneath an arch made by Tudor cottages, and within the church the Sidney chapel contains many memorials to that family.

Leicester Arms, 7 rooms, T551 (B)

Chiddingstone (Kent)

Beautiful 16c and 17c half-timbered houses face the church, notably the fine 16c Castle Inn. Within the grounds of the 18c mock-gothic castle is the 'Chiding Stone', a huge sandstone rock, after which the village is named.

Hever (Kent)

The castle, originally a fortified manor house and home of the Bullen (Boleyn) family, was where King Henry VIII met the ill-fated Anne Boleyn. It was bought and modernized by the wealthy American, William Waldorf Astor. The castle grounds include a maze, composed of more than 1,000 yews, and an Italianate garden.

Edenbridge (Kent)

The High Street of this busy little town contains many ancient buildings – among them the home of a Lord Mayor of London, born in the 15c, whose arms are still to be seen on the doorway.

The home of Anne Boleyn at Hever.

Haxted Water-Mill (Surrey)

The small museum here includes working models and exhibits from a variety of water-mills.

The Route

From Street End to Hollingbourne the minor roads pass through the heart of the Kent Downs. After Leeds there are orchards and hopfields, giving way to pleasant wooded countryside.

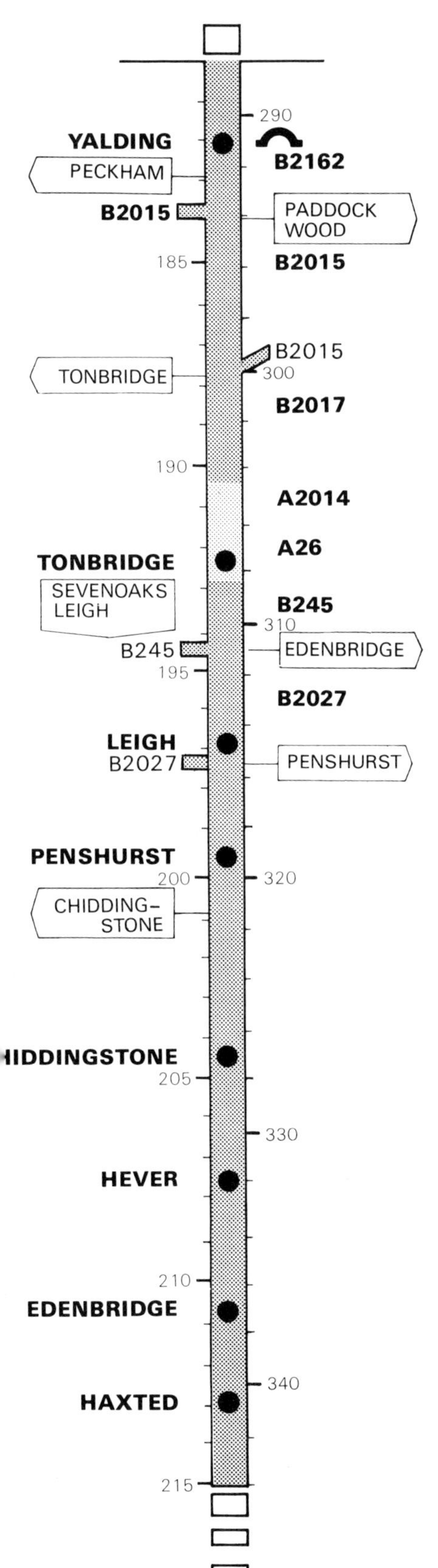

At Yalding turn left (sign East Peckham) and in 0.2 m, after crossing bridges, turn right on to B2162 (sign Peckham). Keep straight for 1.5 m and turn left on to B2015 (sign Paddock Wood). Continue on B2015 for 3.7 m and bear right (sign Tonbridge).

Continue to follow signs Tonbridge on B2017 (later A2014 and A26) for further 4.8 m to Tonbridge town centre.

In Tonbridge take B245 (signs Sevenoaks and Leigh) and in 1.5 m turn left on to B2027 (sign Edenbridge). Remain on B2027 (signs Edenbridge and Leigh) for 2.2 m to Leigh. Here continue straight for 0.6 m and bear left (sign Penshurst). Continue straight for 2.2 m to Penshurst.

Here turn right on to B2188 (sign Tunbridge Wells) and in 0.6 m turn right on to minor road (sign Chiddingstone). In 1.4 m at T junction turn right (sign Chiddingstone). In 0.5 m turn right (sign Chiddingstone) and keep straight for 2.3 m to Chiddingstone.

Here bear right in village and in 0.3 m keep straight (sign Hever). In 1.4 m turn right (sign Hever). In 0.3 m turn right (sign Hever). In 0.7 m turn right (sign Hever) and in 0.2 m turn right for 0.2 m to Hever village.

Retrace route by returning final 0.2 m into village and turn right (sign Edenbridge). In 2.0 m turn right for 0.4 m into Edenbridge town centre. Turn left (sign Haxted) and in 0.2 m turn left (sign Haxted). In further 0.2 m turn right (sign Haxted) for 1.7 m to Haxted water-mill, and here continue straight.

Outwood Post-Mill (Surrey)

The oldest working windmill in England, built in 1665, with sails that measure 59 feet.

Reigate (Surrey)

Nothing remains of the castle in Castle Grounds, but beneath the original site is an underground cave and tunnels known as Barons' Cave – so called because it is said that the barons formulated their plans here before meeting King John at Runnymede, where Magna Carta was signed.

Cranleigh Hotel, 41 West St, 12 rooms, T40600 (B)
Ladbroke Mercury Motel, Reigate Hill, 30 rooms, T46801 (A)

Dorking (Surrey)

Among the older buildings of this market town are the gabled White Horse Inn and the Red Lion. Boxhill, outside the town, towers above the Burford Bridge Hotel where the poet John Keats (1795–1821) stayed while writing his 'Endymion'. Nearby is Flint Cottage, the home of the novelist George Meredith (1829–1909).

White Horse Hotel, High St, 69 rooms, T81138 (A)
Burford Bridge Hotel, Burford Bridge, 30 rooms, T4561 (A) NB lies off the A24 outside the town.

Polesden Lacey (Surrey)

This Regency house, set amidst extensive grounds with flower gardens and many miles of woodland walks, was built on the site of the country home of Richard Sheridan (1751–1816), author of *The Rivals* and *School for Scandal.* King Edward VII was a frequent visitor here, guest of Mrs Richard Greville, whose tomb is to be found in the gardens that she had skilfully planned over many years. Within the house are many fine Dutch and English paintings, as well as rich collections of porcelain, pottery, and silver.

Bookham (Surrey)

The route runs through the very narrow High Street, on the left of which there is parking space behind the pleasant old Royal Oak Inn. Here, incidentally, can be seen details of what must surely be one of the most extraordinary cricket matches on record.

Effingham (Surrey)

Charles Howard (1536–1624), Commander-in-Chief of the English fleet that defeated the Spanish Armada in 1588, lived at Effingham Court Place, the remnants of which are now a farmhouse.

Wisley (Surrey)

The Royal Horticultural Society's famous gardens cover many acres off the A3. They lie to the right of the road but are signed to the left.

The lake in Wisley Gardens.

The Route

The minor road past Polesden Lacey is steep and very narrow. It was found necessary to return by the A3 for the final few miles back to Guildford.

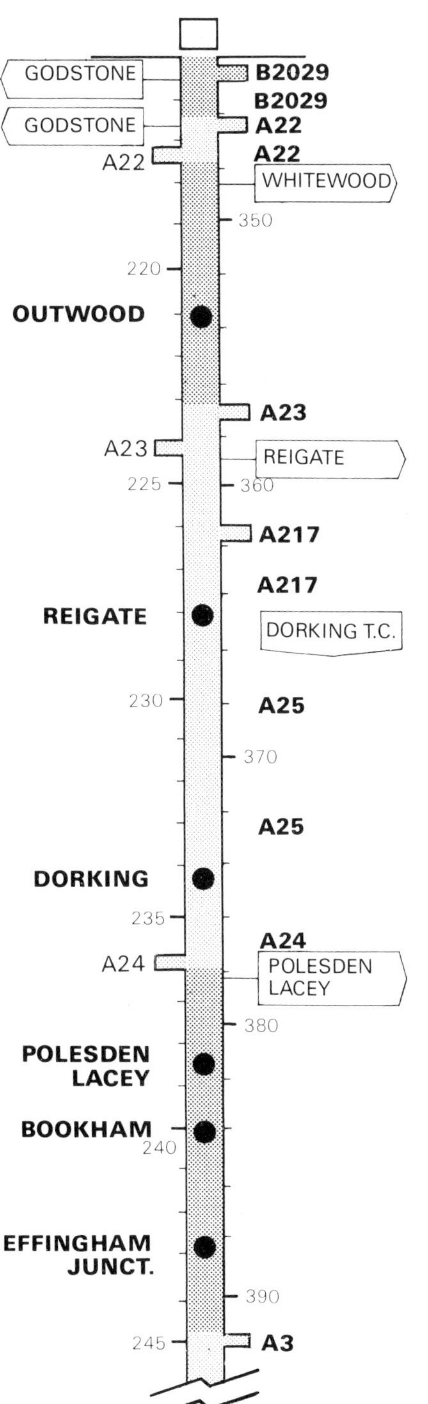

In 2.5 m turn right on to B2029 (sign Godstone). In 1.2 m turn right on to A22 (sign Godstone) and in 0.8 m turn left on to minor road (sign Whitewood). In 1.2 m bear right (sign Horne) and in 0.8 m turn right (sign Outwood) for 1.2 m to Outwood mill.

Here turn left (sign Smallfield) and almost immediately right (sign Redhill). In 2.2 m turn right on to A23 (no sign) and in 0.4 m bear left (sign Reigate). In 1.8 m turn right on A217 for 1.2 m to Reigate town centre. Here keep straight on to A25 (sign Dorking) for 5.7 m to Dorking town centre.

At edge of Dorking take A24 (signs London and Guildford alt. route) and in 1.2 m turn left on to minor road (sign Polesden Lacey). Keep straight for 2.5 m to entry road to Polesden Lacey (on left). Continue straight for 0.7 m and at T junction turn right (sign Guildford). In 0.1 m turn left (sign Guildford) and in 0.1 m at traffic lights turn right (sign Bookham Church). At cross-roads at foot of Bookham High St turn left (no sign).

In 1.3 m turn right (sign Effingham junction) and in 1.7 m just past Effingham junction keep straight (sign Ockham). In 1.2 m keep straight (sign Guildford). In 1.2 m turn left on to A3 (sign Guildford) and keep straight on A3 for 7.0 m into Guildford.

17 *Cheshire, North Shropshire*

THIS ROUTE of some 160 miles starts at the historic city of Chester, making southwards and shortly crossing the Cheshire/Shropshire border. The southernmost point of the route is reached at Much Wenlock, and those wishing to combine this route with Route 10 should note that Bridgnorth, on the latter route, lies some eight miles to the south-east of Much Wenlock along the A458. Thus at its beginning and end the route runs through the county of Cheshire, embracing a pleasant section of North Shropshire in between.

Cheshire extends to the north east almost as far as Manchester and includes towns such as Altrincham and Sale, which can both be described as prosperous Mancunian suburbs. Much of the northern part of Cheshire, particularly that area which clings close to the south bank of the River Mersey, is industrialized. The remaining and greater part of the county, however, is pastoral and continues to provide milk and the world-famous Cheshire cheese as it has done over centuries.

Much of the early part of the route follows the course of the River Dee, which between Farndon and Shocklach defines the Anglo-Welsh border. It is of interest that Farndon was the birthplace of the 16th century historian and map-maker John Speed, son of a London tailor, who summed up Cheshire and its produce in the colourful language of the day: 'The soil is fat, fruitful and rich. The Pastures make the Kine's udders to strout the pail, from whom and wherein the best Cheese of all Europe is made.' Among other famous people to have been born or to have lived in Cheshire are Bishop Heber (1783–1826), author of that well known hymn 'From Greenland's Icy Mountains', who was born at Malpas, and Charles Kingsley (1819–75), one-time Canon of Chester Cathedral, to whom the natural history section of the Grosvenor museum in Chester has been dedicated. Daresbury, just off to the north-east of this route, was the birthplace of Lewis Carroll (1832–98), who immortalized the grinning Cheshire cat.

Passing through Shropshire one thinks of Mary Webb (1882–1927), who was born in the county and whose novels bring it to life, and Alfred Houseman (1859–1936) who wrote most of the poems of *A Shropshire Lad* while occupying the somewhat unglamorous position as clerk at H.M. Patent Office.

Among the larger towns passed in Shropshire those of particular beauty and interest include Whitchurch, Shrewsbury and Much Wenlock. Plenty of delightful rural scenery is encountered, together with many abbeys, churches and ancient houses of historic interest.

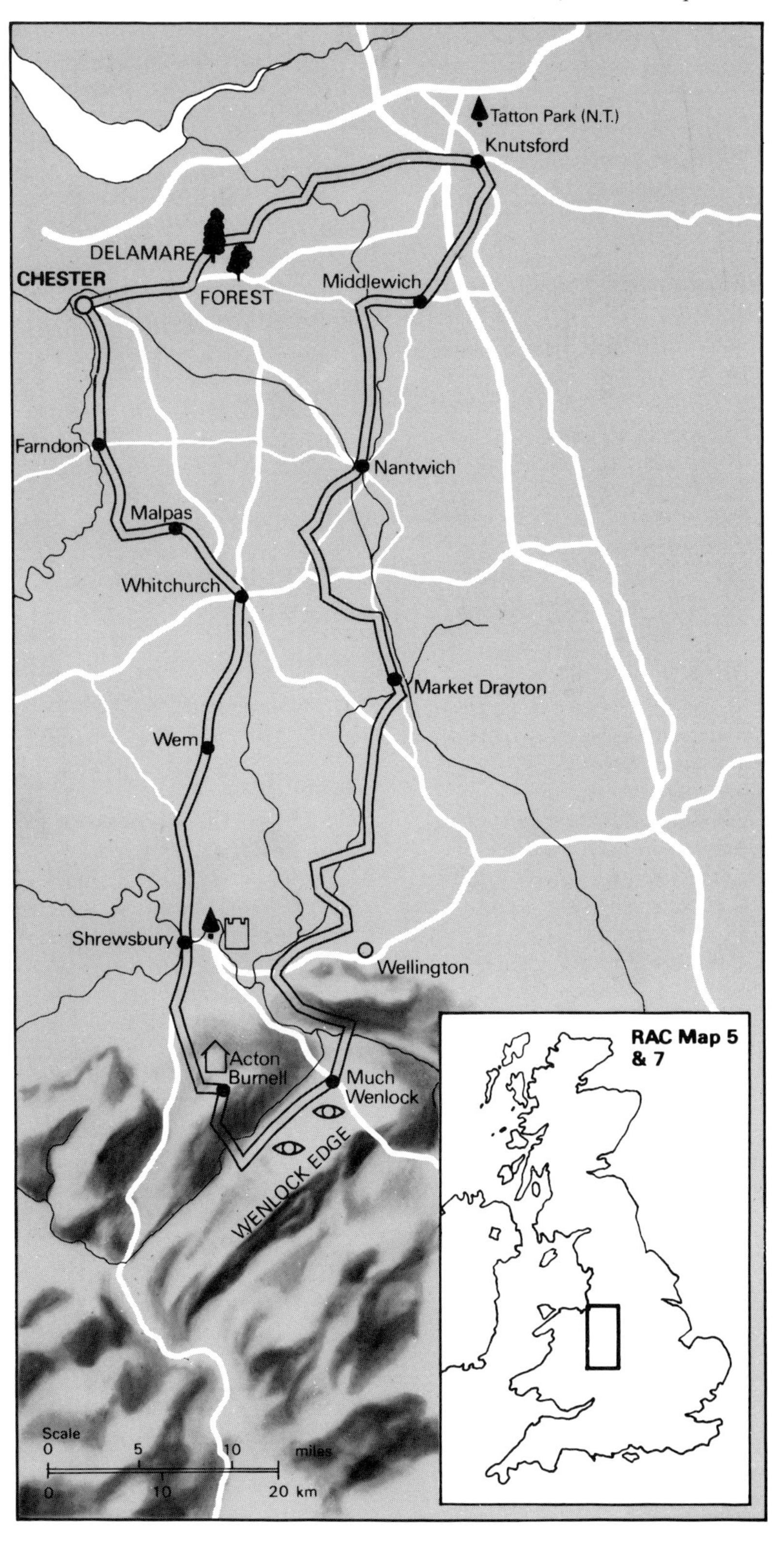
Tatton Park (N.T.)
Knutsford
DELAMARE
CHESTER
FOREST
Middlewich
Farndon
Nantwich
Malpas
Whitchurch
Market Drayton
Wem
Shrewsbury
Wellington
Acton
Burnell
Much
Wenlock
WENLOCK EDGE
RAC Map 5
& 7
Scale
0
5
10
miles
0
10
20 km

Chester (Cheshire)

See Route 1, page 14.

Farndon (Cheshire)

The town stands above the R. Dee, which separates it from Wales and is spanned by a 14c bridge.

Shocklach (Cheshire)

A cluster of houses and an inn make up this little village which, like Farndon, lies just within the English border. Centuries ago, due to its strategic importance, the village boasted a castle, but all that remains now is rubble in a field. For some unaccountable reason the church lies a mile outside the village, but it is worth a visit for its peaceful, remote setting.

Malpas (Cheshire)

The pride of this pleasant hillside town with black-and-white houses and ancient almshouses is undoubtedly the church at St Oswald's with the magnificent Brereton and Cholmondeley chapels. The Brereton monument is a masterpiece of the craftsman's art and is ranked by experts as one of the finest of its kind in existence. The chest tomb is that of Sir Randle Brereton and his wife, and was erected in 1522, eight years before Sir Randle's death. The upright figures around the chest are the weepers, the children of the knight and lady and others who held them in allegiance. The original Brereton crest was a bear – but one of Sir Randle's ancestors, a stalwart knight, was guilty of excess of ardour in battle, pushing an advantage too far. As a result the King, who witnessed this bold deed, rebuked him with the words, 'I shall muzzle that bear', and directed this order to be notified to the Heralds College. This accounts for the muzzled bear at Sir Randle's head and a similar large gargoyle near the church entrance. In the Cholmondeley chapel is another fine chest tomb, erected almost 100 years after the Brereton tomb, with figures that represent Sir Hugh Cholmondeley and his second wife, Mary.

Whitchurch (Salop)

A market town with many old timbered houses and inns. The town's name derives from the 14c church, built in white stone, which collapsed in the early 18c and was immediately rebuilt. In the church is the tomb of John Talbot, Earl of Shrewsbury, who fell at the battle of Bordeaux in 1453, aged 80.

Hollies Motel, Chester Rd, 16 rooms, T2184 (B)
Victoria Hotel, High St, 7 rooms, T2031 (D)
T.O. Shropshire Arts and Crafts Centre, T4232

Wem (Salop)

This market town was destroyed by fire in 1667 and thus few buildings of antiquity are to be found. The ruthless Judge Jeffreys (1648–89) was created Baron of Wem in 1685, living for a time at a house named Lowe Hall. A little white house in Noble Street was the boyhood home of the essayist William Hazlitt (1788–1830).

The Woodlands, Wolverley, Northwood, 8 rooms, T33268 (D)

The Route

Initially the minor roads run southward, parallel to the R. Dee which defines the border with Wales. The Cheshire/Shropshire border is crossed just before reaching Whitchurch, from where the B5476 to Shrewsbury carries little traffic as most vehicles take the nearby A49.

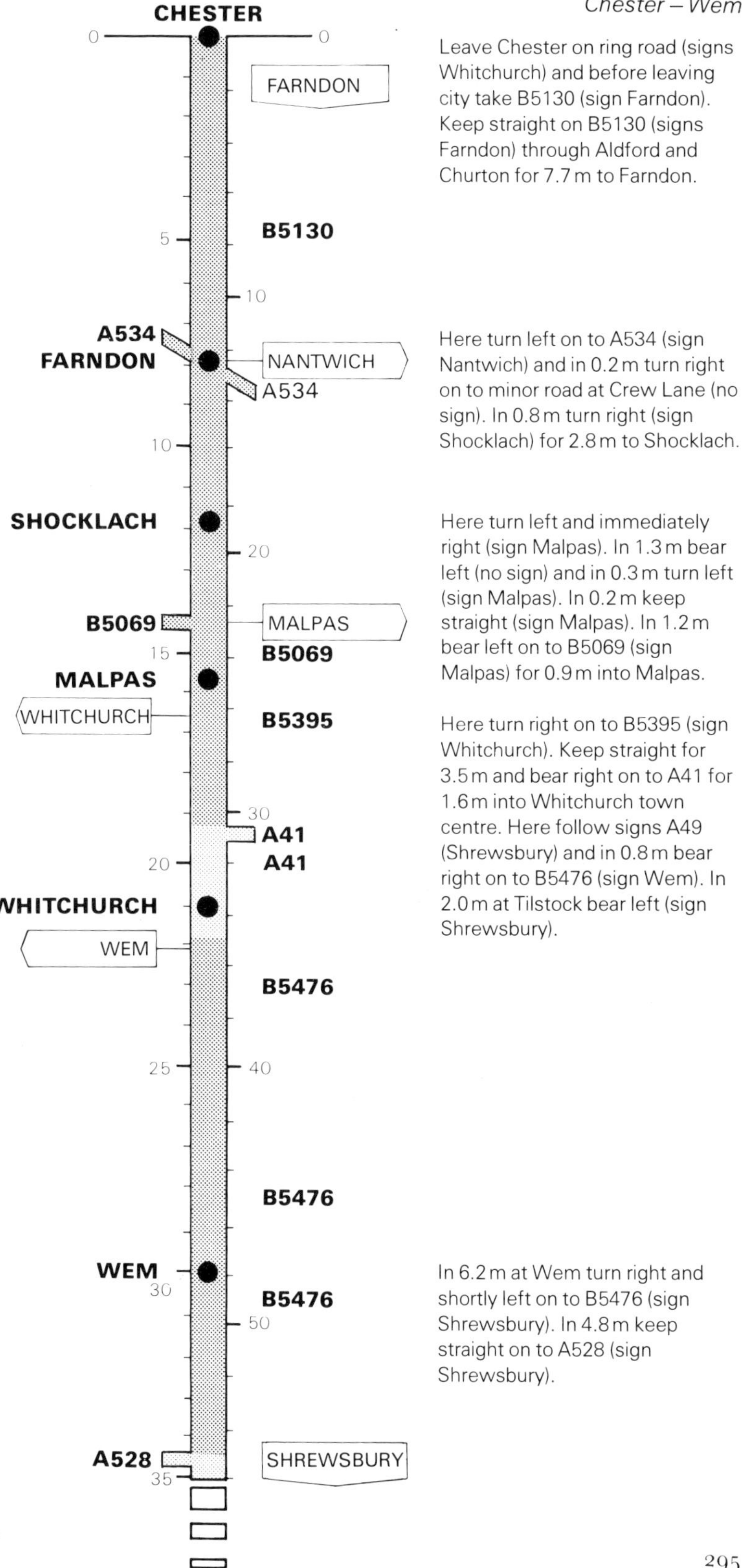

Leave Chester on ring road (signs Whitchurch) and before leaving city take B5130 (sign Farndon). Keep straight on B5130 (signs Farndon) through Aldford and Churton for 7.7 m to Farndon.

Here turn left on to A534 (sign Nantwich) and in 0.2 m turn right on to minor road at Crew Lane (no sign). In 0.8 m turn right (sign Shocklach) for 2.8 m to Shocklach.

Here turn left and immediately right (sign Malpas). In 1.3 m bear left (no sign) and in 0.3 m turn left (sign Malpas). In 0.2 m keep straight (sign Malpas). In 1.2 m bear left on to B5069 (sign Malpas) for 0.9 m into Malpas.

Here turn right on to B5395 (sign Whitchurch). Keep straight for 3.5 m and bear right on to A41 for 1.6 m into Whitchurch town centre. Here follow signs A49 (Shrewsbury) and in 0.8 m bear right on to B5476 (sign Wem). In 2.0 m at Tilstock bear left (sign Shrewsbury).

In 6.2 m at Wem turn right and shortly left on to B5476 (sign Shrewsbury). In 4.8 m keep straight on to A528 (sign Shrewsbury).

Shrewsbury (Salop)

The R. Severn loops round the town with its picturesque half-timbered houses and narrow lanes that the novelist Charles Dickens (1812–70), observing from his bedroom window at the Lion Hotel, described as follows: 'I can look down hill and slantwise at the crookedest black and white houses, all of many shapes except straight shapes.' Points of interest within the town include the Norman castle, built by Roger de Montgomery and restored in 1790; St Mary's Church, 12c with magnificent stained glass windows; Clive House, one-time home of Lord Robert Clive (1725–74), whose statue stands in the Square; the statue of Charles Darwin (1809–82), the scientist who was born here and educated at Shrewsbury's famous school; Rowley House, a museum containing a collection of Roman, prehistoric and medieval material; and the Dingle in Quarry Park, where there are formal gardens laid out by the famous gardener Mr Percy Thrower and where the annual Shrewsbury flower show takes place in August.

Prince Rupert Hotel, Butcher Row, 61 rooms, T52461 (A)
Beauchamp Hotel, The Mount, 25 rooms, T3230 (B)
T.O. The Square, T52019

Condover (Salop)

There are some fine monuments in the church of St Mary and St Andrew, including the marble figure of a young woman, Alice Cholmondeley, carved by her husband Reginald Cholmondeley after a marriage of only a year. Among other monuments are many to the Owen family – and it was Judge Thomas Owen who had the lovely Condover Hall built for his son Roger in the 16c. The Hall can be seen through entrance gates as the road leaves the village. It lies in a 300-acre park and is now a school.

Acton Burnell (Salop)

Although the route turns to the right on entering the village it is worth a diversion of a few hundred yards to see the church and adjoining castle. Acton Burnell Castle, a fortified manor house rather than a castle, with rectangular towers at the four corners, was built in the late 13c for Robert Burnell, Lord Chancellor and Bishop of Bath and Wells, who had served Prince Edward, later Edward I, as his chaplain. In playing fields to the east of the castle are gables of Burnell's earlier house where King Edward's parliament met in 1283. The grey stone church of St Mary was built at the same time as the castle and here is the tomb of Sir Nicholas Burnell (1382), grand-nephew of Robert Burnell.

Much Wenlock (Salop)

This pretty market town with ruins of a Cluniac priory and numerous medieval inns and houses has been described as 'a Rip Van Winkle of a place which has remained asleep since the Middle Ages'. In the covered portion of the Guildhall, once the butter market, Wenlock pottery is sold and there are interesting relics, including stocks designed to accommodate three people – mounted on wheels in order to propel the unfortunate victims around the town. In the upper storey are the oak-panelled council chamber and court room, both still in use. In the High Street is the Talbot Inn where James II once stayed.

Wheatland Fox Hotel, High St, 4 rooms, T292 (D)
T.O. The Guildhall, T727679

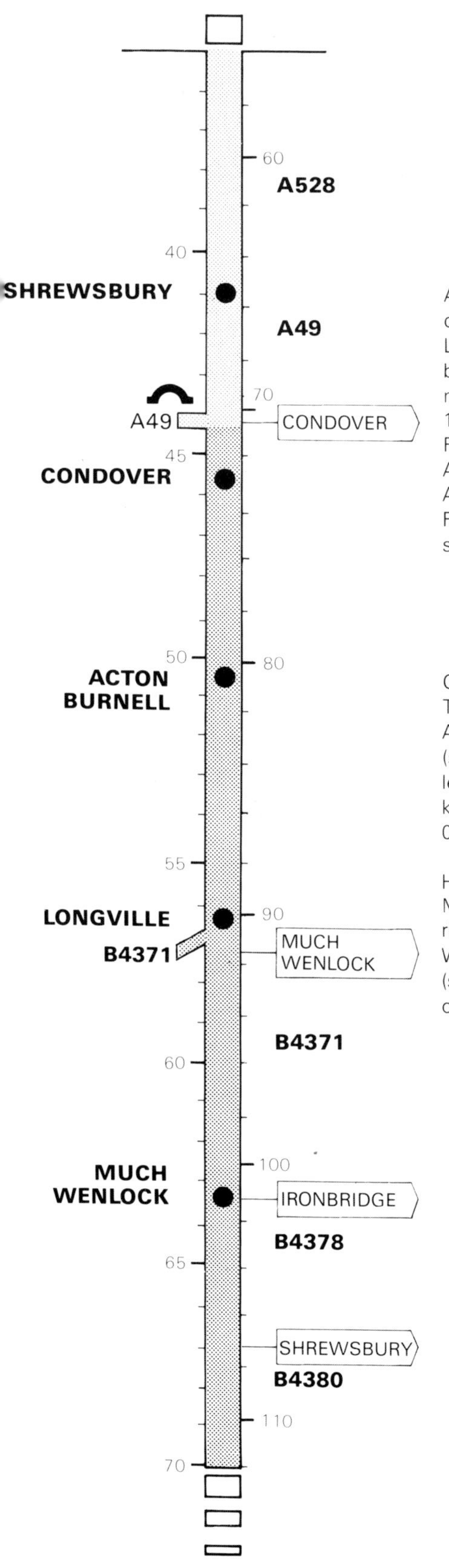

After 6.0 m, in Shrewsbury town centre, take A49 (signs Leominster) and after crossing bridge in 2.9 m turn left on to minor road (sign Condover). In 1.5 m at Condover turn left (sign Frodsley). In 3.4 m turn left (sign Acton Burnell) and in 1.3 m at Acton Burnell turn right (sign Ruckley). In 1.2 m at Ruckley keep straight (sign Broome).

Continue straight for 1.6 m and at T junction turn left (sign Plaish). Almost immediately fork right (sign Plaish). In 1.4 m at Plaish turn left (sign Longville) and in 1.5 m keep straight (sign Longville) for 0.3 m to Longville in the Dale.

Here turn left on to B4371 (sign Much Wenlock) and in 6.4 m turn right. In 0.3 m on entering Much Wenlock turn left on to B4378 (sign Ironbridge). In 3.5 m turn left on to B4380 (sign Shrewsbury).

The impressive ruins of Buildwas Abbey.

The Route

Quiet narrow country roads from Shrewsbury to Longville in the Dale. From here the road runs along the side of Wenlock Edge before descending into Much Wenlock. Further beautiful scenery is encountered for the next few miles – but it then becomes necessary to proceed northwards through several miles of rather flat featureless country in order to avoid the industrial area around Telford.

Buildwas Abbey (Salop)

The Abbey ruins lie in a meadow by the R. Severn, signed to the left some 3½ miles after leaving Much Wenlock. It was founded in 1135 and a surprising amount of the original building remains.

Great Bolas (Salop)

A tiny village tucked away on the R. Tern, consisting of little more than a few houses and Georgian church. But a romantic story of the village's past has been immortalized in one of Tennyson's works, 'The Lord of Burleigh'. In 1791 a servant was employed by the miller here. He soon fell in love and married the miller's daughter, Sarah Hoggins, who was unaware that in fact he was heir to the Earl of Exeter. For two years the couple lived modestly at a nearby farm. Then, on his father's death, the servant became the 10th Earl, and took his wife to the ancestral home in Lincolnshire.

Market Drayton (Salop)

An old market town around which a certain amount of industry has developed over recent years. The town's most famous son is Robert Clive, Clive of India, who was educated at the grammar school here. The school desk on which Clive carved his initials has been retained, as have other memories of the Governor of India – and of the little urchin who ran a protection racket, warning the tradesmen that their windows would be broken if they failed to pay up. Around the town centre are a number of black-and-white houses and a butter market.

Corbet Arms Hotel, High St, 8 rooms, T2037 (B)
Tern Hill Hall Hotel, Tern Hill, 9 rooms, T310 (B)

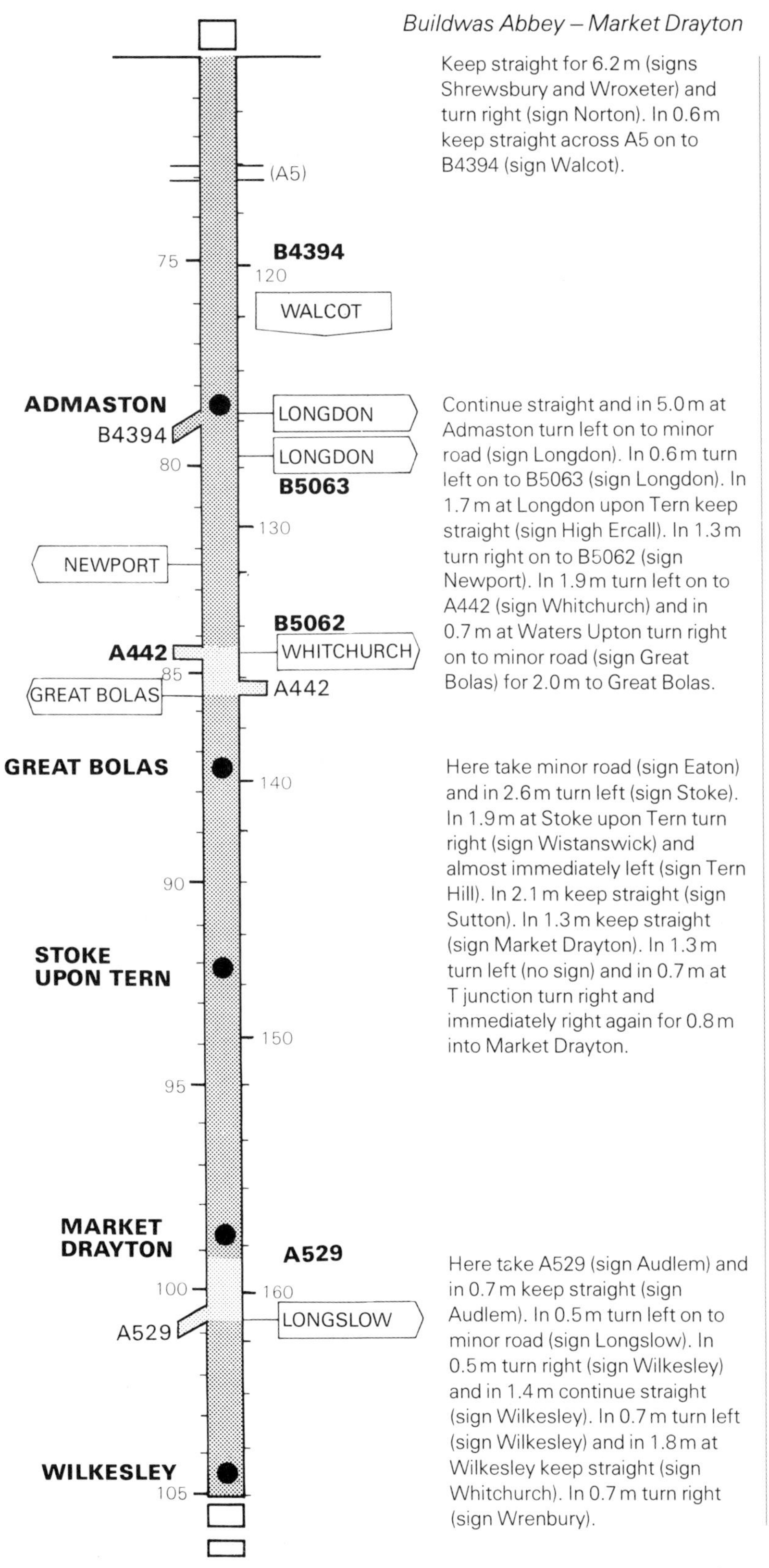

Keep straight for 6.2 m (signs Shrewsbury and Wroxeter) and turn right (sign Norton). In 0.6 m keep straight across A5 on to B4394 (sign Walcot).

Continue straight and in 5.0 m at Admaston turn left on to minor road (sign Longdon). In 0.6 m turn left on to B5063 (sign Longdon). In 1.7 m at Longdon upon Tern keep straight (sign High Ercall). In 1.3 m turn right on to B5062 (sign Newport). In 1.9 m turn left on to A442 (sign Whitchurch) and in 0.7 m at Waters Upton turn right on to minor road (sign Great Bolas) for 2.0 m to Great Bolas.

Here take minor road (sign Eaton) and in 2.6 m turn left (sign Stoke). In 1.9 m at Stoke upon Tern turn right (sign Wistanswick) and almost immediately left (sign Tern Hill). In 2.1 m keep straight (sign Sutton). In 1.3 m keep straight (sign Market Drayton). In 1.3 m turn left (no sign) and in 0.7 m at T junction turn right and immediately right again for 0.8 m into Market Drayton.

Here take A529 (sign Audlem) and in 0.7 m keep straight (sign Audlem). In 0.5 m turn left on to minor road (sign Longslow). In 0.5 m turn right (sign Wilkesley) and in 1.4 m continue straight (sign Wilkesley). In 0.7 m turn left (sign Wilkesley) and in 1.8 m at Wilkesley keep straight (sign Whitchurch). In 0.7 m turn right (sign Wrenbury).

Nantwich (Cheshire)

'Nant' ('riverside vale') and 'wich' ('salt pit') emphasize that the town was once a prosperous salt-producing area. In the 16c there were no less than 216 'wich' houses in and around the town before there was a gradual decline in demand for salt. In 1583 a great fire destroyed much of the ancient town. Queen Elizabeth I organized a collection to rebuild Nantwich, making a personal donation of £2,000 – a deed which inspired the townsmen to express their gratitude with an inscription which can still be seen on a black-and-white building, now a dress shop, near the Square.

Fortunately the parish church of St Mary survived the fire, and the Queen's money was put to good use, for many fine buildings were soon erected – among them the Crown Hotel (1585) in the High Street, where there are a variety of relics of historic interest. A coach driver at this hotel in the 19c was a Mr Piggott, grandfather of the world-famous jockey, Lester Piggott.

Alvaston Hall Hotel, Middlewich Rd, 42 rooms, T64341 (A)
T.O. Beam St, T63914

Knutsford (Cheshire)

Legend has it that the town's name is linked with Canute in that the King (Knut) once forded the river here. In the narrow High Street is a strange building in the Italian style with a tall perpendicular tower known as the King's Coffee House. The building was designed as a memorial to the novelist Mrs Gaskell (1810–65), who was brought up here by an aunt and whose masterpiece *Cranford* (1853) is based on Knutsford and its inhabitants. In a niche on the tower there is a bust of Elizabeth Gaskell. On a pillar are recorded the names of English monarchs from Egbert the Saxon onwards. Near to Knutsford (signed from the centre of the town) is Tatton Hall, one of the most visited houses of all the National Trust properties. The Hall, completed at the beginning of the 19c on the site of a much older house, stands in a park where in addition to formal gardens and woodland there is an orangery, a classical temple, a Japanese garden with a Shinto temple, and a mere where a wide variety of wildfowl are to be seen.

The south front of Tatton Hall.

Rose and Crown Hotel, King St, 11 rooms, T52366 (B)
Longview Hotel, Manchester Rd, 10 rooms, T2119 (C)
T.O. Council Offices, Toft Rd, T2611

The Route

Unspoilt countryside by minor roads from Great Bolas to Winsford. The area around Winsford and Middlewich is now industrialized, and both these towns are skirted before the route turns northwards to Knutsford.

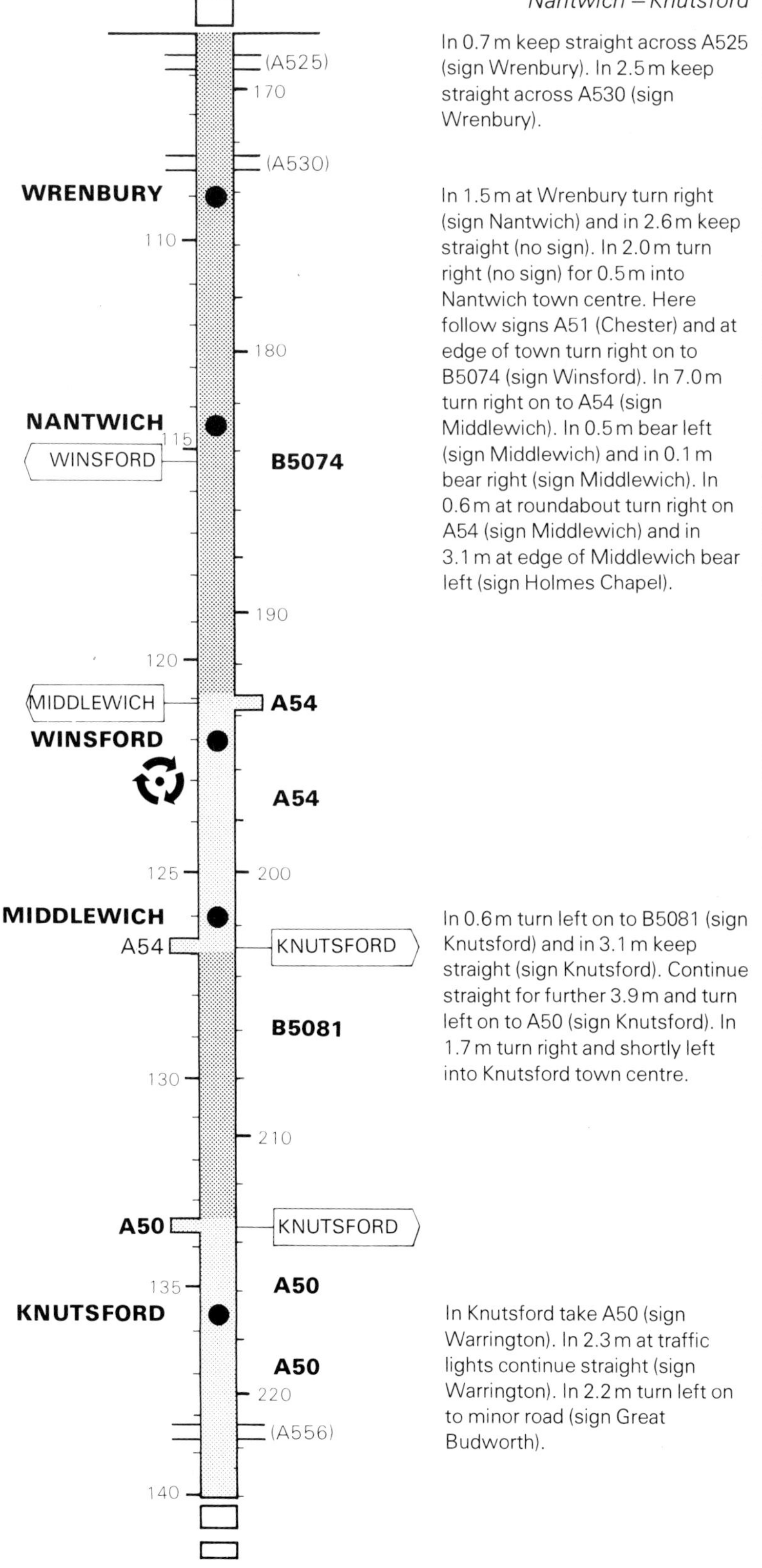

In 0.7 m keep straight across A525 (sign Wrenbury). In 2.5 m keep straight across A530 (sign Wrenbury).

In 1.5 m at Wrenbury turn right (sign Nantwich) and in 2.6 m keep straight (no sign). In 2.0 m turn right (no sign) for 0.5 m into Nantwich town centre. Here follow signs A51 (Chester) and at edge of town turn right on to B5074 (sign Winsford). In 7.0 m turn right on to A54 (sign Middlewich). In 0.5 m bear left (sign Middlewich) and in 0.1 m bear right (sign Middlewich). In 0.6 m at roundabout turn right on A54 (sign Middlewich) and in 3.1 m at edge of Middlewich bear left (sign Holmes Chapel).

In 0.6 m turn left on to B5081 (sign Knutsford) and in 3.1 m keep straight (sign Knutsford). Continue straight for further 3.9 m and turn left on to A50 (sign Knutsford). In 1.7 m turn right and shortly left into Knutsford town centre.

In Knutsford take A50 (sign Warrington). In 2.3 m at traffic lights continue straight (sign Warrington). In 2.2 m turn left on to minor road (sign Great Budworth).

King Charles Tower, high up on Chester's city wall.

Great Budworth (Cheshire)

Black-and-white thatched cottages abound in this lovely Cheshire village. The name Budworth means 'dwelling by the water' – as meres lie on either side of the village, the largest to the west of it. In the church of St Mary and All Saints is the 14c Lady Chapel where Sir Peter Leycester, a great 16c historian is buried. In the Warburton Chapel, 15/16c, there is a fine alabaster effigy of Sir John Warburton (d. 1575). Opposite the church is a pleasant inn, The George and Dragon.

Delamere Forest (Cheshire)

The road passes through the heart of the forest, which still covers some 4,000 acres but at one time was much larger. There is a beautiful reed-fringed pool at Hatchmere and a golf course on the edge of the forest.

The Route

Planning a route back to Chester from Knutsford is no easy task as numerous major roads converge on Chester from the east of the city. However it was found possible to avoid them for a view of Great Budworth and the Delamere Forest prior to taking the A54 for the final ten miles into Chester.

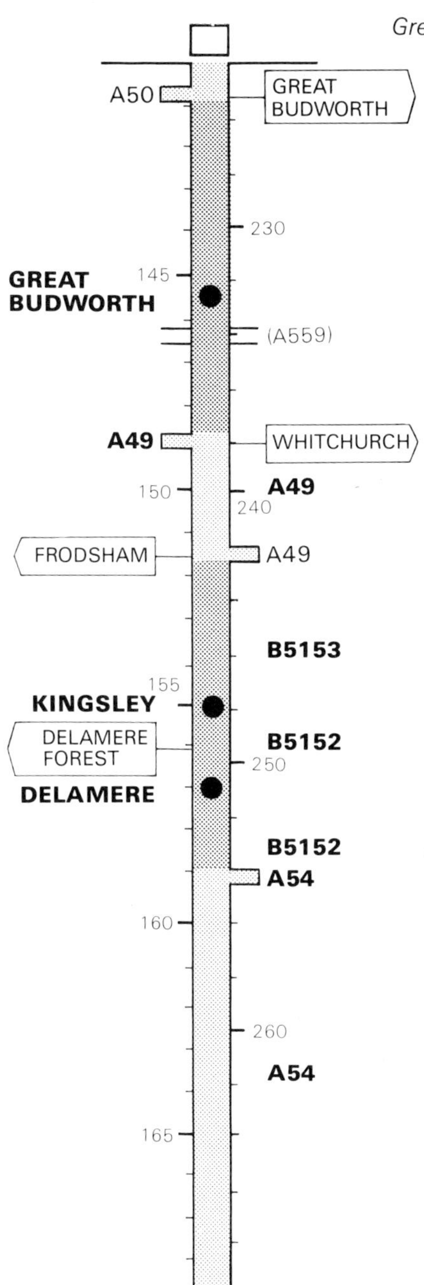

In 0.9 m bear right (sign Great Budworth) and in 2.2 m turn right (sign Great Budworth).

Continue to follow signs Great Budworth for a further 1.9 m to Great Budworth. Here keep straight (sign Comberbach). In 0.9 m at Comberbach) turn left (sign Northwich) and in 0.2 m turn right (sign Runcorn). Almost immediately turn left (sign Runcorn). In 0.8 m keep straight (sign Runcorn). In 0.7 m keep straight (sign Runcorn).

In 0.4 m bear left (no sign) and in 0.2 m keep straight (sign Weaverham). In 0.3 m turn left on to A49 (sign Whitchurch). In 2.2 m turn right on to B5153 (sign Frodsham). Continue straight for 3.9 m and at Kingsley turn left (sign Delamere). In 0.7 m bear right on B5152 (sign Delamere Forest). Keep straight through forest and in 3.5 m turn right on to A54 (later A51) for 10.0 m to Chester.

18 *Staffordshire, Derbyshire*

THIS ROUTE of 175 miles starts and ends at Lichfield, birthplace of Dr Samuel Johnson. It is a compact city with several good hotels, well-tended parks, many old houses of historic interest, and a Cathedral with three lofty spires known, romantically, as the 'ladies of the Vale'.

The road runs northward, crossing the River Dove, into the county of Derbyshire at Tutbury where, from the castle in which Mary Queen of Scots was imprisoned, there are views of the former Royal hunting grounds of Needwood Forest.

Little John's grave at Hathersage church serves as a reminder that the activities of Robin Hood and his merry men were not confined to the Sherwood Forest for, as the ordnance survey maps show, numerous features of the remote Derbyshire moorlands are named after the outlaw. The hamlet of Robin Hood lies a few miles east of Hassop (page 311); Robin Hood's Stride, pillars lying fifty feet apart where, according to legend, Robin crossed from one to the other in a single stride is to be found on Harthill Moor near Elton (page 310); Robin Hood's Well and Little John's Well, together with a four-foot pillar known as Robin Hood's Stoop, are all to be found near Hathersage (page 310); near to Glossop (page 312) are two upright stone pillars known as Robin Hood's Picking Rods; and other fascinating names in the Peak District of Derbyshire include Robin Hood's Chockstone Chimney, Robin Hood's Cave and Robin Hood's Balcony.

A minor road north of Hathersage penetrates the Howden moors, passing three reservoirs – Ladybower, Derwent and Howden – in an area known as Derbyshire's lake district. If time permits it is worth diverting to see this lovely stretch, but that road ends at Howden reservoir, and our continuing route enters Yorkshire momentarily as it proceeds northward past the Strines and Langsett reservoirs.

From here the road runs by Glossop, Hayfield and Chapel-en-le-Frith, circumventing the High Peak district and outstanding features like Bleaklow Hill (2,060 ft) and Kinder Scout (2,088 ft), before reaching Mam Tor (1,698 ft) and the sharp descent to Edale in the beautiful valley through which the River Noe passes. Edale, incidentally, is the southernmost point of the famous Pennine Way, a walk of 250 miles that runs to Kirk Yetholm across the Scottish border.

The return southward is by way of Castleton, famous for its caverns; attractive small towns and villages which include Tideswell, Hartington, Ilam and Thorpe; and the incomparable Derbyshire dales such as Miller's Dale, Beresford Dale, and Dovedale.

Dovedale, home and fishing ground of Izaak Walton, author of *The Compleat Angler*, must certainly be included among England's finest beauty spots; but this two-mile stretch can only be covered on foot, the road only running from Alstonefield to the north of the dale to a point between Ilam and Thorpe at its southern extremity.

Leaving Mayfield the route returns southward through Staffordshire, passing Abbots Bromley, one of that county's most charming villages. These are famous for the ancient tradition of 'well dressing', when garlands of moss and flowers are placed round the wells.

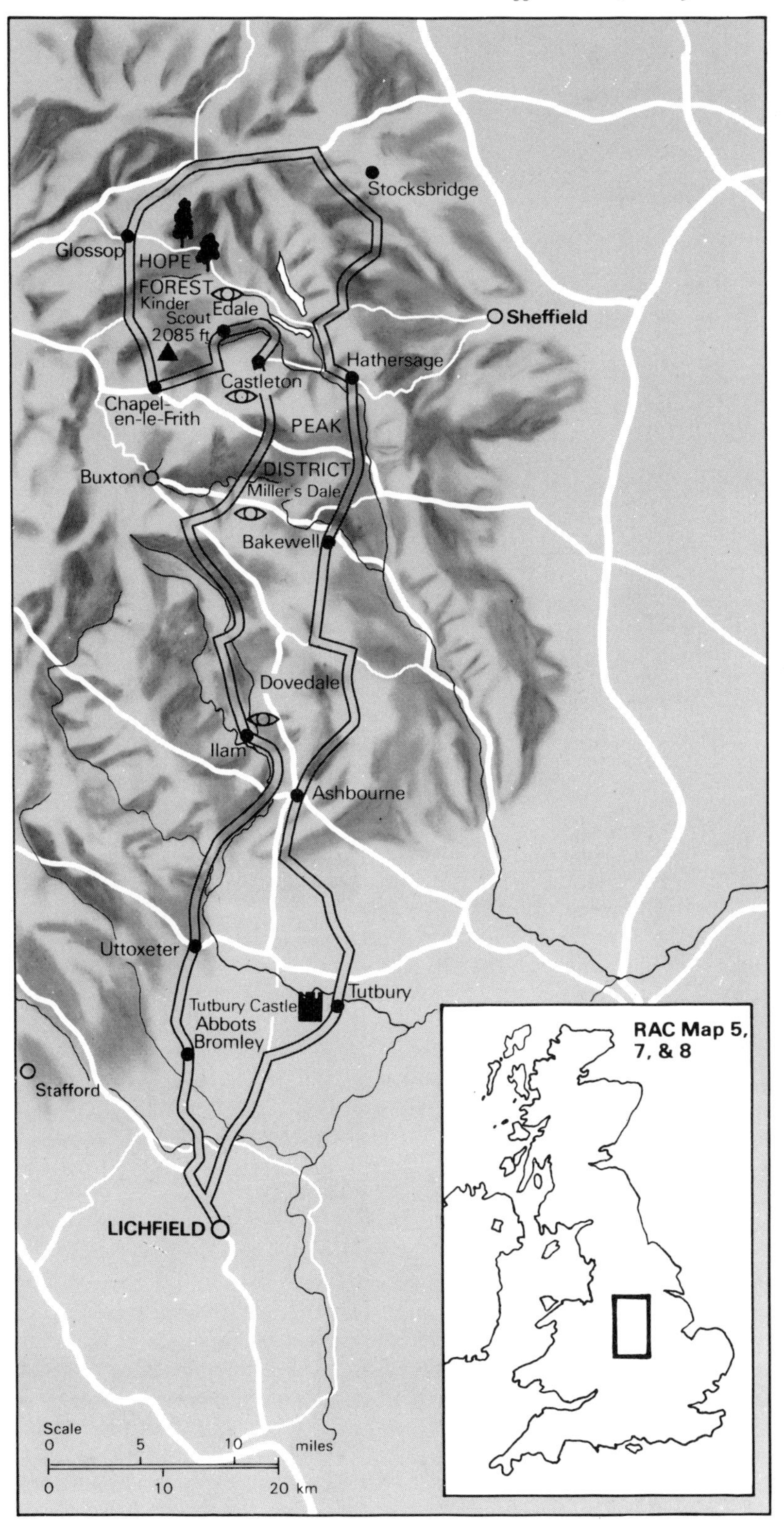
Stocksbridge
Glossop
HOPE
FOREST
Kinder
Scout
2085 ft
Edale
Sheffield
Hathersage
Castleton
Chapel-
en-le-Frith
PEAK
DISTRICT
Buxton
Miller's Dale
Bakewell
Dovedale
Ilam
Ashbourne
Uttoxeter
Tutbury
Tutbury Castle
Abbots
Bromley
Stafford
LICHFIELD
RAC Map 5,
7, & 8
Scale
0 5 10 miles
0 10 20 km

Lichfield's two most famous buildings: Dr Johnson's house (above) and the Cathedral.

Lichfield (Staffs)

Samuel Johnson (1709–84), lexicographer, author and critic was born here, and his statue in the market-place overlooks the house of his birth. This is now a museum containing Johnsonian relics, and on 18 September, the date of the author's birth, an annual service takes place which concludes with the laying of a wreath on the statue by the Mayor of Lichfield. There is yet another statue in the market-place – that of James Boswell (1740–95), Johnson's biographer and member of his intimate circle. A plaque in nearby Beacon St marks the site of the house of the actor, David Garrick (1717–79), who also was a pupil at the old grammar school – now the District Council Chamber. There are memorials both to Johnson and Garrick in Lichfield

Cathedral, where the three lovely spires, the highest of them over 250 feet, are known as the 'Ladies of the Vale'. Among the interesting features within the Cathedral is the sculptor Sir Francis Chantry's most famous work, 'Sleeping Children', a memorial to two children who died in a fire. A large house at the corner of the Cathedral Close was once the home of Erasmus Darwin (1731–1802), botanist and grandfather of Charles Darwin the scientist. Near to the Cathedral are pleasant parks, two pools known as Minter Pool and Stowe Pool, and a number of attractive pedestrianized streets.

Little Barrow Hotel, Beacon St, 24 rooms, T53311 (A)
Angel Croft Hotel, Beacon St, 13 rooms, T23147 (B)
T.O. 9 Breadmarket St, T52109

Tutbury (Staffs)

The town lies on the R. Dove, the most interesting building on the broad main street being the black-and-white Dog and Partridge Inn, once the home of the Curzon family and later a coaching inn. The outstanding feature of the town, however, stands just off the route, to the left. Here are the solid remains of Tutbury Castle, where Mary Queen of Scots spent many years of captivity in the tower which can be climbed for fine views across Needwood forest. Beneath the castle ruins is one of the finest Norman churches in the Midlands, the priory church of St Mary, where services have been held since 1089.

Ye Old Dog and Partridge Hotel, High St, 18 rooms, T813030 (B)

Ashbourne (Derbyshire)

The town lies immediately to the south of Derbyshire's peak district and is known as the Gateway to Dovedale. The huge inn sign across the lovely main street is that of the Green Man and Black's Head Inn, the starting-point for a traditional game of rough and ready football that takes place over a three-mile area of the town on Shrove Tuesdays and Ash Wednesdays. Nearby is the house where Samuel Johnson stayed with his old schoolfriend, John Taylor, who is buried in the fine church with a 215-foot spire known as the Pride of the Peak. In the church is the life-size marble figure of a little girl, Penelope Boothby, who, when she died at the age of six, is reputed to have been able to speak the four languages inscribed on her tomb. The town is noted for its gingerbread, made from a recipe which originated from French prisoners of the Napoleonic Wars.

Green Man Hotel, St Johns St, 17 rooms, T2017 (B)
Clifton Hotel, Station Rd, 13 rooms, T3330 (C)
T.O. 13 The Market Place, T3666

The Route

The narrowest part of this section of the route runs between Elton and Youlgreave – a beautiful stretch but steep and narrow. However, the road signs at Elton direct one to Youlgreave by way of the broader road over a greater distance – and drivers wishing to avoid this pretty but narrow section of the route might consider taking the alternative signed route to Youlgreave.

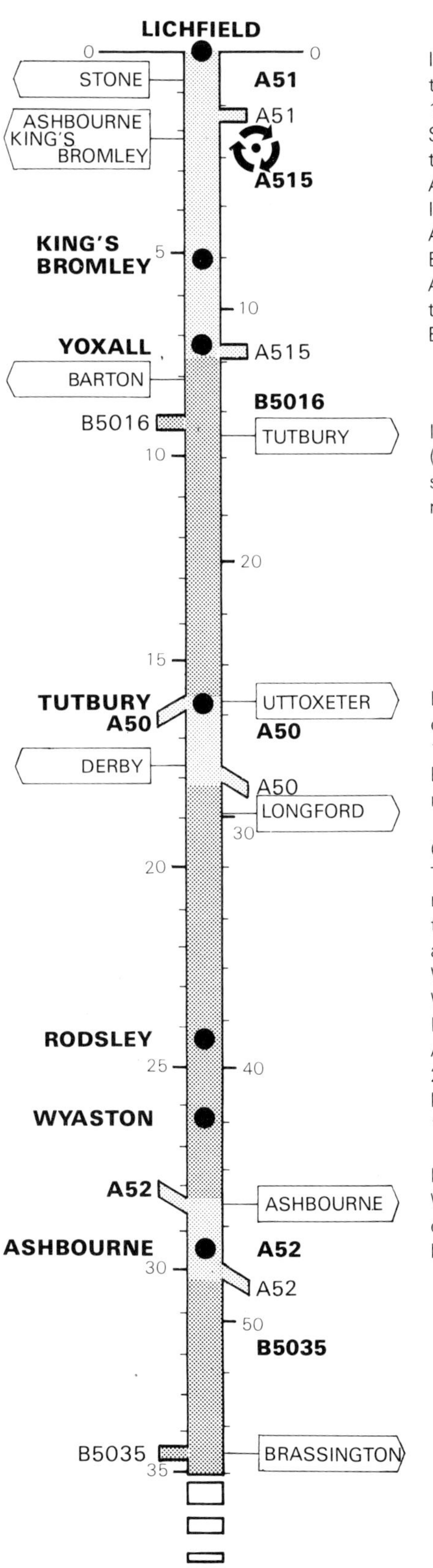

In Lichfield keep straight through town centre (no signs) and in 1.2 m turn right on to A51 (sign Stone). In 0.5 m at roundabout turn right on to A515 (signs Ashbourne and King's Bromley). In 1.4 m keep straight (sign Ashbourne). In 2.0 m at King's Bromley continue straight (sign Ashbourne) and in 2.0 m at Yoxall turn right on to B5016 (sign Barton).

In 2.0 m turn left on to minor road (sign Tutbury) and in 3.2 m keep straight across B5234 on minor road (sign Tutbury).

In 3.7 m entering Tutbury turn left on to A50 (sign Uttoxeter) and in 1.3 m turn right on to A516 (sign Derby). In 0.1 m turn left on to minor road (sign Longford).

Continue straight for 4.8 m and at T junction turn left on to minor road (sign Alkmonton). In 0.5 m turn right (sign Rodsley). In 1.6 m at Rodsley continue straight (sign Wyaston). In 1.5 m turn right (sign Wyaston). In 0.4 m at Shire Horse Inn continue straight (sign Ashbourne). Keep straight for 2.2 m through Osmaston and turn left on to A52 (sign Ashbourne) for 1.0 m into Ashbourne.

In Ashbourne take B5035 (sign Wirksworth) and in 5.4 m bear left on to minor road (sign Brassington).

Elton (Derbyshire)

This village of sturdy 17c and 18c houses is perched 900 feet above sea level. When the old church was rebuilt in 1812 the village ill-advisedly discarded the font, a fine piece of craftsmanship which is now a prize possession of the church in nearby Youlgreave.

Youlgreave (Derbyshire)

Another hilltop town which, like Elton, once had a prosperous lead-mining industry.
YHA, Fountain Square, T518

Bakewell (Derbyshire)

The town nestles beneath wooded hills on the banks of the R. Wye, across which is an impressive 15c bridge of five arches and, on the edge of the town, an even older bridge of the 13c built for pack-horses. In the centre of the town is the Rutland Arms Hotel, where the novelist Jane Austen (1775–1817) wrote her *Pride and Prejudice*. This hotel also has another distinction, for it was here in 1859 that a cook misunderstood the instructions of the housekeeper and unwittingly produced a pudding which proved to be a 'smash hit' – Bakewell Tart. Chatsworth House, seat of the Dukes of Devonshire, lies a few miles to the east of the town in a magnificent deer park and is open to the public on specific occasions.
Milford House Hotel, Mill St, 10 rooms, T2130 (C)
YHA, Flyhill, T2313

Grindleford (Derbyshire)

The road rises sharply out of the village to Sir William Hill (pleasant inn on right) and shortly there are fine views of the Derwent valley before the road descends once more to the river before entering Hathersage.

The 'Waiting Room' at Chatsworth House.

Hathersage (Derbyshire)

The town existed before the Domesday Book, the name possibly deriving from the words 'heather's edge'. St Michael's church enjoys a beautiful position above the town and can be found by diverting to the right off the route. By the porch of the church is the fourteen-foot grave where the body of Little John, Robin Hood's right-hand man, reputedly lies buried. Little John had been brought up in Hathersage, serving his apprenticeship as a nail-maker before joining the rebels under Simon de Montfort at the Battle of Evesham in 1265. Although no definite proof exists that this is the final resting-place of Little John, it is interesting to learn that when, centuries after his death, the grave was opened, it revealed a thigh bone, thirty inches in length, which could only have been that of a gigantic man.
Hathersage Inn, Main Rd, 10 rooms, T50259 (B)
Highlow Hall, 6 rooms, T50393 (D)
YHA, Castleton Rd, T50493

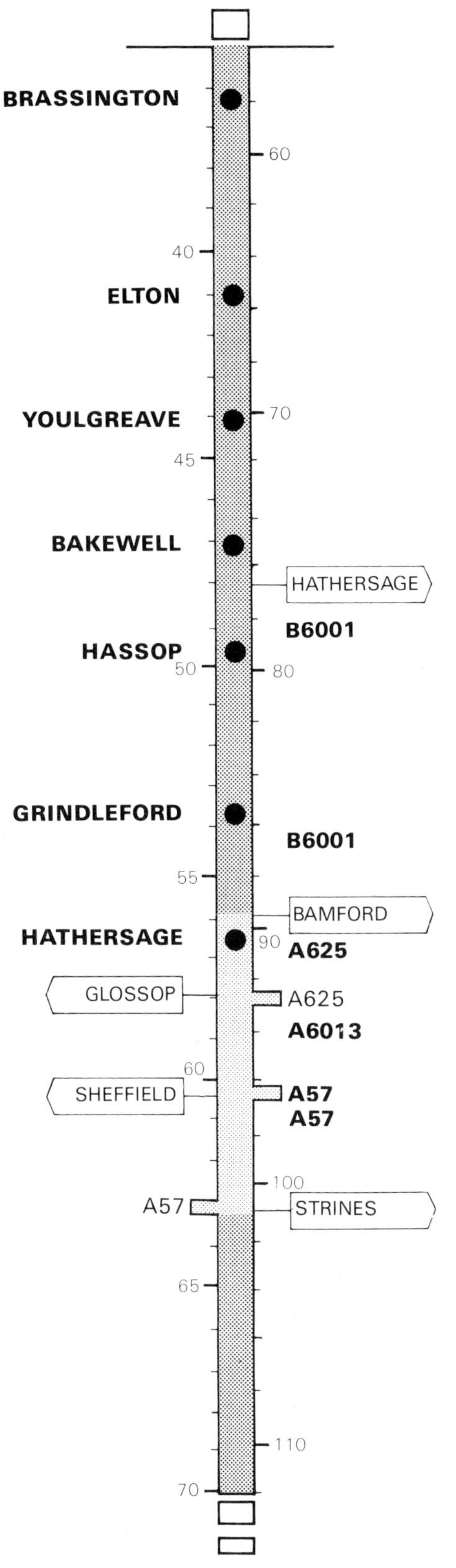

In 1.2 m at Brassington keep straight (sign Longcliffe). In 0.4 m bear left (sign Longcliffe). In 0.6 m keep straight (sign Aldwark) and in 0.3 m keep straight (sign Elton). In 1.9 m continue straight (sign Elton) and in 0.3 m keep straight (sign Elton).

In 1.0 m at Elton turn left (no sign). In 0.2 m keep straight (sign Grafton). In 0.7 m bear right (no sign) for 2.0 m to Youlgreave. Here continue straight (sign Over Haddon) and in 0.7 m at T junction turn right (sign Over Haddon). In 1.0 m keep straight (sign Bakewell) and in 1.3 m turn right into Bakewell town centre.

In Bakewell town centre take A619 (sign Chesterfield) and in 0.8 m turn left on to B6001 (sign Hathersage). Keep straight on B6001 (signs Hathersage) for 1.8 m to Hassop. Here continue straight for 2.0 m and at Calver traffic lights keep straight (sign Hathersage). In 1.9 m at Grindelford turn left (sign Hathersage) and keep straight for 2.7 m into Hathersage.

Entering Hathersage, at T junction, turn left on to A625 (sign Bamford). In 1.7 m turn right on to A6013 (sign Glossop). In 2.7 m turn right on to A57 (sign Sheffield) and in 1.7 m turn left on to minor road (sign Strines). Keep straight and in 3.5 m continue straight (sign Midhope). In 5.2 m bear left.

The Route

The minor road north of Hathersage passes through the moors in the extreme west of Yorkshire, with good views of the Strines and Langsett reservoirs. It was necessary to circumvent the High Peak district by way of the rather busy A628, as owing to the height of the mountains no motorable roads cross them.

Glossop (Derbyshire)

This busy textile town lies only a few miles from Manchester. Those who live here, however, are fortunate that on their doorsteps there are miles of solitude to be found across the expanse of moors, mountains and reservoirs which lie to the east, dividing the Manchester conurbation from that of Sheffield.

Hurst Lee Guest House, Derbyshire Level, 6 rooms, T3354

Hayfield (Derbyshire)

The central part of the village lies off the main road, and the small hotel recommended below, under new management, occupies a quiet position. Paths to the east of the town lead to Kinder Scout (2,088 ft) and a popular ramble leads across the Kinder range down to Edale by way of a track known as Jacob's Ladder.

Royal Hotel, 7 rooms, T New Mills 42721 (D)

Chapel-en-le-Frith (Derbyshire)

The stone-built town, surrounded by lofty hills, is known as the Capital of the Peak District. The town, as the name implies, grew up around the chapel on the edge of the forest, although little remains of the original 13c chapel which occupied the site of the existing church. This is a church with a grim history, for it was here in 1648 that Scottish soldiers who had come to the aid of Charles I were imprisoned. 1,500 of them were held in this confined space, which became known as Derbyshire's 'Black Hole'. Before they were released forty soldiers had died. The town is now semi-industrialized, but a number of old inns and the 17c market cross remain.

Jacob's Ladder, leading to Edale.

Kings Arms Hotel, Market Place, 11 rooms, T2105 (C)
Royal Oak Hotel, Market St, 10 rooms, T2784 (D)

Edale (Derbyshire)

As the road descends from Mam Tor there is a glorious view of the broad valley in which the small village lies. This aerial view is a colourful one as dotted around the fields of the spacious valley are the well-dispersed tents of campers, taking advantage of the fact that most of the farms here provide small camping sites which, to many, are preferable to larger established sites. There are magnificent walks in the surrounding hills and Edale has a fine old inn, the Nag's Head.

YHA, Rowland Cote, Nether Booth, T Hope Valley 70302

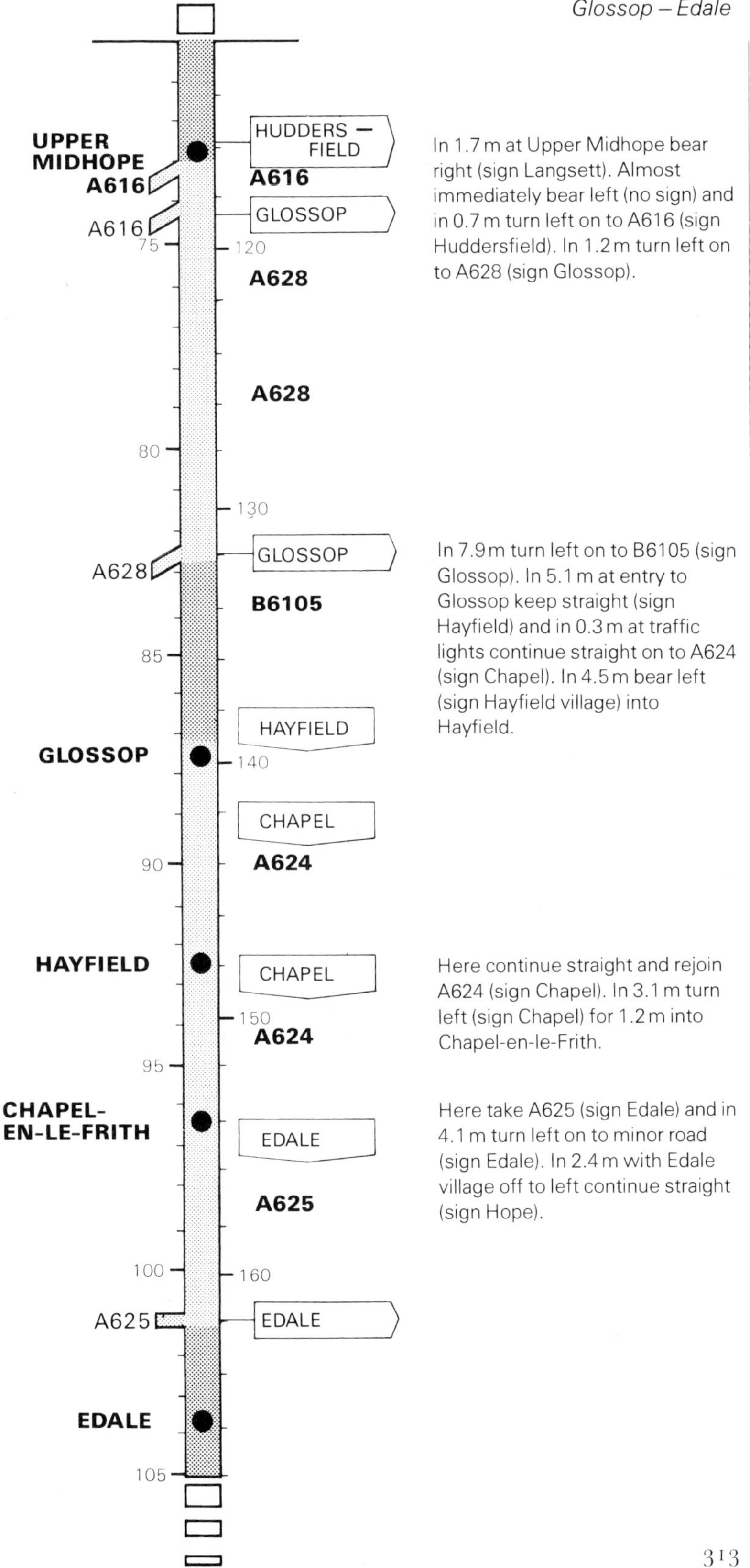

In 1.7 m at Upper Midhope bear right (sign Langsett). Almost immediately bear left (no sign) and in 0.7 m turn left on to A616 (sign Huddersfield). In 1.2 m turn left on to A628 (sign Glossop).

In 7.9 m turn left on to B6105 (sign Glossop). In 5.1 m at entry to Glossop keep straight (sign Hayfield) and in 0.3 m at traffic lights continue straight on to A624 (sign Chapel). In 4.5 m bear left (sign Hayfield village) into Hayfield.

Here continue straight and rejoin A624 (sign Chapel). In 3.1 m turn left (sign Chapel) for 1.2 m into Chapel-en-le-Frith.

Here take A625 (sign Edale) and in 4.1 m turn left on to minor road (sign Edale). In 2.4 m with Edale village off to left continue straight (sign Hope).

Hope (Derbyshire)

Renowned sheep-dog trials take place here in the annual Hope Valley Agricultural show. Just before reaching the village, on the right, is an attractive old inn, the Cheshire Cheese.

House of Anton, Castleton Rd, 5 rooms, T Hope Valley 20380 (B)

Castleton (Derbyshire)

Above the village tower the ruins of the Norman fortress built by William Peveril, the subject of Walter Scott's *Peveril of the Peak*. At the edge of the village, in the face of the cliff beneath the castle, is the massive entrance to Peak Cavern, one of several caverns for which the area is famous. There are guided tours of Peak Cavern by way of passages that lead for a mile into the heart of the hillside. Among other caves to be seen near Castleton are Speedwell Cavern, Treak Cliff Caverns, and the Blue John Caverns, containing the unique Blue John stone which is made into ornaments and jewelry that can be purchased in local shops.

Ye Old Nag's Head Hotel, 10 rooms, T Hope Valley 20248 (B)
Castle Hotel, 6 rooms, T Hope Valley 20578 (B)
YHA, Castleton Hall, T Hope Valley 20195

Tideswell (Derbyshire)

The huge church of St John the Baptist with its tall tower, surmounted by pinnacles, is known as the Cathedral of the Peak. A number of old stone-built houses lie near the church, among them the George Hotel which lies alongside it.

Miller's Dale (Derbyshire)

A tiny village which takes its name from one of Derbyshire's loveliest dales alongside the R. Wye.

Earl Sterndale (Derbyshire)

This remote village beneath high hills is made up of only a small church, a few houses, and a little inn with the strange name 'The Quiet Woman'.

Hartington (Derbyshire)

A village with a spacious square and pleasant inns near the R. Dove, a reach of which flows through the lovely Beresford Dale (signed just off to the left of the road past the village).

Charles Cotton Hotel, 8 rooms, T229 (D)
Bank House, 4 rooms, T465 (D)
YHA, Hartington Hall, T223

Ilam (Staffs)

Attractive estate cottages are grouped round the tall Gothic cross, a memorial to Mrs Watts-Russell, who built this model village in the 19c. She also rebuilt Ilam Hall, part of which is now occupied by the YHA but which, together with the fifty-acre park that surrounds it, is owned by the National Trust and open to the public. The name of the nearby recommended hotel is a reminder of the author of *The Compleat Angler*, who spent many hours fishing in the Dove and surrounding trout streams.

Izaak Walton Hotel, 27 rooms, T261 (A)
YHA, Ilam Hall, T212

The Route

There is a sharp descent to Edale and an equally sharp ascent from Castleton. The road between Alstonefield and Ilam runs parallel to beautiful Dovedale, with its many caves and strange colourful rock formations. This area can only be seen on foot, although the R. Dove can be reached by car if a one-mile diversion is made (sign Milldale on left).

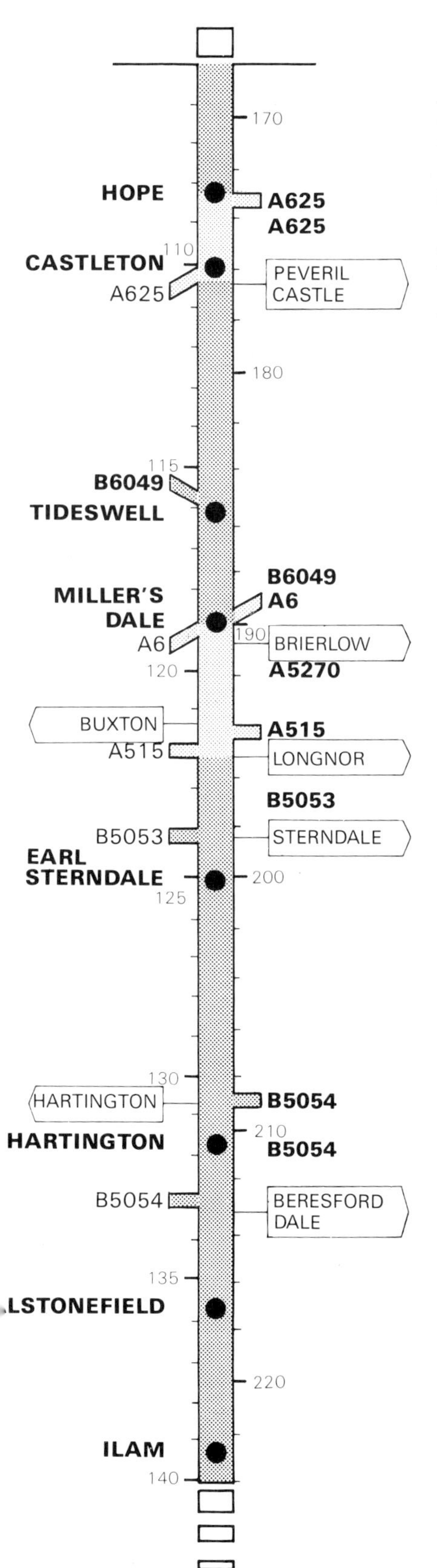

In 4.8 m at Hope turn right on to A625 (no sign) for 1.6 m to Castleton. Here at Castle Hotel turn left (sign Peveril Castle) on to minor road. In 0.4 m bear right and in 2.2 m turn right (signs Little Hucklow). Keep straight for 1.2 m and continue straight (sign Tideswell). In 1.5 m turn right and immediately left on to B6049 (sign Tideswell) for 0.7 m to Tideswell.

In Tideswell continue straight on B6049 (sign Buxton) for 2.5 m to Miller's Dale and here continue straight for 1.4 m and turn right on to A6 (sign Buxton). In 0.5 m turn left on to A5270 (sign Brierlow). In 1.6 m bear right (sign Buxton). In 0.8 m turn right on to A515 (sign Buxton) and in 0.2 m turn left on to B5053 (sign Longnor). In 1.4 m turn left on to minor road (sign Sterndale) for 0.5 m to Earl Sterndale.

Here bear left, in 0.1 m fork left, and in 1.6 m keep straight (signs Pilsbury). In 1.1 m keep straight (sign Hartington) for 3.2 m and turn right on to B5054 (sign Hartington) for 0.7 m to Hartington.

In Hartington take B5054 (sign Warslow) and in 1.2 m turn left on to minor road (sign Beresford Dale). In 0.6 m keep straight (sign Alstonefield) and in further 0.6 m turn left (sign Alstonefield). In 1.7 m at Alstonefield bear right, in 0.6 m turn right and immediately turn left (signs Ilam) for 3.0 m to Ilam. Here turn left (sign Thorpe).

Dr Johnson in a contemporary cartoon (left), *and his bookseller father, Michael Johnson* (right).

Mapleton (Derbyshire)

In common with its neighbour Thorpe, the village lies immediately on the border with Staffordshire. The road to Mayfield passes through the fine deer park of Okeover Hall.

Mayfield (Staffs)

The 14c bridge across the R. Dove, now modernized, is known as the 'Hanging Bridge', for it was here in 1745 that Scottish rebels were hanged after the Jacobite rebellion.

Uttoxeter (Staffs)

It will be remembered that at Lichfield, the starting-point of this route, lived Samuel Johnson in his father's bookshop. Michael Johnson also ran a bookstall in the market-place here, and many years later Samuel remembered with regret the day he refused to come to Uttoxeter to help with the sales. Accordingly he paid penance, standing bare-headed in the rain, and the scene of his contrition is carved in the side of the small stone kiosk where tobacco and confectionery are now sold – the site of his father's stall. Near to this small market town is a fine National Hunt racecourse.

White Hart Hotel, Carter St, 16 rooms, T2347 (B)

Abbots Bromley (Staffs)

A number of pleasant old inns straggle along the main road of the town, famed for its Horn Dance, which according to records has taken place annually since the 17c but probably dates back to pagan times. The team of twelve who take part in the dance is made up of six men wearing reindeer antlers, a man on a hobby horse, a maid marion, a jester, a boy with a crossbow, and two musicians. The dance is performed on the Monday after the Sunday following 4 September.

The Route

Initially by way of the Derbyshire dales, skirting the Derbyshire/ Staffordshire border. The final section of the route from Abbots Bromley to Lichfield crosses flatter, less interesting country.

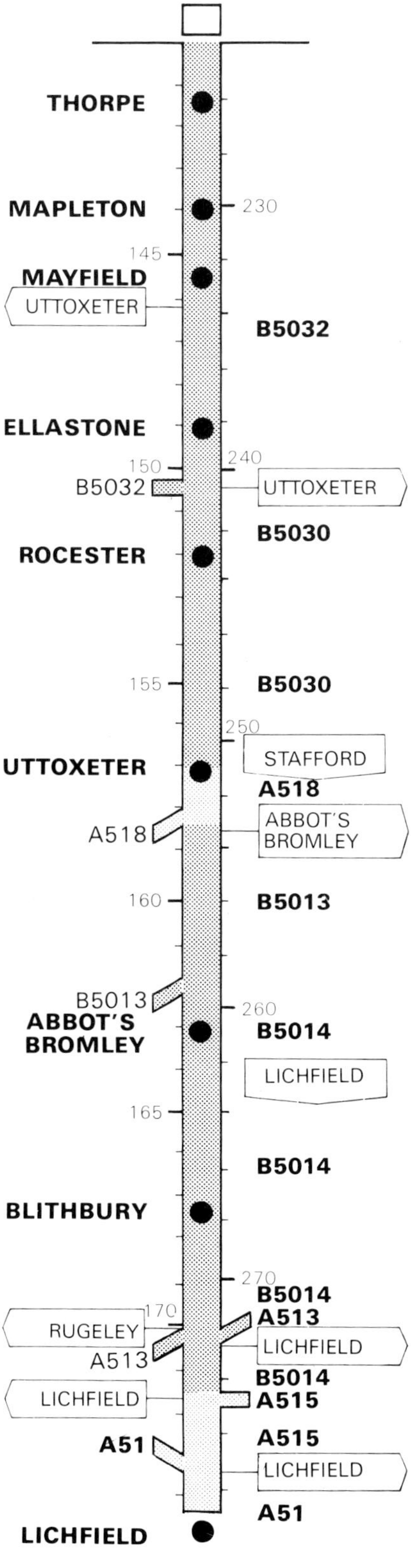

In 1.6 m at Thorpe bear left (sign Tissington) and in 0.4 m turn right (sign Mapleton). In 0.7 m turn right (sign Mapleton) and in 0.8 m at Mapleton turn right (sign Blore). In 0.3 m turn left (sign Mayfield) and in 1.4 m at Mayfield turn left on to A52 and almost immediately right on to B5032 (sign Uttoxeter).

In 3.2 m at Ellastone continue on B5032 (sign Uttoxeter) and in 1.0 m bear left on to B5030 (sign Uttoxeter). In 2.0 m at Rocester bear right (no sign) and then continue on B5030 (sign Uttoxeter) for 4.7 m to Uttoxeter.

In Uttoxeter town centre take A518 (sign Stafford). In 1.0 m bear left on to B5013 (sign Abbot's Bromley). Continue on B5013, later B5014 (signs Abbot's Bromley) for 5.6 m to Abbot's Bromley. Here continue straight on B5014 (sign Lichfield) for 3.0 m to Blithbury. In 2.7 m turn right on to A513 (sign Rugeley) and in 0.3 m turn left (sign Lichfield).

In 2.1 m turn right on to A515 (sign Lichfield) and in 1.5 m turn left on to A51 (sign Lichfield) for 2.0 m into Lichfield.

Index

Abbeycwmhir 258
Abbots Bromley 316
Aberfeldy 152
Abergavenny 241, 244
Abthorpe 78
Achintee 136
Adam, Robert 118, 131
Addison, Joseph 194
Airton 30
Albourne 275
Aldbury 223, 238
Aldeburgh 57, 66
Aldham 68
Alfred the Great 116, 278
Alfwaid of Northumbria 178
Alnwick 172, 180
Alston 175, 186
Alton 204
Alton Barnes 111
Alverdiscott 96
Ambleside 44, 54
Andover 193
Applecross 142
Ardeonaig 152
Ardlui 154
Arimathea, Joseph of 120
Arncliffe 32
Arnold, Matthew 220
Arnold, Thomas 226
Arrochar 132
Ashbourne 308
Ashbury 221, 226
Astor, William W. 288
Athelstan, King 116
Austen, Jane 196, 310
Aviemore 150
Aynho 222
Baconsthorpe Castle 212
Baird, John Logie 131–2
Bakewell 310
Bala 16
Baldwin, Stanley 264
Baliol, Bernard de 190
Baliol, Guy de 190
Bampton 54
Banbury 74, 76
Bangor 12
Barham 276
Barmouth 18
Barnard Castle 190
Barnstaple 92, 96
Barnwell 84
Barrie, James 130
Bath 111, 118
Battle 275, 282
Beaminster 124
Beaulieu 200
Beauly 148
Beaumaris 12
Beccles 207, 210
Beddgelert 20
Beerbohm, Max 194
Bell, Alexander 130
Bell, Henry 132
Bellingham 172, 180
Belloc, Hilaire 192
Betws-y-Coed 22
Beverley 156, 160
Bewdley 262, 264
Bibury 228
Bickleigh 94
Bideford 96
Blackmore, R. D. 94
Blakeney 207, 214
Blanchland 172, 178
Blandford Forum 126
Bledington 234
Blisland 100
Blunden, Edmund 288
Bodinnick 102
Bodmin 92, 100
Boleyn, Anne 244, 288
Bookham 277, 290
Booth, Richard 260
Boothby, Penelope 308
Borrow, George 16, 241
Borrowdale 52
Boscastle 100
Boswell, James 131, 306
Bothwell, James 184
Bowland Bridge 44
Braemore Forest 146
Brampton 175, 186
Bramshaw 198
Brecon 244
Brereton, Sir Randle 294
Bridge of Orchy 134
Bridgnorth 262, 264,
Bridport 112
Britten, Benjamin 66
Broad Hinton 111, 116
Brockenhurst 200
Brompton 160
Bromyard 262, 272
Brontës, the 156
Brooke, Rupert 126
Broughton Mills 48
Browning, Elizabeth 270
Buchan, John 130
Buchanan, Jack 131
Buckingham 222, 236
Buckland in the Moor 108
Bucklers Hard 200
Bucks Green 278
Bude 98
Bungay 208
Burford 221, 228
Burn, Peter 186
Burnell, Nicholas 296
Burnell, Robert 296
Burnham Overy 214
Burns, Robert 130, 134
Burwarton 266
Burwell 57
Bury St Edmunds 60
Bush, William 220
Butler, Samuel 266
Buttermere 50
Buttonoak 264
Cadbury 94
Caernarvon 10, 12, 20
Cairndow 132
Caldbeck 40, 52
Calder Bridge 48
Cambridge 57, 60
Camden, William 106
Camelford 91, 100
Camelot 91
Campbell, Donald 46
Canterbury 276, 286
Capability Brown 160
Capel Curig 22
Capel Garmon 22
Capel-y-Ffynn 260
Cardigan 248
Carlisle, Lady 186
Carmarthen 241, 246
Carrbridge 150
Carroll, Lewis 194, 292
Castle Acre 207, 218
Castle Hedingham 70
Castle Menzies 152
Castle Rising 207, 216
Castleton 166, 314
Catherine of Aragon 82
Cavell, Edith 208
Caxton, William 284
Cayley, Sir George 160
Cerne Abbas 124
Cessford 184
Chantry, Francis 308
Chapel-en-le-Frith 312
Charles I 14, 75, 86, 136, 264, 312
Charles II 96, 226, 264, 268
Charmouth 112, 122
Chaucer, Geoffrey 224
Cheddar 111, 120
Chedworth 222
Chester 10, 14, 292
Chesters 174, 178, 184
Chewton Mendip 120
Chiddingstone 288
Chilham 276, 286
Chipping Camden 221, 232
Chipping Norton 234
Chollerford 172, 178
Cholmondeley, Sir Hugh 294
Churchill, Winston 222
Cilgerran 248
Cirencester 222, 228
Cladich 134
Claude, L. 60
Clifford, Henry 30
Clifton upon Teme 272
Clive, Lord Robert 296, 298
Clovelly 98
Cobbett, William 3, 193, 194, 230, 286
Cobden, Richard 194
Cockermouth 40
Cocking 194
Coddenham 68
Cold Ashby 86
Coleridge, Samuel 52
Colquhoun, Sir James 132
Compton Abdale 232
Condover 296
Coniston 46
Constable, John 60, 68, 232
Cook, James 164, 166
Cornwood 106
Coshieville 152
Cowper, William 75, 80, 168, 212
Crabbe, George 66
Crackington Haven 100
Cranborne 112, 126
Crashaw, Richard 194
Craster 180
Crewkerne 122
Crianlarich 154
Crickhowell 244
Croglin 186
Cromer 207, 212
Cromwell, Oliver 28, 75, 82, 86, 186, 190, 223, 264
Culpeper, Elizabeth 286
Cumberland, Duke of 44
Curtis, William 204
Cuyp, Albert 60
Dagnall 223, 236
Dalmally 134
Darnley, Henry 184
Dartington 106
Dartmouth 93
Darwin, Charles 296, 308
Darwin, Erasmus 308
Daventry 75
Davies, W. H. 3
Deddington 234
Dedham 68
De La Mare, W. 286
Denbigh 22
Dersingham 214
Devils Bridge 241, 252
Dickens, Charles 80, 84, 190, 194, 296
Disraeli, Benjamin 202
Ditchling 274, 280
Dittisham 93, 106
Docking 207, 214
Doddington 286
Dolgellau 12, 18, 256
Dorking 277, 290
Dornie 140, 142
Dover 275
Dowsing, George 62
Drake, Sir Francis 94
Dulverton 92, 94
Dundonnell 146
Dunsfold 194
Dunwich 57, 64
Earl Sterndale 314
East Ayton 162
East Bergholt 68
Eastling 286
East Meon 196
Edale 304, 312
Edenbridge 277, 288
Edgecumbe, Richard 104
Edmund Ironside 116
Edward I 24, 296
Edward II 234
Edward III 198, 216
Edward IV 266
Edward VII 216, 290
Edward the Confessor 275
Edwards, Ifan at Owen 18
Effingham 277, 290
Egbert the Saxon 300
Eglingham 182
Egton Bridge 166
Elgar, Sir Edward 264
Elham 276, 284
Elizabeth I 300
Ellis, Thomas 16
Elmscott 98
Elmshirst, Dr and Mrs 106
Elsdon 180
Elstead 204
Elton 304, 310
Elvington 158
Emborough 120
Ennerdale Bridge 48
Ermington 106
Eskdale Green 46
Ethelbert IV 286
Ethelred the Unready 232
Everingham 158
Evershot 124
Ewelme 220, 224
Exeter 8, 91, 94
Eye 62
Fairfax, Thomas 26
Faringdon 226
Farndon 292, 294
Feetham 36
Feversham, Earls of 168
Finchingfield 58, 70
Finningham 62

Fleming, Alexander 130
Flixton 208
Fordingbridge 200
Forest Green 278
Fort Augustus 128
Fortingall 152
Fort William 136
Fowey 102
Fownhope 268
Freckenham 60
Frensham 193, 204
Fritham 198
Fulbourn 72
Gainsborough, Thomas 60
Gairloch 144
Garelochhead 132
Garrick, David 306
Gaskell, Elizabeth 300
Gaveston, Piers 234
Gay, John 96
George I 138
George V 200
George VI 204
Gibbons, Grinling 194
Glascwm 258
Glastonbury 111, 120
Glencoe 134
Glendower, Owen 244, 252, 258
Glossop 304, 312
Glyn Ceiriog 14
Goathland 166
Godalming 192, 194
Goldsmith, Oliver 128
Goodrich 268
Goya, Francisco 190
Graham, James 136
Grahame, Kenneth 102
Grasmere 40, 44
Grassington 26, 27, 30
Graves, John 52
Great Bolas 298
Great Budworth 302
Great Glen 128
Great Stukeley 82
Greco, El 190
Green How 26
Gresham, Sir John 212
Greta Bridge 190
Greville, Mrs Richard 290
Grewelthorpe 27, 38
Grindelford 310
Grinton 27, 34
Gubbay, Mrs David 278
Guildford 193, 194, 274, 278
Gwbert on Sea 248
Gwilym, Dafydd 252
Gwytherin 22
Hackness 162
Hadleigh 58, 68
Hadstock 72
Halesworth 64
Hallow 264
Hampden, John 224
Hamilton, Lady Emma 196
Hammerton 84
Hampstead Norreys 224
Happisburgh 212
Harbury 88
Hardy, Captain 122
Hardy, Robert 62
Hardy, Thomas 112, 124
Harlech 10, 18
Harleston 208
Hartington 304, 314
Hartland 92, 98
Hartwell 80
Hascombe 194
Hassop 304
Hastings 275
Hastings, Warren 234
Hathersage 304, 310
Hawes 26, 34
Hawick 174, 184
Hawker, R. S. 98
Hawkins, Sir John 94
Hawkridge 94
Hawkshead 40, 44
Hayfield 304, 312
Hay on Wye 260
Hazlitt, William 3, 294
Heber, Reginald 292
Helensburgh 132
Hellidon 86
Helmsley 156, 168
Henry IV 246
Henry VII 104, 200, 262
Henry VIII 82, 84, 214, 232, 280, 288
Hereford 262, 268
Herstmonceux 282
Hever 277, 288
Hexham 172, 178
Higham 68
Hingham 218
Holbein, Hans 194
Holkham 207, 214
Holland, John 106
Hollingbourne 286
Holt 212
Holtby, Winifred 156
Hope 314
Horsey 207
Houseman, A. E. 266, 292
Hovingham 156, 168
Hubberholme 32
Hughes, Thomas 221, 226
Hull, Richard 278
Hunstanton 207
Huntingdon 75, 82
Hurstpierpoint 280
Hutchinson, Mary 160
Hythe 275
Ilam 304, 314
Ingilby, Sir Thomas 28
Ingilby, Sir William 28
Ingleby Greenhow 166
Iona, Isle of 136
Inverary 132
Invergarry 136
Inverness 128, 148
Ivybridge 106
James I 28, 154
James II 296
James Edward, Old Pretender 138
James, G. P. R. 275
James, Henry 282
Jedburgh 174, 184
Jefferson, Thomas 14
Jekyll, Gertrude 194
Jenkins, Henry 38
John of Gaunt 198, 246
Johnson, Michael 316
Johnson, Samuel 3, 131, 304, 306, 316
Jones, Inigo 80, 88
Jousiffe, William 226
Judge Jeffreys 200, 294
Keats, John 132, 290
Kemp, William 70
Kendal 42
Kenilworth 74
Keswick 40, 52
Kettlewell 27, 32
Killin 154
Kilmersdon 118
Kimbolton 82
Kincraig 151
Kineton 76
King Arthur 91, 100, 120
King Ethelwulf 278
King Haakon 132
King Harold 282
King John 200, 262
Kingsbridge 93
Kingsley, Charles 96, 202, 292
Kings Somborne 198
Kingussie 151
Kinlochewe 144
Kirby Hill 190
Kirkby, Malzeard 38
Kirknewton 182
Kirk Yetholm 182
Knaresborough 28
Kneller, Godfrey 102
Knutsford 300
Kyle of Lochalsh 142
Lakeside 44
Lambert, John 30
Lambourn 221, 226
Landor, Walter Savage 76, 241, 260
Langport 122
Lauder, Harry 131
Laughton 280
Lavenham 58
Lavington 111
Laxfield 62
Laxton, William 84
Leamington Spa 74
Ledbury 262, 270
Leigh 276, 288
Leighton Buzzard 236
Leiston 66
Leith Hill 274, 278
Lewes 274, 275, 280
Leyburn 26, 27, 36
Leycester, Sir Peter 302
Lichfield 304, 306
Liddell, Alice 198
Lincoln, Abraham 218
Linton 72
Lisle, Dame Alicia 200
Little John 304, 310
Little Walsingham 207, 214
Livingstone, David 131
Llanbedr 18
Llanberis 20
Llandeilo 240, 246
Llandetty 244
Llandrindod Wells 241, 258
Llangeitho 250
Llangollen 3, 14
Llangower 16
Llanidloes 256
Llanrhaeadr-ym-Mochnant 16
Llanthony 241, 260
Llanuwchllyn 16, 18
Llanwddyn 16
Lloyd George 148
Llyn Clywedog 256
Lochcarron 142, 144
Lode 60
Longparish 202
Longstock 193, 202
Looe 93, 102
Lorna Doone 90, 94
Lostwithiel 92, 102
Lovat, Lord 148
Lovelace, Richard 194
Lowick Bridge 46
Luckington 118
Ludlow 262, 266
Luss 154
Lyme Regis 112
Lymington 200
Lympne 276, 284
Lyndhurst 198
Lynmouth 92
Macdonald, Flora 131
Macdonald, Ramsay 131
Macdonnell, A. G. 204
Machynlleth 241, 252
Macintyre, Duncan 134
Macmillan, Harold 131
Macrae, John 140
Maidstone 276
Malham 27, 32
Mallwyd 12, 241, 256
Malmesbury 111, 116
Malpas 292, 294
Mapleton 316
Market Drayton 298
Market Harborough 86
Market Lavington 114
Marlborough 116
Martock 122
Mary Queen of Scots 36, 152, 184, 304, 308
Masefield, John 270
Masham 27, 38
Mayfield 304, 316
McAdam, John 130
Meare 120
Meavy 104
Menheniot 102
Meredith, George 290
Merlin 100, 116
Middleham 27, 36
Middleton in Teesdale 188
Mildenhall 60
Milton, John 238, 266
Milton Abbas 126
Mitcheldean 270
Mockbeggar 284
Modbury 93, 106
Mold 24
Monmouth, Duke of 111, 118, 200
Montagu, Baron 200
Moore, Sir Henry 106
Mordiford 268
Moretonhampstead 108
Mortimers Cross 266
Morton, H. V. 18
Morwenstow 98
Mottisfont 198
Mousehole 92
Muchelney 122
Much Wenlock 296
Muir of Ord 146
Muker 34
Mulbarton 208
Mundesley 212
Mungrisdale 52
Nantwich 300
Naseby 75, 86
Nayland 68
Needham Market 68
Neenton 266
Nell Gwyn 268
Nelson, Horatio 196
Newbiggin 186
Newbury 220, 226
Newcastleton 184
Newent 262, 270
Newmarket 57
New Quay 250
Newtonmore 151
Norton-St-Philip 118

Index

Norwich 207, 208
Oakford Bridge 96
Ogle, Henry 182
Old Sarum 110, 114
Olney 80
Orford 66
Ormesby St Margaret 210
Oundle 84
Overton 204
Owen, Daniel 24
Owen, Thomas 296
Oxford 220, 224
Paine, Thomas 280
Parr, Katherine 42, 232
Pateley Bridge 26, 28
Patmore, Coventry 200
Pebmarsh 70
Peel, John 52
Penrhyndeudraeth 12
Penshurst 277, 288
Pen-y-Gwryd 22
Penzance 92
Pepys, Samuel 3, 60, 82, 118
Pestalozzi, John 282
Peter the Great 194
Petersfield 192, 196
Pett Bottom 284
Petworth 194
Peveril, William 314
Piddletrenthide 124
Piggott, Lester 300
Pillaton 102
Pitlochry 152
Pitt, William 114
Plockton 140
Plumpton 280
Polperro 102
Polruan 102
Poltimore Arms 96
Pontius Pilate 152
Pontrhydfendigaid 252
Pooley Bridge 54
Porthcurno 92
Postgate, Fr Nicholas 166
Priestley, J. B. 156
Prince Arthur 262
Prince Rupert 26
Pulham Market 208
Queen Anne 96
Queen Mary 256
Queen Victoria 144, 152, 216
Raleigh, Sir Walter 106
Ramsgill 28
Rattlebone, John 116
Ravenstone 80
Reedham 210
Reeth 36
Reigate 277, 290
Rembrandt 194
Reynolds, Sir Joshua 194, 232
Richard II 28, 106
Richard III 36, 104
Richard, Henry 250
Richmond 176
Ripley 28
Ripon 27
Robin Hood 164, 304
Robin Hood's Bay 156, 164
Rockbourne 126
Rockingham 84
Romaldkirk 190
Romney 275
Romney, George 44
Ross on Wye 262, 268
Rosthwaite 52
Rothbury 180
Rowland, Daniel 250
Rothschild, Nathaniel 238
Rubens, Peter 232
Ruckinge 284
Rudgwick 274, 278
Ruggles-Brise, Evelyn 70
Runswick 156
Ruskin, John 14, 40, 46, 52
Rydal, 40
Rye 275, 276, 282
Rylstone 30
St Briavels 262, 270
St Edmund 60
St Ives 92
St Kenelm 272
St Wite 124
Saffron Walden 58, 70
Salisbury 110, 114
Sampford Spiney 104
Sandringham 207, 214, 216
Sandwich 275
Sargent, John 282
Scoraig 146
Scott, Sir Walter 130, 154, 190, 314
Seahouses 180
Sedlescombe 282
Settle 26, 32
Shakespeare, William 74
Shap 54
Shave Cross 124
Shelley, Percy 52
Shere 274, 278
Sheridan, Richard 290
Sheriff Hutton 168
Sheringham 207
Sherston 116
Shiel Bridge 140
Shieldaig 142, 144
Shocklach 292, 294
Shrewsbury 292, 296
Shrewton 111, 114
Shutford 76
Siddons, Sarah 244
Sidmouth 112
Sidney, Sir Philip 288
Simon de Montfort 310
Skipton 27, 30
Slaughter Bridge 100
Sledmere 160
Small Hythe 284
Snowdon, Philip 204
Somerton 122
Southam 88
Southey, Robert 52
South Harting 196
Southwold 57, 64
Spean Bridge 136
Speed, John 292
Staindrop 176
Staithes 156
Stanhope 172, 176
Staverton 86
Staylittle 256
Steele, Richard 194
Stevenson, R. L. 3, 130
Stewkley 236
Stockbridge 202
Stockleigh Pomeroy 8, 94
Stoke 98
Stoke Abbot 124
Stoke Bruerne 80
Stoke by Nayland 68
Stoney Cross 198
Stow on the Wold 234
Stradbroke 62
Strafford, Thomas 86
Stratford on Avon 74
Streatley on Thames 220, 224
Street 120
Street End 276, 286
Stromeferry 142
Swaffham 218
Swaffham Bulbeck 60
Swardeston 208
Sykes, Sir Mark 160
Symonds Yat 262, 268
Talbot, John, Earl of Shrewsbury 294
Talladale 144
Talybont 252
Tal-y-Llyn 256
Tarbet 154
Tavistock 104
Taylor, John 308
Taylor, Rowland 68
Tegryn 248
Tenbury Wells 272
Tenby 241
Tennyson, Alfred 120, 298
Tenterden 276, 284
Terry, Dame Ellen 284
Thackeray, William 194
Thame 223, 238
Theberton 64
Thomas, Dylan 250
Thompson, Robert 160
Thorndike, Russell 276
Thorpe 304
Thrower, Percy 296
Tideswell 304, 314
Tilford 193, 204
Tilshead 111
Tintagel 92, 100
Tiverton 8, 94
Tonbridge 276, 288
Totnes 93, 106
Towcester 80
Trapp 246
Tregarron 250
Trelawney, Jonathan 98, 102
Trescastle 244
Tring 238
Trollope, Anthony 196
Troutbeck 54
Tuckenhay 106
Tummel Bridge 152
Turner, James 168, 232
Turpin, Dick 75, 86
Tutbury 304, 308
Tysoe 76
Uffington 226
Urchfont 114
Uttoxeter 316
Van Dyck, Antony 194
Wade, General George 152
Walberswick 57, 64
Walkington 158
Wall 172, 178
Walliswood 278
Walpole, Robert 60
Walton, Izaak 196, 314
Wappenham 78
Warbeck, Perkin 200
Warburton, Sir John 302
Wark 178
Warnford 196
Warwick 74, 76
Warwick, Richard (the Kingmaker) 168
Watlington 224
Watson, Richard 190
Watts, George Frederick 204
Watts-Russell 314
Webb, Mary 292
Wedmore 111
Welcombe Mouth 98
Wells, H. G. 196
Wells 111
Wells next the Sea 207, 214
Wem 294
Wendover 223, 238
Wensley 26
Wesley, John 30
West Ayton 162
Westbrook, Harriet 52
West Dean 193, 202
Westerdale 166
Westleton 64
Weston Underwood 75, 80
West Wellow 198
Wetherby 26, 28
Wethersfield 70
Wetwang 160
Wherwell 193, 202
Whistler, Rex 198
Whitby 156, 164
Whitchurch 193, 202, 292, 294
Whitchurch Canonicorum 124
Whiteparish 193, 202
Widecombe in the Moor 108
Widemouth 98
Wigmore 266
William the Conqueror 124, 193, 200, 282
William II 198
William III 134, 196
Winchcombe 222, 232
Winchester 193, 196
Winslow 223
Winston 172, 176
Winterton on Sea 210
Winwick 84
Witchampton 126
Withington 222, 230
Woodbridge 66
Woodfalls 193
Woodford 114
Wooler 182
Wootton Bassett 116
Worcester 262, 264
Wordsworth, William 30, 40, 44, 54, 160, 190, 268
Worsley, Sir Thomas 168
Wren, Christopher 224
Yalding 288
York 26, 27, 156, 158
Youlgreave 304, 310
Young Pretender, the 44, 131, 186